By What Authority?

The Literary Function and Impact of Conflict Stories in the Gospel of Matthew

Rebecca Ye-Atkinson

© 2020 Rebecca Ye-Atkinson

Published 2020 by Langham Monographs
An imprint of Langham Publishing
www.langhampublishing.org

Langham Publishing and its imprints are a ministry of Langham Partnership

Langham Partnership
PO Box 296, Carlisle, Cumbria, CA3 9WZ, UK
www.langham.org

ISBNs:
978-1-78368-787-9 Print
978-1-83973-017-7 ePub
978-1-83973-018-4 Mobi
978-1-83973-019-1 PDF

Rebecca Ye-Atkinson has asserted her right under the Copyright, Designs and Patents Act, 1988 to be identified as the Author of this work.

All rights reserved. No part of this publication may be reproduced, stored in a retrieval system or transmitted, in any form or by any means, electronic, mechanical, photocopying, recording or otherwise, without the prior written permission of the publisher or the Copyright Licensing Agency.

Requests to reuse content from Langham Publishing are processed through PLSclear. Please visit www.plsclear.com to complete your request.

Scriptures taken from the Holy Bible, New International Version®, NIV®. Copyright © 1973, 1978, 1984, 2011 by Biblica, Inc.™ Used by permission of Zondervan.

British Library Cataloguing-in-Publication Data
A catalogue record for this book is available from the British Library

ISBN: 978-1-78368-787-9

Cover & Book Design: projectluz.com

Langham Partnership actively supports theological dialogue and an author's right to publish but does not necessarily endorse the views and opinions set forth here or in works referenced within this publication, nor can we guarantee technical and grammatical correctness. Langham Partnership does not accept any responsibility or liability to persons or property as a consequence of the reading, use or interpretation of its published content.

Contents

Acknowledgements vii

Abstract ix

List of Abbreviations xi

Chapter 1 1
Introduction and Methods
    1.1 Research Question and Purpose of the Investigation 1
        1.1.1 Research Question 1
        1.1.2 Purpose of the Investigation 3
    1.2 Conflict Stories in Previous Studies 6
        1.2.1 Conflict Stories in Different Form Categories 6
        1.2.2 Studies of Conflict Stories in the Gospel of Matthew 12
        1.2.3 Evaluation of Previous Studies 14
    1.3 Methodology in the Current Study 20
        1.3.1 Conflict Stories: Terminology and Criteria for
             This Study 20
        1.3.2 Tools of Literary Criticism Applied in This Study 23
    1.4 Scope of Methodology Applied in the Thesis 42
    1.5 Structural Plan of the Book 43

Chapter 2 45
Conflict Stories in Matthew 9: Jesus, the Supreme Authority
    2.1 Analysis of Individual Pericopae: Matthew 9:1–8, 9–13,
        14–17 46
        2.1.1 Matthew 9:1–8 46
        2.1.2 Matthew 9:9–13 53
        2.1.3 Matthew 9:14–17 60
    2.2 Conflict Stories in Context of Matthew 5–9 67
        2.2.1 The Wider Context: Matthew 5–9 67
        2.2.2 Conflict Stories in Matthew 8–9 70

Chapter 3 75
*Conflict Stories in Matthew 12: This Generation Encounters
the Lord of the Sabbath*
    3.1 Analysis of Individual Pericopea: Matthew 12:1–8, 9–14,
        22–37, 38–45 76
        3.1.1 Matthew 12:1–8 76

        3.1.2 Matthew 12:9–14 87
        3.1.3 Matthew 12:22–37 98
        3.1.4 Matthew 12:38–45 109
    3.2 Conflict Stories in Context 119

Chapter 4 121
    Conflict Stories in Matthew 13, 15, 16 and 19: The Parting of the Ways
    4.1 Analysis of Individual Pericopea: Matthew 13:53–58;
         15:1–9; 16:1–4; 19:1–9 121
        4.1.1 Matthew 13:53–58 121
        4.1.2 Matthew 15:1–9 131
        4.1.3 Matthew 16:1–4 140
        4.1.4 Matthew 19:1–9 147
    4.2 Conflict Stories in Context Matthew 13–20 155

Chapter 5 157
    The Jerusalem Conflict Stories: Whose Son Is the Christ?
    5.1 Analysis of Individual Pericopea: Matthew 21:14–17,
         23–27; 22:15–22, 23–33, 34–40, 41–46 157
        5.1.1 Matthew 21:14–17 157
        5.1.2 Matthew 21:23–27 165
        5.1.3 Matthew 22:15–22 173
        5.1.4 Matthew 22:23–33 180
        5.1.5 Matthew 22:34–40 187
        5.1.6 Matthew 22:41–46 194
    5.2 Conflict Stories in the Context of Matthew 21–25 203

Chapter 6 205
    Summary and Conclusions
    6.1 Conclusion and Findings 206
    6.2 Summary 221

Appendix 1 225
    Jesus in Dialogue with Other Characters in the Gospel of Matthew

Bibliography 231

Acknowledgements

This book is a revised version of my doctoral dissertation under the same title (University of Edinburgh, 2014). During 2018 and 2019 I was able to partially revise and update the chapters as well as improve the format.

For the completion of the work, I am deeply indebted to many people without whom I would not have been able to begin, continue and finish this study. In particular, I am indebted to the late Dr Grant Osborne as well as Dr David Pao, who not only guided me to see the beauty of the New Testament text but also inspired me to further explore the field of gospel studies.

To Dr Earl and Bette Reeves, Da'an and Doris Tzuoo, our loving friends who have embraced us as part of their family, faithfully prayed for us, and generously supported us – I wish to express my heartfelt gratitude.

I also wish to express my sincere appreciation to our "Edinburgh family" – Dr John and Irene Hannah, Pastor Ian Ching and Angel Low. They have been supportive in more ways than I can express here. They encouraged and walked with us during our most challenging years in completing this study.

Our dear friend, Dr David Knight, meticulously proofread the final draft despite his busy schedule. His comments and corrections have been indispensable. Of course, any remaining errors remain solely my responsibility.

Last but not the least, I want to express thanks to my family. To my three children, Kereb, Nahum and Iona, who have truly been a wonderful joy and blessing to my life. To my husband, Jason, who in his profound love and patience, encouraged and helped me each step of the way. This book is dedicated to him.

Abstract

The purpose of this book is to explore the significance of conflict stories in the Gospel of Matthew from a literary critical perspective. The key research question the thesis has attempted to answer is, *how do conflict stories function in Matthew's narrative?*

Because their interest is often limited to the *Sitz im Leben* behind the Matthean text, previous studies attempting the similar pursuit view conflict stories as transparent accounts of Matthew's polemical program against the Jews or Judaism. Thus they have neglected a vital purpose of the author, that is, besides his interest to record or preserve what happened in history, the gospel author is also interested to arouse or affirm the readers' faith in Jesus through his preservation and redaction of his sources, which is an inseparable part of the author's theological program. How exactly then has his literary work achieved this purpose?

Assuming the literary unity of the Matthean text, this study has treated the Matthean text as a mirror and explored literary nuances reflected by the textual "surface." Under such a premise, the narrative analysis of this thesis has highlighted three foci:

1. The connection which each conflict makes with its narrative context;
2. How the Hebrew Scripture interacts with the author's composition or redaction of the stories; and
3. The literary impact these stories have on the implied reader.

This study selects a total of seventeen conflict stories in Matthew based on three criteria (Matt 9:1–8, 9–13, 14–17; 12:1–8, 9–14, 22–37, 38–45; 13:53–58; 15:1–9; 16:1–4; 19:1–9; 21:14–17, 23–27; 22:15–22, 23–33, 34–40, 41–46):

1. The presence of an attitude of hostility or challenge in the setting of the narrative (either explicit or implied);
2. The presence of a question of an accusation or a challenge; and
3. The question or the accusation is usually followed by a reply of Jesus.

In conclusion, the literary analysis of this study suggests the two most important functions of Matthean conflict stories.

1. Conflict stories function, either individually or in clusters, as kernels of the Matthean plot to advance the narrative forward in order to reach its climax in the passion narrative.
2. The christological focus in conflict stories is consistently concerned not only with the superiority of Jesus over the opponents, but more importantly with the nexus between the divine status of Jesus and him being the messianic figure.

List of Abbreviations

Modern Publications

ABD	*Anchor Bible Dictionary.* Edited by D. N. Freedman. 6 vols. New York, 1992
BDAG	Bauer, W., F. W. Danker, W. F. Arndt, and F. W. Gingrich. *Greek-English Lexicon of the New Testament and Other Early Christian Literature.* 3rd edition. Chicago, 1999
Bib	*Biblica*
BiblSac	*Bibliotheca Sacra*
BNTC	Black's New Testament Commentaries
BTB	*Biblical Theology Bulletin*
BZ	*Biblische Zeitschrift*
CBQ	*Catholic Biblical Quarterly*
CBQMS	Catholic Biblical Quarterly Monograph Series
CTR	*Criswell Theological Review*
DJG	*Dictionary of Jesus and the Gospels.* Edited by J. B. Green and S. McKnight. Downers Grove, 1992
FRLANT	Forschungen zur Religion und Literatur des Alten und Neuen Testaments
ICC	International Critical Commentary
Int	*Interpretation*
JAAR	*Journal of the American Academy of Religion*
JBL	*Journal of Biblical Literature*
JETS	*Journal of the Evangelical Theological Society*

JRH	*Journal of Religious History*
JSNT	*Journal for the Study of the New Testament*
JSNTSup	Journal for the Study of the New Testament: Supplement Series
JSOTSup	Journal for the Study of the Old Testament: Supplement Series
JTS	*Journal of Theological Studies*
NICNT	New International Commentary on the New Testament
NIGTC	New International Commentary on the Greek Testament
NTS	*New Testament Studies*
NTTS	New Testament Tools and Studies
NovT	*Novum Testamentum*
NovTSup	Novum Testamentum Supplements
RB	*Revue biblique*
ResQ	*Restoration Quarterly*
SBL	*Society of Biblical Literature*
SJT	*Scottish Journal of Theology*
Str-B	Strack, Hermann L., and Paul Billerbeck. Kommentar zum Neuen Testament aus Talmud und Midrasch. 6 vols. Münchem: Beck, 1922–61.
TDNT	*Theological Dictionary of the New Testament.* Edited by Gerhard Kittel and Gerhard Friedrich. Translated by G·. W. Bromiley. 10 vols. Grand Rapids, 1964–76
TNTC	Tyndale New Testament Commentaries
THKNT	Theologischer Handkommentaz zum Neuen Testament
WBC	World Biblical Commentary
WUNT	Wissenschaftliche Untersuchungen zum Neuen Testament
ZKT	*Zeitschrift for Katholische Theologie*
ZTK	*Zeitschrift for Theologie und Kirche*

Apocrypha

1–2–3–4 Macc	1–2–3–4 Maccabees
Wis	Wisdom of Solomon

Old Testament Pseudoepigrapha

1–2–3 Enoch	1–2–3 Enoch
Jub.	Jubilees
Pss.Sol.	Psalms of Solomon
Test. Iss.	Testament of Issachar

Early Christian Literature

1 Clem.	1 Clement
Hipp. *Refut.*	Hippolytus *Refutation of All Heresies*
Justin Martyr	
Dial.	Dialogue with Trypho

Classical and Hellenistic Literature

Jos.	Joesephus
Ant.	Antiquities of the Jews
War	The Jewish War
Philo	
Decal.	*De Decalogo*

Dead Sea Scrolls and Related Texts

CD	Cairo Damascus Document
1QH	Thanksgiving Hymns from Cave 1
1QS	Manual of Discipline from Cave 1
11QTemple	Temple Scroll from Cave 11

Orders and Tractates in Mishnaic and Related Literature

Gen. Rab	Genesis Rabbah
Ex. Rab	Exodus Rabbah
b. Shab	Babylonian Shabbat

t. Shab	Tosephta Shabbat
m. Hag.	Mishnah Hagiga

Other Rabbinic Works

Mek. Ex.	Mekilta Exodus
Pesiq.	Pesiqta
Sifra Deut.	Sifra Deuteronomy
Sifra Lev.	Sifra Leviticus

Targumic Material

Tg. Isaiah	Targum Jonathan to Isaiah

CHAPTER 1

Introduction and Methods

1.1 Research Question and Purpose of the Investigation

1.1.1 Research Question

Within the overall narrative in the Synoptic Gospels, there is a group of short stories involving dialogues between Jesus and other characters that frequently culminate with a saying of Jesus. Although this unique literary form has been recognized by modern biblical scholars, these stories are known collectively by different terms (see following discussion in section 1.2 "Conflict Stories in Previous Studies"). The dialogues usually consist of two or more parties. One party is Jesus; the other involves a variety of characters including: John the Baptist, Jesus's disciples, the devil, evil spirits, the poor/sick/needy, Jewish leaders, John's disciples, members of the crowd, and finally, Pilate (see appendix 1). This study will specifically examine dialogue stories in the Gospel of Matthew between Jesus against his opponents, usually the Jewish leaders. These stories will be labeled *conflict stories* in the study. They refer to short narratives that involve hostility between a question or accusation and a reply. The detailed criteria for determining the form of such stories will be discussed in section 1.3.1 "Conflict Stories: Terminology and Criteria for this Study." According to the criteria, there are in total seventeen conflict stories in Matthew.

In the simplest terms, the research question of this study is: *how do conflict stories function in Matthew's narrative?* There are two main factors that attract my attention to conflict stories particularly in Matthew. First, despite

Matthew's extensive use of Jesus's monologues,[1] he nevertheless retains all of the conflict materials from his sources (see table 2 "Conflict Stories in Matthew and Their Parallels").[2] Additionally, Matthew inserts an additional conflict (21:14–17). Two stories in Mark are altered by Matthew (Mark 12:28–34, 35–37) so that they take the form of conflict stories (22:34–40, 41–46). Does Matthew simply want to preserve his original sources? Recent redaction-critical studies suggest that in fact Matthew presents those conflicts much more vividly than his sources.[3] If this is the case, is Matthew redacting these stories more colorfully simply for literary aesthetics, or are there other reasons for these elaborations? Do conflict stories contribute to the overall plot development of Matthew? If yes, then, what literary functions do conflict stories serve for the Matthean narrative? Although these questions are not completely overlooked within literary-critical studies of the gospels, scholars have explored the topic narrowly and insufficiently.[4] Therefore, a comprehensive literary-critical analysis of conflict stories in Matthew remains to be carried out, and it is this task that my study seeks to accomplish.

Second, comparing all other kinds of dialogue stories in Matthew, the conflict stories appear with highest frequency (classified as such because of mutual hostility between dialogue parties, see appendix 1). Seventeen of the fifty-two dialogue encounters narrated are between Jesus and his opponents, the religious leaders.[5] Outside of such encounters, there are no other direct interactions between these parties in the Matthean narrative. Consequently,

---

1. Matthew uses impressive and long monologues in five major blocks to present Jesus's views on various issues including: the Torah, discipleship, mission, and eschatology (Matt 5–7, 10, 13, 18, 24–25).

2. This study will follow two-source theory as a working hypothesis. For a detailed justification see "The Source of Matthew" in W. D. Davies and D. C. Allison, *A Critical and Exegetical Commentary on the Gospel According to Saint Matthew, 1–7*, 3 vols., ICC (Edinburgh: T & T Clark, 1988), 97–127.

3. The most recent redaction-critical study is by Boris Repschinski, *The Controversy Stories in the Gospel of Matthew: Their Redaction, Form and Relevance for the Relationship between the Matthean Community and Formative Judaism* (Gottingen: Vandenhoeck & Ruprecht, 2000). His work will be discussed further in section 1.2.2.2.

4. Detailed discussion of related studies will be offered later under the section "Conflict Stories in Previous Studies."

5. Classification of all but one of these stories remains largely undisputed (discussion of classification criteria will be discussed below). The disputed one is in Matt 8:18–20 because scholars have not reached a broad consensus whether it is an 'unfriendly' or neutral encounter. This story will be excluded by the study because the attitude of the scribe is not hostile toward Jesus (8:19).

it may be asked, why does the portrayal of religious leaders in Matthew appear to be only hostile? An answer that scholars most readily give is that this characteristic reflects a strained relationship between Matthew's community and the Judaism of his time, whether the nature of relationship is *intra* or *extra muros*.[6] Nevertheless, the purpose of the author for such a consistently negative portrayal of the Jewish leaders within the narrative remains unclear. In other words, it does not solve the problem of explaining the authorial intention for the related stories – what purposes does the author intend to achieve for his overall narrative in redacting, arranging, and inserting conflict stories within respective contexts?

1.1.2 Purpose of the Investigation

The basic assumption of this study is that the Gospel of Matthew as a whole bears a uniformity of style. This presumes that the author is more than a collector of sources but a creative artist of literary composition.[7] In fact, the text of Matthew reflects the author's creative art in composing, developing, redacting and organizing historical and biographical events.[8] Moreover, the author intends to arrange those events in such a sequence that is most suitable for evoking the audience's (and the reader's) response to the identity and authority of the central character Jesus.[9] This coincides with what Aune suggests for the function of the gospels: "Rhetorically, the Gospels are primarily

---

6. The terms *intra* and *extra muros* Judaism are explained by W. D. Davies. They describe the engagement of Matthew with Judaism and the Old Israel. Such an engagement, if takes place within Judaism as a dialogue, is *intra muros*; however, it would be *extra muros* if the engagement is "an appeal or apologetic to the Synagogue from a church that was already outside it." William D. Davies, *The Setting of Sermon on the Mount* (Cambridge: Cambridge University Press, 1966), 290.

7. Many scholars have noted the literary skills of Matthew. For example, Ulrich Luz lists several literary techniques used by Matthew and suggests that the final form of the first gospel "presupposes a high degree of literacy among at least some members" of the reading community of Matthew's day. (*The Theology of the Gospel of Matthew* [Cambridge: Cambridge University Press, 1995], 3–6).

8. David Aune suggests that the compilation of Matthew is more like a "literaturization of historical and biographical composition." David Aune, *The New Testament in Its Literary Environment* (Philadelphia, PA: Westminster Press, 1987), 65. However, this is not a definition of the genre of the Gospel of Matthew. There are numerous discussions on the issue of genre (of the gospels) that are worth noting; most prominent among them is Richard Burridge, *What Are the Gospels?: A Comparison with Graeco-Roman Biography*, 2nd ed. (Grand Rapids, MI: Eerdmans, 2004).

9. It is especially true for Matthew and Luke who use "one source the backbone of the narrative, supplemented by other sources..." move "closer toward the biographical and

persuasive literature, using various strategies to persuade their audiences that the crucified and risen Jesus is the Messiah, the Son of God. The Gospels, then, are fundamentally Christian literary propaganda."[10]

Therefore, in addition to describing the words and deeds of the characters, the author also often produces his own commentary on the narrative events to persuade the reader. For example, all of the "formula" quotations in Matthew are such authorial commentaries.[11] Seen from this perspective, the Gospel of Matthew is first and foremost written for individuals and communities that are both real and conceptual for the author. When conflict stories are viewed under such an overall function of the gospel, the purpose of this study then, is *to explore the specific significance of conflict stories in the gospel from a literary-critical perspective in order to discern the author's intention for the conflict stories and their impact on the implied reader.*

This study will approach the Matthean text synchronically. That means the study employs literary critical analysis as the primary tool to investigate the text. However, it will inevitably incorporate insights concluded from redaction- and historical-critical approaches. This is because the former sheds light on the authorial intention of the text and the latter helps to illuminate *a priori* assumptions of the author about the audience as the gospel is written against the backdrop of its historical, cultural and literary context.

The following diagram illustrates a synchronic approach to the conflict stories in Matthew. The Gospel of Matthew as well as its sources is situated within an overarching frame of "Context," represented by the brackets. The letters "X" and "Y" stand for issues of contention in Mark and Q that are used by Matthew, but they do not necessarily have the form of a conflict story (e.g. Mark 12:28–34, 35–37; Q/Luke 10:25–28; 20:41–47). The order of X's and Y's demonstrates their different positioning in Matthew.

---

historiographical expectations of pagan readers . . ." and make "many linguistic and stylistic improvements in Mark." Aune, *New Testament*, 65.

10. Aune, 59.

11. As Stanton writes in regards to the distinctive "formula" quotations, "These quotations are all theological 'asides' or comments by the evangelist . . . the evangelist uses Scripture to underline some of his most prominent and distinctive theological concerns." G. N. Stanton, "Matthew," in *It Is Written: Scripture Citing Scripture: Essays in Honour of Barnabas Lindars, SSF*, eds. D. A. Carson and H. G. Williamson (Cambridge: Cambridge University Press, 1988), 205.

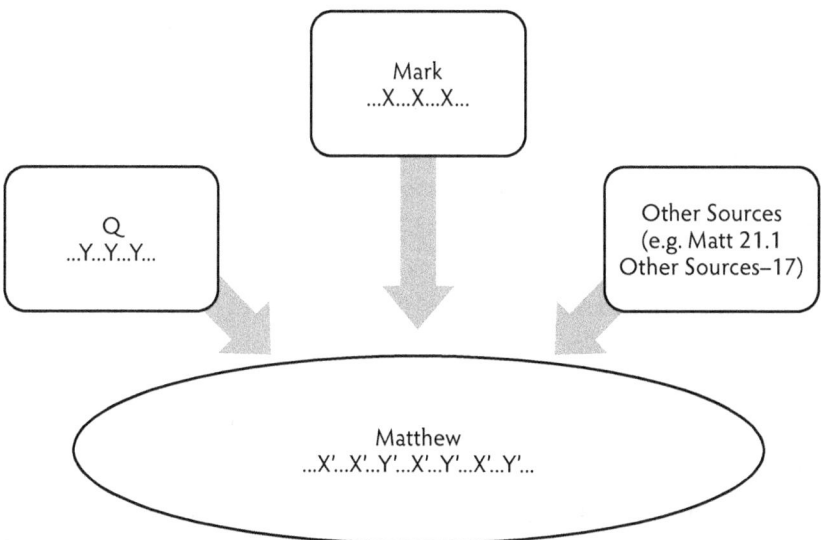

Context of Culture, History, the Hebrew Scripture[12] and Greco-Roman Literature
(X= conflict materials in Mark; Y= conflict materials in Q)

This diagram is not intended to demonstrate a precise process of how Matthew retains and redacts conflict materials from Mark, Q and other sources. Instead, it simply reflects three perspectives that this study examines in relation to the Matthean conflict stories. They are listed below in order of their descending importance for the analysis, as follows:

1. First and foremost, the ordering and placement of X's and Y's within their immediate context as well as overall narrative arrangement shall receive primary attention;
2. The process of how X or Y are redacted into X's and Y's;
3. The cultural, historical and literary context of conflict stories will be consulted only when they illuminate the understanding of the function of conflict stories.

---

12. The term "the Hebrew Scripture" in this study refers to the Scripture of Israel that was possibly available or known to Matthew. It includes the Greek version of the Scripture (i.e. LXX) and does not necessarily mean that the Scripture is in the Hebrew language.

In what follows, I will first briefly survey the process of how the form of conflict stories has been categorized by previous studies. Studies that have investigated conflict stories in the Gospel of Matthew will also be discussed. The definition of conflict stories in the current study will emerge after considering how previous studies have approached the generic category of these pericopae. Then, I will propose several literary-critical tools by introducing their categories and theories that will be applied in this study. An introduction to the plan of this thesis will be presented at the end of this chapter.

1.2 Conflict Stories in Previous Studies

This section briefly surveys literature that identified the form of conflict stories. The authors are arranged chronologically according to the dates of the first edition of their original work. The discussion, however, is not intended to be a comprehensive evaluation of their work. Rather, the focus will be on the contribution of each author in recognizing and establishing criteria for conflict stories as a particular form. This is because their work contributes to the selection and definition of conflict stories in this study. At the end of the section, an overall evaluation of these studies in relation to the current analysis will be provided.

1.2.1 Conflict Stories in Different Form Categories

1.2.1.1 Martin Dibelius

In modern scholarship, Martin Dibelius's work, *Die Formgeschichte des Evangeliums*,[13] was the first to pay attention to the literary form of different stories in the gospels. He uses the term "paradigm" to denote a narrative type to which conflict stories belong and suggests five criteria in identifying a story as a paradigm:

1. It has a beginning and end which are independent of its context within a given gospel;
2. It is succinct without detailed characterization;
3. It has religious or edificatory style;
4. It is didactic, emphasizing the final reply of Jesus;

---

13. This survey is based on the English translation of the second German edition of the book (published in 1919), *From Tradition to Gospel* (New York: Scribners, 1934).

5. It has a preaching point, such as a general phrase, an exemplary act of Jesus, or a comment from Jesus's audiences.[14]

Dibelius's criteria derive from his emphasis on the function of the form. It is to "bring out the decisive act of Jesus . . . what Jesus said or did."[15] Therefore, these paradigms, for Dibelius, become the key traditions of Jesus that early Christian missionaries preserved and proclaimed in their teaching.[16] Although he suggests that the origin of the form of these paradigms is closest to the Hellenistic *chreia*, the paradigm remains unique.[17] From his form-critical analysis, he concludes that the more closely stories follow the form of the paradigm, the older they are.[18]

1.2.1.2 Martin Albertz

Martin Albertz's form-critical study is the first monograph focusing on conflict stories.[19] Unlike Dibelius, Albertz adopts the term "controversy dialogues" and argues that their structure is composed of two elements:

1. Exposition (exposition) is when the author introduces the setting of the story and the questioner(s).
2. Gespräch (dialogue) consists of the question(s) directed to Jesus and Jesus's speech in reply.[20]

Albertz additionally notes that the closing remarks within some narratives could further act as a third element. Beyond the structural analysis, what most interests him is the formal origin of these dialogues. Just as Israelite prophets engaged in verbal battle with false prophets, societal leadership, or occasionally the people in the Old Testament, Albertz considers the shape of controversy dialogues were similarly fashioned by the evangelists.[21] Even though he assumes that some adaptation or expansion may have happened

---

14. Dibelius, *From Tradition to Gospel*, 44–58.
15. Dibelius, 68.
16. Dibelius, 69.
17. Dibelius, 152–158.
18. Dibelius, 61.
19. Martin Albertz, *Die synoptishen Streitgespräche: ein Beitrag zur Formgeschichte des Urchristentums* (Berlin: Trowitzsch, 1921).
20. Albertz, *Die synoptishen Streitgespräche*, 86–87.
21. Albertz, 163.

in the history of transmission, Albertz nonetheless believes that controversy dialogues generally reflect disputes between the historical Jesus and his opponents. He differs fundamentally from Dibelius by attributing the tradition of paradigm to the *Sitz im Leben* of the historical Jesus and his opponents rather than to early Christian kerygma.

1.2.1.3 Rudolf Bultmann

Rudolf Bultmann investigated a much wider category of apophthegms and also uses the term "controversy dialogues" to denote one of three sub-categories of apophthegm.[22] Bultmann suggests that controversy dialogues consist of two parts:

1. The starting-point lies in some action or attitude which is seized on by the opponent and used in an attack by accusation or by question;[23]
2. The reply to the attack follows more or less a set form, with special preference for the counter-question or the metaphor, or even both together. Nevertheless, like the attack, it can also consist of scripture quotation.[24]

For Bultmann, the *reply* is more important than the starting-point. His work forms a useful comparison to Dibelius and Albertz. Bultmann is to some extent similar to Dibelius in that both consider the most important part of controversy dialogues is Jesus's reply. However, for Bultmann, this is because he believes the most original form of the controversy dialogues lies within the sayings of Jesus. In this regard, Bultmann resonates with Albertz, but he identifies the *Sitz im Leben* of these stories as Palestinian Jewish Christian

---

22. The survey is based on the English translation of the second German edition of the book (*Geschichte der synoptischen Tradition*, published in 1931; the first edition was published in 1921). Rudolf Bultmann, *The History of the Synoptic Tradition*. 2nd ed. ,translated by John Marsh (New York: Harper, 1968), 11–69; the other two categories include *scholastic dialogues* and *biographical apophthegms*.

23. Bultmann, *History of the Synoptic Tradition*, 39.

24. Bultmann, 41.

churches.²⁵ He believes that it was their concerns towards the law which eventually gave rise to the formation of controversy dialogues.²⁶

1.2.1.4 Vincent Taylor

Vincent Taylor labeled these pericopae "pronouncement stories." He defines their literary form as stories that "quickly reach their climax in a saying of Jesus which was of interest to the first Christians because it bore directly upon questions of faith and practice."²⁷ To this extent, he agrees with Bultmann that the reply of Jesus deserves most attention. Although similarly adopting a form-critical approach, Taylor differs considerably from both Dibelius and Bultmann in two ways. First, while both Dibelius and Bultmann argue for the creativity of early churches (Greek-speaking or Palestinian Jewish) in shaping and inventing conflict stories, Taylor suggests otherwise. He insists that it was the practical needs among early churches which "*kindle recollections and prompt the relating* of His [Jesus's] words and deeds."²⁸ In other words, he endeavors to link the stories back to the historical Jesus. Second, Taylor limits his form analysis only within gospel stories, rather than seeking analogies in Hellenistic or Jewish literature. According to Taylor, pronouncement stories consist of:

1. Brief narratives introduced by a question or portrayal of events; and
2. Finished with a pronouncement of Jesus which the early church had found related to their contemporary setting.²⁹

1.2.1.5 Arland Hultgren

The next forty years following the work of Taylor did not see much attention devoted to conflict stories. It was not until 1979 that Arland Hultgren rekindled scholarly interests in this form of pericopae within the Synoptic Gospels. By that time Hultgren had the advantage of combining a newer

---

25. He does acknowledge that the apophthegms are somewhat similar to the form of Hellenistic stories, hence the term "apophthegms." Bultmann, 11.
26. Bultmann, 41.
27. Vincent Taylor, *The Formation of the Gospel Tradition*, 2nd ed. (London: Macmillan, 1935), 23.
28. Taylor, *Formation*, 37; italics added.
29. Taylor, 65.

method – redaction criticism – with form criticism. Hultgren uses the term "conflict stories," but his identifying criteria are conceptually close to those suggested by Albertz and Bultmann:

1. Introductory narrative;
2. Opponent's question or attack;
3. Dominical saying.[30]

Like Bultmann and Dibelius, Hultgren studies the form of conflict stories in their Hellenistic and Jewish literary contexts. Yet unlike his forebears, he concludes that they are too unique to be stylistically dependent on these literary genres, and therefore are a form "composed by early Christian storytellers specifically to suit their needs of the newly developing Christian movement."[31]

The two approaches – redaction and form criticism – assisted Hultgren in advancing the above-mentioned studies in two key areas. First, by comparing conflict stories among Synoptic Gospels, he notes that the narrative component of conflict stories seems to have attracted a greater degree of the redactors' interest, much more than previously noticed.[32] Second, Hultgren demonstrates how Jesus's sayings are dependent on the discourse context of the narrative. To this extent, some sayings cannot be understood outside of their immediate narrative setting and Hultgren identifies these short narratives as "unitary conflict stories."[33] Other sayings, however, may have been circulated independently. Therefore, he uses the term "non-unitary conflict stories" to denote those stories where the opponent's question and other narrative elements are composed to create a setting for such sayings.[34] Whether or not this distinction is valid will be discussed later; here it is simply worth noting his efforts to investigate the form of conflict stories in their literary context.

---

30. Arland Hultgren, *Jesus and His Adversaries: The Form and Function of the Conflict Stories in the Synoptic Tradition* (Minneapolis: Augsburg, 1979), 53; cf. Hultgren's summary of Bultmann's criteria on p. 29.
31. Hultgren, *Jesus and His Adversaries*, 39.
32. Hultgren, 52.
33. Hultgren, 67.
34. Hultgren, 100.

1.2.1.6 Robert Tannehill

Although Robert Tannehill follows Taylor's terminology, "pronouncement stories," he defines the term slightly differently. A "pronouncement story is a brief narrative in which the climactic (and often final) element is a pronouncement which is presented as a particular person's response to something said or observed on a particular occasion of the past."[35] Conflict stories then belong to this larger category of "pronouncement stories." According to Tannehill, a pronouncement story consists of two elements:

1. The pronouncement (i.e. the response), and
2. its setting (the *stimulus*,[36] i.e. the occasion provoking such a response).[37]

As Tannehill recognizes, pronouncement stories generally correspond with Bultmann's "apophthegms,"[38] therefore they include conflict stories broadly. Tannehill establishes a taxonomy of six categories: correction stories, commendation stories, objection stories, quest stories, inquiry stories, and description stories.[39] The criteria by which Tannehill classifies these stories depend on different relationships between the story's setting and Jesus's response at the end of the story, that is, the response to the setting.[40] The value of this taxonomy is that it helps to distinguish the shift from one attitude to another as the story encourages such.[41] He claims that the six categories can encompass most of the pronouncement stories in ancient Mediterranean literature. The current study will draw several insights from Tannehill. For example, by highlighting the importance of the dialogue form in the Synoptic Gospels, he makes note of highlighting pronouncement stories as "acts of communication between writers and readers."[42] Furthermore, upon investigating the literary effect of Jesus's sayings, Tannehill argues that "the

---

35. Robert Tannehill, "Introduction: The Pronouncement Story and Its Types," *Semeia* 20 (1981): 1.
36. Tannehill, "Pronouncement Story," 6.
37. Tannehill, 1.
38. Tannehill, 1.
39. Tannehill, 6.
40. Robert Tannehill, "Tension in Synoptic Sayings and Stories," *Interpretation* 34, no. 2 (1980): 145.
41. Tannehill, "Tension," 145.
42. Tannehill, "Pronouncement Story," 4.

pronouncement story is shaped to have a particular impact upon the reader."[43] In the analysis of conflict stories, my study will also examine how the reader responds to the impact of conflict stories.

1.2.2 Studies of Conflict Stories in the Gospel of Matthew
1.2.2.1 Stanley Saunders

Saunders's unpublished PhD dissertation, "No One Dared Ask Him Anything More," aims to be a literary analysis of the function of the conflict stories in the Gospel of Matthew.[44] He primarily uses the term "controversy stories,"[45] and his criteria for conflict stories follow Hultgren closely:

1. An introductory narrative that serves as a transition, provides a setting, or indicates the basis for the dialogue that follows;
2. A question or challenge put to Jesus (or, in 22:41–46, a challenge Jesus directs to his opponents); and
3. A response consisting of a maxim or proverb, a parable, an allegory, an argument from scripture, etc.[46]

Based on these criteria, Saunders determines sixteen controversy stories in Matthew. The most unique feature of his work is that he no longer treats conflict stories in isolation but attempts to analyze them within the literary context. In terms of the selection of conflict stories, Saunders's study largely overlaps with the present investigation. However, he excludes the story of 13:53–58 which is included in the present investigation. Moreover, Saunders considers the trilogy of parables (21:28–32, 33–46; 22:1–14) as part of a conflict story (21:23–27). These are not included in the present study because they do not meet my formal criteria of conflict stories. There are two purposes explicitly stated by Saunders's study. First, it intends to test the accuracy of the interpretation that "Matthew transmits stories about fasting, about Sabbath practice, about table fellowship, etc., in order to map out the

---

43. Tannehill, "Tension," 144–145.

44. Stanley Saunders, "'No One Dared Ask Him Anything More': Contextual Readings of the Controversy Stories in Matthew" (PhD diss., Princeton Theological Seminary, 1990).

45. Saunders is not consistent in the use of the terminology. Throughout the thesis, the term "controversy storie'" is used, but in several occasions he also uses "challenge stories" without any explanation; see, for example, "No One Dared," 114, 116, 464.

46. Saunders, 114–115.

Christian position on these issues."[47] His investigation appropriately leads to a negative conclusion. Unfortunately, however, his second purpose – to describe carefully Matthew's use of the conflict stories[48] – is not so successfully achieved. More evaluation of his work will be offered in the next section, section 1.2.3 "Evaluation of Previous Studies."

1.2.2.2 Boris Repschinski

Focusing on the Gospel of Matthew, Boris Repschinski has produced the most recent monograph devoted to conflict stories where he labels these pericopae as "controversy stories." He embraces Bultmann's criteria for story selection but divides them into four points. For Repschinski, controversy stories should include:

1. an action or attitude;
2. which is used by the opponents;
3. in an attack by question or accusation;
4. The attack is followed by a reply, often including a counter-question or a scripture quotation.[49]

In view of the hostile behavior present in the stories, Repschinski then adds two pericopae to Bultmann's original fifteen-story set, Matthew 13:53–58 and 21:14–17, which were considered by Bultmann as biographical apophthegms.[50] Therefore, his study has seventeen controversy stories in total. Because of his particular interest in observing how Matthew shapes those stories, Repschinski primarily employs redactional criticism but also incorporates form critical approaches. A key question Repschinski seeks to answer is whether Matthew's gospel reflects its origin inside or outside of Judaism. As a conclusion, he argues that the Matthean controversy stories indeed reflect a struggle *intra muros* vis-à-vis Judaism.[51]

---

47. Saunders, 6–7.
48. Saunders, 7.
49. Repschinski, *Controversy Stories*, 62.
50. Bultmann, *History*, 31, 34.
51. Repschinski, *Controversy Stories*, 343.

1.2.3 Evaluation of Previous Studies

Antagonism between Jesus and the Jewish leaders in the gospels has long been studied by biblical scholars. Perhaps inspired by curiosity concerning this polemical aspect of Jesus's story, numerous publications in the past decades attempted to explain how and why this antagonism became a prominent feature, especially of the first gospel. Such explanations are approached from the perspectives of source, form and redaction criticism, either to seek the "oldest" tradition before the written form of the text, or to discern the evangelist's theology from his redaction of the sources available to him.[52] Other scholars, casting their net wider, have focused on examining first century Christian communities or early Jewish sectarianism by incorporating socio-scientific approaches as an additional analytical tool.[53] Their purpose is to locate the evangelists amid the wider phenomenon of post-70 CE reformulation of

---

52. Just to name a few, for example, in addition to the scholars discussed above, there are also Sjef van Tilborg, *The Jewish Leaders in Matthew* (Leiden: Brill, 1972); David E. Garland, *The Intention of Matthew 23* (Leiden: Brill, 1979); Peter Briscoe, "Faith Confirmed through Conflict," in *Back to the Sources. Biblical and Near Eastern Studies in Honor of Dermot Ryan*, eds. Kevin J. Cathcart and John F. Healey (Dublin: Glendale, 1989), 104–118; Andrew Overman, *Matthew's Gospel and Formative Judaism* (Minneapolis: Fortress, 1990); Stanton, "Matthew's Christology and the Parting of the Ways," in *The Parting of the Ways A.D. 70 to 135*, ed. James D. G. Dunn (Tübingen: Mohr Siebeck, 1992), 99–116; Scot McKnight, "A Loyal Critic: Matthew's Polemic with Judaism in Theological Perspective," in *Anti-Semitism and Early Christianity: Issues of Polemic and Faith*, eds. Craig A. Evans and Donald Hagner (Minneapolis: Fortress, 1993), 55–79; Richard E. Menninger, *Israel and the Church in the Gospel of Matthew* (New York: Peter Lang, 1994); Samuel Byrskog, *Jesus the Only Teacher: Didactic Authority and Transmission in Ancient Israel, Ancient Judaism and the Matthean community* (Stockholm: Almqvist & Wiksell, 1994); Kenneth G. Newport, *The Sources and Sitz im Leben of Matthew 23* (Sheffield: Sheffield Academic Press, 1995); Douglas R. Hare, "How Jewish Is the Gospel of Matthew," *CBQ* 62 (2000): 264–277; Paul Foster, *Community, Law and Mission in Matthew's Gospel* (Tübingen: Mohr Siebeck, 2004).

53. For example, Marcus Borg, *Conflict, Holiness and Politics in the Teaching of Jesus* (New York: E. Mellen, 1984); Ed P. Sanders, *Jesus and Judaism* (Philadelphia: Fortress, 1985); R. R. Hann, "Judaism and Christianity in Antioch: Charisma and Conflict in the First Century," *JRH* 14 (1987): 341–360; Irving Zeitlin, *Jesus and the Judaism of His Time* (Oxford: Polity Press, 1988); Amy-Jill Levine, *The Social and Ethnic Dimensions of Matthean Salvation History* (Lewiston: Edwin Mellen, 1988); Bruce Malina and Jerome Neyrey, *Calling Jesus Names* (Sonoma, CA: Polebridge, 1988); D. L. Balch ed., *Social History of the Matthean Community* (Minneapolis: Fortress, 1991); Anthony Saldarini, *Matthew's Christian-Jewish Community* (Chicago: University of Chicago Press, 1994); Evert-Jan Vledder, *Conflict in the Miracle Stories* (Sheffield Academic Press, 1997); W. Horbury, *Jews and Christians in Contact and Controversy* (Edinburgh: T & T Clark, 1998); David Sim, *The Gospel of Matthew and Christian Judaism* (Edinburgh: T & T Clark, 1999); Warren Carter, *Matthew and the Margins* (Sheffield: Sheffield Academic Press, 2000); Howard W. Clark, *The Gospel of Matthew and Its Readers* (Bloomington, IN: Indiana University Press, 2003).

religious ideology and the sectarianism that accompanied the struggle to redefine self-identity of each sectarian group.

All of these studies have contributed to our understanding of the historical Jesus or the theology of the evangelists, and they generally share the common feature in that they treat the text as a window.[54] This means that, through this window, one hopes to obtain an insight into the immediate environment of the text, be it linguistic context, literary source, ideological reality, or social-political locale, which is viewed as the key to unlocking the meaning of the text. Due to the historical emphasis of these inquiries, they are generally placed under the framework of "historical-critical paradigm."[55]

The historical-critical paradigm has dominated gospel studies in the past century. While it has been exceedingly fruitful, there are two significant drawbacks. First, exegetical methods within this paradigm start with the historical setting from which the text took its genesis. Consequently, by overemphasizing the tradition behind words, phrases, sentences of the text, the essential narrative integrity of the gospel tends to be either rejected or ignored.[56] Second, by anchoring the meaning of the gospel within its historical setting, historical critics often conclude that the theology of the text reflects the life and belief of the specific historical community behind the text. An inevitable risk may arise in that they might lose their insight on the evangelist's fundamental purpose for writing the gospel. For example, Matthew did not intend to describe what life was like in first-century Palestine to his readers,

---

54. Murray Krieger in his *A Window to Criticism* uses "window and mirror" metaphors to illustrate different focuses and major developments in modern literary criticism. He views one of the functions of the language "as window to the world," which means the meaning of the text lies through and beyond the text to another time and space; *A Window to Criticism: Shakespeare's Sonnets and Modern Poetics* (Princeton: Princeton University Press, 1964), especially 3–4. Such a metaphor is then followed by many other scholars from both biblical studies and beyond; for example, Norman R. Peterson, *Literary Criticism for New Testament Critics* (Philadelphia: Fortress, 1978), 19; Hans Frei, *The Eclipse of Biblical Narrative: A Study in Eighteenth and Nineteenth Century Hermeneutics* (New Haven: Yale University Press, 1974), 135, 280–281; Powell, *What Is Narrative Criticism?* (Minneapolis: Fortress, 1990), 8.

55. This term derives from Peterson's concept of "historical-critical tradition." Although he does not use the exact words "historical-critical paradigm," he believes that "this tradition constitutes the fundamental 'scientific paradigm' of biblical studies." *Literary Criticism*, 9.

56. I do recognize that for some biblical scholars, not only the unity of the gospel is not to be assumed, but some have built their entire career by demonstrating that the gospel is a collection of fragmented traditions, for example, Karl Schmit, *Der Rahmen der Deschichte Jesu* (Berlin: Trowitzsch, 1919).

or even to reveal his community's identity; rather, the author was primarily writing a story about the person of Jesus for "general circulation."[57]

The previously mentioned scholars, with the exception of Tannehill and Saunders, all could be placed under the category of the "historical-critical paradigm." Dibelius, Albertz, Bultmann, Taylor and Hultgren each dismantle the stories to seek their origin or how they were formed in the pre-literary stages. In its comprehensiveness and specificity, Bultmann's study serves as a milestone for form-critical analysis in the field of gospel studies. While these scholars vary in their assumptions, emphases, terminology and conclusions, they nonetheless share three characteristics in common. First, they all adopt form-critical methods to determine the form of short narratives that usually ended with a saying of Jesus. Second, they study conflict stories across the gospels, rather than locating them within the narrative frame of one particular gospel. Third, as mentioned above, they all share a common aspiration to employ the text as a window through which to gain insight into the *Sitz im Leben* of the text, either in terms of its history of transmission or the history of the evangelists' community.

Besides the two drawbacks under the framework of "historical-critical paradigm," one of the most significant limitations shared among these scholars is their failure to recognize the drama of exchange between Jesus and his opponents and its impact on the readers. Although Hultgren mentions this flaw,[58] it is Tannehill who initiates the change to focus on the tension of conflicts and their impact on the reader.[59] Therefore, while Tannehill also uses form-critical methods to analyze conflict stories across the gospels, his study marks a significant departure from the form-critical investigation. This is because Tannehill employs communication theory and draws attention to the form as an essential communicative element between the author and the reader.

---

57. In his article, "For Whom Were Gospels Written," Bauckham has convincingly argued for a general gospel audience against the assumption that each gospel is written for a particular, enclosed community. In *The Gospels for All Christians: Rethinking the Gospel Audiences*, ed. Richard Bauckham (Grand Rapids, MI: Eerdmans, 1998), 9–48.

58. Hultgren, *Jesus and His Adversaries*, 51.

59. Tannehill in his earlier book, *The Sword of His Mouth*, clearly recognizes the tension embedded with the narrative, ". . . the impact [of the story] comes not through convincing portrayal of character but through the tension which is expressed in the structure of the story itself . . . We find in these stories, then, another variety of tensive language, one in which the tension assumes narrative form, with two speaking and acting persons as the poles." Tannehill, *The Sword of His Mouth* (Missoula, MT: Scholars Press, 1975), 153–154.

He does briefly address the narrative settings of the conflict stories; his focus, however, rests with the categorization of their types, seeking how different types demonstrate different value conflicts.⁶⁰ Furthermore, his categories run the risk of being too specific which often results in subjective classifications that may cause overlapping and some confusion. For example, Tannehill considers both Matthew 12:38–42 and 16:1–4 to be "corrections stories," yet they can also be categorized as "objection stories."⁶¹

In contrast to Tannehill, Repschinski focuses on Matthew's authorial intention, paying further attention to the final form of the text. One of the most interesting findings in the study is his demonstration of how Matthew consistently redacts his sources to create more discourses, thereby highlighting the dialogical nature of the controversy stories.⁶² However, his approach – redactional criticism – limits his reading of the Matthean conflict stories primarily in relation to Mark. Repschinski also adds discussions of the form-critical analysis (ch. 6) and narrative features of conflict stories (ch. 7), but they are brief and continue serving his purpose of determining the *Sitz im Leben* of Matthew.⁶³

Previous studies, except for Saunders, have therefore failed to investigate the literary function of these pericopae for the narrative program of each gospel. In terms of the Gospel of Matthew, what remains unaddressed is a detailed analysis into the nature and purpose of conflict stories as they appear within the total narrative structure of Matthew. Saunders's work claims to analyze the literary function as such.⁶⁴ However, his primary assumption is that conflict stories "offer an opportunity to explore the nature of the relationship between Matthew's vision for the Christian community and competing Jewish and Christian sects."⁶⁵ That leads his study to focus on the nature of

---

60. Tannehill, "Varieties of Synoptic Pronouncement Stories," *Semeia* 20 (1981): 119.
61. Tannehill, "Varieties," 103.
62. Repschinski, *Controversy Stories*, 264–265.
63. Repschinski's form-critical analysis in ch. 6 concludes, for example, that the form of conflict stories is a combination of Greek chreia and contests in dialogue. Repschinski, *Controversy Stories*, 292–293. His discussion on the narrative settings and characters in ch. 7 concludes that conflict stories are vehicles through which Jesus and his disciples claim leadership in Israel, 320–321, 341–342. It unfortunately does not shed new light on the function of conflict stories.
64. Saunders, "No One Dared," ii, 7.
65. Saunders, ii.

Matthew's polemic: whether conflict stories reflect Matthew's "intra-familial, even prophetic critique" of Judaism, or "rhetoric typical of documents oriented toward community building" with "an identity independent of competing Judaism[s]."[66] To this extent, Saunders's work is similar to Repschinski's study.

The present study is similar to Saunders's to the extent that it also aims to investigate the literary function of conflict stories. There are, however, several vital differences between the two. First, this study refines Saunders's observation on the Matthean Christology emerged from the conflict stories. Saunders's key finding on the Christology is summarized in his conclusion: "The controversy stories in Matthew have a consistently Christological focus. Matthew uses them to depict the character of Jesus' mission, the nature and surpassing power of his authority, and the focus of his ministry on the realization of God's will for mercy."[67]

Whilst this statement is relevant for the conflict stories in Matthew, because it is so broad, it could just as well be applied to conflict stories in all of the Synoptic Gospels. Saunders's observation fails to describe the distinct christological focus in Matthew's presentation of the conflict stories. This study refines Saunders's work by offering another insight: the christological focus in the Matthean conflict stories is particularly concerned with the nexus between the divine status of Jesus and his being the Davidic Messiah. Second, there is a major methodological weakness in Saunders's study. That is, it does not provide a framework of literary critical methods nor does it apply clearly defined tools of literary analysis. For example, he mixes concepts such as plot, character, sources, and literary components together, considering them to be genre characteristics that he calls "generic repertoire."[68] Therefore, while claiming to use literary-critical approaches, his application becomes rather superficial, lacking both coherent definitions as well as in-depth investigation. In contrast to Saunders, this study will consult with current literary theories and systematically analyze conflict stories with contemporary literary critical

---

66. Saunders, 486, also 478–489.

67. Saunders, 465.

68. Saunders, 86–101. Moreover, he fails to directly interact with his contemporary literary theories. Instead, he relies on the limited categories applied by a few Matthean scholars in their own studies, such as Kingsbury and Anderson; in his own words, "I rely on Capel Anderson's work throughout this discussion of character in Matthew," 98, fn 80; see other examples on 87, 92, 100, 103.

tools. Moreover, inquiry into the *Sitz im Leben* of Matthew will be bracketed outside of the focus. Third, as mentioned above, there are differences in the selection of conflict stories (see discussions in section 1.2.2.1 "Stanley Saunders"). Whereas Saunders includes sixteen stories (plus three parables), my study will analyze seventeen conflicts. The following table (table 1) provides a summary of previous studies on the conflict stories in the gospels.

Table 1. Summary of Previous Studies

Scholars (year)	Terminology	*Sitz im Leben*	Structure	Authenticity
Dibelius (1919)	Paradigm	Greek-speaking Jewish churches	5 criteria	No
Albertz (1921)	Controversy dialogues	Historical Jesus	2+1 elements	Yes
Bultmann (1921)	Controversy dialogues	Palestinian Jewish Christian churches	3 criteria	No
Taylor (1935)	Pronouncement stories	Historical Jesus	2 criteria	Yes
Hultgren (1974)	Conflict stories	Early Christian storytellers	3 criteria	No
Tannehill (1981)	Pronouncement stories	Greek-speaking Roman world	2 elements	N/A[69]
Saunders (1990)	Controversy stories	(possibly) *intra muros* of Judaism[70]	3 criteria	No
Repschinski (2000)	Controversy stories	Struggles *intra muros* of Judaism	4 criteria	No

---

69. This is not a concern for Tannehill, as he writes, "no attempt will be made to separate material of early and late origin, beyond noting that certain scenes (especially inquiries), though marked as separate narrative episodes by a change of setting and/or characters, comment on material in a previous scene, indicating that they did not have an independent origin." Tannehill, "Varieties," 102.

70. I added "possibly" because Saunders does not claim to have solved such an issue. "No One Dared," 486.

1.3 Methodology in the Current Study
1.3.1 Conflict Stories: Terminology and Criteria for This Study

While the selection of the conflict stories in the present study primarily depends on the criteria of Bultmann and Repschinski, its purpose differs fundamentally from their research. The present study will explore the Gospel of Matthew as an integral literary unit and apply literary-critical methods to analyze this string of stories within their narrative context of Matthew and their final narrative impact on the reader.

As a result, what most distinguishes this research from previous studies is that, while treating conflict stories as a unique literary form isolated from other thematic stories in Matthew (e.g. parables, miracle stories), this research does not focus on their pre-gospel traditions. To this extent, instead of attempting to employ the text as a window, this study regards the text more as a mirror within which 'meaning' is reflected by *what* the text says and *how* it is said.[71] Such an approach is succinctly described by Powell as the approach where "the critic determines to look at the text, not through it, and whatever insight is obtained will be found in the encounter of the reader with text itself."[72]

I choose to use the term "conflict stories" for two main reasons. First, by using "story" I intend to highlight the narrative nature of the text under investigation.[73] A story, by definition, is dramatic in nature and its drama can be found in the movement, change and conflict of the events and characters involved. Second, I use "conflict" to underline the intensified hostility within each story, even though "controversy" is also widely used. The criteria of selecting conflict stories for this study are slightly different from those of Bultmann and Repschinki. Instead of using "an attitude or an action of Jesus or his disciples," I will take account of:

---

71. The metaphor of "mirror" used here is described by Krieger "as an enclosed set of endlessly faceted mirrors ever multiplying its maze of reflections but finally shut up within itself." Krieger, *Window to Criticism*, 3. Krieger, however, later endeavors to mix the sharp division between the window and the mirror, and insists that eventually the mirror will become windows as well (4).

72. Powell, *What Is Narrative Criticism?*, 8.

73. This is similar to Hultgren's reason for choosing the word "stories." *Jesus and His Adversaries*, 52.

1. The presence of an attitude of hostility or challenge in the setting of the narrative (either explicit or implied);
2. The presence of a question of an accusation or a challenge; and
3. The question or the accusation is usually followed by a reply from Jesus.

The result is in accordance with Repschinski's set of seventeen stories: 9:1–8, 9–13, 14–17; 12:1–8, 9–14, 22–37, 38–45; 13:53–58; 15:3–9; 16:1–4; 19:1–9; 21:14–17, 23–27; 22:15–22, 23–33, 34–40, 41–46. The following table (table 2) provides the list of conflict stories in Matthew with parallel materials in Mark and Luke.

Table 2. List of Conflict Stories in Matthew with Their Parallels in the Synoptic Gospels

	Matthew	Mark	Luke
1	9:1–8 Healing of the Paralytic	2:1–12	5:17–26
2	9:9–13 Eating with Tax Collectors and Sinners	2:15–17	5:29b–32
3	9:14–17 Question about Fasting	2:18–22	5:33–35
4	12:1–8 Plucking Grain on Sabbath	2:23–28	6:1–5
5	12:9–14 Healing on Sabbath	3:1–5	6:6–10
6	12:22–37 The Beelzebub Controversy	3:22–30	11:14–23
7	12:38–45 Asking for Signs from Heaven	8:11–12	11:29–32
8	13:53–58 A Prophet without Honor	6:1–6	
9	15:1–9 Hand Washing Tradition	7:1–8	
10	16:1–4 Asking for Signs from Heaven	8:11–12	11:29–32
11	19:3–9 Question on Divorce	10:2–9	
12	21:14–17 Jesus at the Temple		
13	21:23–27 Question about Authority	11:27–33	20:1–8
14	22:15–22 Paying Taxes to Caesar	12:13–17	20:20–26
15	22:23–33 Question on Resurrection	12:18–27	20:27–40
16	22:34–40 Question on Greatest Commandment	12:28–34*	10:25–28*
17	22:41–46 Whose Son Is the Christ?	12:35–37*	20:41–47*

* Strictly speaking, these stories are not "conflict stories" but reflect conflict materials that are altered by Matthew to be conflict stories.

There are several conflict stories in Matthew that may formally meet these criteria but will not be included by this study. They are: the three temptations of Jesus in 4:1–11 and the trial of Jesus before the Sanhedrin in 26:62–64. This omission is due to two reasons. First, the temptation story (4:1–11) and the Passion narrative (Matt 26–28) belong to what Bultmann classifies as "historical stories and legends,"[74] differing from "the sayings of Jesus" to which other conflict stories belong.[75] The dialogue between Jesus and the high priest is part of the longer trial scene where there are multiple parties involved in the hostile encounter (26:59–68). Moreover, one of the dialogue parties in the temptation story is the devil who is not a human figure. Therefore, the two excluded stories display compound characteristics in terms of their form and content, which deserve separate treatment and distinguish them from the rest of seventeen conflict stories. Second, these stories are not included by most scholars mentioned above.[76] To maintain the continuity of the object of the present study with that of previous scholarship, they will not be included.

While each individual story will be examined in terms of its textual linguistics, more importantly, each story will be analyzed within the surrounding context and its situation within the overall narrative framework of Matthew. Repschinski spares only a handful of pages at the end of his book on narrative analysis of the conflicts. However, he admits, "a thoroughgoing narrative analysis of the controversy stories in Matthew's Gospel would take up more space than this chapter can allow for."[77] My research intends to underline the integrity of these conflict narratives in their own right, as well as explore how this series of conflicts serves the author's broader theological purpose. Some specific questions could be asked. For example: Could Hultgren's "non-unitary stories" really be independent of their textual surroundings? How do conflict stories advance the plot line and what purpose do they serve for Matthew's theology?

---

74. Bultmann, *History*, 254–257.

75. Bultmann, 39.

76. See Taylor, *Formation*, 44–62; 77–78; Saunders, "No One Dared," 5–6, 114–15; Repschinski, *Controversy Stories*, 62; Albertz is an exception as he includes Matt 4:1–11 as a *Streitgespräch*.

77. Repschinski, *Controversy Stories*, 294.

1.3.2 Tools of Literary Criticism Applied in This Study

Beginning in the 1970s, and already flourishing by the 1980s, the literary-critical approach came to the stage of biblical studies as a possible remedy to the drawbacks of the historical-critical paradigm.[78] Peterson describes this shift to literary-critical approach as the "revolutionary chang" to the fundamental scientific paradigm of biblical studies.[79] In contrast to the historical-critical approach,[80] the literary-critical approach has several underlying assumptions. First, instead of assuming the text is a collection of fragmented oral or textual traditions, the literary-critical approach assumes the text to be a unity. Second, it treats the text as a mirror, assuming that meaning (of the text) is reflected within the text itself. Third, the literary-critical approach assumes the importance of the reader and therefore takes into consideration of the relationship between text and the reader. In fact, the mirror approach of literary criticism itself is not as novel as it may sound. Some scholars suggest that it was an applied technique from early as by Horace, a poet from the first century BCE.[81]

Because literary criticism covers a vast number of methods and theories, one modern literary critic, M. H. Abrams, proposes a functional typology to categorize several basic types of literary criticism:

1. *Expressive* type: author-centered, attentive to the views of the author;
2. *Pragmatic* type: reader-centered, attentive to the impact caused by the text on the reader;
3. *Objective* type: text-centered, attentive to the self-sufficient world of text itself;
4. *Mimetic* type: reference-centered, attentive to the accuracy of the representation by the text to the outer world.[82]

---

78. Although "literary-critical approach" is used here as a singular term, it encompasses a wide range of hypothesis, theories related to study the text as literature. In this study, "literary criticism" is also used interchangeably with "literary-critical approach."

79. Peterson, *Literary Criticism*, 9.

80. For the sake of pairing up with the term "literary-critical approach," in this study "historical-critical approach" is used interchangeably with "historical-critical paradigm."

81. Edgar V. McKnight, "Literary Criticism," in *Dictionary of Jesus and the Gospels* (Downers Grove: InterVarsity Press, 1992), 473–480.

82. Quoted by Powell, *What Is Narrative Criticism?*, 11. Cf. M. H. Abrams, *The Mirror and the Lamp: Romantic Theory and the Critical Tradition* (New York: W.W. Norton, 1953), 8–29.

It should be noted that Abrams's typology defines literary criticism in its broadest sense, thus his *mimetic* type and part of the *expressive* type could include what we discussed above regarding historical-critical approach. However, biblical scholars at large adopt the narrower definition of literary criticism which only covers reader-centered (*pragmatic* type) and text-centered (*objective* type) methods.[83] It is this narrower definition that is under discussion in the current study. Even so, surveying the whole discipline of literary-criticism will not be realistic due to the scope of the current study, therefore, I will only highlight specific methods that either have been applied to or are relevant to gospel studies, and they will be discussed in the following sections in this order: narrative criticism, reader-response criticism, and speech-act theory.[84]

Before introducing the literary-critical tools applied to this study, two preliminary matters are worth noting. First, it is necessary to point out that the shift from historical-critical paradigm to literary-critical approach within biblical studies is not a disjunctive movement. Rather, the advance of redaction and composition criticism has built a bridge for this shift. Paying attention to the authorial intention in redacting their sources, a question will inevitably arise: if minute redaction of certain passages tells us about the *theology* of the evangelist, then what does the whole arrangement of materials tell us about the *intention* of the evangelist? From answers to these questions we have seen the movement toward the claim for the integrity of gospel narratives.[85] Second, it must be emphasized that although this study employs the literary-critical approach, it by no means indicates that such an approach opposes or invalidates the historical-critical approach. Instead, I will argue that the literary approach offers alternative perspectives for reading the text, which, although separate from the historical approach, may nonetheless incorporate and evaluate the findings of historical approach, as Malbon so aptly reminds us:

---

83. Powell, *What Is Narrative Criticism?*, 12.

84. A comprehensive bibliography on literary criticism surveying titles that are published up to 1992 is compiled by Powell. Mark A. Powell, *The Bible and Modern Literary Criticism: A Critical Assessment and An Annotated Bibliography* (Westport: Greenwood Press, 1992).

85. Moore offers a detailed account of how this shifting process came about with redaction and composition criticism as bridge; see Stephen Moore, *Literary Criticism and the Gospels* (New Haven: Yale University Press, 1989), 4–8.

Reading the text with no reference to history or other texts is impossible; and, of course, focusing on the internal relations of the text has its own dangers. Yet there is still something to be said for preliminary investigations of the text and of history in relative isolation, so that the two may thereafter inform each other rather than risk forming or deforming each other initially.[86]

1.3.2.1 Narrative Criticism

Anyone who makes use of narrative criticism cannot evade the work of Seymour Chatman[87] and Wayne Booth[88] who set the foundational agenda for modern narrative critics. First, Chatman and Booth both highlight the distinction between the historical author of a literary work and the implied author which can be constructed only from the text (see discussion on "implied author" below). Second, they both call attention to the rhetoric of the story, believing that how the story is told is itself as significant as the actual content of a story.[89] This idea should not be strange to biblical scholars since redaction critics have already recognized that authorial intention can be detected through the author's shaping of his sources. In addition, building on Booth's idea of the implied author, Chatman offers another contribution which became widely accepted by both literary critics and biblical scholars. Chatman uses a diagram to describe the process of narrative-communication and suggests that "only the implied author and implied reader are immanent to a narrative ... The real author and real reader are outside the narrative transaction ..."[90] The significance of these distinctions will be shown in the following discussion of the implied author and the implied reader.

---

86. Elizabeth S. Malbon, *In the Company of Jesus: Characters in Mark's Gospel* (Louisville: Westminster John Knox Press, 2000), 115.

87. Seymour Chatman, *Story and Discourse: Narrative Structure in Fiction and Film* (Ithaca: Cornell University Press, 1978).

88. Wayne Booth, *The Rhetoric of Fiction* (Chicago: University of Chicago Press, 1961).

89. Booth, *Rhetoric of Fiction*, 149; also Chatman, *Story and Discourse*, 19.

90. Chatman, 151.

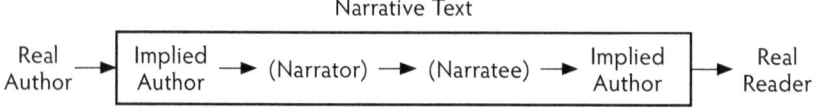

Narrative criticism treats the New Testament narrative text as a communication device between author and reader,[91] concerned only with the final form of the text, and focusing on the world internal to it.[92] In what follows I will introduce key categories of narrative criticism which will be used in this study, including: implied author and implied reader (narrator and narratee), plot, character, order and sequence, rhetoric and story, setting and mood, and point of view.[93] And I will summarize each of these categories briefly together with scholars who either initiated or have had significant influence on them.

The implied author and narrator: The concept of "implied author" was coined by Booth who defines it as "an ideal, literary, created version of the real man, he is the sum of his own choices."[94] This concept has been further developed since then, but the basic assumption remains the same. That is, the implied author is only discernible from the text and may not be entirely corresponding to the historical author. Booth argues the primary reason for this is because a given literary work only presents one version of the historical author's self – the implied author.[95] As a consequence, it becomes less important for narrative critics to inquire into the *Sitz im Leben* of the historical author than to focus on the text itself. To this extent, the narrator serves

---

91. The term "narrative criticism" was designated by Rhoads for the first time in 1980 (remaining unpublished until 1982); see David Rhoads, "Narrative Criticism and the Gospel of Mark," *JAAR* 50 (1982): 411–434.

92. Malbon, "Narrative Criticism," in *Searching for Meaning: An Introduction to Interpreting the New Testament*, ed. Paula Gooder (Louisville, KY: Westminster John Knox Press, 2009), 80.

93. For detailed discussion on some of these categories, see Powell, *What Is Narrative Criticism?*, 11–75. Also cf. Janice Capel Anderson, *Matthew's Narrative Web: Over, and Over, and Over Again* (Sheffield: Sheffield Academic Press, 1994), 26; Malbon, "Narrative Criticism," 81–86.

94. Booth, *Rhetoric of Fiction*, 75. Cf. Booth, *Critical Understanding* (Chicago: University of Chicago Press, 1979), 269.

95. Some illustrations are given by Booth; "Just as one's personal letters imply different versions of oneself, depending on the differing relationships with each correspondent and the purpose of each letter, so the writer sets himself out with a different air depending on the needs of particular works." *Rhetoric of Fiction*, 75.

as the spokesperson or the "voice" of the implied author.[96] Yet the implied author and the narrator can be separated under the circumstances when the narrator is dramatized, that is, when he becomes a character of the narrative, or, if he is unreliable.[97] Because the narrator of the Gospel of Matthew is not only reliable but also endowed with 'omniscience'[98] in the earthly realm,[99] he becomes almost indistinguishable from the implied author.[100] In this study, therefore, I shall use Matthew, the (implied) author and the narrator interchangeably. For the sake of simplicity, I will also designate the author with a third person masculine singular pronoun "he."[101]

The implied reader and narratee: The implied reader is not only a crucial concept for narrative criticism, but is vital for reader-response criticism. Yet the implied reader is one of the least agreed upon concepts within literary criticism. This study follows the definition popularized by Wolfgang Iser, which suggests that the implied reader be understood as that which "incorporates both the prestructuring of the potential meaning by the text, and the reader's actualization of this potential through the reading process."[102] Iser's definition is rephrased by Kingsbury with a more human-like feature; therefore, the implied reader is the "imaginary person in whom the intention of the text is to be thought of as always reaching its fulfillment."[103] As a result, the implied reader is the counterpart to the implied author (as shown by Chatman's narrative text diagram above) and is to be distinguished from the historical audience/reader to whom the narrative was originally directed. Furthermore, just like the implied author, the implied reader is more of a

---

96. Powell, *What Is Narrative Criticism?*, 25.

97. Powell, 25–26.

98. Similar to what the authors describe about the narrator of the Gospel of Mark. David Rhoads, Joanna Dewey and Donald Michie, *Mark as Story: An Introduction to the Narrative of a Gospel*, 2nd ed. (Minneapolis: Fortress, 1999), 39.

99. Which means that the narrator apparently is only knowledgeable about things on earth, but the things of heaven and hell are explained through the mouth of characters within the narrative. Powell, *What Is Narrative Criticism?*, 26.

100. Anderson, *Matthew's Narrative Web*, 29.

101. According to Rhoads, Dewey and Michie, the narrator is more of a function rather than a personal character for the author. *Mark as Story*, 39. However, for the sake of rhetoric simplicity, I designate the narrator with a third person masculine singular pronoun "he."

102. Wolfgang Iser, *The Implied Reader: Patterns of Communication in Prose Fiction from Bunyan to Beckett* (Baltimore: Johns Hopkins University Press, 1974), xii. The original work was published in German in 1972.

103. Jack D. Kingsbury, *Matthew as Story*, 2nd ed. (Philadelphia: Fortress, 1988), 38.

literary construct rather than real person(s) and the ideal goal for narrative critics is to read the text as the implied reader reads it.[104] In other words, the implied reader is a role the real reader needs to play as the implied author envisions them.[105] Reconstructing this hypothetical reader is essential for investigating the possible impact of the narrative text because it helps the literary critic to identify the meanings that the author intends to achieve or the response he strives to evoke in the reader upon reading the text.[106] Like the implied author, the implied reader can be, yet not exclusively, constructed from the narrative and is to be different from the narratee. The narratee is the one whom the narrator is speaking to in the narrative, such as Theophilus in Luke-Acts. He can also be a character in the story or be unidentified.[107] This study shall only focus on "the implied reader" and will use the term interchangeably with "the reader."

It is assumed in this study that the implied reader has *a priori* understandings of the text. Most significantly, these understandings encompass a background knowledge of the Gospel of Matthew that may or may not be explicitly mentioned in the text. The fact that the author frequently cites Hebrew Scripture, especially the prophetic sayings (e.g. 1:22; 2:5, 17; 3:3; 4:4, 6, 10, 14; 8:17), suggests the implied reader is envisioned by the author as to be not only more or less familiar with such literature but also holds it in high regard. One may also speculate on *a priori* understanding of the implied reader from historical evidence external to the text. The gospel text itself is a document completed at a time far removed from modern day readers. Given the implied reader is a role envisioned by the author,[108] readers today are required to resort to all available historical evidences to reconstruct the original context of the gospel so that they may acquire informed impressions

---

104. Cf. Chatman, *Story and Discourse*, 150; or, as Kingsbury suggests, the implied reader is the "imaginary person in whom the intention of the text is to be thought of as always reaching its fulfillment." *Matthew as Story*, 36.

105. Anderson, *Matthew's Narrative Web*, 28. The implied reader in this sense is similar to Umberto Eco's definition of the "Model Reader," which refers to a model of the possible reader, foreseeable by the author, "supposedly able to deal interpretatively with the expressions in the same way as the author deals generatively with them." Umberto Eco, *The Role of the Reader* (Bloomington: University of Indiana, 1979), 7.

106. David B. Howell, *Matthew's Inclusive Story: A Study in the Narrative Rhetoric of the First Gospel* (Sheffield: Sheffield Academic Press, 1990), 42.

107. Powell, *What Is Narrative Criticism?*, 26–27.

108. Eco, *Role of the Reader*, 7.

of such ancient texts and obtain possible expectations of the author for the implied reader. For example, if one is not aware that a key characteristic of the Sadducees is their rejection of resurrection, then it is puzzling to understand for what the reason they are mentioned repeatedly in Matthew 16:1–12, a passage preceding Jesus's first prediction of his death and resurrection. However, the modern reader can only discover such a knowledge of the Sadducees by the implied reader from combined historical sources, including other New Testament texts or even the writings of Josephus.[109]

The three elements of implied author, narrative (text) and implied reader form the overarching framework for narrative critics to investigate the text. The relationship within the communication process is also illustrated in the following diagram by Powell,[110] which is essentially a modification of Chatman's narrative text diagram:

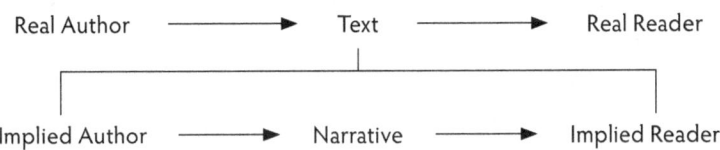

After determining how we understand the implied author and narrator versus the implied reader and the narratee, then it is possible to come to other categories.

Plot: Plot is the most important element of narrative criticism that this study will focus on. There are two reasons for this. First, as Brooks accurately observes, plot "... is the principle of interconnectedness and intention which we cannot do without in moving through the discrete elements – incidents, episodes, actions – of a narrative."[111] Conflict stories, being discrete elements of Matthew's narrative, must be analyzed in terms of their relationship with the Matthean plot in order to determine their literary function. Second, scholars have observed that, especially in transmitting oral literature into written

---

109. For a detailed discussion, please see section 4.1.3 in chapter 4.
110. Powell, *What Is Narrative Criticism?*, 19.
111. Peter Brooks, *Reading for the Plot: Design and Intention in Narrative* (Cambridge, MA: Harvard University Press, 1984), 5.

material, maintaining the plot of the traditional narrative is "of necessity."[112] In other words, a narrative without a minimal plot becomes incomprehensible to the reader;[113] therefore, a storyteller must strive to maintain the interest of the reader in the narrative. The Gospel of Matthew consists of both written materials (Mark and Q) and possibly other oral traditions, but it is composed with great mastery of the author and becomes a distinct literary work in its own right. As previous studies have shown that Matthew consistently heightens the dialogical nature of the conflict stories,[114] it is evident that conflict stories are important for the plot development because in each story the author slows down his narrative time[115] to make these dramatic scenes take on a decisive role in the action of the narrative.[116]

Although scholars have not agreed upon a precise definition for plot, several leading literary critics offer the following descriptions:

> The events in a story are turned into a plot by its discourse, the modus of presentation. The discourse can be manifested in various media, but it has an internal structure qualitatively different from any one of its possible manifestations. That is, plot, story-as-discoursed, exists at a more general level than any particular objectification . . . Its function is to emphasize or de-emphasize certain story-events, to interpret some and to leave others to inference, to show or to tell, to comment or to remain silent, to focus on this or that aspect of an event or character.[117]

> A plot is a set of rules that determines and sequences events to cause a determinate affective response. Thus 'plot' is restricted to creating 'stories' from the infinite flux of experience . . . Plotting, like the use of syntax, is a profound mental process which we

---

112. Robert Scholes and Robert Kellogg, *The Nature of Narrative* (New York: Oxford University Press, 1966), 12.

113. Brooks, *Reading for the Plot*, 5.

114. Repschinski, *Controversy Stories*, 264–265.

115. It refers to the "length-of-narrative," a concept in contrast to "duration-of-story" termed as "story time." Gérard Genette, *Narrative Discourse* (Ithaca, NY: Cornell University Press, 1980), 88. Chatman uses different terms – "story time" and "discourse time" – but they refer to the same concept. Chatman, *Story and Discourse*, 62f; cf. detailed discussion of story time and plotted time in Peterson's *Literary Criticism*, 49–80.

116. Genette, *Narrative Discourse*, 86–112, especially 110.

117. Chatman, *Story and Discourse*, 43.

use in making sense of experience. Real incidents apart from a plot are affectively meaningless. Only by imposing a plot on them can we make them affectively meaningful.[118]

[Plot is] the intelligible whole that governs a succession of events in any story . . . This provisory definition immediately shows the plot's connecting function between an event or events and the story. A story is *made out of* events to the extent that plot *makes* events *into* a story. The plot, therefore, places us at the crossing point of temporality and narrativity . . .[119]

. . . the organizing line of plot is more often than not some scheme or machination, a concerted plan for the accomplishment of some purpose which goes against the ostensible and dominant legalities of the fictional world, the realization of a blocked and resisted desire. Plots are not simply organizing structures, they are also intentional structures, goal-oriented and forward-moving . . . to speak of plot is to consider both story elements and their order. Plot could be thought of as the interpretive activity elicited by the distinction between *sjuŽet* [events] and *fabula* [story], the way we *use* the one against the other . . . Plot is thus the dynamic shaping force of the narrative discourse.[120]

Based on these descriptions and definitions, it is possible to discern five main characteristics of plot. It involves (1) sequence[121] or order of events and (2) changes in development. It must (3) retain logical connection (e.g. causation, conflict), (4) be purposeful and meaningful;[122] and (5) require the reader's vital role (in perceiving the plot).[123]

---

118. Kieran Egan, "What Is a Plot?," *New Literary History* (1978): 470.

119. Paul Ricoeur, "Narrative Time," in *On Narrative*, ed. W. J. T. Mitchell (Chicago: University of Chicago Press, 1981), 167.

120. Brooks, *Reading for the Plot*, 12–13.

121. James L. Resseguie, *Narrative Criticism of the New Testament: An Introduction* (Grand Rapids: Baker Academic, 2005), 197.

122. Cf. M. H. Abrams, *A Glossary of Literary Terms*, 7th ed. (Boston, MA: Heinle & Heinle, 1999), 173.

123. Cf. Brooks, *Reading for the Plot*, 14; also Abrams, *Glossary of Literary Terms*, 224.

The Plot of Matthew and the Conflict Stories: What then is the main plot in Matthew? From the outset, it should fit within the meta-narrative frame of God's salvation history, which is likely the *a priori* understanding of history in the mind of the author and the reader. The storyline of the meta-narrative frame is simple. That is, God created humanity but they rebelled against Him (e.g. Gen 1–3). God then promised to save humanity through Abraham (e.g. Gen 12) and will eventually fulfil that promise through his messianic servant (e.g. Isa 40–55). With this in view, if one attempts to incorporate the five characteristics of a plot, then the plot of Matthew which focuses on a central figure, Jesus, can be summarized as this: God sent Jesus as the Messiah (1:1, 17), the Son of God, in order to save the people from their sins (1:18, 20–23), but the leaders of Israel rejected Jesus as the Messiah by plotting to kill him (e.g. 2:3–4, 13, 16; 12:14; 26:14–16, 59). The plot then reaches its resolution in the crucifixion and resurrection of Jesus (Matt 27–28:15),[124] where Jesus emerges as the ultimate winner of the conflict and fulfils God's salvific plan for all the nations (28:16–20).[125] This is a general summary of the Matthean plot, which seems to be also largely comprehensive of the plot of other gospels. However, the main task of this study is to investigate how conflict stories contribute to the overall development of the Matthean plot. For the purpose of this study, then, the next question is: what is the overall development of the plot specific to Matthew?

In the development of his plot Matthew seems to demonstrate a continuity and discontinuity of Jesus's ministry through a discernable watershed section in Matt 12–13 (for details see discussions in chapters 3 and 4). The continuity lies in the author's close connection between the life of Jesus with the history of Israel. This feature is exemplified, for example, by Matthew's prologue (1:1–17) and his characteristic use of the introduction formula to the Hebrew Scripture quotations in the gospel. In the light of such connections, Jesus's life and mission are continuous with an inherited Jewish tradition. Conversely, the discontinuity is also in plain view, the Matthean Jesus ushers

---

124. Kingsbury, "The Plot of Matthew's Story," *Int* 46 (1992): 355.

125. This summary is similar to Matera's description of Matthew's plot, "In the appearance of Jesus the Messiah, God fulfils his promises to Israel. But Israel refuses to accept Jesus as the Messiah. Consequently, the Gospel passes to the nations." Matera, "Plot of Matthew's Gospel," 243.

in a new kingdom paradigm that is incompatible with the paradigm which the Jewish leaders represent.

Prior to Matthew 12–13, the continuity of Jesus's ministry with Judaism appears to be the primary tone of the narrative. As evidence of this, most of the formulaic Matthean sayings occur in Matthew 1–13 (1:22; 2:15, 17, 23; 3:3; 4:14; 8:17; 12:17; 13:14, 35). From Matthew 14 to the Passion narrative starting in Matthew 26, the discontinuity of Jesus's ministry is much more pronounced in two ways. First, the author pays more attention to the polarization of Jesus and his opponents. In contrast to the christological focus of Matthew 1–13, the following section demonstrates a focus on the stubbornness of the Jewish leaders and the severe consequences they face. For example, the conflict in 15:1–9 is less focused on the authority of Jesus but highlights the negative characterization of the Pharisees. Additionally, immediately following the last block of conflict stories in Matthew 21–22, the author arranges the last discourse in Matthew 23 together with Matthew 24–25 where almost the entire section is devoted to Jesus's monologue. The author highlights through both sections (i.e. conflict story block Matt 21–22 and discourse block Matt 23–25) the deadly antithetical nature of the relationship between Jesus and the Jewish leaders which paves the way for the Passion narrative.

Second, the exclusion of the Jewish leaders and inclusion of Gentiles in Jesus's ministry becomes an important ecclesiological concern to the author. For example, in Matthew 10 Jesus gives the disciples clear instructions to go to "the lost sheep of Israel" (10:5–6), whereas in Matthew 15 he grants the Canaanite woman's request even though the words "the lost sheep of Israel" are reiterated in the story (15:24–28). The conflict between Jesus and the Jewish leaders over a hand washing tradition (15:1–20) is starkly juxtaposed with the faith of the Canaanite woman (15:21–28). These two are also bracketed by two feeding stories, where the four thousand in the second feeding story is likely referring to Gentiles. In Matthew 16–20 the author records Jesus's teaching on the horizontal dimension for relationships of the kingdom such as suffering, perseverance, humility, compassion, mercy, forgiveness, unity, and patience (16:13–20:28). Such a kingdom is inevitably divisive to those who retain a hardness of heart but is inclusive of those who express their faith in the person of Jesus.

My investigation in chapters 2–5 reveal that although scholars have long recognized the tension between this continuity and discontinuity, the conflict stories further accentuate the tension in the plot development of Matthew. The conflict stories serve to emphasize the identity of Jesus as the Davidic Messiah of the Jewish expectation (e.g. 9:14–17; 12:22–24; 21:14–17; 22:41–46). Similarly, the authority of Jesus and his kingdom is shown to clash with and be often antagonistic to the Jewish leaders, resulting in their consistent rejection of Jesus (e.g. 9:1–8, 9–13, 14–17; 12:22–37; 13:53–58; 15:1–9; 19:3–9; 21:23–27).

Closely related to this, the author's theological purpose for the conflict stories is seen from his scrupulous redaction of the sources as well as the "insertion" of unique materials and the arrangement of the materials within the overall narrative sequence.[126] An example in Matthew is the story of "The Sign of Jonah." The same story (12:38–45; 16:1–4) when put in a different location in the narrative sequence entails a rather different function. Therefore, conflict stories in Matthew are like a miniature of the whole gospel to the extent that they embody a movement of both plot and emotion. In other words, they are not to be read as a static set of stories through which we know something about the author's hostility to the Jews; instead, they are to be read as the author's tool to evoke a certain understanding or emotion in the reader regarding the person of Jesus and the movement he started.

Plot and Character: Characters are the actors in the narrative; they are human or non-human, individuals or a character group. Plot and character are two necessary elements to form the narrative world of the gospels.[127] Characters are agents of the plot because their actions advance the plot, but plot also governs the process of characterization.[128] For example, conflict stories in Matthew largely contain two characters, Jesus and the religious leaders (a character group). As the plot develops, these two characters are defined more and more into opposition against each other. In regards to characterization: How does Matthew shape these characters? In conflict stories, for

---

126. As literary critics point out, the order, sequence, and location of narrative materials in a text can significantly influence the meaning of the text. Perry rightly mentions, "Literary texts may effectively utilize the fact that their material is grasped successively; this is at times a central factor in determining their meanings. The ordering and distribution of the elements in a text may exercise considerable influence on the nature, not only of the *reading process*, but of the *resultant whole* as well." Menakhem Perry, "Literary Dynamics: How the Order of a Text Creates Its Meanings," *Poetics Today* (1979): 35.

127. Moore, *Literary Criticism*, 15–16.

128. Resseguie, *Narrative Criticism*, 197.

example, characters are revealed mostly through their speech, but sometimes also through their silence (e.g. 22:33). Characters can be portrayed through what others comment about them, such as the narrator and the opposing dialogue party in conflict stories. Questions remain to be resolved: What is Matthew's purpose to shape characters in such a way? How does the degree of characterization vary and how does it relate to plot development?[129] All these questions will be initially dealt with at the level of each pericope, with a subsequent synopsis emerging only after all seventeen stories are analyzed within the total narrative framework of Matthew.

Order or Sequence: As a feature of the plot, the order or sequence of events in any narrative is endowed with a "temporal duality."[130] That means, the length of time within the story (i.e. story time) and the length of time of the author's telling the story (i.e. narrative time)[131] determine the order or sequence of events in a narrative. An author can arrange and rearrange the order of events through literary devices, such as repetition, flashback, foreshadowing, or back reference.[132] If, as Tannehill rightly suggests, "I mention a respect for the text as a unique unity (a unity which may exist at various levels, from individual pericope to Gospel to, perhaps, the Bible as a whole) which discloses its full meaning and value only through the interaction of its parts,"[133] then how the author organizes each pericope in connection

---

129. Merenlahti defines the degree of characterization as "the extent to which characters stand out as mere functional agents as opposed to individual personalities." Petri Merenlahti, "Characters in Making: Individuality and Ideology," in *Characterization in the Gospels: Reconceiving Narrative Criticism*, eds. David Rhoads and Kari Syreeni (Sheffield: Sheffield Academic Press, 1999), 55; also cf. Fred. W. Burnett, "Characterization and Reader Construction of Characters in the Gospels," *Semeia* 63 (1993): 1, 19.

130. The term is used by Genette in *Narrative Discourse*, 33.

131. Genette particularly points out the importance of this temporal duality for oral narrative; it "is a typical characteristic not only of cinematic narrative but also of oral narrative, at all its levels of aesthetic elaboration, including the fully 'literary' level of epic recitation or dramatic narration." Genette, *Narrative Discourse*, 33.

132. Back reference refers to "new material appearing in the course of a text can go on developing previously constructed frames – fill them or extend them. This is called backward reference. The elementary back reference is when additional use is made of material from previous stages of the text for the sake of an additional new frame that can fit in without contradiction with what was previously constructed. This reference will be strongly felt if, in the context of the new frame, not only are new unexploited aspects of old reconstructed items uncovered, but additional meanings constructed out of the verbal material itself." Perry, "Literary Dynamics," 59.

133. Tannehill, *The Sword of His Mouth: Forceful and Imaginative Language in Synoptic Sayings* (Missoula, MT: Scholars Press, 1975), 201.

with its surrounding context should dominate how the reader would perceive the meaning of the text. For example, Matthew follows Mark's order of events closely in the first six conflict stories (9:1–8//Mark 2:1–12; 9:9–13//Mark 2:15–17; 9:14–17//Mark 2:18–22; 12:1–8//Mark 2:23–28; 12:9–14//Mark 3:1–5; 12:22–37//Mark 3:22–30). Yet unlike Mark's continuous narration from the conflicts regarding fasting to plucking grain on the Sabbath (Mark 2:18–28), Matthew inserts 9:18–11:30 in between the two conflicts. The Matthean Sabbath conflicts, therefore, should be analyzed in light of their relationship with Matthew 10–11.

Rhetoric and Story/Narrative: Just as the order of events in a narrative has a "temporal duality," approaching a narrative also rests at two levels. *The rhetoric level* refers to the manner by which a story is told. It includes techniques the author uses, including, for example, repetition, irony, figure of speech, simile and metaphor. *The story/narrative level* refers to the content of the story. It includes "actions, happenings, characters or items of setting."[134] Booth argues that it is inevitable for the author to employ literary devices even if he pursues objectivity in the writing.[135] Following Chatman and Booth, narrative critics today generally agree that not only the content of the story, but the rhetoric of the author also delivers meaning and has impact on readers.[136]

Not all agree on the terminology of "rhetoric," however. For instance, Powell follows Chatman's term "discourse,"[137] Howell uses "narrative"[138] as Culpepper,[139] and Resseguie follows Booth's term "rhetoric."[140] There are two reasons why this study employs the term *rhetoric*. First, the term "discourse" can be confused with another nuance of the word associated with the Gospel of Matthew, that is, the five discourse blocks as opposed to stories: Matthew 5–7, 10, 13, 18, 24–25. Second, although Culpepper and Howell intend to use "narrative" to avoid the word "discourse" for the above same reason, the

---

134. This follows the structuralist theory, see Chatman, *Story and Discourse*, 19.

135. Booth, *Rhetoric of Fiction*, 149–150.

136. For example, Howell, *Matthew's Inclusive Story*, 95–96; also, Susan S. Lanser, *The Narrative Art: Point of View in Prose Fiction* (Princeton, NJ: Princeton University Press, 1981), 99ff.

137. Powell, *What Is Narrative Criticism?*, 23; cf. Chatman, *Story and Discourse*, 19ff.

138. Howell, *Matthew's Inclusive Story*, 95.

139. Alan Culpepper, *Anatomy of John: A Study in Literary Design* (Philadelphia: Fortress, 1983), 53.

140. Resseguie, *Narrative Criticism*, 197. Cf. Booth, *Rhetoric of Fiction*.

word narrative is now more commonly used for the overall genre of gospels as stories; therefore, it seems a little odd to insert a narrower meaning to narrative. Additionally, the rhetoric of Matthew needs to be related to how this gospel differs and redacts conflict stories from his sources. In the analysis of each conflict story, this study will approach the text from both the rhetoric level and story level.

Setting and Mood: These are two minor yet interesting elements of a story. Setting "is the background against which the narrative action takes place,"[141] which includes physical, spatial, social-cultural or religious dimensions.[142] Mood refers to "the elements of the story which evoke tacit emotional responses on the part of the reader – the texture of the storyteller's language, the patterned nuances of vocabulary."[143] In regards to setting and mood, what is most relevant for studying the conflict stories includes, for example, the author's description of the location of the story (e.g. Jesus's hometown, the temple, a field), or the author's citation of or allusion to the Hebrew Scripture. The latter is particularly important for Matthew because scriptural citation or allusion appears frequently in Jesus's answer to the opponents. It functions to lead the reader "to respond in one way and not another: that is, the reader's reactions to any event may be shaped by anticipations generated by linguistic elements which appeared earlier in the narrative."[144] Matthew's citation of Isaiah 42:1-4 (12:18-21) before the Beelzebub conflict (12:22-37), for example, has oriented the reader's mood to the following conflicts where Jesus takes on the mission of justice, not only to the Jews but also to the Gentiles.

Point of view: Point of view is controlled by the narrator or the author to signify his perspective(s), and is central to evaluating the characters and narration in the literary text.[145] But why is point of view relevant for studying the conflict stories? This is because the author's point of view "is one of the major determining factors in how a reader appropriates and actualizes a

---

141. Resseguie, 87.

142. Camery-Hoggatt, *Irony in Mark's Gospel: Text and Subtext* (Cambridge: Cambridge University Press, 1992), 52; also Resseguie, *Narrative Criticism*, 87.

143. Camery-Hoggatt, 52.

144. Camery-Hoggatt, 54.

145. Uspensky, *A Poetics of Composition: The Structure of the Artistic Text and Typology of a Compositional Form*, trans. V. Zavarin and S. Wittig (Berkeley: University of California Press, 1973), 167–172.

story."[146] The author of Matthew consistently leads the reader to share a point of view similar to that of the narrator and Jesus. As a result, the reader tends to side with or to be sympathetic to Jesus in their judgment of each conflict.

The concept of "point of view" is first developed by two influential literary critics, Gérard Genette[147] and Boris Uspensky.[148] When literary critics examine the point of view of their text, they mostly refer to the five dimensions categorized by Uspensky.[149] However, in this study, I will only focus on the *phraseological, psychological* and *evaluative planes*, of which the latter two are described by Powell as "the standards of judgment by which readers are led to evaluate the events, characters, and settings that comprise the story."[150] This is because throughout the Matthean conflict stories, the author has displayed his careful choices of words in light of his redactions (phraseological plane). Moreover, the author also provides descriptions of characters' inner feelings or perceptions of (psychological plane) as well as his own commentary on the events (evaluative plane). An example of the evaluative point of view in Matthew is where the evangelist only presents one evaluative point of view that is shared by the narrator and Jesus, a feature that confirms the reliability of the narrator. As for the other two dimensions, spatial and temporal planes—while not absent in the stories, they are of less importance for the purpose of this investigation.

1.3.2.2 Reader-Response Criticism

A communication process will not complete until "the 'message' of a text has reached its destination; that is, until it is comprehended by a reader."[151] This study assumes that the reader of the narrative actively engages with the text so

---

146. Howell, *Matthew's Inclusive Story*, 38.
147. This concept is discussed in his work, *Narrative Discourse*, 185–189.
148. Uspensky devotes his entire book *A Poetics of Composition* to this concept.
149. These five dimensions include: (1) Phraseological plane – author/narrator's choice of words in telling the story; (2) Spatial plane – place from which actions and characters are narrated; (3) Temporal plane – time from which actions and characters are narrated; (4) Psychological plane – what the author/narrator describes as the inner feelings, motives, thoughts and perceptions of characters; (5) Evaluative or ideological plane – overriding perspective summing up the four dimensions above. Uspensky, *Poetics of Composition*, 1–100.
150. Powell, *What Is Narrative Criticism?*, 24.
151. Howell, *Matthew's Inclusive Story*, 38.

as to contribute to the meaning-making of the text.¹⁵² As a result, in addition to narrative criticism, this study will also draw insights from reader-response criticism. However, until the present day, among scholars no real agreement has been achieved on what reader-response criticism is – it seems to cover a range of criticisms.¹⁵³ Generally speaking, reader-response criticism "encompasses a range of criticisms which emphasize the role of readers as active agents in completing the meaning of a text by the way they read it."¹⁵⁴ Two key questions of reader-response criticism are (1) who is the reader and (2) what is the relationship between the reader and the text? Some biblical scholars prefer audience/hearer to reader on the assumption that the gospels were originally written for aural occasions. Therefore, this study will use "reader" and "audience" interchangeably.

For the purpose of this study, I will consider the dialectical relationship between the reader and the text, recognizing that "meaning is thus a product of the dynamic of reader and text interaction."¹⁵⁵ The reason for incorporating dialectical reader-response criticism is to allow a wider construct for the reader. As an inherent experience, the *a priori* assumption and knowledge of the reader needs to be taken into consideration for investigating a historical narrative. For example, from Matthew's repeated use of the introductory formulae ἵνα πληρωθῇ τὸ ῥηθὲν, one could imagine such a characteristic of the reader. That is, regardless of whether or not the (implied) reader is Jewish, he or she is expected to have a certain degree of familiarity or reverence toward the Hebrew Scripture.¹⁵⁶

---

152. According to Powell, however, there may be some critics taking an extreme position that totally abandons the role of the text and place the meaning of the text solely within the creativity of the reader. Powell, *What Is Narrative Criticism?*, 16–17. For these critics, then, the reader no longer *participates* in determining the meaning but generates the meaning themselves.

153. Robert M. Fowler, "Reader-Response," in *Searching for Meaning: An Introduction to Interpreting the New Testament*, ed. Paula Gooder (Louisville, KY: Westminster John Knox Press, 2009), 127.

154. Fowler, "Reader-Response," 127.

155. Resseguie, "Reader-Response Criticism and the Synoptic Gospels," *Journal of the American Academy of Religion* 52 (June 1984): 307.

156. This judgment is along the same logic expressed by Eco; "To organize a text, its author has to rely upon a series of codes that assign given contents to the expressions he uses. To make his text communicative, the author has to assume that the ensemble of codes he relies upon is the same as that shard by his possible reader. The author has thus to foresee a model of the possible reader (hereafter Model Reader) supposedly able to deal interpretatively with the expressions in the same way as the author deals generatively with them." Eco, *Role of the Reader*, 7.

1.3.2.3 Speech-Act Theory

Speech-act theory is not a new approach to biblical scholars, and its contribution to biblical studies has already been appreciated by scholars such as Daniel Patte[157] and Hugh White.[158] But why is the theory relevant at all? This study will incorporate speech-act theory out of consideration of its most prominent contributions. First, speech-act theory allows historical factors – the shared *presupposition pool* – to determine the possible illocutionary force (for definition, see below discussion).[159] Regardless of the precise genre of the gospels, today there are very few scholars who would deny that the gospels do reflect some history (even though many still debate as to how historical they are). This fact should alert literary critics of the gospels not to 'absolutize' textual literary meaning as *the only* meaning. Rather, one must consider "how the methods peculiar to each perspective [of historical and literary criticisms] may both contribute to a fuller understanding of Matthew's Gospel."[160] For instance, the meaning of a simple utterance 'I will come out of the closet . . .' has to depend on when and where this speech is given. If the reader does not share the same presupposition pool with the speaker, then it will likely cause some confusion. Therefore, speech-act has to consider *a priori* assumptions, which are not in the text yet are "part of the communication of the meaning by that text."[161] It then allows the investigation to approach the text with historical inquiry but not in the same way as historical-critical approach.[162]

Furthermore, related with the shared presupposition pool, there are "rules which users of the language assume to be in force in their verbal dealings with each other; they form part of the knowledge which speakers of a language

---

157. Daniel Patte, "Speech Act Theory and Biblical Exegesis," *Semiea* 41 (1988): 85–102.

158. Hugh White, "Introduction: Speech-Act Theory and Literary Criticism," *Semeia* 41 (1988): 1–24.

159. Presupposition pool refers to the set of presuppositions which the speaker and hearer share, "constituted from general knowledge, from the situative context of the discourse, and from the completed part of the discourse itself." T. Venneman, "Topics, Sentence Accent, Ellipsis: A Proposal for their Formal Treatment," in *Formal Semantics of Natural Language: Papers from a Colloquium Sponsored by the King's College Research Center, Cambridge*, ed. E. L. Keenan (Cambridge: Cambridge University Press, 1975), 134.

160. Anthony C. Thiselton, "Reader-Response Hermeneutics, Action Models, and the Parables of Jesus," in *The Responsibility of Hermeneutics,* eds. Roger Lundin, Anthony C. Thiselton, and Clarence Walhout (Grand Rapids: Eerdmans, 1985), 82ff, 106.

161. Patte, "Speech Act Theory," 90.

162. White, "Introduction," 2.

share and on which they rely in order to use the language correctly and effectively, both in producing and understanding utterances."[163] These rules are related to linguistic or psychological factors that need to be met in order for the utterance to make sense. For instance, the speech-act of a promise will only make sense if the speaker (1) is able to carry out the promise; (2) sincerely intends to do so; and (3) understands that the promise is what the hearer wishes for.[164] Therefore, in the Matthean conflict stories, to discern what impact the words of Jesus have for other characters and the reader, it is also necessary to explore what these rules are behind the verbal exchange.

Why is speech-act theory relevant for studying conflict stories in Matthew? It is because conflict stories involve direct interactions between characters more than other forms of narratives, such as parables, miracles or Jesus's discourses. If the premise of speech-act theory is "to say something is to do something,"[165] then as far as conflict stories are concerned, speech-act theory can offer useful insights into the intricacies of the interactions between Jesus and the opponents. Moreover, in considering the relevance of speech-act theory to Matthew, Thiselton suggests that "Matthew's Christology demonstrates a relation to speech-act theory perhaps more clearly than Mark, not least because Matthew's interest lies in the authority of Jesus' *words and teaching.*"[166] Given the fact that this study specifically investigates Jesus's words and teaching in conflict stories within the Gospel of Matthew, speech-act theory will serve as a functional method of analysis.

Just like the duality of time in a narrative, speech-act also happens on two levels. At the rhetoric level, it is performed by the implied author regarding the total speech-act communication of his work. The other is at the story level performed by the character(s). For two reasons, this study will focus on the latter, that is, on the speech-act performed by Jesus. First, focusing on the rhetoric level of speech-act requires the theory as its primary analytical tool; therefore, the whole narrative of Matthew rather than conflict stories needs

---

163. These rules are defined as "appropriateness conditions or felicity conditions" by Mary L. Pratt. Pratt, *Toward a Speech Act Theory of Literary Discourse* (Bloomington, IN: Indiana University Press, 1977), 81.

164. Cf. Pratt, *Speech Act Theory*, 81.

165. Derek Tovey, *Narrative Art and Act in the Fourth Gospel* (Sheffield: Sheffield Academic Press, 1997), 70.

166. Thiselton, *New Horizons in Hermeneutics: The Theory and Practice of Transforming Biblical Reading* (Grand Rapids, MI: Zondervan, 1992), 288.

to be analyzed. Such a focus, however, is beyond the scope of the current study. Second, analyzing the speech-act of Jesus helps to discern the messianic consciousness of the character.

The theory itself, however, was first introduced by an Oxford philosopher of language, John. L. Austin, who differentiates between the "performatives" and "constatives" within speech (or utterance).[167] It is further developed by Searle who identifies five types of illocution.[168] However, in conflict stories, two of the five categories seem most observable in the speech-act of Jesus. They are conflicts which tell the reader who Jesus is (assertive speech-acts)[169] and what his mission will be (commissive speech-acts)[170] which are most relevant to this study (e.g. see discussion of 9:1–8, 9–13, 14–17; 12:1–8, 9–14; 21:14–17). These categories help the study to discern that the meaning of an utterance goes beyond simply presenting a propositional fact. Therefore, they inspire the current study to seek the multidimensional implications of conflict stories in Matthew.

1.4 Scope of Methodology Applied in the Thesis

Having presented the various methods employed by this study, it is necessary to point out that these methods will not be equally applied in each section. Primarily, this study uses narrative critical tools to analyze each conflict story. For example, the discussion of each story will be divided into two sections: the setting of the story and the conflict scene proper. Such a division helps

---

167. Both terminologies are established by J. L. Austin. *Constatives*, according to Austin, are utterances describing a state of affairs which must be evaluated as either as true or false. *Performatives*, on the other hand, refer to the saying itself perform an act; see his major work *How to Do Things with Words*, 2nd ed. (Oxford: Clarendon Press, 1975), 5.

168. John R. Searle uses plain language to describe these five categories of illocutionary acts: "We tell people how things are (Assertives), we try to get them to do things (Directives), we commit ourselves to doing things (Commissives), we express our feelings and attitudes (Expressives), and we bring about changes in the world through our utterances (Declarations). Searle, *Expression and Meaning: Studies in the Theory of Speech Acts* (Cambridge: Cambridge University Press, 1979), viii.

169. Assertives are defined by Searle as speech-acts that commit the speaker him/herself "to something's being the case, to the truth of the expressed proposition." Searle, *Expression and Meaning*, 12. For example, they include the act of describing, suggesting, claiming, etc.

170. Commissives are defined as speech acts that "commit the speaker to some future course of action." Searle, *Expression and Meaning*, 12. Examples are the acts of promising, threatening, vowing, etc.

to distinguish how the author describes the immediate context of the conflict (e.g. location of the story, inner thoughts of the dialogue party) from the polemical verbal exchange within each scene. Moreover, the authorial intention is explored both from the content of the conflict (story) and the sequence or the manner of how the story is told by the author of Matthew (rhetoric) in discussions of each conflict. As a result, the redactional features of Matthew receive much interest, and more importantly, how the author arranges certain conflict within the flow of the Matthean narrative and the author's own insertion will also be investigated (e.g. 9:13; 12:6–7; 21:14–17).

Two other methods, reader-response criticism and speech-act theory are applied as the subsidiary methods in this study. Admittedly, the reason for this is because a thoroughgoing application of these methods to the gospel's conflict stories deserves a monograph of their own. Given the limited scope of this study, therefore, it is not possible to apply all methods in equal weight. Nonetheless, the advantage of reader-response criticism and speech-act theory is that they both closely complement narrative criticism. A key strength of reader-response criticism is that it enquires into the possible impact of the text on the reader.[171] Therefore, in determining the "meaning" of the text, this study will consider the response potentially intended to evoke from the reader by the author. Second, speech-act theory entails consideration for underlining rules which dialogue partners must share in order to produce effective and meaningful utterances. For the purpose of this study, investigation will be made to uncover the background knowledge shared by Jesus and his opponents particularly in conflicts where the authority of Jesus is being established by the narrative (e.g. 9:1–8, 9–13; 12:1–8, 9–14).

1.5 Structural Plan of the Book

Chapters 2–5 form the bulk of this study. Among the seventeen conflict stories in Matthew, there are three groups of conflicts, each of which contains stories closely linked with each other by the author's arrangement. They are: Matthew 9:1–8, 9–13, and 14–17 included in chapter 2; 12:1–8, 9–14, 22–37,

---

171. Reader-response criticism in general looks into response of all possible readers, including the real reader, the implied reader, the reader of certain historical era, or the modern reader. However, this study limits the scope to "the implied reader."

and 38–45 included in chapter 3; 21:14–17, 23–27; 22:15–22, 23–33, 34–40, and 41–46 included in chapter 5. There are four conflict stories scattered across Matthew 13–20, and they will be included in chapter 4. The conclusion in chapter 6 provides a summary and a synopsis of the findings of the study.

CHAPTER 2

Conflict Stories in Matthew 9
Jesus, the Supreme Authority

The first three conflict stories appear in Matthew 9 arranged in an uninterrupted sequence. One of the most intriguing features about these conflict stories is that even though they are located within the "miracle chapters" of Matthew (Matt 8–9),[1] only one of three conflict stories involves Jesus's miraculous deeds. Even so, as will be shown in the discussion below, the miracle in the first conflict story is not the focus of the story. What then is the author's purpose of including three conflict stories within the "miracle chapters"? In other words, what is the function of the first conflict stories in the narrative of Matthew 8–9?

In this chapter, each conflict story will be analyzed first and their relationship with each other will be discussed in light of their wider literary context, including Matthew 4–9. This first round of clashes between Jesus and the Jewish leaders sets the tone for the remaining long series of conflicts because Jesus' identity is most clearly fine-tuned in the conflicts from here onward.

---

1. This is noted by Heinz Joachim Held, "Matthew as Interpreter of the Miracle Stories," in *Tradition and Interpretation*, Günther Bornkamm, Gerhard Barth, and Heinz Joachim Held (London: SCM Press, 1963), 246; also by Kingsbury, "Observations on the 'Miracle Chapters' of Matthew 8–9," *CBQ* 40 (1978): 559.

2.1 Analysis of Individual Pericopae: Matthew 9:1–8, 9–13, 14–17

2.1.1 Matthew 9:1–8

2.1.1.1 Matthew 9:1: The Setting of the Story[2]

Matthew 9:1–8 is the first conflict story in the Gospel of Matthew. Because the story setting is an integral part of the narrative, the analysis includes 9:1 as part of the story even though some scholars consider 9:2 as the beginning of the conflict story.[3] The author employs a shift of location to provide an important geographical setting for the story.[4] The preceding narrative concludes with the fear of Jesus by the Gentile township in 8:34, which itself may not be a surprising outcome to the reader.[5] However, when Jesus moves to τὴν ἰδίαν πόλιν (9:1),[6] the reader is surprised to discover that Jesus encounters an even

---

2. See Chatman's discussion on "setting," *Story and Discourse*, 138ff; see also Powell's chapter on "setting," in *What Is Narrative Criticism?*, 69–83.

3. Such as Urich Luz, *Matthew 8–20*, trans. James E. Crouch, 3 vols. (Minneapolis, MN: Fortress, 2001–2007), 26; also Repschinski, *Controversy Stories*, 62. Repschinski follows the division of Bultmann and both do not consider the narrative setting or conclusion as an integral part of the story. Bultmann, *History*, 39–41.

4. Rhoads, Dewey and Michie divide "setting" into cosmic, temporal, geographical, cultural-political, spatial categories, each of which may serve many functions; for details see *Mark as Story*, 63–72.

5. It is not surprising because the antagonism between Gentiles and Jews was generally assumed in the Matthean reader's mind, as it was a popular view of the Jewish people during Second Temple Judaism.

6. Matthew's redaction of Mark 2:1 by substituting "Capernaum" with "his *own town*" is intentional in order to emphasize the upcoming rejection to be unexpected and ironic. In fact, the geographical setting "his own town" generally acts in the narrative as a literary motif that signifies a place of Jewish opposition or rejection in the first gospel. With the exception of 4:13 where the narrator introduces Capernaum as Jesus's primary residence, every other occurrence of "his own town" (or rendered as "Capernaum/ his home town," see 8:5; 9:1; 11:20–24; 13:54; 17:24) is located in a context where the Jewish rejection is either predicted (as in 8:14ff) or present. Moreover, it is significant for this present study that two of these occurrences take place in conflict stories (9:1–8; 13:53–58). Capernaum as the geographical setting here has the function of "evoking associations." Rhoads, Dewey and Michie, *Mark as Story*, 63. The association between a location and a theme in a literary work is also suggested by Bal: "If spatial thinking is indeed a general human tendency, it is not surprising that spatial elements play an important role in fabulas. It is . . . possible to make a note of the place of each fabula, and then to investigate whether a connection exists between the kind of events, the identity of the actors, and the location." Mieke Bal, *Narratology: Introduction to the Theory of Narrative*, 2nd ed. (Toronto: University of Toronto Press, 1997), 215.

more fervent rejection (9:3–4).[7] To this extent, the setting in 9:1 begins the story by preparing the reader for the subsequent rejection of Jesus.[8]

2.1.1.2 Matthew 9:2–8: The Conflict Scene Proper

The beginning (9:1) and the ending[9] (9:8) form the frame of the conflict story.[10] Writing in 9:2b that it is Jesus who now does the "seeing" (ἰδὼν ὁ 'Ιησοῦς . . .), the narrator subtly aligns readers to the psychological point of view of Jesus, even as the narrator himself fades away.[11] It is not until 9:8, where the narrator summarizes the reaction of the crowd, that the reader again feels the presence of the narrator or the third person perspective.[12] Within this frame, the

---

7. It needs to be noted also that not long before 9:1–8 where Capernaum is mentioned, a gentile centurion gives Jesus high honor, and Jesus contrasts the Gentile's faith with Israel's rejection.

8. Matt 9:1 is in fact a transitional verse which concludes the story in 8:28–34 (e.g. 9:1a) and begins a new story in 9:1–8 (e.g. 9:1b). But for the purpose of structure outline, I include the whole 9:1 as the beginning of the current conflict story.

9. End or ending, end/ending, defined by Abram, "follows from what has gone before but requires nothing more [about the story]." Abram, *Glossary*, 226. Earlier, Matthew had cleverly faded out the narrator's perspective in several stages causing a "disappearance" of the narrator between 9:2–7. The first of these occurs in 9:2a where Καὶ ἰδοὺ begins the sentence in combination with the "descriptive imperfect" προσέφερον in order to intensify the vividness of the scene; cf. Stanley E. Porter, *Idioms of the Greek New Testament*, 2nd ed. (Sheffield: Sheffield Academic Press, 1994), 34. Additionally, there is a dramatic slowing down of the narrating time/speed in this verse compared to 8:33–34 and 9:1, where a long process (in the story world) is narrated only in a few words.

10. This is according to Alter's definition; the *frame* helps to "make immediately apparent in the passage . . . the highly subsidiary role of narration in comparison to direct speech by the characters." Robert Alter, *The Art of Biblical Narrative* (New York: Basic Books, 1981), 65; cf. his more detailed discussion on "Narration and Dialogue" in 63–87.

11. Through the use of ἰδού, the reader from now on would *watch* what to come through Jesus's eyes; see Gary Yamasaki, *Watching a Biblical Narrative: Point of View in Biblical Exegesis* (New York: T & T Clark, 2007), 191. Luz recognizes that the fact that "Jesus stands alone" is a "characteristic of the narrative," though he does not explain its significance. Luz, *Matthew 8–20*, 26.

12. The crowd is in awe and praises God. The verb ἐφοβήθησαν has a variant reading ἐδόξασαν from C, L, Q and a few minuscules (N-A 27th ed. p21) τὸν δόντα ἐξουσίαν τοιαύτην τοῖς ἀνθρώποις in the ending is unique to Matthew (see par. Mark 2:12 and Luke 5:25–26). However, it is still debatable as to how much the crowd understands the identity of Jesus. Some scholars interpret the crowd's attributing the authority to the plural "men" as a misunderstanding on the part of the crowd, for it seems that at this stage they only recognize the authority but not a *new* person with this authority. See Luz, *Matthew 8–20*, 28. Cf. J. R. C. Cousland, *The Crowds in the Gospel of Matthew* (Boston: Brill, 2002), 131, also footnote 41. Others see the plural form as a hint to the Matthean community's acquirement of the authority to forgive sins; see discussion in Repschinski, *Controversy Stories*, 71. However, according to the narrative flow, Repschinski's interpretation is unlikely because it will require reading back what happens later in the narrative (16:19; 18:18) to earlier stories 9:8. It is probable that at this stage, the crowd understands the

conflict scene of 9:2–7[13] is shaped by the author into a chiastic structure and centers upon the verbal exchange between the scribes and Jesus (C & C′).[14] In comparison to its Markan parallel, the Matthean account is comparatively brief, omitting Mark's detailed description of the people's efforts to deliver the paralytic as well as the crowd's reaction to his being healed (Mark 2:3–4, 12).[15] These redactional omissions have resulted in placing greater emphasis upon the centre of the conflict scene (C & C′).

> *Frame (9:1)*
> A   προσέφερον αὐτῷ παραλυτικὸν ἐπὶ κλίνης βεβλημένον (9:2a)
> B   ὁ Ἰησοῦς ... εἶπεν τῷ παραλυτικῷ ... (9:2b)
>   C   τῶν γραμματέων εἶπαν ἐν ἑαυτοῖς ... (9:3)
>   C′ ἰδὼν ὁ Ἰησοῦς ... εἶπεν ... (9:4–6a)
> B′ τότε [ὁ Ἰησοῦς] λέγει τῷ παραλυτικῷ ... (9:6b)
> A′ καὶ [παραλυτικος] ἐγερθεὶς ἀπῆλθεν εἰς τὸν οἶκον αὐτοῦ (9:7)
> *Frame (9:8)*

As is evident from the chiastic structure, both the healing act and its effect (A, B, B′, A′) are merely peripheral events. In fact, the words of Jesus that cause a bed-ridden person to walk again are already rather typical of his speech-acts so far (cf. 8:3, 13, 16, 26, 32; 9:22).[16] At first, Jesus's initial

---

message but does not yet fully understand the messenger. It is also interesting that the narrator does not provide any reaction from the scribes, which will change in later conflict stories.

13. Genette discusses "scene" in great detail, see his *Narrative Discourse*, 109–110. His main point is that "the contrast of tempo between detailed scene and summary almost always reflected a contrast of content between dramatic and nondramatic . . ." This is certainly the case in 9:1–8. Similarly, Alter describes that "a proper narrative event occurs when the narrative tempo slows down enough for us to discriminate a particular scene," *Art of Biblical Narrative*, 63.

14. This observation coincides with Repschinski's claim that "at the center of Matthew's structure and redaction is the controversy in which the miracle is the minor part . . .," even though he does not offer a chiastic structure and his evidence only rests on his observation that Matthew has a "tighter structure." Repschinski, *Controversy Stories*, 74–75. For discussion of criteria of recognizing a chiasmus, see Craig Blomberg, "The Structure of 2 Corinthians 1–7," *CTR* 4, no. 1 (1989): 5–7.

15. In fact, it is so brief that it prompts scholars to speculate Matthew might have presupposed the reader's familiarity with the details in Mark; Davies and Allison, *Matthew 8–18*, 88. Cf. David Hill, *The Gospel of Matthew*, New Century Bible Commentary (London: Marshall, Morgan & Scott, 1972), 170.

16. A modern-day analogy would be when a minister says "Now I pronounce you man and wife" in the front of the church, resulting in the fact that the couple is married. For a general introduction to Austinian speech-act theory, see chapter 1.

utterance to the paralytic Θάρσει, τέκνον, ἀφίενταί σου αἱ ἁμαρτίαι (9:2b) is quite at odds with the crippled man's more immediate and more obvious crippled state.[17] Yet Matthew directs the attention of his reader to note that the act of forgiving is completed by Jesus's speech.[18] To be precise, the effect of his speech-act – ἀφίενταί σου αἱ ἁμαρτίαι – such that, Jesus is not simply describing a state of affairs which awaits evaluation; instead, the forgiving act is performed.[19] It is commonly agreed that the voice of ἀφίενταί is a divine passive usually implying God as the subject, yet Matthew clarifies later in the context of the conflict story the subject of this passive verb is in fact Jesus (C & C′).[20] Likewise, his words perform the healing act by commanding the paralytic to "stand up and go home" (9:6b).[21] The effect of both utterances (i.e. the perlocutionary force) is demonstrated through the physical healing of the paralytic (9:7).

It is worth noting that, without the intervening conflict story (C, C′), the remaining dialogue and healing account (A, B, B′, A′) reflect a seamless narrative. Evidently, Jesus's first utterance to the paralytic ἀφίενταί σου αἱ ἁμαρτίαι was so especially offensive to the scribes that they accuse Jesus of blasphemy (9:4). Accordingly, the narrative proceeds to its climax where the elemental message of the story is revealed.

At the centre of the story, there is an unexpected twist marked by the hostile exchange between Jesus and the scribes (C, C′) that seems a straightforward

---

17. This is because unlike in other healing stories where Jesus commends a person's faith (cf. 8:10–13; 9:22, 27–30; 15:28), here he simply encourages the paralytic and addresses his sins as being forgiven (9:2b).

18. The present tense in ἀφίενταί (9:2b), according to Thiselton, is typical for a performative utterance. Thiselton, *New Horizons*, 286.

19. The authoritative force of the words of Jesus is underscored by the lenses of speech-act because in the story world, Jesus is not assumed by other characters to have such an authority to forgive the paralytic. Yet the narrative tells the reader that Jesus does not simply speak empty words but his words achieve a visible result. In Matt 8–9 especially, there is a concentration of word-spoken-as-act in miracle stories.

20. As Davies and Allison recognize, 9:6 disallows the interpretation that Jesus only "declares" God's forgiveness but clearly points to the Son of Man as the one who forgives; *Matthew 8–18*, 89; also cf. Robert Gundry, *Matthew: A Commentary on His Literary and Theological Art* (Grand Rapids: Eerdmans, 1982), 163.

21. Austin and Searle classify an utterance of "command" into a sub-category of speech-act, but under different label: "exercitive" for Austin and "directive" for Searle. Austin, *How to Do Things*, 154–155; Searle, *Expression and Meaning*, 13–23.

conflict story.²² What does Matthew intend to achieve by including the first conflict in a miracle story? How does he portray Jesus in interacting with the scribes and what are the implications of the author's portrayal of the interaction between these characters?

A perusal of 9:1–8 in its context helps to discern that this conflict story serves two functions. The first and primary function is to draw attention to Jesus as an authority who assumes God's prerogative. Because ἀφίενταί σου αἱ ἁμαρτίαι is stated in a passive voice, it gives rise to debates whether Jesus is speaking for himself or as an intermediary for God.

A literary reading of the text, however, shows that the author intends the reader to understand that Jesus is the one who forgives the sins of the paralytic.

First, Jesus's authority to forgive sins is expressed explicitly by the purpose clause: ἵνα δὲ εἰδῆτε ὅτι ἐξουσίαν ἔχει ὁ υἱὸς τοῦ ἀνθρώπου ἐπὶ τῆς γῆς ἀφιέναι ἁμαρτίας. It is plausible, as Yang suggests, that the title ὁ υἱὸς τοῦ ἀνθρώπου is used here not simply as a self-designation but also points to "Jesus' authoritative eschatological mission as the fulfiller of God's ultimate will."²³ Such an interpretation is precisely what the scribes understood and consequently causes their objection. In the Matthean account, the author omits the questions in Mark 2:7, τί οὗτος οὕτως λαλεῖ ... τίς δύναται ἀφιέναι ἁμαρτίας εἰ μὴ εἷς ὁ θεός, and inserts οὗτος with the affirmative statement βλασφημεῖ. Instead of wondering τί οὗτος οὕτως λαλεῖ, the opponents seem to have recognized that Jesus is speaking about himself forgiving sins²⁴ and so accuse him of blasphemy (9:3).²⁵ Their charging of him with blasphemy derives from their perception that Jesus is acting in the place of God.

---

22. Even though the scribes do not address the accusation *directly* at Jesus, as I interpret ἐν ἑαυτοῖς as "in their hearts" based on its context in 9:4 τὰς ἐνθυμήσεις αὐτῶν and ἐν ταῖς καρδίαις ὑμῶν, their accusation is known to Jesus (and hence the reader who is watching the scene through Jesus's eyes).

23. See Yong-Eui Yang's detailed discussion of the Matthean use of the Son of Man in *Jesus and the Sabbath* (Sheffield: Sheffield Academic Press, 1997), 192.

24. That Matthew omits Mark's questions (Mark 2:7) and only retains the statement of accusation logically is a step further in their speculation of Jesus's offence. In other words, the scribes no longer doubt or question if Jesus is speaking for himself but are convinced of such an offence.

25. In first century Palestine, forgiveness of sins can only be granted by God and through the accepted procedure. For example, see G. F. Moore, *Judaism in the First Centuries of the Christian Era: The Age of the Tannain*, 3 vols. (Cambridge, MA: Harvard University Press, 1927–1930), 1: 535; "Forgiveness is a prerogative of God which he shares with no other and deputes to none." In practice, therefore, it is only associated with the priest in the Temple

Second, the divine authority of Jesus in this story is implied by his speech-act in 9:2b. The basis for the speech-act depends on the conventions of the "world" where his words are spoken.[26] Even though Jesus's claim to forgive sins may not be accepted by his opponents, it is precisely the author's intention to show that "the *operative effectiveness* of 'My son, your sins are forgiven' (Mark 2:5; Luke 5:20; cf. Matt 9:2) depends on *a state of affairs about the identity, role and authority of Jesus*."[27]

Therefore, although the pronouncement of Jesus to the paralytic could be seen as only speaking on God's behalf, the author clearly intends to depict Jesus assuming a divine status. Seen from the context of the conflict, such an intention is hardly surprising. From the outset the reader has been repeatedly conditioned to presuppose the divine authority of Jesus: he is conceived by the Holy Spirit (1:18, 20, 23) and is the Son of God (2:15; 3:17; 4:3, 6; cf. 8:28–29).

The secondary function of this conflict story is that it seeks to expose the illegitimate authority of the scribes and therefore underscore the supremacy of Jesus over that of the scribes. This is initially achieved by the author's depiction of their opposition to Jesus. As the context shows, the sheer fact of accusing Jesus has already placed the scribes in an unfavorable light before the reader (9:3). The secretive manner by which the scribes charge Jesus (εἶπαν ἐν ἑαυτοῖς) additionally communicates to the reader the illegitimacy of their accusation.[28] More importantly, the author exposes their illegitimacy by characterizing the scribes' corrupted state of mind in the speech of Jesus. In his reply to the scribes the key word πονηρὰ is intentionally added by the author as his negative assessment of them (9:4).[29] The fact that the word πονηρὰ is embedded in the speech of Jesus is significant because the narrator

---

of Jerusalem, through appropriate sacrifice rituals. The fact that *only* God himself has the prerogative to forgive sins comes from the Old Testament tradition, e.g. Exod 34:6–7; Pss 103:3; 130:4; Isa 43:25; 44:22; Jer 31:34; Dan 9:9. Even the Messiah is not expected to forgive sins but to be the means whereby God would forgive in the end times (Isa 53:4–6). Also cf. G. H. Twelftree, "Blasphemy," in *Dictionary of Jesus and the Gospels*, 76.

26. See Austin's four detailed qualifications for a speech-act in *How to Do Things*, 26–37.

27. Thiselton, *Thiselton on Hermeneutics: Collected Works with New Essays* (Grand Rapids: Eerdmans, 2006), 106; emphasis original.

28. It is secretive because the scribes did not openly pronounce the charge but their thoughts may be seen by their "body language and whispering together." R. T. France, *The Gospel of Matthew*, New International Commentary on the New Testament (Grand Rapids: Eerdmans, 2007), 346.

29. Van Tilborg, *The Jewish Leaders*, 28. Cf. Mark 2:8; Luke 5:22.

has,³⁰ all along, given his character a "badge of reliability"³¹ and aligned the reader's ideological point of view with that of the reliable character.³² Thus, the direct attack of the reliable character on the moral authority of the scribes in 9:4, which follows three unfavorable characterizations of them,³³ serves to convince the reader to conclude that πονηρὰ is a correct evaluation of the scribes and that their authority is without legitimacy.

Since Jesus was not the only "miracle worker" in the first-century Palestine, the healing and exorcism miracles narrated thus far are insufficient to establish his supremacy and something more is needed.³⁴ Accordingly, the author shapes the rhetorical question in 9:5 so as to indicate clearly that the authority to forgive sins is much greater than the power to perform miracles (9:2b, 5, 6b). By using the purpose clause ἵνα δὲ εἰδῆτε ὅτι . . . (*so that* you might know . . .) the author reveals in the final speech of Jesus to the scribes that the purpose of the earlier utterance to the paralytic was in fact to affirm the authority of Jesus as greater than what the scribes had presumed (9:6a).

---

30. As mentioned in chapter 1, in Matthew the narrator/author presents only one evaluative point of view shared by the narrator/author and Jesus, and the narrator/author is likewise reliable.

31. This term originally is used by Booth (*Rhetoric*, 18), which Anderson borrows to refer to Jesus; *Matthew's Narrative Web*, 56.

32. The ground for this claim comes primarily from the contexts proceeding to our story. From chs. 1 to 4, the narrator asserts Jesus as Ἰησοῦ χριστοῦ υἱοῦ Δαυὶδ υἱοῦ Ἀβραάμ (1:1), conceived of the πνεύματος ἁγίου (1:18) which is confirmed by ἄγγελος κυρίου (1:20). Soon the narrator says that Jesus is anointed by [τὸ] πνεῦμα [τὸν] θεοῦ (3:16). Furthermore, the narrator particularly uses a cluster of fulfillment quotations as direct commentary to the reader: 1:23/Isa 7:14; 2:6/Mic 5:2; 2:15/Hos 11:1; 2:18/Jer 31:15; 3:3/Isa 40:3; 4:15–16/Isa 9:1–2, to demonstrate that Jesus's life is a fulfillment of Scripture. Even though 3:3/Isa 40:3 is referring to John the Baptist, the purpose is to establish John's reliability to elevate Jesus's identity, cf. 3:11. It needs to be noted that the context following 9:1–8 also provides evidences; however, I only list evidences from previous passages primarily to show the effect of a narrative read in sequence.

33. The narrator has introduced the scribes three times before. They first appear as the co-conspirators of Herod (2:3–6). Then at the end of Jesus's Sermon on the Mount, the narrator describes them as having no authority compared to Jesus (7:28–29). In the third instance, the narrator has Jesus declining a scribe's request to follow him (8:19–20).

34. In comparison to Jesus's first speech-act to the paralytic (9:2b), the healing speech-act "get up and go home" (9:6b) seems to be much more common for their day, and the New Testament alone offers many examples of people exercising miraculous powers (besides Jesus or his followers); cf. Matt 12:27; Acts 8:9–24; 13:6–11; 16:16; 19:19. Therefore, Jesus's healing authority alone would not be necessarily superior to that of the scribes.

2.1.1.3 Summary of 9:1–8 in Its Immediate Narrative and Rhetorical Context

At its core, the narrative of 9:1–8 is a conflict story rather than a miracle story,[35] and it is the first of the initial three conflict stories (9:1–8, 9–13, 14–17), all of which are placed within a cluster of ten miracles performed by Jesus.[36] Within the *inclusio* of 4:23 and 9:35, the issue of authority appears as a central theme.[37] Literary analysis of this conflict reveals something specifically about Jesus's authority. The author Matthew intends to draw attention to Jesus as an authority who assumes God's prerogative, acting in the place of God. Through this conflict, therefore, Jesus's supremacy is underscored and, additionally, the illegitimacy of scribes' authority is highlighted.

2.1.2 Matthew 9:9–13

2.1.2.1 Matthew 9:9–10a: The Setting of the Story

Unlike Mark, Matthew avoids reiterating the ministry of Jesus to the seaside crowd (Mark 2:13) in order to closely link the 9:9–13 pericope to the previous story.[38] Thus, following the forgiveness and healing of the paralytic, 9:9 and 9:10a immediately provide the context of the second conflict story.[39] The

---

35. As demonstrated in the chiastic structure, the center of the story really lies in the conflict with a miracle framing the conflict. Also see Held's description, "In the Matthean narrative the element of the miracle story recedes markedly into the background . . . thus the glorifying of God no longer refers so much to the miracle itself as to the power of Jesus to which it witness, namely to forgive sins . . . in this way, however, the new relating of the healing of the paralytic by Matthew is seen to be a well-thought-out construction on the basis of the saying of Jesus about his authority to forgive sins." Held, "Matthew as Interpreter," 176–177.

36. Even though some scholars group 9:18–33 as three miracle stories, they consist of four miracles performed by Jesus. Davies and Allison, *Matthew 1–7*, 122–123.

37. This assertion comes from two observations. First, chs. 5–7 demonstrate Jesus's authority to interpret the Law, concluded by 7:28–29. In 8:5–13, a Gentile is contrasted with people of Israel over his acknowledgment of Jesus's authority. Jesus's claim to have authority in 9:1–8 marks the beginning of the climax of the miracle chapters. Second, the issue of authority occurs in the introduction of a new section (10:1), unifying the section between 4:23 and 9:35 with the following context. Almost identical word for word, 4:23 is said to be the prologue foreshadowing Jesus's public ministry and 9:35 is the retrospection of the text in between; see Charles H. Lohr, "Oral Techniques in the Gospel of Matthew," *CBQ* 23 (1961): 413–415. Therefore, chs. 8–9 are juxtaposed to the Sermon on the Mount (chs. 5–7) by an *inclusio* between 4:23 and 9:35, which places chs. 5–7 and 8–9 into a wider yet coherent literary unit. Davies and Allison also consider these two verses form an *inclusio*; *Matthew 1–7*, 411. Cf. Kingsbury, "Observations," 566–567.

38. Repschinski, *Controversy Stories*, 75.

39. The unity between 9:9 with 9:10–11 is also attested by Held from another angle. He believes that Jesus's pronouncement in 9:13 of "calling sinners" makes a christological statement

spatial setting of the story is indicated in 9:10a – a meal inside someone's house (ἀνάκειμαι), while the psychological setting of the story is established by the call of Matthew in 9:9. Arguably, the latter (9:9) forms a narrative unit on its own. This is because the identity of Matthew – a setting element – as a tax collector prepares the reader for the next story in which Jesus welcomes tax collectors.[40] The call of Matthew also creates a certain mood in the mind of the reader that Jesus has exercised his authority by actively calling "unworthy" people to follow him.[41] Despite that, within the story world a Jewish person's association with tax collectors directly opposes the social convention, at the rhetorical level the call of Matthew prepares the reader for "a world to consider in their imagination."[42] In such a world impressed on the reader, Jesus is showing astonishing mercy to those who would normally be thought of as outside of the realm of God's salvation.

More importantly, the call of Jesus to follow him is a directive speech-act[43] demonstrating his institutional authority.[44] In commanding the tax collector to follow him Jesus acts as Matthew's master. Unlike call narratives in

---

which ties calling Matthew and inviting sinners/tax collectors to the feast together as evidence of the "Messiah of deed." Held, "Matthew as Interpreter," 258.

40. Matthew the tax collector as a setting element is an indication for the call story to be the setting because although this tax collector is an important character in the call story, he is unimportant for the conflict story but simply belongs to the character group "tax collectors" and can be presumed present at the conflict scene; see Chatman's discussion of "setting element" in *Story and Discourse*, 141.

41. Cf. Chatman, "A normal and perhaps principal function of setting is to contribute to the mood of the narrative," *Story and Discourse*, 141. In this case, Jesus's calling such a man to be his disciple, according to France, "was a daring breach of etiquette, a calculated snub to conventional ideas of respectability, which ordinary people no less than Pharisees might be expected to balk at." France, *Gospel of Matthew*, 351.

42. Rhoads, Dewey and Michie, *Mark as Story*, 72.

43. Directive speech-acts are "attempts by the speaker to get the hearer to do something," Searle, *Expression and Meaning*, 13; Jesus's call as a command has the illocutionary force of getting the hearer Matthew to follow him.

44. Thiselton differentiates *institutional* authority from *causal* authority and asserts that the former is of "extra-linguistic nature" and the latter only "rests on little more than the force of self-assertion." Christology in the New Testament, according to Thiselton, "represents an affirmation of the former and a denial of the latter, and it is this which gives rise to reticence if or when Jesus *asserts* propositions *about himself*, rather than *acts* and speaks as himself." *Thiselton on Hermeneutics*, 100.

the Jewish Scripture[45] or an individual's entry into a rabbinic school,[46] the absolute authority of Jesus is displayed by his sole initiative and the unconditional obedience of the respondent. The authoritative position of Jesus is also highlighted by the author's redaction of Mark 2:14. In contrast to the tax collector, who is referred to only as ἀνθρώπου, Jesus is explicitly identified by name ὁ Ἰησοῦς (9:9).[47] Moreover, the author retains the Markan use of the historical present λέγει thereby indicating the long-lasting force of Jesus's words on the reader.[48]

2.1.2.2 Matthew 9:10b–13: The Conflict Scene Proper

The narrative scene 9:10b–13 is composed of a hostile exchange between Jesus and another group of religious leaders over the issue that Jesus eats with "the tax collectors and sinners." The verb ἰδοὺ functions in 9:10b much like it does in 9:2a. It not only marks the vividness of the story scene, but also aligns the reader's psychological point of view from the narrator to that of the verb's subject, here being the Pharisees (9:11a).[49] Thus the reader is prompted to adopt their question as genuine:[50] Indeed, why *does* Jesus eat with the tax collectors and sinners?

Interestingly, the author alters the Markan account of ὅτι (Mark 2:16) to διὰ τί (9:11) in order to mould their question to be "slightly more pointed."[51] In addition, Matthew also intensifies the conflict and divergence between Jesus and the Pharisees by reducing "the scribes and the Pharisees" in Mark to just "Pharisees," and by inserting as the Pharisees' reference to Jesus "your teacher." It should be noted that throughout the preceding Matthean narrative the reader has already established a negative impression of the Pharisees.

---

45. Although commentators believe Elijah's call of Elisha to be the prototype of stories of individuals being called to discipleship in Jewish tradition (1 Kgs 19:19–21), it is different from Jesus's call stories in that Elisha requests a condition (and thus granted) before following Elijah.

46. In order to enter a rabbinic school, the initiative usually comes from the prospective pupil rather than the Rabbi himself; Arthur J. Droge, "Call Stories," *ABD*, 1:821.

47. Cf. Gundry, *Matthew*, 166.

48. Cf. Luz, *Matthew 8–20*, 31; Gundry, *Matthew*, 166.

49. See examples in Gary Yamasaki, *Watching a Biblical Narrative*, 191.

50. The question is genuine because the Pharisees' question also assumes the illegitimacy of Jesus's action, whereas the reader may not necessarily assume so, yet they need an explanation for such an action.

51. Repschinski, *Controversy Stories*, 77.

Consequently, in the reader's mind their attack on Jesus has already been tainted with little trust from the outset.

In the story world, however, the attack from the Pharisees does not arise without legitimate reasons. To start with, first-century tax collectors were widely thought of as a dishonest and despised people group.[52] Even in Matthew's gospel their low moral status is equated with that of either the Gentiles or immoral people (5:46; 18:17; 21:31). Similarly, "the sinners" fared worse as they were considered to be "blatant violators of the law."[53] That the Pharisees would separate themselves from "the tax collectors and sinners" and question those Jews who associate themselves with such dubious types is well justified and completely compatible with their usual conventions. Yet, rather than affirm the Pharisaic standard of inclusion/exclusion, the story demonstrates two ways in which Jesus directly opposed it.

First, Jesus shows an inclusive attitude for the tax collectors and sinners to be part of his community. Eating and reclining with tax collectors and sinners is essentially enjoying table fellowship together.[54] In this substantial meal, likely a banquet,[55] Jesus recognizes that the social outcast such as tax collectors and sinners can have esteemed status in his presence. By closely engaging with them, Jesus continues fulfilling Isaiah's prophecy (8:17, cf. Isa 53:4).[56] Moreover, this story immediately follows the call of Matthew to become Jesus's disciple. Such a narrative arrangement conveys to the reader that "the tax collectors and sinners" will also have the opportunity to be included in the community of Jesus.

---

52. John R. Donahue argues that tax collectors in the gospels are portrayed negatively primarily because of their dishonesty, "Tax Collectors and Sinners: An Attempt at Identification," *CBQ* 33 (1971): 59. Also, in Roman and Hellenistic literature they are grouped with the worst kind of people such as robbers, murderers, thieves, beggars (Cicero, *Off.* 15:51; Diog, *Ep.* 36:2; Dio Chrys, *Or.* 14:14); in the New Testament "tax collectors" are likened to sinners, Gentiles or immoral people (e.g. Mark 2:15; Matt 9:10; 11:19; 21:31; Luke 7:34; 15:2; 18:11); see discussions of Donahue on "Tax Collector," in *ABD*, 6:337.

53. Craig S. Keener, *A Commentary on the Gospel of Matthew* (Grand Rapids: Eerdmans, 1999), 295.

54. See Dennis E. Smith, "Table Fellowship," in *ABD*, 6:303.

55. As Keener suggests, "the term 'recline' indicates that this was no ordinary meal (Palestinian Jews normally sat on chairs) but a banquet (when people reclined), probably in the teacher's honor." Keener, *Matthew*, 296.

56. However, as I shall discuss later in this chapter, the author is not just confirming the image of the Servant of God in Jesus but gradually transforms to a figure with much more authority.

Second, by offering himself as a way of salvation, Jesus claims the place of God and creates a new community through his speech-act. Jesus's action in this conflict story demonstrates an authority that is consistent with his authority to forgive sins in the previous story. Sin no longer has power over Jesus, instead, he has all the authority to overcome and remove sin – an authoritative position solely belonging to God himself.

In the first part of his rebuttal to the Pharisees, Jesus responds with the following statement: it is not the healthy who need a doctor, but the sick. Here, Jesus uses a proverbial saying that has several Hellenistic parallels and was likely known to his opponents.[57] The saying describes a state of affairs in which Jesus and his opponents represent two fundamentally opposing positions (9:12).[58] On the one hand, because "the Pharisees' holiness paradigm concentrates on separation and insulation from those things that have the power to defile,"[59] their approach to sin is inevitably passive. Jesus, however, is a like a physician; he is one who actively engages with anyone regardless of the character of their spiritual maladies.[60] In this respect, the character of Jesus in this story of calling and dining with sinners is entirely consistent with the image of Jesus portrayed in earlier healing stories where he touches the leper and the sick (8:3, 15). Jesus's action completely invalidates the Pharisaic understanding that holiness and salvation is only possible through repentance by restitution, sacrifice and obedience to the law.[61] Consequently, the Pharisees take offense at this. The implication of the portrayal of Jesus in the story is indeed significant because from now on Jesus more evidently acts in the place of God.[62] Just like God who does not stay away from the sins of the people, Jesus also actively deals with them for the purpose of their salvation (cf. 1:21).

---

57. See, for example, Plutarch, *Apoph. lac.* 230F; Diog. Laert. 6.1.1.

58. This part of Jesus's rebuttal is his *assertive* speech-act which has a word-to-world direction of fit; see Searle's discussion on "direction of fit." *Assertive* type of illocution, according to Searle, is to "commit the speaker to something's being the case, to the truth of the expressed proposition." Searle, *Expression and Meaning*, 3, 12. Therefore, the Matthean author uses the saying to continue evoking Isa 53:4 as well as echo the context of this conflict story (8:17).

59. David E. Garland, *Reading Matthew: A Literary and Theological Commentary on the First Gospel* (New York: Crossroads, 1993), 103; also see Borg, *Conflict, Holiness and Politics*, 135.

60. Carter, "Jesus' 'I Have Come' Sayings in Matthew's Gospel," *CBQ* 60 (1998): 55.

61. Davies and Allison, *Matthew 8–18*, 102.

62. Cf. Ernst Fuchs, *Studies of the Historical Jesus* (London: SCM Press, 1964), 20ff.

That Jesus offers himself as a way of salvation can also be seen in the second part of his rebuttal (9:13). The insertion of Hosea 6:6 is the most significant redaction by Matthew in this story.[63] The direct quotation from the prophet Hosea is used as the divine mandate of Jesus to establish his new community, and thus, Jesus calls the world to correspond to the truth of his words.[64] In this new realm, salvation is based on a relationship to Jesus alone, in contrast to the law-abiding boundary upheld among the Jews (as represented by the Pharisees). If the major theme of the book of Hosea is that God desires true love and a marriage relationship with his people,[65] then Hosea 6:6 should be understood as a call to God's salvation. It is only possible because God has covenantal loyalty to his people and not because sacrifices are a mechanism by which one can manipulate God into action.[66] The logic for the author Matthew is that, similarly, salvation is only possible for the "the tax collectors and sinners" because of Jesus's love and mercy for them, and is not preconditioned by cultic rituals or literal observance of legal rules. Consequently, the command of Jesus to Pharisees that they "go and learn" what Hosea says indicates, therefore, that the Pharisaic view of holiness actually fails to meet the fundamental command for covenantal loyalty from Israel's God.

The ἦλθον saying which follows γάρ is a promise that has already occurred through his healing and forgiving activities (Matt 8–9) and not just for the future. As a speech-act, the ἦλθον saying has the illocutionary force of committing Jesus himself to the saving act, which is predicted by the angels at his birth (1:21–23) and has been exemplified by the healing story in 9:1–8. The conjunction γάρ commences a causal clause[67] which justifies the previous

---

63. The quotation of Hos 6:6 does not appear anywhere else in the New Testament, and only appears in two of Matthew's conflict stories. Cf. Davies and Allison, *Matthew 8–18*, 98; also Luz, *Matthew 8–20*, 33.

64. This part of Jesus's rebuttal is his *directive* and *commissive* speech-act which has a world-to-word direction of fit. *Directive* type of illocution is "attempts by the speaker to get the hearer to do something" such as invitations or commands. *Commissives* are "those illocutionary acts whose point is to commit the speaker to some future course of action." Searle, *Expression and Meaning*, 13–14; also see Searle's discussion on 'direction of fit,' *Expression and Meaning*, 3.

65. Bo H. Lim and Daniel Castelo, *Hosea*, The Two Horizons Old Testament Commentary (Grand Rapids, MI: Eerdmans, 2015), 39–40.

66. Douglas Stuart, *Hosea-Jonah*, WBC 31 (Dallas: Word Books, 1987), 110.

67. Richard A. Edwards, "Narrative Implications of *Gar* in Matthew," *CBQ* 52 (1990): 647–648.

command of Jesus to the Pharisees and his association with the tax collectors and sinners.

What then is the relationship between eating with the tax collectors and sinners and the ἦλθον saying? It is likely, as Carter suggests, that the ἦλθον saying particularly reminds the reader of God's earlier commission to Jesus that he shall save his people from their sins and manifest God's presence among men (1:21–23).[68] Therefore, in the call to Jesus's table fellowship, it is possible that Matthew intends "to blend the eschatological banquet and marriage motifs to declare to Israel the exile is over . . ."[69] Moreover, the call to discipleship (9:9) and table fellowship together mark the assembly and establishment of the caller's community. Here Jesus takes the initiative to exercise his institutional authority of showing mercy and thereby to establish *his own community*. In other words, Jesus redefines who "his people" are. In the presence of Jesus God's mercy is now being extended beyond the community of Israel to include even those who were previously excluded. In both "calls" in the conflict story the author implies a Christology,[70] because "the self-involving aspects of Jesus's pronouncements imply christological presuppositions."[71] Such an understanding is consistent with the surrounding context of the story. The "sinners" that are called, the "sick" who need a doctor, and the healed paralytic – they have all become objects of Jesus's healing/saving acts, and, thus, their inclusion into the kingdom of God is possible.

2.1.2.3 Summary of 9:9–13 in Its Immediate Narrative and Rhetorical Context

In the second conflict story, the center of the contention is the close association between Jesus and those who are deemed to defile the Jewish community. Such an association opposes the social-religious convention of their day. If Jesus in the first conflict story begins to demonstrate his divine status as God,

---

68. Carter, "'I Have Come,'" 62. Gathercole suggests similarly that "I have come" saying is "*not* that Jesus is referring to a specific occurrence of 'calling,' but rather that this is the whole purpose of his mission." Simon Gathercole, *The Preexistent Son: Recovering the Christologies of Matthew, Mark, and Luke* (Grand Rapids: Eerdmans, 2006), 158.

69. Philip Long, *Jesus the Bridegroom: The Origin of the Eschatological Feast as a Wedding Banquet in the Synoptic Gospels* (Eugene, OR: Pickwick, 2013), 192.

70. Thiselton, *Thiselton on Hermeneutics*, 104. Even Bultmann admits, "to call" implies a Christology, *Theology of the New Testament*, vol. 1 (London: SCM Press, 1952), 43.

71. Thiselton, *Thiselton on Hermeneutics*, 78.

whereby he has the institutional authority to forgive sins, then through the second conflict story, the author demonstrates that Jesus establishes a new community based on this authority status. This is evident in the act of Jesus showing mercy to the excluded, which reverses the community boundary upheld by the Pharisees. In this new community, it is no longer a relationship to the law that demarcates God's community primarily, but rather a relationship to Jesus.

The story is tightly knitted to the first conflict not only in terms of its close proximity, but also because they share similar themes, such as Jesus's mercy for marginalized people. Jesus displays an inclusive attitude for the tax collectors and sinners to be part of his community. Jesus acts in the place of God by offering himself as a way to salvation and, in effect, performs speech-acts that create a new community. Together with the first conflict, the present story prepares the reader for the climactic christological message in the next conflict.

2.1.3 Matthew 9:14–17

2.1.3.1 The Setting of the Story

Jesus and his challengers apparently are still at the banquet in the house;[72] the disciples, sinners, tax collectors, and Pharisees are all present together. Unlike in Mark, the transition to this story is immediate in Matthew – a simple τότε leading directly to the verbal exchange between Jesus and his challengers – giving the reader an impression that "the meal with the sinners gives rise to the present discussion as well" and that "this would locate the dialogues of eating with sinners and of the disciples' fasting practice in the same room."[73] Accordingly one may assume that the spatial setting of the last conflict story – a banquet – is the same setting for the current conflict story.

2.1.3.2 Matthew 9:14–17: The Conflict Scene Proper

Apart from introducing dialogue partners, the narrator's role is minimal in this story. The content of the actual conflict consists only of a verbal exchange

---

72. Davies and Allison, *Matthew 8–18*, 107, footnote 112; also cf. Edwards, *Matthew's Story of Jesus* (Philadelphia: Fortress, 1985), 30.

73. Repschinski marks this as a key redactional feature of the Matthean account in 9:14–17, *Controversy Stories*, 90; cf. 83.

between Jesus and his challengers. Matthew redacts Mark by making it clear that it is the disciples of John who raise the challenge. Indeed, there may well have been conflict between them since, following the example of their master, John's disciples typically call people to repentance through fasting. Yet, from the phrase διὰ τί ἡμεῖς καὶ οἱ Φαρισαῖοι we may understand that the Pharisees are also included in the challenging party, even though they themselves utter no question during the scene.[74]

A number of commentators believe that the conflict reflects a friction between the fasting practices of Jewish tradition and that of Jesus or the later church.[75] Literary analysis of the scene, on the other hand, suggests that the story necessitates a christological interpretation. According to this interpretation, the conflict underlines a key aspect of Jesus's authority consistent with the earlier two conflict stories, namely, that Jesus not only acts in the place of God but his authority is entirely incompatible with the existing authority structure.

How does the author in this conflict achieve his objective of highlighting a christological message? From the following two aspects, one can discern the author's careful crafting toward this objective.

First, Matthew portrays Jesus as the central figure assuming a messianic and supreme authority. The portrayal can be seen from the author's redaction features. Matthew substitutes νηστεύειν (Mark 2:19b) in Jesus's reply with πενθεῖν and places the verb before "bridegroom" to not only increase the parallelism with verse 15e,[76] but also to emphasize the act of mourning (9:15b). Because "fasting might be a religious practice, but mourning is much more directed toward a person," the author is able to highlight more the person of bridegroom than a Jewish ritual through the redaction.[77]

---

74. Repschinski goes as far as considering the Pharisees as the real opponents of Jesus in this story, *Controversy Stories*, 85.

75. Bultmann, *History*, 19. Dibelius, *From Tradition to Gospel*, 65. Francis W. Beare, *The Gospel according to Matthew* (Oxford: Basil Blackwell, 1981), 229ff. See detailed discussion of the tradition history and integrity of this story in Joseph F. Wimmer, *Fasting in the New Testament* (New York: Paulist Press, 1982), 85ff. Michael G. Steinhauser locates the sayings in 9:16–17 in particular in the break between Christianity and Judaism, but has difficulty conceiving how the sayings might have functioned in the ministry of Jesus, except as an affirmation of the radical newness of the Jesus's kingdom. Steinhauser, *Doppelbildworte in den synoptischen Evangelien: Eine form- und traditions-kristische Studie* (Würzburg: Echter Verlag, 1981), 63ff.

76. Davies and Allison, *Matthew 8–18*, 109; also Repschinski, *Controversy Stories*, 86.

77. Repschinski, 86.

This way, the author Matthew redacts Mark's account in order to underline the person of Jesus as the center of the reader's attention.

The author also assigns to Jesus an image otherwise solely applied to God in the Jewish tradition.[78] Matthew redacts the reply of Jesus and links fasting with mourning,[79] defending the disciples' non-fasting action in an analogy that the wedding guests cannot mourn at the presence of the bridegroom. This logic enables the reader to recognize that Jesus likens himself to the bridegroom in the setting of a wedding banquet,[80] and that his disciples are like the "guests/friends of the bridegroom" (9:15). Such a portrayal of Jesus is consistent throughout Matthew that Jesus is implied to be the bridegroom in parables of the wedding feast (cf. 22:1–14; 25:1–13).[81]

Yet, Jesus's claim should be surprising to Matthew's reader since God is the only one denoted to be the husband or the bridegroom of Israel according to the Hebrew Scriptures (e.g. Isa 49:18; 54:5–6; 62:4–5; Jer 2:2, 32–33; 3:1–11, 20; 31:32; 33:11; Ezek 16:8–52; Hos 2:1–3:5). How can a person claim himself to have a God-like role? Nonetheless, by quoting the prophet Hosea in the immediate context (9:13) and in the current conflict Jesus makes an analogy of himself as the bridegroom (9:15), it seems very possible that the author

---

78. Cf. G. K. Beale and D. A. Carson, *Commentary on the New Testament Use of the Old Testament* (Grand Rapids: Baker Academic, 2007), 35. George Buchanan also states, "Reference to a 'bridegroom' in religious, Jewish contexts almost always is a code name for the Messiah. The contract that God made with his people was a wedding contract: God was the groom and the Israelites were the bride." Buchanan, *The Gospel of Matthew*, 2 vols. (Lewiston, NY: Mellen Biblical Press, 1996), 1:417.

79. The replacement of 'fasting' in Mark with 'mourning' is clearly a Matthean redaction; Davies and Allison, *Matthew 8–18*, 109; also Repschinski, *Controversy Stories*, 86.

80. Beare believes that it is not only a clear indication that Jesus implies himself being the bridegroom "at the wedding feast seen as the inauguration of kingdom of God," but also that "the feast is already going on, and the disciples of Jesus are there as guests." Beare, *Matthew*, 229.

81. For example, France, *Gospel of Matthew*, 356; D. J. Williams, "Bridegroom," *DJG*, 88. Even though Herbert Basser's claim that Matthew uses hypostatic concepts of mystical traditions to refer to "bridegroom," nonetheless, he clearly considers Jesus as the bridegroom in his interpretation. Basser, *The Mind behind the Gospels: A Commentary to Matthew 1–14* (Boston: Academic Studies Press, 2009), 231. Besides the first evangelist, other gospel writers such as John (John 3:29) also use a deliberate identification of Jesus with the bridegroom; also Paul in describing the church as the bride of Christ in 2 Cor 11:2 and Eph 5:25 implies that Jesus is the bridegroom. Also Rev 19:7–9; 21:2. On the other hand, Carter proposes two meanings for "bridegroom": (1) "the term bridegroom is a rare image for God (Isa 62:5); (2) it also describes the people God clothed with the 'garments of salvation' and 'robe of righteousness' (Isa 61:10)." Carter, *Matthew and the Margins*, 222–223. In the context of Matt 9:15, however, the bridegroom clearly cannot be "the people of God."

intends for the audience to understand this implicit christological claim:[82] this Jesus enjoys the same divine status as Israel's God.

Moreover, the portrayal of Jesus is infused with both the images of a bridegroom and of the Messiah at the eschatological banquet.[83] As already mentioned, the context of this conflict story is the banquet introduced in the previous story (see 1.3.1). Therefore, it is reasonable to believe that in this story the author connects Jesus's table fellowship with the analogy of a wedding banquet,[84] which is used by Jesus to describe a joyful moment in contrast to mourning (9:15b). The joyful banquet is likely to evoke in the reader's mind the great messianic banquet where God's people rejoice at the presence of the Messiah,[85] although, in Jesus's analogy, it is the bridegroom who receives the attention. Such an association between the images of a bridegroom and the Messiah, however, is unusual because it is both absent in the Hebrew Scripture and scarce in later Jewish literature.[86] Interestingly, while all Synoptic Gospels preserve the saying (cf. Mark 2:19-20; Luke 5:34-35), it is Matthew who makes the clearest link between the presence of the bridegroom and joy (i.e. *contra* mourning; 9:15). Furthermore, Jesus's antithetical

---

82. As already mentioned in the discussion of the previous conflict story, the overall theme of the marriage metaphor in Hosea needs to be taken into consideration. Ryan Eagy's study particularly argues for a close link between the marriage metaphor in Hosea 2 where God is the bridegroom and Hosea 6 where God desires lovingkindness from his people. Eagy, "Matthew 9:9-17 and the Divine Bridegroom of Hosea," *ET* 128 (2017): 525-526. His conclusion is sound: "Jesus's claim to be the bridegroom must be read as a claim to divinity. Jesus claims he is the God of Hosea, who is now with his people," 526.

83. *Contra*. Long, who comments that "It is important to observe here that Jesus is not necessarily equating his role as messiah with the metaphor of bridegroom, as is frequently assumed" in his analysis of the Markan parallel of our current story, *Jesus the Bridegroom*, 194. However, Long seems to contradict himself. On the one hand, he believes that "The meal shared with Levi is described as a wedding fest because it is hosted by the bridegroom" (190) (i.e. the banquet in Mark 2:18-22/Matt 9:14-17 is the same as in Mark 2:13-17/Matt 9:9-12); on the other hand, he argues both that Jesus's table fellowship is associated with messianic banquet (189) and that Jesus's role as the host Messiah is not necessarily associated with bridegroom (194).

84. Long, 190-191, 193.

85. Cf. "Jesus is the groom of God's people in the coming messianic banquet foreshadowed in their table fellowship (22:2; 25:10-13)," Keener, *Matthew*, 300, also footnote 93; "In the symbolic language of the East the wedding is the symbol of the day of salvation . . .," Jeremias, *The Parables of Jesus*, rev. ed. (London: SCM Press, 1963), 117.

86. Gundry, for example, assumes that Jesus invented the comparison between the Messiah and bridegroom and applied the metaphor to himself; *Matthew*, 170; Jeremias originally suggests that such a connection is absent also in the literature of late Judaism but later finds an exception in *Pesiq.* 149a; *Parables of Jesus*, 52, also footnote 13.

saying marks the distinction between the present joyful period and future mourning when he is taken away from them (i.e. Jesus is absent from their midst).[87] In other words, the joyful messianic banquet is defined in relation to the person of Jesus rather than determined by chronology, because the joyful and celebrating state in Jesus's earthly presence with the disciples is continuous[88] and not just a future hope.[89] Likewise, the contrast in fasting practices between Jesus's disciples and his challengers is not so much due to chronological boundaries, but with whom they associate themselves, namely, either with Jesus or without him.

The above discussion outlines a key point the author makes through this conflict. That is, even though the reply of Jesus in 9:15 is not an explicit confession of his messiahship, Matthew does convey an implicit Christology to the reader – Jesus has both the role of the Messiah and the status usually reserved for God.

Second, the supreme status of Jesus, which creates a new community (the disciples), is entirely incompatible with the old community as represented by his opponents (in this case represented by John's disciples and Pharisees).[90] This is made plain by the contrasting analogies of new versus old cloths and wine/wineskins. At first glance, the two contrasting analogies seem to have little to do with the question of fasting since the communities of Jesus and his opponents both fast (cf. 4:2; 6:16–18).[91] However, it is precisely the common theme behind fasting/not fasting and new versus old that links 9:15 and

---

87. Many scholars hold this interpretation. Hill, for example, states that "this is a thinly veiled allegory of the death of Jesus," *Matthew*, 176–177. Others, see, for example, Beare, *Matthew*, 229; Gundry, *Matthew*, 170; J. P. Meier, *Matthew* (Wilmington: Glazier, 1980), 95; Daniel Patte, *The Gospel according to Matthew: A Structural Commentary on Matthew's Faith* (Philadelphia: Fortress, 1987), 130.

88. The verb ἐστιν as the present indicative form is likely used here for a present action, highlighting a continuous situation in progress; see discussion of present tense forms in Porter, *Idioms*, 29. Also see Fanning's category of "progressive or descriptive or specific present": "the aspectual viewpoint of the present is reflected in this use by the close focus on the internal process or state without reference to the beginning or end-point of the situation." Buist M. Fanning, *Verbal Aspect in New Testament Greek* (Oxford: Clarendon Press, 1990), 199–200.

89. France suggests that in fact joy "characterizes the whole of Jesus' earthly ministry, not just a hope in the future," *Gospel of Matthew*, 356.

90. Patte, *Matthew*, 131; Luz, *Matthew 8–20*, 37.

91. Luz, *Matthew 8–20*, 37; Beare even argues that 9:16–17 should be regarded as a "supplement" to 9:14–15: *Matthew*, 231. Their apparent disjunction is also noted by other Christian traditions, such as *Gospel of Thomas* (Saying 104/Matt 9:15 and 47b/Matt 9:16–17), which separates them into different story units.

9:16–17 together. That is, Jesus's presence on earth has brought about the beginning of a new eschatological world that is incompatible with the old.

This is because of the two functions of the analogy of the bridegroom at a wedding banquet (9:15): (1) this analogy governs the next two analogies about the old/new cloth and wine/wineskins. To be sure, though verse 16 and verse 17 are two separate sayings, they nonetheless convey the same message,[92] that is, "they are matter-of-fact observations about the danger of mixing the old and the new."[93] Placing all three analogies together, the author invites the reader to actively engage in seeking the common element among them. The common element is the first analogy, which explains Jesus's (and his disciples') actions as sensible *because of who he is*.[94] While garments or wine may symbolize a new eschatological age,[95] the crucial point in Jesus's analogy of mending garments and pouring wine is, in fact, on the disastrous results of mixing new and old together.[96] By highlighting the unmatchable situation between the old and new immediately following an implicit message of who Jesus is (i.e. the new bridegroom), the author entails that the reason for the followers of Jesus not to fast is precisely that he inaugurates a new community, and that this new community brought by his presence is entirely incompatible to that of the old (i.e. as represented by the Pharisees or John's disciples); and (2) the analogy also helps to illustrate the incompatibility

---

92. Buchanan, *Matthew*, 1:418; also Patte, *Matthew*, 131. Saunders, "No One Dared," 184.

93. Beare, *Matthew*, 231.

94. Edwards, *Matthew's Story*, 30–31.

95. Wine and garments are also eschatological symbol for the new cosmos and the New Age; Jeremias, *Parables of Jesus*, 117.

96. Many scholars build elaborate interpretations over vv. 16–17 (especially over vv. 17: καὶ ἀμφότεροι συντηροῦνται) as to whether Jesus meant to replace Judaism with Christianity; see Floyd V. Filson, *The Gospel According to Saint Matthew* (London: A & C Black, 1977), 120; Hill, *Matthew*, 177 (although Hill believes that Matthew inserts his own view in vv. 17–18 to contrast Jesus's saying that Judaism is to be preserved not abolished); or, the Matthean redaction "both new and old are preserved" conveys the author's intent to preserve things in the past; see Davies and Allison, *Matthew 8–18*, 115; D. J. Harrington, *The Gospel of Matthew*, Sacra Pagina, vol. 1 (Collegeville: Liturgical Press, 1991), 129. Jeremias believes that the mixing wine describes foolish actions; new wine is the traditional metaphor of the New Age. Items such as tent, sheet, and garment are common symbols of the cosmos. He suggests this as the context of Mark 2:21: the old world's age has run out; it is compared to the old garment which is no longer worth patching with new cloth; the New Age has arrived. Jeremias, *Parables of Jesus*, 117–118, also 130. However, seen from the immediate context of vv. 17–18, it seems that the question of preservation of Judaism with Christianity is irrelevant to the interpretation of 9:17–18 in that the preserved "both" refer to new wine and new wineskins; see Luz, *Matthew 8–20*, 37; Repschinski, *Controversy Stories*, 88.

of the two, because at the presence of the bridegroom (i.e. Jesus's earthly presence) the eschaton has begun.[97] Jesus answers a question targeted at the disciples' ongoing action (9:14b: . . . οὐ νηστεύουσιν[98]) by articulating a clear contrast between the *present/continuous* status quo (μὴ δύνανται . . . μετ' αὐτῶν ἐστιν ὁ νυμφίος) and a *future* condition (ἐλεύσονται . . . νηστεύσουσιν). According to Fuller, the description of a present matter ἐφ' ὅσον μετ' αὐτῶν ἐστιν ὁ νυμφίος suggests that "the nearness of God is *now* a reality precisely in his drawing near in Jesus' eschatological ministry."[99] Furthermore, Jesus's earthly presence with those who follow him has already launched such a jubilant eschatological atmosphere that "they [the parables] use all the resources of dramatic illustration to help men to see that in the events before their eyes . . . God is confronting them in His kingdom, power and glory."[100] Therefore, even though Jesus intends for the disciples to fast in the future, probably after his crucifixion (9:15c, d),[101] such a practice "is based on the absence of the Bridegroom, not Jewish tradition."[102]

2.1.3.3 Summary of 9:14–17 in Its Immediate Narrative and Rhetorical Context

Matthew 9:14–17 is so closely connected to 9:9–13 that the two stories share the same setting – the banquet.[103] The third conflict story continues a series of questions following the Pharisees' challenge to Jesus's eating with "inappropriate" guests. On this occasion, however, the main challengers become John's disciples (though the Pharisees are still implied as challengers in 9:14).[104] Jesus is challenged for his disciples' behavior, but as a teacher responsible for

---

97. Jeremias's comment that "realized eschatology" is the meaning of Mark 2:19 can also be applied to Matt 9:15 as well; *Parables of Jesus*, 117. Cf. C. H. Dodd, *The Parables of the Kingdom*, rev. ed. (London: Fontana Books, 1961), 198.

98. This current action is also to be understood as a present continuous as "Why do your disciples not fast in general?" Hill, *Matthew*, 176.

99. Reginald. H. Fuller, *The Foundation of New Testament Christology* (London: Lutterworth Press, 1965), 106.

100. Dodd, *Parables of the Kingdom*, 197–198.

101. Keener, *Matthew*, 300; Carter, *Matthew and the Margins*, 223.

102. Hultgren, *Jesus and His Adversaries*, 82.

103. The image of a banquet as the connection between two stories also refers to the heavenly banquet because Jesus's "calling" in the previous story implies more than a prophetic calling but bears a heavenly connotation. Gathercole, *Preexistent Son*, 158.

104. As "John's disciples advocate a concern of the Pharisee," Luz, *Matthew 8–20*, 36.

his disciples, the real target is Jesus himself. This conflict follows immediately after two conflicts which have already demonstrated Jesus's supreme authority and divine identity, namely, (1) the Son of Man assumes God's prerogative to forgive sins (9:1–8); (2) Jesus manifests God's presence on earth and offers himself as a way to save people from their sins (9:9–13). In relation to the previous two conflict stories, the author seems to present a climactic christological message to the reader in this third conflict: *Jesus is the eschatological Messiah who also enjoys God's divine status, but the community Jesus creates around him is incompatible with the old Israel.*

2.2 Conflict Stories in Context of Matthew 5–9

Literary analysis of gospel texts requires that each story under investigation should not be isolated from its literary context and needs to be examined in relation to its immediate and wider contexts in order that the author's message is understood within the overall framework. In the last section, each conflict story has already been dealt with in relation to its immediate context. The following will take a close look at how to understand these three conflicts as a literary unit within the wider context of the Matthew 5–9 narrative unit.

2.2.1 The Wider Context: Matthew 5–9

Given that all of the first three conflict stories in Matthew were already included in Mark's account, why did Matthew redact and retell them in his gospel? The answer lies in the arrangement of these conflict stories in their wider literary context which includes Matthew 8–9, the so-called "miracle chapters,"[105] and Matthew 5–7 (Sermon on the Mount). It is necessary, however, to first inquire into the author's purpose in these chapters before inquiring as to how the wider literary context shapes the interpretation of the three stories.

Besides establishing the literary unity of Matthew 5–9,[106] scholars have also dealt extensively with their subject matter and thereby almost

---

105. Cf. Kingsbury, "Observations," 559.

106. The earliest attempt to establish literary unity of Matt 5–9 is by J. Schneiwind, *Das Evangelium nach Matthäus*, 9th ed. (Göttingen: Vandenhoeck & Ruprecht, 1960), 103ff. Following Schneiwind, there are also W. Grundmann, *Das Evangelium nach Matthäus*, 5th ed. (Berlin: Evangelische Verlagsanstalt, 1981), 110, 245–246; Held, "Matthew as Interpreter," 249; Christopher Burger, "Jesu Taten nach Matthäus 8 und 9," *ZKT* 70 (1973): 281–282; William

unanimously divided these chapters into Jesus's words and deeds,[107] corresponding to two types of literary genre: (1) Matthew 5–7 records Jesus's words which are recognized as discourse material, where narration time and story time overlap,[108] and, (2) Matthew 8–9 is composed of short stories which are narrative material. From the outset, however, it must be noted that the author's *purpose* for his literary work exists largely at the rhetoric level. It is to be distinguished from the *subject matter* existing mainly at the story level.

In Matthew 8–9, the author has clearly redacted, selected, and arranged his source materials into a "new" composition. Scholars such as Kingsbury and Thompson attempted to discover what Matthew intends to do especially in these chapters. Kingsbury, for example, believes that the author presents Jesus as the Messiah and the Son of God in both the Sermon on the Mount and the miracle chapters. The latter, in particular, function as an invitation for Matthew's community to approach this Son of God with their own petitions for help in time of distress and affliction.[109] Thompson, on the other hand, proposes that the author's composition provides "continuous movement between various episodes" in order to "complete Matthew's initial portrayal of Jesus' ministry in Galilee and prepare both for the mission of the twelve disciples and for the reactions of Israel to the messianic activity of Jesus and his disciples."[110] While both views are plausible, from the literary critical point of view, neither attempt seems wholly satisfactory. For instance, Matthew's juxtaposition of discourse and narrative materials has not been fully explored. Moreover, the titular significance of Son of God in the miracle chapters may be over-influenced by Kingsbury's reading of Matthew

---

G. Thompson, "Reflections on the Composition of Mt 8:1–9:34," *CBQ* 33 (1971): 365–388. However, J. D. Kingsbury goes further and includes Matt 4:17 as the beginning and 11:1 as the end of a narrative unit; "Observations," 566–567.

107. The division between Jesus's "words" and "deeds" was first proposed by Schniewind (*Matthäus*, 36) who influenced many scholars after him, such as Thompson, "Reflections," 367. Here I use these two words for the sake of convenience; however, as argued elsewhere in this chapter, many of Jesus's words of authority should be regarded not simply as verbal utterances, but as speech-acts, because as Saunders rightly points out, "Matthew is not seeking in these chapters (5–9) merely to depict the word/act dimensions of Jesus' activity." Saunders, "No One Dared," 130.

108. In fact in the discourse in Matt 5–7 the narration time is equal in length with the story time and the author seems to be presenting Jesus's teaching word by word.

109. Kingsbury, "Observations," 565, 572.

110. Thompson, "Reflections," 387–388.

1–4, and the function of Matthew 8–9 cannot be determined for Kingsbury without the presupposition of a persecuted Matthean community. Likewise, Thompson's proposal does not sufficiently investigate the author's purpose beyond compositional considerations and Matthew's theological intention is left unexamined.[111]

Since the first evangelist is known for his technique of integrating discourse and narrative materials together, Bauer in his study of the structure of Matthew proposes three observations regarding the relationship between discourse and narrative materials from which we may discern the author's purpose for Matthew 5–9. Based on Bauer's observations, this literary analysis proposes that the author's purpose is the *elaboration and exposition of Jesus's supreme and God-like authority* by supplying a selection of Jesus's teaching stories and miracle (including conflict) stories in the early part of his gospel.

1. *"Not only are the discourses integrated into the material that follows in each case, but the lack of clear, decisive beginnings to the discourses indicates that these discourses are also integrated into the material that precedes."*[112] The Sermon on the Mount immediately follows the end of the last narration that "large crowds . . . followed him" (4:25) and starts with "Jesus saw the crowds" using a simple connective δὲ (5:1).[113] It indicates that the audiences of the Sermon on the Mount are the ones Jesus called and healed in the preceding narrative (4:18–21, 25; 5:1), who, as disciples, have subjected themselves to Jesus's authority[114] or have acknowledged his authority by following him.[115]

2. *"The formula which is repeated at the end of the discourses is transitional in nature."*[116] With regard to the author's purpose for chapters 5–9, the ending of the Sermon on the Mount is particularly interesting (7:28–29). It is

---

111. Luz believes that Matthew is telling a "theological" story of Jesus in chs. 8–9 which goes deeper than the surface level of miracles and dialogues that are geographically or chronologically connected to each other. Luz, *Matthew 8–20*, 2.

112. David. R. Bauer, *The Structure of Matthew's Gospel: A Study in Literary Design* (Sheffield: Almond Press, 1989), 129. However, for the purpose of my own argument, I altered Bauer's original order of the three observations.

113. See usage of δὲ in Porter, *Idioms*, 208.

114. It is demonstrated by Jesus's "sitting down" and his disciples' "coming to him" in the setting of the Sermon on the Mount.

115. For example, 4:25: large crowds "followed" him; see different usage of "follow" in Kingsbury's discussion in "The Verb Akolouthein as an Index of Matthew's View of His Community," *JBL* 97, no. 1 (1978): 56–73.

116. Bauer, *Structure of Matthew*, 129.

transitional because, on the one hand, it sums up chapters 5–7 where Jesus teaches with clear authority over the interpretation of the law and Jewish traditions. Yet, on the other hand, the ending also prepares the reader to expect a *different* authority. It informs the reader that the amazement of the crowds is the result of the authoritative teaching of Jesus but not of the scribes (7:29).[117] Soon after, in chapters 8–9, the reader encounters three conflict stories which each confirm this expectation and present Jesus as a different authority figure. Moreover, throughout the following miracle narratives in Matthew 8–9, the reader encounters several occurrences of the word ἐξουσία (8:9; 9:6, 8; cf. 10:1). Consequently, in the reader's mind, the authority of Jesus is undoubtedly a major theme of chapters 8–9 which is also present in chapters 5–7.

3. "*The notion that the discourses are integrated into the flow of the surrounding narrative is indicated also by an examination of the contexts of each of the discourse.*"[118] The arrival of God's kingdom proclaimed by Jesus in the earlier narrative (4:17) is also a major theme emphasized in the Sermon on the Mount. This kingdom comes not only with Jesus's teaching, but also with his powerful speech-acts of healing, exorcism and speech-acts in conflict with other religious authorities. The above analysis shows the author's christological emphasis upon Jesus's authority, which is the key message in all conflict narratives.

In summary, based on the observations of Bauer, closer examination of the integration between discourse and narrative materials makes it possible to discern that the author has a theological purpose in chapters 5–9. That is, by providing a selection of Jesus's teaching and miracles, Matthew intends to elaborate and clarify that Jesus's authority is so supreme that he acts in the place of God.

2.2.2 Conflict Stories in Matthew 8–9

Having determined the author's purpose for the wider context of chapters 5–9, we now turn to identifying the specific purpose of chapters 8–9. There have been many attempts to divide chapters 8–9 into different units under various

---

117. In the story world, the scribes certainly have authority based on their knowledge of the Mosaic law or Jewish traditions, therefore οὐχ ὡς οἱ γραμματεῖς αὐτῶν in 7:29 does not mean that Jesus has authority but the scribes lack authority, but Jesus's authority is not like that of the scribes; see similar interpretation in Beare, *Matthew*, 200; also Luz, *Matthew 1–7*, 390.

118. Bauer, *Structure of Matthew*, 130.

themes, such as Christology, discipleship, faith and debates.[119] However, a literary critical reading of the chapters shows that such divisions were probably of less importance to the author than the concern to develop the presentation of Jesus's image from the *Servant* of God to that of the Messiah who possesses divine authority as God *himself*. Indeed as much is echoed in Matthew's opening statement wherein Jesus is "Immanuel (God with us)," and, in Matthew 1–4, he is identified as the "Son of God."

The image of the Servant of God, as presented in chapter 8, does not fully capture the identity of Jesus portrayed in chapters 8–9. After the first three healing miracles (8:1–4, 5–13, 14–15) Matthew inserts a fulfillment quotation (8:17)[120] in addition to the summary report of Jesus's healing activities (8:16).[121] In itself, Matthew 8:17 could suggest Jesus was the Isaianic Servant of God (cf. Isa 53:4); however, the metaphor of the suffering, obedient and humiliated Servant is so far absent from Jesus's ministry.[122] Therefore, while the initial impression of Jesus in the reader's mind as the Servant of God may be reasonably warranted by the author's quotation of Isaiah 53:4, it cannot be the central image portrayed by chapters 8–9. The development of Jesus's image in the narrative then leads the reader to expect something more about his identity beyond simply being the Servant of God.

In the early part of chapters 8–9, Jesus is demonstrated to have such a great power that merely by λόγῳ ("with a word," 8:16) he can heal the sick, calm the storm and drive out demons (e.g. 8:3, 8, 13, 16, 26, 32). Thus, the reader may also share the astonishment of the gentile centurion who recognizes Jesus as a man of ἐξουσία (cf. 8:10).[123] As apart from Jesus's teaching authority

---

119. For example, Thompson, "Reflections," 368–387; H. J. Held, "Matthew as Interpreter," 169–181; C. Burger, "Jesu Taten nach Matthäus 8 und 9," 284–287.

120. Davies and Allison, *Matthew 8–18*, 7–8.

121. Held argues that "the summary report speaks less about individual deeds of Jesus at a particular place and time than about his healing activity generally, and the quotation from Isaiah 53:4 is intended to interpret all his works of healing." Held, "Matthew as Interpreter," 172.

122. France finds that "in view of the concentration elsewhere in the New Testament on the theme of vicarious suffering and redemption in Isaiah's vision of the Servant, it is remarkable that neither of these two quotations (Isaiah 53:4 and 42:1–4) [in Matthew] focuses on this theme, either in the specific words quoted or in the context of Jesus' ministry to which they are related." France, *Matthew: Evangelist and Teacher* (Downers Grove: InterVarsity Press, 1989), 300–301. Kingsbury, on the other hand, rejects Servant-Christology within chs. 8–9 on the ground that Matthew presents Jesus more as the Son of God in these chapters. "Observations," 565.

123. This is significant because the word ἐθαύμασεν is usually reserved for description of others' amazement toward Jesus's power.

which may be more readily recognized by Jewish audiences (7:28–29)[124] – and his miraculous powers – the narrative so far has not yet revealed what *kind* of authority Jesus possesses. The next two miracle stories (8:23–27, 28–34) further vex the reader: Jesus even has power over "the winds and the waves" (8:22), while the demons address him as "Son of God" (8:29). Therefore, alongside the disciples on the boat (8:27), Matthew's audiences may also raise the question: who is this Jesus? What kind of power is this?

The author seems to have anticipated this puzzlement. It is worth noting that, in the first century, Jesus was not the only one who reportedly possessed miraculous powers.[125] Thus, in the following conflict stories, the author begins to distinguish between power and authority and point to what this great power reveals.[126]

To be sure, the three conflict stories pose a challenge to the interpretation of chapters 8–9: they do not neatly fit within the overall genre of "miracles." One may reasonably argue that the healing of the paralytic is a miracle. However, as already noted above (see analysis of 9:1–8), the healing scenario only provides the occasion for Jesus to rebuke his challengers: the Son of Man has authority to forgive sins (9:8). So, why did the author insert the conflict stories in the midst of the miracle chapters?

Analysis of the individual pericope demonstrates that the reader encounters a Jesus who makes proclamations neither about the law nor about God. Instead, Jesus declares characteristics of himself that are the prerogatives of God: he has authority to forgive sins, to save sinners, and is identified as the eschatological bridegroom. In these stories, the reader meets a Jesus in whom "there is an immediate confrontation with God's presence and his very

---

124. Their identity of being Jewish is implied by οἱ γραμματεῖς αὐτῶν in 7:29.

125. For example, Acts mentions Jewish magicians like Simon and Elymas (Acts 8:9–24; 13:6–11).

126. Sociologists have long recognized a great differentiation between power and authority. For example, following Max Weber, Dahrendorf asserts that "power is merely a factual relation, authority is a legitimate relation of domination and subjection. In this sense, authority can be described as legitimate power." Dahrendorf further explains that "power is the 'probability that one actor within a social relationship will be in a position to carry out his own will despite resistance, regardless of the basis on which this probability rests'"; whereas authority (*Herrschaft*) is the "probability that a command with a given specific content will be obeyed by a given group of persons." Dahrendorf, *Class and Class Conflict in Industrial Society* (Stanford: Stanford University Press, 1959), 166.

self."[127] Thus, the three conflict stories give the impression that they convey an *implicit* Christology revolving around Jesus's authority,[128] that is, Jesus is to be identified as the Messiah who acts in the place of God.[129]

Seen within a larger context, therefore, the conflict stories in Matthew 8-9 help the author to effectively elucidate that Jesus not only has miraculous power but that this power is of such great legitimacy that it is equated with God's own authority.[130] Employing conflict, the narrative of Matthew 8-9 develops the image of Jesus from the Servant of God (e.g. 8:1-17) to the Messiah acting in the place of God.[131]

---

127. Fuller, *Foundation*, 106.

128. According to Fuller, "an examination of Jesus' words – his proclamation of the Reign of God, and his call for decision, his enunciation of God's demand, and his teaching about the nearness of God – and of his conduct – his calling men to follow him and his healings, his eating with publicans and sinners – forces upon us the conclusion that underlying his word and work is an *implicit Christology*," *Foundation*, 106 (italics added).

129. Against Jeremias who argues that because "the allegorical representation of the Messiah as a bridegroom is completely foreign to the whole of the Old Testament and to the literature of late Judaism," Jesus's hearers would not have understood the image of bridegroom as the Messiah in Matt 25:1ff. However, Jeremias immediately contradicts himself by saying that ". . . the parable (i.e. 25:1ff) conceals a Messianic utterance of Jesus which only his disciples could understand," *Parables of Jesus*, 52–53.

130. It is therefore not surprising then when Jesus begins to assume such authority, whether in a miracle (9:1–8) or in his action (of calling/eating with tax-collectors and sinners and of not fasting), it becomes offensive to those religious leaders who would embark on challenging Jesus from here on throughout the Matthean narrative.

131. Thompson, "Reflections," 383. Kingsbury goes as far as arguing for Jesus being Israel's Messiah and Son of God who has divine dignity and authority ("Observations," 565–566), but our analysis seems to point to a "higher" christological message by the author.

CHAPTER 3

Conflict Stories in Matthew 12

This Generation Encounters the Lord of the Sabbath

There are four conflict stories in Matthew 12. Compared to the first three conflict stories in Matthew 9, the four stories in Matthew 12 continue the challenge to the identity and authority of Jesus, but the antagonism is more intense. The more Jesus's identity and authority are revealed, the more hostile his opponents become. As a result, Matthew's narrative in this section contains the first explicit mention of Jesus's manner of death, but at the same time, his opponents are warned that they will receive eschatological judgment from God.

Four conflict stories occupy most of Matthew 12, but the sequence is interrupted by the prophecy of Isaiah 42:1–4, which is the key to the interpretation of the four conflicts. In fact, as the following analysis shows, these conflicts illustrate the Isaianic prophecy of the Messiah's justice. This justice entails that Jesus carries out his mission by bringing κρίσις to all who will either reject him or acknowledge him. Therefore, structurally Matthew 12 is situated as the transitional point of the plot development of the whole gospel. It prepares for the theme of acceptance/rejection being fully demonstrated by the parable discourse of Matthew 13.[1]

---

1. In fact, Howell suggests that "The plotting device of acceptance/rejection actually divides the discourse [Matt 13] in half and places it in its context in the Gospel," *Matthew's Inclusive Story*, 141.

This chapter continues looking at the question: why does the author use the Sabbath as a contention point for his plot development? Or in terms of literary criticism, what is the function of these conflict stories in the narrative of chapters 10–13? How does the author achieve his goal?

This chapter will first examine each conflict story as well as their relationship with each other. Then all four stories will be examined in the light of their wider literary context, which includes both Matthew 11 and 13. A brief summary will be provided at the end of this chapter.

3.1 Analysis of Individual Pericopea: Matthew 12:1–8, 9–14, 22–37, 38–45

3.1.1 Matthew 12:1–8

3.1.1.1 Matthew 12:1: The Setting of the Story

By inserting a typical Matthean marker ἐν ἐκείνῳ τῷ καιρῷ at the start of the story,[2] the author links 12:1ff closely with the preceding context, even though the temporal indicator "the Sabbath" sets the story apart from Jesus's previous sayings (11:25–30) chronologically in the story world.[3] These conflict stories (vv. 1–8) and verses 8–14 are tied to the sayings by their shared topic – Sabbath being a "light burden."[4] The connecting phrase ἐν ἐκείνῳ τῷ καιρῷ then "bring(s) the gaps in the time continuum to the reader's attention."[5]

In the setting of the story, Matthew emphasizes Jesus as the key character. The author replaces the personal pronoun αὐτόν in Mark with ὁ Ἰησοῦς[6] and introduces Jesus's action in an independent clause before turning to the disciples.[7] What is also different from Mark is that Matthew adds a description of the disciples' being hungry as the cause of their action to pluck the grain and eat. The significance of this redaction will be discussed in the next section.

---

2. The phrase ἐν ἐκείνῳ τῷ καιρῷ does not occur in any other gospels but is used three times in Matthew (11:25; 12:1; 14:1); cf. John Hicks, "The Sabbath Controversy in Matthew: An Exegesis of Matthew 12:1–14," *ResQ* 27 (1984): 80. According to *BDAG*, τῷ καιρῷ refers to "a period characterized by some aspect of special crisis," see "καιρός," *BDAG*, 498.

3. Yang, *Jesus and the Sabbath*, 166; Davies and Allison, *Matthew 8–18*, 305.

4. France, *Matthew*, 457; Harrington, *Matthew*, 171.

5. Shimon Bar-Efrat, *Narrative Art in the Bible* (Sheffield: Almond Press, 1989), 159.

6. Gundry, *Matthew*, 221.

7. Whereas in Mark 2:23 and Luke 6:1 Jesus's action seems to be accompanying the disciples' action in the infinitive construction; see discussion in Saunders, "No One Dared," 210.

3.1.1.2 Matthew 12:2–8: Conflict Story Proper

The Pharisees appear for the second time in Matthew's conflict stories. They are characterized as the opponents of Jesus and address the accusation of the disciples to their master. While the nature of the accusation and the temporal setting of the Sabbath lead many commentators to analyze the legitimacy of the disciples' action according to the Jewish law (e.g. whether the disciples did break a Sabbath law that prohibited reaping on the Sabbath,[8] or whether Jesus's defence is valid in view of rabbinic rhetoric[9]) a literary critical investigation of the text within its context sheds a somewhat different light on the thrust of the passage.

This analysis finds that, rather than focusing on the legality of the disciples' action on the Sabbath, the author aims to reveal the identity of Jesus more specifically as the Messiah who assumes the divine authority of God, which is contrary to the authority of the Pharisees. Such a finding is based on analysing how Matthew arranges the text and how his composition and redaction highlight the christological nature of the conflict. The following four points substantiate the discovery.

First, in Matthew's account, Jesus's reply is directed at the significance of the temple rather than that of the Sabbath laws. This Sabbath conflict is mentioned in all Synoptic Gospels (par. Mark 2:23–28; Luke 6:1–5), but Matthew has the longest account. In particular, the author inserts a second example of the service of the priests in the temple in addition to David's story and the sayings in 12:6–7.[10] One significant problem arises with the addition of the second example: namely, the two examples appear unconnected with each

---

8. Etan Levine, "The Sabbath Controversy according to Matthew," *NTS* 22 (1975/76): 480–483.

9. D. M. Cohn-Sherbok, "An Analysis of Jesus' Arguments Concerning the Plucking of Grain on the Sabbath," *JSNT* 2 (1979): 311–341.

10. Matthew is the only evangelist who includes the priests' Sabbath service in the temple and uses the expression οὐκ ἀνέγνωτε twice in Jesus's rebuking examples of the Pharisees' accusation. This seems to be contrary to the Matthean narrative style of being succinct, as if he considers David's story in his source (Mark and Q) as an insufficient defence. Some scholars believe that it is because Matthew wants to add a halakhic argument to Jesus's defence; see Lena Lybaek, *New and Old in Matthew 11–13: Normativity in the Development of Three Theological Themes* (Gottingen: Vandenhoeck & Ruprecht, 2002), 160, footnote 72. Cf. Michael D. Goulder, *Midrash and Lection in Matthew* (London: SPCK, 1974), 328. Others argue from Matthean community point of view that it is due to the fact that unlike Mark's Roman gentile community, David's story alone is not persuasive for Matthew's Jewish-Christian audience; see Hicks, "Sabbath Controversy," 84, footnote 21.

other and not in complete concord with their context (v. 1, v. 8) from a narrative point of view. On the one hand, David's story seems to have nothing to do with Sabbath law since its origin in the Hebrew Bible (1 Sam 21:7) has no reference to the Sabbath in the text. David's alleged offence in the temple is that he ate the bread "which was not lawful for them to do, but only for the priests."[11] Whether David is in breach of Sabbath law is not the point as far as the Matthean context is concerned.[12] On the other hand, although the priests serving in the temple does relate to the Sabbath, it is not related to hunger, unlike the case in David's story. This apparent disjunction leads some scholars to conclude that Matthew's argument is illogical.[13]

However, because the two examples are introduced by the same phrase οὐκ ἀνέγνωτε and connected by the particle ἤ, one cannot but assume that the author regards the two examples to be connected with each other in some way.[14] For example, one could posit that each example is linked with *half* of the accusation and that they therefore together form a logical defence on Jesus's part for the disciples: David's story deals with hunger and the priests' temple service deals with the Sabbath.[15] Or, is it possible that something fundamental is shared by both examples?

This analysis proposes that the link tying both examples together is the locale of both incidents – the temple. Both texts specifically refer to the temple. In David's story, on the one hand, he and his companions ate the showbread in τὸν οἶκον τοῦ θεοῦ. Although at the time of David, τὸν οἶκον τοῦ θεοῦ refers to the tent housing the Ark of the Covenant and not yet a proper temple like the one in first-century Jerusalem. The priests in the second example, on the

---

11. Gerhard Barth, "Matthew's Understanding of the Law," in *Tradition and Interpretation*, Günther Bornkamm, Gerhard Barth, and Heinz Joachim Held (London: SCM Press, 1963), 81, footnote 4.

12. Robert Banks, *Jesus and the Law in the Synoptic Tradition* (Cambridge: Cambridge University Press, 1975), 115; Lybaek, *New and Old*, 160. Basser suggests that because of this, David's story has nothing to do with the Lord of the Sabbath saying, *Mind behind the Gospels*, 283. Although some scholars infer the link to the Sabbath from the reference to the shewbread in Midrash, for example, H. L. Strack and P. Billerbeck, *Kommentar zum Neuen Testament aus Talmud un Midrasch, Bd. I: Das Evangelium nach Matthäus* (Müchen: Beck, 1956), 618ff.

13. For example, Basser, *Mind behind the Gospels*, 283; J. W. Doeve also agrees that "the nature of the infringement is not quite the same" in both examples. Doeve, *Jewish Hermeneutics in the Synoptic Gospels and Acts* (Assen: Van Gorcum, 1954), 106–107.

14. Hence, for example, Lybaek suggests the link is the mention of the temple and priests, *New and Old*, 160; also Saunders, "No One Dared," 209.

15. Such is the case argued by Basser, *Mind behind the Gospels*, 282–283.

other hand, were also ἐν τῷ ἱερῷ. One must bear in mind that in the mind of Matthew's reader, τὸν οἶκον τοῦ θεοῦ or τῷ ἱερῷ is not to be understood simply as a physical building. Instead, it represents the presence of God[16] and points to his authority.[17] Therefore, if the actions of David and of the priests are deemed innocent while taking place in the temple (as indicated in the text v. 5 and v. 7), they can only be deemed so in the eyes of God who, according to the audience, is the ultimate and exclusive authority in the temple and none other.[18] If this is the *a priori* understanding of Matthew's audience, then the fundamental issue linking the two examples in Matthew's mind is the temple.

Secondly, the subject of μεῖζόν ἐστιν refers to Jesus. Once it is established that Matthew intends the temple as the key link between the two examples in Jesus's defence, then the insertion of verse 6 begins to make sense. This is because the temple is precisely the referent Jesus uses for his comparison τοῦ ἱεροῦ μεῖζόν ἐστιν ὧδε. But the question remains: how does the temple link lead one to conclude that the neuter singular subject of μεῖζόν is referring to Jesus, especially given the fact that some scholars suggest an impersonal rendering of μεῖζόν ἐστιν (i.e. "*something* is greater than the temple")?

Those who argue for μεῖζόν as "*something* is greater" encounter the inevitable problem of fitting the explanation into the context of Jesus's defence. If, for example, this "something" refers to the service performed by Jesus's disciples,[19] then David's story as the first example of defence becomes ir-

---

16. Donald Verseput, *The Rejection of the Humble Messianic King: A Study of the Composition of Matthew 11-12* (Frankfurt am Main: Verlag Peter Lang, 1986), 162.

17. Joachim Gnilka suggests that for Matthew's readers the temple, which was already destroyed, signifies the place where one meets God ('der Bezugspunkt zu Gott'), *Das Matthäusevangelium* (Freiberg: Herder, 1986), 1: 444. It should hold true even when the temple was not destroyed.

18. It is no wonder then, that in commenting on the Sabbath conflict stories, Chilton and Neusner say that "Jesus claim is ultimately concerned with where and what is the temple" and that "the holy place has shifted to the circle made up of the master and his disciples" in this Sabbath conflict story. Bruce Chilton and Jacob Neusner, *Judaism in the New Testament: Practices and Beliefs* (London: Routledge, 1995), 142; however, I cannot quite follow their accompanying statement that "what we do in the Temple is the opposite of what we do everywhere else," 142.

19. See, among others, Davies and Allison, *Matthew 8-18*, 313; Doug Moo, "Jesus and the Authority of the Mosaic Law," *JSNT* 20 (1984): 16-17, citing b.*Sabb*. 132b; Victor Hasler, *Amen: Redaktionsgeschichtchtliche Untersuchung zur Einführungsformel der Herrenworte "Wahrlich ich sage euch"* (Zürich: Gotthelf, 1969), 87; Birger Gerhardsson, "Sacrificial Service and Atonement in the Gospel of Matthew," in *Reconciliation and Hope: New Testament Essays on Atonement and Eschatology presented to L. L. Morris on his 60th Birthday*, ed. Robert J. Banks (Exeter: Paternoster Press, 1974), 28.

relevant because neither David nor his men performed any services in the temple. Moreover, by plucking and eating the grain, the disciples can hardly be considered to be performing priestly services.[20] Others argue that this "something" refers to the kingdom of God,[21] but the problem remains: why do we prefer a further context (vv. 41–42) whereas a more immediate context (vv. 4–5 and 8) within the same pericope can shed light on its interpretation? Still others interpret "something" as the community of disciples,[22] or mercy.[23] However, neither seems to be appropriate. On the one hand, in Jesus's *qal wahomer* argument (see a detailed discussion of *qal wahomer* offered in the following paragraph, point number 3), neither the community of disciples nor "mercy" can be easily inferred from the text as being greater than the temple; and on the other hand, either explanation would make the christological saying of verse 8 incongruous with the context.

Therefore, a christological interpretation of τοῦ ἱεροῦ μεῖζόν ἐστιν ὧδε (12:6b) appears to be the more plausible option: *one* (Jesus) is greater than the temple. This conclusion is based on a close investigation of the structure and context of verse 6: (1) grammatically a neuter adjective can be applied to persons when the emphasis is on the quality of the person and it can be found elsewhere in the New Testament.[24] Therefore, from the outset a personal interpretation of μεῖζόν is possible; (2) verses 6–8 form a unit of thought.

---

20. Verseput, *Rejection of the Humble King*, 165.

21. This is due to the context in 12:41–42 as Hicks suggests, "Sabbath Controversy," 86. Also, Eduard Schweizer, *The Good News According to Matthew*, trans. David Green (Atlanta: John Knox, 1975), 278; Beare, *Matthew*, 271.

22. Hill, *Matthew*, 211, citing Thomas Manson, *The Sayings of Jesus: As Recorded in the Gospels According to St. Matthew and St. Luke Arranged with Introduction and Commentary* (London: SCM Press, 1966), 187.

23. Luz, *Matthew 8–20*, 182; Paul Gaechter, *Das Matthäus Evangelium* (Innsbruck: Tyrolia, 1963), 391; Herman C. Waetjen, *The Origin and Destiny of Humanness: An Interpretation of the Gospel According to Matthew* (Corte Madera, CA: Omega, 1976), 143; Akira Ogawa, *L'histoire de Jésus chez Matthieu: La signification de l'histoire pour la théologie matthéenne* (Frankfurt am Main: Lang, 1979), 126.

24. For example, see Luke 16:15; Heb 7:7. When the neuter adjective is applied to persons, it "lays down an absolute and universal principle based on the distinction and separateness, each in its own sphere, of the natural and supernatural orders," Maximilian Zerwick and Joseph Smith, *Biblical Greek: Illustrated by Examples* (Roma: Editrice Pontificio Istituto Biblico, 1963), 47. Also see Gundry, *Matthew*, 223; Lybaek, *New and Old*, 161; cf. Verseput, *Rejection of the Humble King*, 164–165.

This is contrary to those who argue for a unity of verses 5–7.[25] The fact that verses 5–7 have been inserted due to Matthew's redactional activity does not automatically make them a complete thought. Rather, a skilled author would probably pay more attention to how this insertion can be harmonized with the rest of the existing narrative – and this is, according to our analysis, what happens with Matthew's insertion of verses 5–7. It is likely, as many have suggested, that verse 5 is intended as a halakhic argument complementing a haggadic example (v. 4).[26] Besides, the author inserts λέγω δὲ ὑμῖν and omits καὶ ἔλεγεν αὐτοῖς (cf. Mark 2:27 and Luke 6:5) to begin his conclusion of verses 6–8, with verse 7 functioning as an interpolation;[27] (3) the author compares Jesus to the temple through a *qal wahomer* argument. The parallel relationship can be seen in the following chart:

David + his companions	(hungry + eat)	in the House of God
Priests	(serving on the Sabbath)	in the Temple
--------	--------	--------
The disciples	(hungry + eat on the Sabbath)	before Jesus

By virtue of the *qal wahomer* argument, the disciples are placed parallel to David (and his companions) and the priests, while Jesus is parallel to the Temple (including the House of God). Consequently, even as David and the priests are both in the presence of a superior authority (the Temple), so also the disciples are under the superior authority of Jesus. While some commentators suggest a parallel between Jesus and David,[28] or a parallel between the

---

25. David Hill, "On the Use and Meaning of Hosea VI.6 in Matthew's Gospel," *NTS* 24 (1977): 107, 115; cf. Reinhart Hummel, *Die Auseinandersetzung zwischen Kirche und Judentum im Matthäusevangelium* (München: Kaiser Verlag, 1963), 43.

26. Lybaek, *New and Old*, 160, footnote 72; cf. Goulder, *Midrash*, 328.

27. Basser suggests that v. 7 functions just as a kind of footnote to the argument in Matthew's sources just like interpolations function as footnotes in the rabbinic literature, *Mind behind the Gospels*, 294. The connection between v. 8 and v. 6 can also be seen as v. 8 further qualifies v. 6; Lybaek, "Matthew's Use of Hosea 6:6," in *The Scriptures in the Gospels*, ed. Chris. M. Tuckett (Leuven: Leuven University Press, 1997), 493.

28. Hicks, "Sabbath Controversy," 81–82; Gundry, *Matthew*, 222–223; Saunders, "No One Dared," 213; also Garland, *Reading Matthew*, 138.

services of priests and those of Jesus and the disciples,[29] the context shows that such suggestions can be problematic. The text explicitly says it is the disciples who are ἐπείνασαν[30] and ἐσθίειν, and they are the ones similar to David who is also ἐπείνασεν and ἔψαγον, so the parallel is not between Jesus and David but between the disciples and David.[31] Furthermore, the disciples are comparable to the priests not in terms of offering some form of services but in terms of the occasion – both occur on a day intended to be set apart as holy (i.e. Sabbath), and both are in the presence of a higher authority. The logic is, therefore, *that just as the priests' action on the Sabbath is deemed blameless in the presence of God, so is that of the disciples' action in the presence of Jesus*.[32] In a claim comparing himself to the temple, Jesus acts in the place of God by presenting himself as one who assumes the authority of God, a speech-act similar to the pronouncement in the first conflict (9:6). As such, the words

---

29. This service of Jesus and the disciples according to Hill is the worship of God, also he cites Gerhardsson, that it is the "perfect spiritual sacrifice that Jesus and his disciples are offering." Hill, "Hosea VI.6 in Matthew," 115, footnote 3, citing Gerhardsson, "Sacrificial Service and Atonement," 28.

30. Matthew inserts "hungry" to describe the disciples. Many commentators hold that the author intends to increase the parallelism between Jesus's scenario and David with his men in 1 Sam 21:1-6, e.g. Garland, *Reading Matthew*, 137; Repschinski, *Controversy*, 95; France, *Matthew*, 457; Gundry, *Matthew*, 221; Verseput, *Rejection of the Humble King*, 158, 160; Hill, "Hosea VI.6 in Matthew," 114. Others, however, believe that the insertion shows that the disciples break the Sabbath law out of need; see Luz, *Matthew 8-20*, 180; or, at least not to violate the Jewish prohibition of fasting on Sabbath, see Keener, *Matthew*, 353.

31. Verseput, *Rejection of the Humble King*, 161; also Hill, "Hosea VI.6 in Matthew," 114, citing Ernst Lohmeyer, *Das Evangelium des Matthäus* (Göttingen: Vandenhoeck & Ruprecht, 1958), 184, and Alan McNeile, *The Gospel According to Matthew: The Greek Text with Introduction, Notes, and Indices* (London: Macmillan, 1952), 168. Cohn-Sherbok argues first for a parallel between Jesus and David ("Analysis," 34) but later contradicts himself by compare David and his men to Jesus's disciples in the same article ("Analysis," 35). Therefore, I disagree with scholars, such as Yang (*Jesus and the Sabbath*, 302) and Garland (*Reading Matthew*, 138) who interpret v. 6 along the lines of Jesus being greater than David as well as the temple. This is because (1) David is not comparable to the temple – they are not on the same level nor were they compared in the Scripture; (2) nowhere in the text does it say anything about "greater than David."

32. Also as Lybaek states, "the point of correspondence between the temple priests and the disciples is their being without guilt despite breaking the Sabbath law," "Matthew's Use of Hosea 6.6," 493.

of Jesus (12:6) match the world of the reader[33] and expresses to a high degree his own belief in the truth of such a claim.[34]

Then we come to the third evidence to substantiate the discovery that in 12:1–8 the author aims to reveal the identity of Jesus more specifically as one who has the divine status of God. It is the use of Hosea 6:6 interposed between verse 6 and verse 8. This quotation from Hosea is unique to Matthew and is used for the second time as a redaction to Mark's parallel (Mark 2:23–28). Again, the Hosea quotation is situated in a similar context to that in 9:9–13 where Jesus quotes the Scripture to rebuke the Pharisees. As in 9:13, the quotation is introduced by τί ἐστιν to call attention to its meaning.[35] Therefore, in 12:7, the Hosea quotation should be interpreted not only within its own context but also through the lenses of its earlier use in 9:9–13.

According to Luz's suggestion, the use of Hosea 6:6 in 12:7, just as in Matthew 9:13, should be understood dialectically. It is not that God chooses mercy over sacrifice but "wants mercy *more* than sacrifice."[36] In fact, the Hosea quotation has nothing to do with whether the disciples are right or wrong in their plucking the grain.[37] Instead, the quotation highlights God's initiative to relate to his people. The notion of "covenant-loyalty" in Hosea 6:6, defined by Hill as "devotion and fidelity to Jahweh," is also evident in the Matthean quotation.[38] In Hosea 6, through the prophet God reminds Israel that sacrifice is secondary to ἔλεος, which is the essence of the covenant both on the part of God and for his people.[39] The key difference between ἔλεος and θυσίαν probably lies in the direction of the relationship. The direction of ἔλεος

---

33. This is another *assertive* type of illocution to "commit the speaker to something's being the case, to the truth of the expressed proposition," Searle, *Expression and Meaning*, 12. This part of Jesus's response has a word-to-world direction of fit; see Searle's discussion on "direction of fit," 3.

34. Unless Jesus is hypothesizing that he is the Lord of the Sabbath, his claim can be seen as an insistence on his identity/authority that he truly believes to have; see distinction between "suggesting, insisting, and hypothesizing" as illocutionary acts in Pratt, *Toward Speech Act Theory*, 83.

35. Or to emphasize the need for understanding, Lybaek, *New and Old*, 163.

36. Luz, *Matthew 8–20*, 182.

37. Similarly, Hill argues that the Matthew is not really concerned with justifying disciples' action with examples or Hosea 6:6 but against his argument that it is only relevant to Matthew's church regarding the love commandment, "Hosea VI.6 in Matthew," 116.

38. Hill, "Hosea VI.6 in Matthew," 109–110.

39. Seow, C.L. "Hosea, Book of," *ABD* 3: 291–297.

is a two-way relationship based on God's ἔλεος toward man so that man can manifest his ἔλεος toward his neighbors. But the direction of θυσίαν is one-way and is often abused by man's attempt to invoke God to do certain things.[40] The dialectical message of mercy over sacrifice then should be: sacrifice cannot manipulate God to bring about salvation because salvation is only available through God's initiative to extend his love to the people, therefore, the best sacrifice to God is to demonstrate one's ἔλεος to both God and His people. If, as is likely, the Matthean Jesus has this "covenant-loyalty" in mind when he quotes Hosea 6:6 again in 12:7, then the quotation pertinent to the unit of verses 6–8 is used to emphasize God's own initiative to grant mercy to his people, and that mercy is personified by the presence of Jesus, the Messiah.

More importantly, both verse 6 and verse 8, as the context immediately preceding and following the Hosea 6:6 quotation in verse 7 are christological statements. This Son of Man, like God, has divine authority: he is greater than the temple and he rules over the Sabbath. Together with the citation of Hosea 6:6, the author portrays a Jesus who not only rebukes the Pharisees for their ignorance of the law but, more importantly, expresses the will of God as part of his own integral character.

The parallel between the two contexts where this Hosea passage is quoted in Matthew additionally confirms the above interpretation. In both contexts, the Hosea quotation is situated within a christological statement declaring the divine nature of Jesus's authority. In Matthew 9, the Hosea quotation is followed by a christological punch line that points out Jesus's redemptive mission divinely appointed by God (9:13; cf. 1:21–23). Here in Matthew 12 the Hosea quotation is used once again preceding a christological statement that Jesus as the Son of Man has the same divine authority as God over the Sabbath. Seen in this context, the line of thought between verse 6 and verse 7 is not broken as van Tilborg claims.[41] Rather, the logic is indeed coherent: the will of the Father is sandwiched between two pronouncements of Jesus's identity and authority.[42] It not only affirms the persuasive force of the christological point of the story but also convicts the Pharisees of obduracy. This is

---

40. Sacrifice is one-way because including Sabbath observance it refers to ritual behavior conducted only by man toward God.

41. "That the line of thought is broken between Mt 12.6 and Mt 12.7," *Jewish Leaders*, 116.

42. Luz, *Matthew 8–20*, 183.

because the implication of εἰ δὲ ἐγνώκειτε in 12:7 points out the status quo of the Pharisees, namely, they have completely missed the point. Although εἰ δὲ ἐγνώκειτε echoes the manner of teacher-pupil in the call to "go and learn" in 9:13,[43] it goes further to demonstrate both that the Pharisees are ignorant of the Scriptures and that their failure has made them unable to discern reality.

What is this reality then according to Matthew's narrative? It is, Jesus pronounces, that the disciples are τοὺς ἀναιτίους, just like David with his men and the priests in the temple. This pronouncement further confirms that Jesus does not take the role of a defence lawyer attempting to justify the disciples' behaviour through either precedent.[44] Instead, Jesus is acting as a judge because the disciples' innocence is due not to his eloquent defence but to his own pronouncement of their innocence.[45] The impact on the reader is that, even before Matthew finishes the narration of this conflict story, they would probably recognize the implication of the story. That is, Jesus is not arguing against the Pharisees on an equal footing but acting in the place of God who passes a judgment: the disciples are innocent, but Pharisees are obdurate and have lost their cause. The second quotation from Hosea 6:6 advances the plot by showing that Pharisees indeed did not learn what this Scripture means even after being told so (cf. 9:13).

The fourth evidence substantiating the discovery that in this Sabbath conflict the author aims to reveal Jesus's divine status is the concluding verse: the "Son of Man is the Lord of Sabbath" (12:8).[46] It appears that all the previous words in response to the Pharisees' accusations are accumulated for this final "punch line" of the story. Matthew's redactional changes bring to prominence the notion of Jesus's *authority* that he is the Lord of the Sabbath. Matthew inserts an explanatory γάρ to begin a causal clause (12:8),[47] and he further

---

43. Lybaek, *New and Old*, 163.

44. Similarly, Banks points out that the author has no intention to justify the action of the disciples based on an Old Testament precedent, *Jesus and Law*, 116.

45. Verseput argues that that is a pronouncement of the disciples' status; *Rejection of the Humble King*, 167. If this is the case, then according to speech act theory, Matthew presents Jesus with an institutional authority that only belongs to God, because "many declarations have appropriateness conditions requiring that the speaker be endowed with institutional authority to perform the act in question, as with marrying, excommunicating, or sentencing someone to prison," Pratt, *Speech Act of Literary Discourse*, 83.

46. See Yang's discussion of Son of Man, *Jesus and the Sabbath*, 191–192.

47. See Edwards' discussion of the use of γάρ in Matthew, "Narrative Implications of *Gar* in Matthew," 647–648.

changes the word order. Unlike in Mark 2:28, the two appositional concepts κύριος and ὁ υἱὸς τοῦ ἀνθρώπου now stand at both ends of the saying[48] and the authoritative concept κύριος appears first in the sentence,[49] which specifically denotes the divine nature of Jesus's authority.[50]

However, for Matthew's reader, who else but God himself can be both greater than the temple and Lord of the Sabbath?[51] To be sure, according to the Hebrew Bible, it is God who has the exclusive authority over the Sabbath[52] (e.g. Exod 16:23, 25; 20:10; 31:15; 35:2; Lev 23:3; Deut 5:14) and it is most definitely described by God as "*my* Sabbath" (e.g. Exod 31:13; Lev 19:3, 30; 26:2; Isa 56:4; 58:13). If this is an accepted notion in the mind of the reader, then the scandalous nature of Jesus's words is highlighted.[53] The sayings of verse 6 and verse 8 should astonish the people in the story world (perhaps including Matthew's first audiences),[54] because a *man* now has the authority of God himself. It is no surprise then that the Pharisees' determination to destroy Jesus in verse 14 should conclude these two Sabbath stories. Jesus's claim for himself is evident and it enrages them.[55]

3.1.1.3 Summary of 12:1–8 in Its Immediate Narrative and Rhetorical Context (11:2–12:50)

Matthew 12:1–8 immediately follows chapter 11:25–30 where the author presents Jesus as the Son who is given all things by the Father and is able to grant rest. Such a narrative arrangement obliges the reader not to read the pericope simply as an isolated legal dispute resembling rabbinic debate over

---

48. Gundry, *Matthew*, 224.

49. Hicks, "Sabbath Controversy," 88; also Davies and Allison, *Matthew 8–18*, 316.

50. See Kingsbury's detailed discussion on κύριος where he particularly mentions 12:8 as an example of divine authority; Kingsbury, *Structure*, 106.

51. In accordance with Hummel, Verseput proposes that "the terium comparationis between Jesus and the temple lies not in Jesus' greater glory but in the simple fact of his superior authority over the Sabbath," *Rejection of the Humble King*, 165, footnote 113, citing Hummel, *Die Auseinandersetzung*, 42; see also Gundry, *Matthew*, 223–224.

52. Yang, *Jesus and the Sabbath*, 51.

53. Therefore, I agree with France's interpretation that this is a good example to show that the "Son of Man" cannot refer to humanity in general as some scholars would propose; France, *Matthew*, 463.

54. As Luz correctly states, for any Jewish ears the authority as Lord of the Sabbath does not belong to Jesus; Luz, *Matthew 8–20*, 183.

55. Keener, *Matthew*, 356.

ritual or oral Sabbath law. The connecting point between 11:25-30 and 12:1-8 is the Sabbath but the focus should be on Jesus's authority, a prominent point in both pericopae.

In this story Matthew adds verse 5 to form a *halakhah* so that recourse to David's story of eating food reserved for priests (12:3-4) and priestly service not inciting guilt (12:5) both centre on the location of the two events – the temple, which is the link between the two examples and which signifies the presence of God. Moreover, the *one* (who is greater than the temple) refers to Jesus. Through this Sabbath conflict, the author attempts to demonstrate Jesus's divine status as manifested in his lordship over the Sabbath.[56] Relating this to the message of the context of 11:25-30, Jesus, like God, can give true rest to the people.

3.1.2 Matthew 12:9-14

3.1.2.1 Matthew 12:9: The Setting of the Story

Matthew's redaction of the story setting (12:9) reveals his intention to minimize distraction and focus instead the spotlight on the actual conflict itself.[57] Rather than retaining Mark's description of Pharisees' watching (Mark 3:2a) and Jesus's words to the sick man, the author only provides a spatial setting, τὴν συναγωγὴν αὐτῶν. The setting appears with such a haste that the reader immediately encounters the conflict scene between the Pharisees and Jesus, which is fashioned into a direct speech and takes most of the narrative time.

The brief setting is also one of the several reasons to connect the story of 12:9-14 closely to the first Sabbath conflict in verse 1-8. Furthermore, even though verses 9-14 qualifies as an independent unit,[58] the relationship between 12:1-8 and verses 9-14 is evidently inseparable because: (1) the issue of contention still revolves around the Sabbath law; (2) the main verb in

---

56. Or more accurately, as Chilton and Neusner claim, "The Sabbath celebrates creation and commemorates God's completion of the work of creation with the sanctification of the day of rest, the paramount celebration in the way of life set forth by the Torah. Jesus instructs the Christian community that he is the Lord of the Sabbath, meaning, acts of service take precedence over the requirements of sanctification of that day. But that is because Christ gives rest and restoration: he is the Sabbath." Chilton and Neusner, *Judaism*, 135.

57. See detailed discussion on Matthew's redactional activity in Repschinski, *Controversy*, 107-108.

58. It qualifies as an independent unit because it fits the criteria stated in the introductory chapter, page 21.

question, ἔξεστιν, is shared by both pericopae; (3) following 12:1–8 and especially τὴν συναγωγὴν αὐτῶν, the Pharisees are not named separately but implied (vv. 10b, 11a).[59] Their presence is finally confirmed by Φαρισαῖοι in 12:14; (4) the story is introduced by μεταβὰς ἐκεῖθεν, which is a typical Matthean marker of linking narratives.[60] The theological significance of the close connection between these two stories will be discussed in the next section.

3.1.2.2 Matthew 12:10-14: The Conflict Scene Proper

If, as is likely, Luz is correct in discerning a chiastic structure in the story form, then this conflict story resembles the first conflict (9:1–8, the healing of the paralytic). It centers on the hostile encounter between Jesus and Pharisees (12:10b–12:12) and is framed by a miracle (12:10a and 12:13).

The Chiastic Structure[61]

A   Καὶ μεταβὰς ἐκεῖθεν **ἦλθεν** εἰς τὴν συναγωγὴν αὐτῶν: (12:9)
  B   καὶ ἰδοὺ **ἄνθρωπος χεῖρα** ἔχων ξηράν. (12:10a)
    C   καὶ ἐπηρώτησαν αὐτὸν λέγοντες:
       Εἰ **ἔξεστι τοῖς σάββασιν** θεραπεύειν; (12:10b)
       ἵνα κατηγορήσωσιν αὐτοῦ. (12:10c)
       ὁ δὲ εἶπεν αὐτοῖς· Τίς ἔσται ἐξ ὑμῶν
       ἄνθρωπος ὃς ἕξει
      D   πρόβατον ἕν, καὶ ἐὰν ἐμπέσῃ τοῦτο τοῖς
         σάββασιν εἰς βόθυνον,
         οὐχὶ κρατήσει αὐτὸ καὶ ἐγερεῖ; (12:11)
         πόσῳ οὖν διαφέρει ἄνθρωπος προβάτου. (12:12a)
    C′ ὥστε **ἔξεστιν τοῖς σάββασιν** καλῶς ποιεῖν. (12:12b)

---

59. See also Repschinski, *Controversy*, 107, footnote 56. In my view, the immediate context in the narrative overwhelmingly points to Pharisees; therefore, I find it difficult to support the claim by Verseput that the opponents should include a wider range of people, namely, "the entirety of unbelieving Judaism" since Pharisees are not specifically mentioned; *Rejection of the Humble King*, 178.

60. See similar expression in Matt 11:1 and 15:29; Repschinski, *Controversy*, 107; Yang, *Jesus and the Sabbath*, 197.

61. Produced according to Luz's description, bold letters are the similar "catchwords," *Matthew 8–20*, 186; for discussion of criteria of recognizing a chiasmus, see Craig Blomberg, "Structure of 2 Corinthians 1–7," 5–7.

B'   τότε λέγει τῷ **ἀνθρώπῳ**· Ἔκτεινόν σου τὴν **χεῖρα**.
     καὶ ἐξέτεινεν,
     καὶ ἀπεκατεστάθη ὑγιὴς ὡς ἡ ἄλλη.   (12:13)
A'   **ἐξελθόντες** δὲ οἱ Φαρισαῖοι συμβούλιον ἔλαβον κατ'
     αὐτοῦ ὅπως
     αὐτὸν ἀπολέσωσιν.   (12:14)

This conflict is the first occasion where the Pharisees take the initiative to challenge Jesus directly. Its importance is evident because Matthew redacts the conflict scene into a dialogue[62] rather than retaining Jesus's monologue as in his sources (Mark 3:4; cf. Q/Luke 6:9).

The Question

After telling the reader about the Pharisees' question regarding the Sabbath observance, Matthew pauses, just like Mark and Luke, by retaining an authorial commentary pointing out their inner thoughts, ἵνα κατηγορήσωσιν αὐτοῦ. It discloses to the reader two things, one explicit and the other implicit.

First, the authorial commentary explicitly demonstrates a characteristic of the Pharisees. Namely, they are not truthful – they ask Jesus a question simply *in order to* accuse him (v. 10c, ἵνα). So far in Matthew, the narrator reveals the negative trait of the Pharisees' character only twice, both through the method of "showing" (3:7 and 9:34).[63] Here in 12:10, however, is the first time the narrator tells the audience in a candid statement about the Pharisees' character by commenting on their evil motive. In a narrative, this method of telling,[64] according to Alter, informs the reader that by opposing Jesus, the character trait of the Pharisees is wicked.[65]

---

62. This assertion is based on Alter's analysis of dialogues in the Hebrew Bible; "As a rule, when a narrative event in the Bible seems important, the writer will render it mainly through dialogue, so the transitions from narration to dialogue provide in themselves some implicit measure of what is deemed essential, what is conceived to be ancillary or secondary to the main action," *Art of Biblical Narrative*, 182; this principle, I believe, can also be applied to Matthew's writing.

63. Both "showing" are through the direct speech of characters, John the Baptist (who calls them a "brood of vipers" in 3:7) and the Pharisees themselves (by accusing the reliable character Jesus of "casting out demons by the prince of demon" in 9:34). For distinction between "showing" and "telling" method in characterization, see Booth, *Rhetoric of Fiction*, 3–9.

64. This is the first time in the Matthean story where the author *tells* the reader the negative trait of the Pharisees.

65. Alter, *Art of Biblical Narrative*, 117.

Second, the authorial commentary implicitly shows that the Pharisees anticipate from Jesus a wrong answer (i.e. "yes") according to their tradition. The reason for anticipating such an answer is because in the previous stories Jesus is shown to be merciful (9:12; 12:7: "I desire mercy, not sacrifice").[66]

The Answer

Because Matthew redacts his source by inserting ἔξεστιν in the Pharisees' question (12:10b; cf. Mark 3:2b), the question is turned into a halakhic challenge[67] and the legal focus of the Sabbath dispute becomes more explicit.[68] Yet, Jesus does not respond to the question directly. Instead, there is a unique Matthean insertion of an example in Jesus's rhetorical question by building an argument from rescuing a fallen sheep (the lesser) to healing a sick man (the greater) (12:11–12). Many commentators agree that this debate form is an argument *a fortiori* or fits the Jewish *qal wahomer*.[69] However, the nature of Jesus's answer (i.e. whether it is Jewish halakhic remains highly disputed),

---

66. From the witness of three gospels we can infer that Pharisaic tradition at Jesus's time considers that a non-life-threatening healing is not permitted on Sabbath; Yang, *Jesus and the Sabbath*, 200; see also Banks, *Jesus and Law*, 124. This attitude seems to be in accordance with some rabbinic practices from later periods. There was no definitive stipulation on the matter of Sabbath healing among different groups or periods of Judaism; see Borg, *Conflict, Holiness and Politics*, 161; Verseput, *Rejection of the Humble King*, 181. Based on rabbinic writings, however, one can assume the prohibition of healing, with the exception of when life is in immediate danger; see Yang, *Jesus and the Sabbath*, 199. For evidence of these rabbinic practices which allow the sick or injured to be treated on the Sabbath day only if life were in danger, see, for example, I. Abrahams, *Studies in Pharisaism and the Gospels*, vol. 1 (Cambridge: Cambridge University Press, 1917), 129–135.

67. Hicks, "Sabbath Controversy," 89.

68. Banks, *Jesus and the Law*, 123–124. This is in line with the first evangelist's preference as ἔξεστιν is not an uncommon word for gospel writers but has the most occurrences in the first gospel. Among all twenty-two occurrences of ἔξεστιν in all four gospels, nine are in Matthew (12:2, 4, 10, 12; 14:4; 19:3; 20:15; 22:17; 27:6). Others include e.g. Mark 2:24, 26; 3:4; 6:18; 10:2; 12:14; Luke 6:2, 4, 9; 14:3; 20:22; John 5:10; 18:31.

69. For *qal wahomer* argument, among others, see Verseput, *Rejection of the Humble King*, 181; Phillip Sigal, *The Halakhah of Jesus of Nazareth According to the Gospel of Matthew* (Atlanta: SBL, 2007), 166; also David Daube, *The New Testament and Rabbinic Judaism* (London: Athlone Press, 1956), 67–71; cf. Davies and Allison, *Matthew 8–18*, 313. Basser believes it belongs to the standard intra-Jewish debate form even though he argues for a gentile identity of the narrator, *Mind behind the Gospels*, 280, 288, 295; cf. xiii; Harrington, *Matthew*, 173; for *a fortiori* argument, see Yang, *Jesus and the Sabbath*, 203–204; Davies and Allison, *Matthew 8–18*, 319; France, *Matthew*, 465.

Conflict Stories in Matthew 12

and the understanding of the form and nature of Jesus's argument has caused much confusion among interpreters.[70]

But what is so significant about understanding the form and nature of Jesus's argument? How is it understood in the eyes of the implied reader? The following analysis, detailed by three points, shows that Jesus's answer in 12:11–12 uses Jewish *qal wahomer* debate form. However, it cannot be deemed as halakhic.

First, the fact that Jesus's answer in 12:11–12 fits the form of *qal wahomer* is relatively straightforward. As a typical debate form in Judaism, *qal wahomer* needs to include two items relating to each other as of major and minor importance.[71] Jesus clearly argues his case using a lesser valued sheep to more valued human being (v. 12b: . . . ὥστε ἔξεστιν τοῖς σάββασιν καλῶς ποιεῖν; cf. 6:26; 10:31). Another premise for *qal wahomer* is that "a certain restrictive or permissive law is connected" with respect to one of the two items.[72] This premise, although less obvious from external evidences, can still be applied to Jesus's argument concerning a hypothetical example of pulling a sheep out of a pit on the Sabbath (12:11). The logic of *qal wahomer* can be shown as the following:

---

70. Some maintain that in 12:11–12 Jesus uses the *qal wahomer* argument in order to establish a *halakah* (Hicks, "Sabbath Controversy," 89; also Sigal, *Halakhah in Matthew*, 166–168). Yet others reject it being neither *qal wahomer* nor halakhic. For example, Yang not only rejects it being *qal wahomer*, he also states that, "it is rather anti-halakhic in pointing out the inconsistency and inhumanity of their [the Pharisees'] halakhic system" (*Jesus and the Sabbath*, 204 footnote 278). Although Banks does not use either term, *qal wahomer* nor halakhic, he upholds Jesus's argument as unsuitable from a Jewish scribal point of view (*Jesus and the Law*, 127). Moreover, Cohn-Sherbok argues that because Jesus misuses rabbinic reasoning, he is not a skilled debater within mainstream Judaism. This in turn explains why Jesus often provokes the indignation and hostility of Pharisees and Sadducees (Cohn-Sherbok, "Analysis," 40). Still others, such as Davies and Allison, state that Matthew clearly employs *qal wahomer* (as well as *a fortiori*) in 12:5–7, thus "Matthew's Jesus stands securely within the Jewish legal framework" (*Matthew 8–18*, 313). However, they view the examples in 12:11–12 differently in that "the First Gospel's legal debates remain relatively unsophisticated," even though 12:11–12 is still considered an argument *a fortiori* therefore is likely a *qal wahomer* (*Matthew 8–18*, 319).

71. David Instone-Brewer, *Techniques and Assumptions in Jewish Exegesis before 70 CE* (Tübingen: Mohr Siebeck, 1992), 17. Qal wahomer also refers to "an inference from the less to the more important, and vice versa, from the more to the less important," Cohn-Sherbok, "Analysis," 37.

72. Cohn-Sherbok, "Analysis," 37.

Rescue a fallen sheep	on the Sabbath	(permissible)
---------------------		--------------------
Man > sheep		
Heal the sick man	on the Sabbath	(permissible)

The premise for this *qal wahomer* (i.e. it is permissible for Jesus's audiences to rescue fallen animals on Sabbath), is entailed by the logic of Jesus's rhetoric itself. At the very outset, it needs to be noted that the Hebrew Bible has no clear teaching on rescuing animals out of a pit on the Sabbath.[73] The only extant evidence contemporary to Jesus's time from Qumran prohibits lifting an animal out of the pit or water on Sabbath.[74] Rabbinic tradition in the Talmud, on the other hand, allows rescuing an animal on the Sabbath if it is in distress.[75] This ambiguity causes some scholars to propose that either the Matthean Jesus appeals to the common practice of the wider audiences instead of Pharisaic tradition,[76] or he complies with a lax halakhic observance evident in Galilee.[77]

While it is understandable to speculate from external evidence what Jewish tradition around Jesus's time was like in regard to rescuing animals from a pit, such traditions are diverse if not even contradictory. Our current text – the internal evidence – seems to offer an alternative and a more relevant insight. Because the way the question is framed rhetorically, τίς ἔσται ἐξ ὑμῶν[78]

---

73. Although there are clear teachings in the Hebrew Bible on lifting a fallen animal or caring for one's animal, e.g. Deut 22:4; Prov 12:10.

74. CD 11:13–14; 4Q251 2:5–6; see more discussions in Yang, *Jesus and the Sabbath*, 202–203.

75. Cf. *b. Sab.* 128b; *t. Sab.* 15.1; also see discussion in Basser, *Mind behind the Gospels*, 295; also Yang, *Jesus and the Sabbath*, 202–203.

76. Manson, *Sayings of Jesus*, 189; Hare, *Matthew*, 133; also Verseput argues that Jesus appeals to the practice of the individual by asking "which one of you . . .," *Rejection of the Humble King*, 180–181.

77. Verseput, *Rejection of the Humble King*, 181; Lohse, "Worte," 88; Geza Vermes, *Jesus the Jew: A Historian's Reading of the Gospels* (New York: Macmillan, 1973), 54–57.

78. The phrase τίς ἔσται ἐξ ὑμῶν is typical of Jesus's saying (cf. 7:9–11; Luke 14:5; 17:7; 15:4), though uncommon within rabbinic tradition; Verseput, *Rejection of the Humble King*, 180; cf. Heinrich Greeven, "Wer unter euch . . . ?" *Wort und Dienst* 3 (1952): 100; Jeremias, *Parables of Jesus*, 103; Eduard Lohse, "Jesu Wort über den Sabbat," in *Judentum, Urchristentum, Kirche; Festschrift für Joachim Jeremias*, ed. Walther Eltester (Berlin: Töpelmann, 1960), 79–89,

ἄνθρωπος ὃς ἕξει πρόβατον ἕν⁷⁹ καὶ ἐὰν ἐμπέσῃ τοῦτο τοῖς σάββασιν εἰς βόθυνον, οὐχὶ κρατήσει αὐτὸ καὶ ἐγερεῖ, one must presume that it is a common practice among those Pharisees (and probably among Matthew's first readers) that they would rescue a fallen sheep on the Sabbath.⁸⁰ If the answer is negative, then Jesus's argument of using "how much more . . ." does not stand on any logical ground and simply falls flat before his audience in the story world. Additionally, seen from the overall context of the Matthean narrative, a portrayal of a paradoxical teacher does not correspond to Matthew's ongoing efforts to portray this characteristic of Jesus who holds a supreme authority in his itinerant ministry (cf. 7:29). Therefore, the logic of the rhetoric itself requires such a premise for the *qal wahomer* that it is permissible for Jesus's audiences to rescue fallen animals on Sabbath.⁸¹

Second, even though Jesus's argument in 12:11-12 indeed fits the debate form of a *qal wahomer* argument,⁸² as argued above, it cannot be considered as halakhic.⁸³ The key reasons lie in Jesus's change of wording in 12:12b. The major reason is the parallel structure of Jesus's answer to the question which makes the replacement of θεραπεῦσαι with καλῶς ποιεῖν noteworthy. The Jewish *halakhah* is generally understood as rulings, legal statements or discussions that derived primarily from the written Torah but also include

---

especially 87. Verseput also purports that this phrase likely evokes the audience's reflection so that they would naturally side with Jesus, 180.

79. Several scholars argue for the importance of the indefinite article e≠n here, interpreting the man as a poor farmer who owns only *one* sheep, possibly echoing Nathan's story in 2 Sam 12:1-4. Verseput, *Rejection of the Humble King*, 180-181; Luz, *Matthew 8-20*, 187-188; Basser, *Mind behind the Gospels*, 5. If this is the case, then the sense of urgency in rescuing the animal and the preciousness of the sheep in the story only increase in Jesus's saying. Others consider ἕν as simply a Semitic expression; Hagner, *Matthew 1-13*, 333; Beare, *Matthew*, 272.

80. This argument is contrary to Sigal's belief that these Pharisees are pietistic Jews who hold strict views of Sabbath observance represented in Jubilees and Qumran documents; *Halakhah in Matthew*, 185. However, his argument is based on a logic jump, see discussion, for example, on 183. Cf. Yang, *Jesus and the Sabbath*, 264.

81. Luke 14:5, although referring to a son or an ox, should also be considered as an evidence of this premise among the contemporaries of Jesus.

82. Pace Yang, who argues against *qal wahomer*; Yang, *Jesus and the Sabbath*, 204, footnote 278. I think Yang misunderstood Cohn-Sherbok's argument because the invalidity derives from the lack of comparability between the priests and Jesus's disciples (in the case of first Sabbath conflict) and not from lacking Torah reference. In fact, Cohn-Sherbok agrees that the argument corresponds *formally* to a *qal wahomer*, see "Analysis," 38-39.

83. Although Jesus uses the usual halakhic example found in rabbinic texts, such as sheep or ox (Keener, *Matthew*, 358, note 58), it does not naturally render the argument itself also a *halakhah*.

oral Torah that deals with every aspect of Jewish life.[84] If it were a *halakhah*, then the expected answer from Jesus should have been that "it is lawful to *heal* on the Sabbath," in order to correctly respond to his opponents' halakhic question.[85] Yet this is not the case. Instead, Jesus concludes with ὥστε ἔξεστιν τοῖς σάββασιν καλῶς ποιεῖν. The conjunction ὥστε shows that this conclusion is drawn from the preceding *qal wahomer* argument. But the expected word "heal" is replaced by καλῶς ποιεῖν, a concept that not only includes the former[86] but also expands to all activities that are good in God's eyes. It is precisely this replacement that disqualifies Jesus's argument from being halakhic. This is because the "legality" by which the conclusion is reached (12:12b: ὥστε ἔξεστιν τοῖς σάββασιν καλῶς ποιεῖν) is no longer based on "an actual precept promulgated in Scripture."[87] Rather, as the narrative shows, it is precisely based on Jesus's own authority as the Lord of Sabbath which ultimately defines ἔξεστιν. On a minor note, lack of any rabbinic parallels further indicates the peculiarity of such an argument.[88]

Having determined the form and nature of Jesus's argument in 12:11–12, the key question naturally follows: why did the author insert such a line in his own narrative account? To be sure, as shown above, the premise of the *qal wahomer* – the audiences (including the Pharisees) in the story world are permitted to rescue fallen animals on Sabbath – can only lead to "healing the sick" but not necessarily "to do good on Sabbath." If this is the case, then upon what basis does the validity of this saying ὥστε ἔξεστιν τοῖς σάββασιν καλῶς ποιεῖν stand? And what does the author intend to achieve?

There are two possible explanations. The first one is that the character Jesus acts preposterously, making up statements that cannot match any reality. But this solution contradicts Matthew's characterization of Jesus elsewhere in the narrative. The context of the narrative leads to the other plausible answer. That is, the author intends to show that the validity of the saying rests upon

---

84. Gary Porton, "Halakhah," *ABD* 3:26–27. See detailed discussions specifically on the Sabbath *halakhah* in Sigal, *Halakhah in Matthew*, 172–185.

85. Hicks, "Sabbath Controversy," 89; also see my previous discussion under the section *the Question*, pages 89–90.

86. This fact qualifies Jesus's argument as *qal wahomer* even according to Cohn-Sherbok's criteria for the conclusion of *qal wahomer*, "Analysis," 37.

87. Daube, *New Testament and Rabbinic Judaism*, 68.

88. Banks, *Jesus and Law*, 124.

Jesus's own authority, which is explicitly stated in verse 8 (the Son of Man is the Lord of the Sabbath). As such, Matthew implies that Jesus's words in verse 12b inherently have the similar status as the Torah.[89] Three pieces of contextual evidence are worthy of consideration.

First, as argued in the previous section (under the heading *the Setting*), though 12:1–8 and verses 9–14 belong to two independent pericope in terms of their form as conflict stories, the author nonetheless intends to tie the two stories closely together.[90] As a result, the explanatory force of γάρ (12:8) should continue to the saying of 12:12b. That is to say, the reader is compelled to read the Sabbath healing story with the saying "for the Son of Man is the Lord of Sabbath" (12:8) still resounding in his ears. Seen from the perspective of speech-act theory, the climactic saying (12:8) is to be understood with assertive illocutionary force.[91] This means, the saying ὥστε ἔξεστιν τοῖς σάββασιν καλῶς ποιεῖν needs to be interpreted in light of verse 8 as a declaration from someone who just asserted such an authority to say so.[92]

Second, the author portrays Jesus arguing from the form of *qal wahomer* but the argument is too peculiar to be halakhic, so the reader is left to ponder the true authority of Jesus's words. Given the fact that the narrative context has shown a Jesus who claims to be the Lord of Sabbath and the author quotes Hosea 6:6 again to emphasize God's desire for mercy (12:7; cf. 9:9),[93] the reader is compelled to link the conclusion of the *qal wahomer*, "it is lawful to do good on the Sabbath," with Jesus's own authority.

Last, but not least, in Matthew's narrative, Jesus's last answer reflects the scriptural background of the story. The Sabbath tradition as well as Hosea

---

89. It is also in accordance with Hagner who interprets that Jesus himself becomes the law-giver, not law interpreter of the will of God, Hagner, *Matthew 1–13*, 331. Also Verseput argues that "Jesus' answer does indeed constitute a verdict upon what is permissible on the Sabbath," *Rejection of the Humble King*, 178.

90. Cf. Yang, *Jesus and the Sabbath*, 302.

91. The assertive illocutionary force, as argued in detail in 3.1.2.1, refers to the speaker Jesus represents, the current state of affairs being the reality.

92. Following Searle's summary of general categories of illocutionary acts, here Jesus tells the audience what things are (assertives: v. 8) and brings about changes in the world through his utterances (declarations: v. 12b), *Expression and Meaning*, viii.

93. Davies and Allison, *Matthew 8–18*, 321. Barth also states that "the saying 'I desire mercy and not sacrifice' thus means here in the first place that God himself is the merciful one, the gracious one, and that the Sabbath commandment should therefore be looked upon from the point of view of his kindness"; "Matthew's Understanding," 83.

6:6 quotation features the celebration of creation and commemoration of covenantal relationship with God.[94] Keeping the Sabbath ultimately represents how man as creation is related to God the creator (i.e. to imitate God who is good,[95] to be holy[96]). So keeping the Sabbath is not about when one can or cannot do something. The author's insertion of Jesus's answer, ὥστε ἔξεστιν τοῖς σάββασιν καλῶς ποιεῖν, indeed reflects such an essence of the Scripture, and therefore, in effect corresponds to Jesus's earlier claim to be the Lord of Sabbath and to be merciful (12:7; cf. 9:9) and is not simply an ethical command for service.[97]

Contrasting Outcomes: Jesus Restoring, Pharisees Destroying
Only after answering his opponents does Jesus turn to the sick man and heal him (v. 13). As mentioned in *the Setting*, this conflict is similar to the first conflict story (9:1–8) not only in terms of their structure, but also in terms of the means by which Jesus heals. He simply speaks and the withered hand is restored.[98] Notice the phrase ὑγιὴς ὡς ἡ ἄλλη as Matthew's own insertion indicates "the success and completeness of the cure."[99] Contrary to some scholars who argue that the healing result validates Jesus's pronouncement,[100] here it is proposed instead that the healing result is actually the consequence of both performative utterances "for the Son of Man is the Lord of the Sabbath" (assertive) and "so it is lawful to do good on Sabbath" (declarative).[101] In other words, this conflict displays the development of the plot from the establishment of the authority of Jesus (evident in the previous conflicts: 9:1–8, 9–13, 14–17) to the ramifications of such an authority. The proposal concurs

---

94. See Yang's summary on Sabbath both in the Hebrew Bible as well as in Judaism to the first century CE, *Jesus and the Sabbath*, 299–300; also see detailed discussions in Chilton and Neusner, *Judaism*, 136–138.
95. Chilton and Neusner, 136.
96. Yang, *Jesus and the Sabbath*, 51, 299.
97. Pace J. W. Leitch, "Lord also of the Sabbath," *SJT* 19 (1966): 430.
98. This is different from the healing in Matt 8:3, 15; 9:25.
99. Hagner, *Matthew 1–14*, 334.
100. Repschinski, *Controversy*, 107, footnote 53.
101. In the speech-act terminology it is the perlocutionary act of the two sayings. Perlocutionary act, by definition, is "what we bring about or achieve *by* saying something, such as convincing, persuading, deterring," Austin, *How to Do Things*, 109. Applied in this conflict story, then, the perlocutionary act refers to the healing achieved as the Lord of Sabbath declares that to do good is permissible on the Sabbath.

with Verseput's comment, "instead of proving himself to be the Lord of the Sabbath, Jesus behaves as one whose credentials are already confirmed, speaking with an authority in accordance with his position."[102]

The story does not simply end with the restoration of the man's hand. Another opposite outcome follows. The Pharisees made a decision to αὐτὸν ἀπολέσωσιν, after having failed to find a reason to accuse Jesus. The author places two words of opposite meaning and imagery, ἀπεκατεστάθη and ἀπολέσωσιν, in close proximity and in effect creates an irony in the narrative (vv. 13, 14). The person who is accused of breaking the Sabbath in fact restores (and heals), but the so-called the "guardians of the Sabbath" collude in destruction. Because of the close link with the previous story, the murder plot in verse 14 may also reflect the Pharisees' reaction to the early christological announcement (v. 8).[103] In other words, it is likely that they indeed understand the supreme authority of Jesus as the real issue of contention.[104] The murder plot (12:14), therefore, is another authorial commentary that confirms the author's characterisation of "evil" Pharisees (v. 10b).

3.1.2.3 Summary of 12:9–14 in Its Immediate Narrative and Rhetorical Context (11:2–12:50)

The story of 12:9–14 should be interpreted in light of the first Sabbath conflict in 12:1–8. The above analysis has shown that the story of the Sabbath healing is not an example of Jesus's halakhic teaching on the Sabbath observance. Even though the logic of Jesus's argument suits the form of a *qal wahomer*, its validity rests on Jesus's own authority, which is declared in the previous conflict (12:6, 8). Instead, this conflict should be seen as an illustration of Jesus's lordship over the Sabbath and Matthew presents Jesus again as one who is divine and acts in the place of God. In other words, this conflict story complements the first Sabbath story of 12:1–8 in that it demonstrates the *consequence* of Jesus being the Lord of the Sabbath.

---

102. Verseput, *Rejection of the Humble King*, 176.

103. Yang, *Jesus and the Sabbath*, 212.

104. Just as Hagner correctly remarks, "the tragedy is not the failure to accept Jesus' argument but the failure to be receptive to Jesus as the one who brings the kingdom," *Matthew 1–13*, 334.

More specifically, the saying ὥστε ἔξεστιν τοῖς σάββασιν καλῶς ποιεῖν is anchored in the christological pronouncement[105] in 12:8 and it is based only on Jesus's own messianic authority[106] thus cannot be deemed as simply a *halakhah*.[107] The authority expressed in Jesus's words, ἔξεστιν τοῖς σάββασιν καλῶς ποιεῖν, which declares an all-encompassing command, is exemplified by his merciful act – a healing miracle. God's will of desiring mercy manifested in Jesus's authority distinguishes itself from that of the Pharisees. Therefore, their plot to destroy is provoked by recognizing the supreme authority evident in the person of Jesus that threatens their own authority.[108]

3.1.3 Matthew 12:22–37

3.1.3.1 Matthew 12:22–23: The Setting of the Story

The setting of the conflict story beginning with τότε is a healing miracle (12:22–23), which in several ways resembles the earlier passage in Matthew 9:27–34. First, similar to his redaction in 9:27–34,[109] Matthew again inserts into the story the characteristic of blindness (and its reversal as the result of healing).[110] Second, as in the earlier narrative, the crowd's reaction to the healing result becomes a trigger for the conflict,[111] causing the Pharisees to attribute Jesus's healing power to Beelzebub, the prince of demons.

---

105. It is christological because, as Thiselton rightly states, "the self-involving aspects of Jesus' pronouncement imply Christological presuppositions," *New Horizon*, 285.

106. W. Rordorf, *Sunday: The History of the Day of Rest and Worship in the Earliest Centuries of the Christian Church*, trans. A. A. K. Graham (London: SCM Press, 1968), 69–71.

107. "To do good in Sabbath" is even against possible ongoing halakhic traditions of Jesus's day because of its broad scope while the halakhic traditions are striving to be meticulously specific.

108. Thus, unlike the reason given by Cohn-Sherbok that it is Jesus's lacking the rhetoric skill of Pharisees which provoked their opposition, "Analysis," 40.

109. The similarity lies in the key fact that the characteristics of blindness/seeing is inserted in both passages, even though Matthew's redaction in 9:27–34 is adding the healing of two blind men in a separate story.

110. Although Hagner argues that 12:22–32 is influenced by the story in 9:32–34 because Matthew has a special interest in τυφλός, (*Matthew 1–13*, 340), or as others believe Matthew simply prefers doublets (Davies and Allison, *Matthew: 8–18*, 334), it is still remarkable that Matthew's addition counters the Matthean tendency of abbreviating the narrative of his sources. Examining the context surrounding the motif pair in 12:22–24, it is likely that the author adds τυφλός intentionally in order to evoke the Isaianic motif of "hearing and seeing" – the reversal of the blind and mute (cf. Isa 29:18; 35:5–6), and more importantly, to correspond to the reversal of the blind in Isa 42:6–7, 16.

111. Repschinski, *Controversy*, 133. Also, as Novakovic argues, because of the presence of the aorist participle ἀκούσαντες, it is the crowd's reaction that becomes the source of the conflict

Nonetheless there are two interesting different nuances between the two episodes. First, the author uses the verb ἐξίσταντο for the crowd's reaction (12:23), which expresses a much stronger feeling than ἐθαύμασαν in 9:33.[112] Second, the crowd becomes aware of Jesus's messianic identity by asking a more poignant question (μήτι οὗτός ἐστιν ὁ υἱὸς Δαυίδ) than a simple comment of surprise in 9:33 (οὐδέποτε ἐφάνη οὕτως ἐν τῷ Ἰσραήλ).[113] Although in a question form, Jesus is named by the crowds specifically as the Son of David.[114]

Whether or not 12:22–24 and 9:27–34 refer to the same incident is not germane,[115] because for the purpose of literary critical study, the key issue is, for what purpose does the author tell similar stories again? Its significance for the author will be discussed in section 3.1.3.3 in relation to the wider context of this conflict story. However, the passage 9:27–34 will be referred to so long as it is relevant for our analysis.

---

and not the miracle itself. Lidija Novakovic, *Messiah, the Healer of the Sick: A Study of Jesus as the Son of David in the Gospel of Matthew* (Tübingen: Mohr Siebeck, 2003), 82.

112. The Greek word ἐξίστημι refers to "the feeling of astonishment mingled with fear..." (*BDAG*, 350), whereas θαυμάζω refers to a more general sense of "wonder, marvel and be astonished" (*BDAG*, 444). Also see Joseph A. Comber, "Jesus and the Jews in Matthew 11 and 12" (PhD diss., University of Chicago, 1975), 73. Verseput similarly suggests that the verb ἐξίστηνι, together with πάντες, "represent an intensification over the previous reactions of the crowds," *Rejection of the Humble King*, 214.

113. Saunders, "No One Dared," 242.

114. The title "Son of David" occurs more frequently in Matthew's gospel than in the rest of the whole New Testament. Seven of his nine uses are peculiar to Matthew. Mark and Luke both share the double use of the title in the story of Bartimaeus, but the discussion is mainly about whether the Messiah is the Son of David, otherwise they make no use of the title. In Matthew's gospel, here is the first time the title Son of David is spoken of by the crowds, whereas Mark (10:47) and Luke (18:38) keep this title for much later in their narratives. Although there is a plethora of meanings attached to the title, "the popular use of Son of David comes mainly in Matthew, for his purpose is to expound in a meaningful way to a Jewish audience how Jesus was identified with the coming Messiah." Donald Guthrie, *New Testament Theology* (Downers Grove: InterVarsity Press, 1981), 354. See discussion on the Son of David as a messianic title in Jewish tradition in Josephy Fitzmyer, *Essays on the Semitic Background of the New Testament* (London: Chapman, 1971), 113–126.

115. Those who believe they refer to the same healing include, for example, Beare, *Matthew*, 276; Luz, *Matthew 8–20*, 199; Gundry, *Matthew*, 230; Saunders, "No One Dared," 239.

3.1.3.2 Matthew 12:24–37: The Conflict Scene Proper

Pharisees' Accusation: 12:24

Within the conflict scene, the Pharisees' reaction presents another similarity to 9:27–34.[116] Both stories narrate their grudge to attribute Jesus's healing power to the prince of demons. Matthew arranges it in such a fashion that οὗτός appears in the beginning of both 12:23b and 12:24b, highlighting the contrasting effect between the reactions of the Pharisees and of the crowd. The accusation appears to challenge Jesus's source of power, but essentially it is an attack on Jesus's own identity. The words δαιμόνια and ἐκβάλλω will be echoed several times in Jesus's condemnation of the Pharisees (12:26, 27, 28, 29, 43, 45).[117]

Jesus's Judgment: 12:25–37

The verses below are divided for the purpose of references.

12:25	εἰδὼς δὲ τὰς ἐνθυμήσεις αὐτῶν εἶπεν αὐτοῖς·		a
	Πᾶσα βασιλεία μερισθεῖσα καθ' ἑαυτῆς ἐρημοῦται, καὶ		b
	πᾶσα πόλις ἢ οἰκία μερισθεῖσα καθ' ἑαυτῆς οὐ σταθήσεται.		c
12:26	καὶ εἰ ὁ Σατανᾶς τὸν Σατανᾶν ἐκβάλλει,		a
	ἐφ' ἑαυτὸν ἐμερίσθη·		b
	πῶς οὖν σταθήσεται ἡ βασιλεία αὐτοῦ;		c
12:27	καὶ εἰ ἐγὼ ἐν Βεελζεβοὺλ ἐκβάλλω τὰ δαιμόνια,		a
	οἱ υἱοὶ ὑμῶν ἐν τίνι ἐκβάλλουσιν;		b
	διὰ τοῦτο αὐτοὶ κριταὶ ἔσονται ὑμῶν.		c
12:28	εἰ δὲ ἐν πνεύματι θεοῦ ἐγὼ ἐκβάλλω τὰ δαιμόνια,		a
	ἄρα ἔφθασεν ἐφ' ὑμᾶς ἡ βασιλεία τοῦ θεοῦ.		b
12:29	ἢ πῶς δύναταί τις εἰσελθεῖν εἰς τὴν οἰκίαν τοῦ ἰσχυροῦ		a
	καὶ τὰ σκεύη αὐτοῦ ἁρπάσαι,		b
	ἐὰν μὴ πρῶτον δήσῃ τὸν ἰσχυρόν;		c
	καὶ τότε τὴν οἰκίαν αὐτοῦ διαρπάσει.		d

---

116. Here Matthew has an interesting redaction, replacing "some of them" (in Q 11:15) with "the Pharisees"; such a redaction "... shapes the controversy story into an attack specifically on them," Repschinski, *Controversy*, 133.

117. Comber, "Jesus and the Jews," 73–74.

12:30	ὁ μὴ ὢν μετ' ἐμοῦ κατ' ἐμοῦ ἐστιν,	a
	καὶ ὁ μὴ συνάγων μετ' ἐμοῦ σκορπίζει.	b
12:31	διὰ τοῦτο λέγω ὑμῖν,	a
	πᾶσα ἁμαρτία καὶ βλασφημία ἀφεθήσεται τοῖς ἀνθρώποις,	b
	ἡ δὲ τοῦ πνεύματος βλασφημία οὐκ ἀφεθήσεται.	c
12:32	καὶ ὃς ἐὰν εἴπῃ λόγον κατὰ τοῦ υἱοῦ τοῦ ἀνθρώπου,	a
	ἀφεθήσεται αὐτῷ·	b
	ὃς δ' ἂν εἴπῃ κατὰ τοῦ πνεύματος τοῦ ἁγίου,	c
	οὐκ ἀφεθήσεται αὐτῷ	d
	οὔτε ἐν τούτῳ τῷ αἰῶνι οὔτε ἐν τῷ μέλλοντι.	e
12:33	Ἢ ποιήσατε τὸ δένδρον καλὸν καὶ τὸν καρπὸν αὐτοῦ καλόν,	a
	ἢ ποιήσατε τὸ δένδρον σαπρὸν καὶ τὸν καρπὸν αὐτοῦ σαπρόν·	b
	ἐκ γὰρ τοῦ καρποῦ τὸ δένδρον γινώσκεται.	c
12:34	γεννήματα ἐχιδνῶν, πῶς δύνασθε ἀγαθὰ λαλεῖν πονηροὶ ὄντες;	a
	ἐκ γὰρ τοῦ περισσεύματος τῆς καρδίας τὸ στόμα λαλεῖ.	b
12:35	ὁ ἀγαθὸς ἄνθρωπος ἐκ τοῦ ἀγαθοῦ θησαυροῦ ἐκβάλλει ἀγαθά,	a
	καὶ ὁ πονηρὸς ἄνθρωπος ἐκ τοῦ πονηροῦ θησαυροῦ ἐκβάλλει πονηρά.	b
12:36	λέγω δὲ ὑμῖν	a
	ὅτι πᾶν ῥῆμα ἀργὸν ὃ λαλήσουσιν οἱ ἄνθρωποι	b
	ἀποδώσουσιν περὶ αὐτοῦ λόγον ἐν ἡμέρᾳ κρίσεως.	c
12:37	ἐκ γὰρ τῶν λόγων σου δικαιωθήσῃ,	a
	καὶ ἐκ τῶν λόγων σου καταδικασθήσῃ.	b

In contrast to the first time that the Pharisees arraigned Jesus for working with the power of demons, this time the author's rhetorical composition presents a Jesus who not only refutes his opponents' charge as logically faulty (12:25–28), but more importantly, he launches a tirade of condemnation on the Pharisees (12:29–37). Therefore, in this conflict story, it is Jesus's response following the Pharisees' accusation that features significantly in the author's composition. Besides numerous repetitions of words and phrases from previous chapters, such as 3:7ff, 9:34; 7:15–20 and 10:25,[118] the text also shows an elaborate parallelism: v. 25//26, v. 27a//28a, v. 30a//30b, v. 31b//31c, v. 32ab//32cd, v. 33a//33b, v. 33c//34b, v. 35a//35b, v. 37a//37b.[119]

Two things are worth noting in Jesus's first refutation (12:25–28). First, the emphasis is clearly on the clause ἐν πνεύματι θεοῦ because the seemingly conditional expression (12:28a) in fact has already been affirmed in the prophecy of Isaiah (12:18b citing Isa 42:1b: θήσω τὸ πνεῦμά μου ἐπ' αὐτόν) and becomes the first concluding counter-argument. Thus, it is indeed ἐν πνεύματι θεοῦ that Jesus casts out demons.[120] Second, placing ἡ βασιλεία τοῦ θεοῦ[121] and the verb ἔφθασεν[122] closely with ἐν πνεύματι θεοῦ, the author explicitly adds eschatological overtones to the portrayal of Jesus who otherwise on this occasion is simply expected to defend the origin of his healing power.[123]

---

118. Howell comments that, "[t]he effect of this repetition is that the implied reader sees Jesus' repudiation of the Jewish leaders as being justified after the second incident (12:22–25). Their opposition and rejection has persisted and has perhaps even grown (12:14)," *Matthew's Inclusive Story*, 139–140.

119. Cf. Saunders, "No One Dared," 238.

120. The Spirit here is linked with the bestowing of the Spirit in 12:18 where the Spirit of God is upon Jesus; see discussion in John Nolland, *The Gospel of Matthew: A Commentary on the Greek Text*, NIGTC (Grand Rapids: Eerdmans, 2005), 500; also Luz, *Matthew 8–20*, 204. Moreover, both the contrast and the word order presented by the parallel between v. 27a and v. 28a shift the accent on the phrase.

121. Here the phrase is against the usual Matthean expression of "kingdom of heaven," and only appears four times in the whole gospel (the other three times are 19:24; 21:31, 43). Scholars offer many explanations (see Davies and Allison, *Matthew 8–18*, 339), though Davies and Allison's own reasoning sounds most likely; "βασιλεία τοῦ stands in conscious parallelism to πνεύματι θεοῦ and in antithesis to βασιλεία αὐτοῦ (sc. Satan, v. 27)," Davies and Allison, *Matthew 8–18*, 339; similarly Verseput, *Rejection of the Humble King*, 228; McNeile, *Matthew*, 176; Grundmann, *Matthäus*, 329, footnote 5; Goulder, *Midrash*, 332, footnote 64.

122. The verb ἔφθασεν is significant and its interpretation is often divided into two main views, either as "has already come" or "come first"; see review in Davies and Allison, *Matthew 8–18*, 342, and Werner G. Kümmel, *Promise and Fulfilment: The Eschatological Message of Jesus* (London: SCM Press, 1984), 105–109. I agree with the first interpretation because the verb demonstrates a full expression of the kingdom's presence; cf. Verseput, *Rejection of the Humble King*, 229.

123. Verseput argues, "the Spirit of God was not without certain eschatological overtones. According to expectation, the Messiah would be endowed with the Spirit (Isa 11:2; Pss. Sol. 17:37; 18:7; 1 Enoch 49:2–4; 62:2; T. Levi 18:7; T. Judah 24:2; Tg. Isa 42:1–4 . . . In that day, among the people of God, an eschatological renewal was expected to take place at the instigation of the Spirit," *Rejection of the Humble King*, 226–227. Although Allison is more cautious, nonetheless he comments on 12:28 that, ". . . these logia do at least allow us to imagine a plausible scenario in which Jesus could have spoken of God's kingdom as present. And it is an

Jesus's refutation in the next section (12:29–37) begins with an analogy of plundering someone's house. Because of its close proximity to ἡ βασιλεία τοῦ θεοῦ (12:28), the οἰκία most likely symbolizes the kingdom.[124] Matthew 12:29 and 30 should be read together, complementing 12:28, as the consequence of God's kingdom coming upon the people.[125] This passage initiates a transition in the whole of Matthew's gospel because the apparent competition of authority is now turning into the image of opposing kingdoms.[126] The conflict is no longer between two groups but between the kingdom of God and the kingdom of Satan. By using the impersonal or inclusive pronouns ὁ and ὅς in subsequent verses (12:30 and 12:32),[127] not only the audiences in the story world but also the implied reader seems to be involved in reflecting upon Jesus's words. In this transitional passage (12:29–30), the Matthean Jesus presents two polarized positions, implicating there will not be room for indecisive fence riders (12:29–30).[128] The phrase τοῦ πνεύματος τοῦ ἁγίου is evoked again[129] in relation to the Pharisees' accusation (12:31–32), but this time it is Jesus who takes on the role of an accuser, asserting that the Pharisees commit an unforgivable sin (12:32). Because of their evil words, according to Jesus, they will be condemned on the day of judgment (12:33–37).

Comparing to all previous conflict stories, this one has two distinct features. First, it seemingly repeats a healing miracle that triggers the conflict.

---

apocalyptic scenario." Allison, *Constructing Jesus: Memory, Imagination, and History* (Grand Rapids: Baker Academic, 2010), 113.

124. Davies and Allison, *Matthew 8–18*, 342.

125. As a consequence of the kingdom's arrival, "Jesus claims a specific act of binding prior to his ministry of exorcism," and Matthew recalls his audience to an earlier episode of Jesus's defeating Satan in the temptation story; Keener, *Matthew*, 365; also Jeremias, *Parables of Jesus*, 122; Johannes Weiss, *Jesus' Proclamation of the Kingdom of God* (Philadelphia: Fortress, 1971), 81; against France, *The Gospel According to Matthew: an Introduction and Commentary* (Downers Grove: InterVarsity Press, 1985), 210.

126. In the next section (3.1.3.3), I will argue that the whole transition passage covers from Matt 12 through to the end of Matt 13.

127. For more, see Howell, *Matthew's Inclusive Story*, 221–222.

128. As Basser rightly puts, "No longer can this figure of Satan in Matthew be seen as the accusing and testing angel of the Lord, but rather as the king of that evil realm that opposes God's rule. We have here complete and utter dualism – the war between the divine and Satan . . . There is no middle ground," *Mind behind the Gospels*, 302. The literary impact cannot be underestimated because it ushers in a watershed in the gospel for the parting of the ways between Jesus's group and the rest of the pious Jews and initiates the transition of Jesus's mission eventually toward all nations.

129. The word "the Spirit" is used three times in this story (12:28, 31, 32).

Second, it adds an unusually long response of Jesus.[130] What does the author intend to achieve through this composition? What exactly is the message to the reader? In order to answer these questions, one must first explore the conflict story in its narrative context where the author has an unusual redaction to the storyline, the quotation of Isaiah 42:1–4 in 12:18–21.

3.1.3.3 Quotation of Isaiah 42:1–4 and Its Interpretive Role for the Conflict Story

The conflict in 12:22–37 starts with the Greek adverb τότε, which, according to McNeil, assumes the force of the Hebrew "*waw* consecutive." It shows that the event happens in due sequence to its immediately preceding context,[131] which in the current case is the longest Scripture quotation in Matthew (cf. Isa 42:1–4).[132] Other scholars support this grammatical point in their study of Matthew 12. Most prominent is Jerome Neyrey, for instance, who argues that "the text of Isa 42 which is cited in Matt 12:18–21 has many points of contact with the whole of the narrative in Matt 12"[133] and thus is "intended by Matthew to illuminate the whole of the narrative in chapter 12, not just vv. 14–16."[134] Similarly, Richard Beaton proposes that Matthew's citation of Isaiah 42:1–4 here is closely associated with both its preceding and subsequent context.[135] These studies, despite their different nuances, all coincide in one

---

130. This is in fact the longest response of Jesus among all conflict stories.

131. McNeile, "Τότε in St. Matthew," *JTS* 12 (1911): 127–128.

132. "This is not only against Matthew's economical tendency in his quoting of the Scriptures, but also is probably Matthew's independent translation of the Hebrew with LXX and targum influence," Gundry, *The Use of the Old Testament in St Matthew's Gospel* (Leiden: Brill, 1967), 111–116.

133. See Jerome H. Neyrey, "The Thematic Use of Isaiah 42.1–4 in Matthew 12," *Bib* 63 (1982): 472. These eight points are:
   (1) God's commissioning in 12:18a,b – 12:8, 28,40;
   (2) Whose spirit? In 12:18c – 12:24, 25–32, 43–45;
   (3) Believers, especially Gentiles in 12:18d – 12:41–42, 46–50;
   (4) Refusal to give a sign in 12:19a – 12:38–39;
   (5) Refusal to hear in 12:19b – 12:38–42;
   (6) Healing role of the Servant in 12:20a,b – 12:9–13, 15, 22;
   (7) Judgment upon unbelievers in 12:20c – 12:31–32, 33–37, 41–42;
   (8) Names of God's Servant in 12:21 – 12:8, 23, 31–32, 40.

134. Neyrey, "Thematic Use of Isaiah 42:1–4," 459. Though he also denies a direct link between 12:18b/20c and the first half of Matt 12; 465.

135. Richard Beaton, *Isaiah's Christ in Matthew's Gospel* (Cambridge: Cambridge University Press, 2002), 172. Besides Neyrey and Beaton, Cope also argues, though partially, for the interrelationship between 12:18–21 and its following verses; see Lamar Cope, *Matthew:*

point. That is, because of the allusive echoing with the intertext Isaiah 42, the text of Matthew 12:18–21 and 12:22–37 form a literary unity.[136]

However, the question remains: how does the Isaiah quotation influence the narrative of 12:22–37? As far as the storyline is concerned, 12:22–37 seems to have little to do with the Isaiah quotation.[137] Also, the words of Jesus in 12:25–45 can hardly fit the image of that gentle and quiet servant of God portrayed in 12:18–21. So, what is the function of 12:18–21/Isaiah 42:1–4 for its following narrative? Among other things, the following evidence demonstrates that the author attempts to achieve two main goals by arranging the current conflict story immediately following the Isaiah quotation (12:18–21).

First, corroborated by its following narrative (12:22–24), the quotation places a sharper focus on Jesus's identity as the coming Messiah so that the healing miracle becomes a sign of Jesus's messiahship. This is shown by Matthew's messianic tone in the Isaiah quotation. The context of this quotation, the whole passage of Isaiah 42, is the first servant song in Deutero-Isaiah that describes a royal servant who carries a messianic mission to the nations. However, the text of 12:18 is probably a combination of quotation and allusion of Isaiah 42:1, 41:8–9a, and 11:2a, 4.[138] Moreover, there is a strong intertextual link between Isaiah 42 and Isaiah 11:41 because they are both infused with the messianic use of the Day of the Lord (cf. Isa 35, 61). It is very likely, as Lybaek argues, that "Matthew understands Isa 42 in messianic terms" just like the Targumic usage of the Isaianic servant language. In *Tg. Isa.* 42:1, the

---

A Scribe Trained for the Kingdom of Heaven (Washington: Catholic Biblical Association of America, 1976), 46. Similarly, Keener writes that "the quotation especially looks forward to the conflict in the following narrative, showing the lowly character of Jesus' first coming (21:5) and especially the final line reinforcing Matthew's theme of the gentile mission" (Keener, *Matthew*, 360). W. R. G. Loader believes 12:18–21 plays a programmatic role for Jesus's ministry, "Son of David, Blindness, Possession and Duality," *CBQ* 44 (1982): 576.

136. Allusive echo is a property of echo in Hays's terms of intertextuality. It "functions to suggest to the reader that text B should be understood in light of a broad interplay with text A, encompassing aspects of A beyond those explicitly echoed." Richard Hays, *Echoes of Scripture in the Letters of Paul* (New Haven: Yale University Press, 1989), 20. Hays is not the only one holding this view, as other scholars have also recognized the significance of the wider context of a cited passage in the Second Temple Jewish exegesis; see, for example, a comprehensive discussion by Instone-Brewer, *Techniques*, especially his discussion on 167.

137. Luz, *Matthew 8–20*, 202.

138. Lybaek, *New and Old*, 93–94.

text reads "my servant, the Messiah . . ."[139] Furthermore, the Isaiah quotation is immediately followed by the author's insertion of the blindness to form the doublet of blind and mute. The reversal of the blind and mute as a typical messianic motif in Isaiah further strengthens Matthew's objective to signify the arrival of messianic age.[140]

The author's intention to highlight Jesus's identity as the coming Messiah can also be seen from the narrative text. The fact that the miracle leads the crowd to wonder[141] whether Jesus is possibly the Son of David together with the negative response of the Pharisees indicates that Jesus's messianic identity is precisely the point of contention.[142] The phrase θήσω τὸ πνεῦμά μου ἐπ' αὐτόν (12:18b) affirms the fact that Jesus drives out demons by the Spirit of God. It is logically linked to 12:28a as an affirmative answer to the crowds' question in 12:23 (i.e. Jesus is the Davidic messiah). In the presence of Jesus, God's kingdom has indeed arrived (12:28b).[143] In addition, the pronounced themes in the passage of 12:17–37, such as God's chosen servant, spirit-endowed, and the Son of David, are all of messianic nature. These themes function to link the entire passage of 12:17–37 back to the messianic theme in 11:3–5[144] as well as to the baptism account in Matthew 3.[145] After pointing

---

139. Other examples are the translation of servant in Isa 43:10 and 52:13; cf. Ezek 37:24, see J. Jeremias, "παῖς θεοῦ," *TDNT* 5:681. Also see Chilton, *The Isaiah Targum: Introduction, Translation, Apparatus and Notes* (Wilmington: M. Glazier, 1987), 81–83. For more discussion see Lybaek, *New and Old*, 98–101.

140. It alludes to its intertexts such as Isa 35:5–6, 42:7, 16. Just as God's servant opens the blind eyes in Isa 42:7, Jesus the meek servant also makes the blind to see in 12:22–24.

141. Just like the miracle doublets in 9:27–34, here is not the act of individual healings themselves, but the final healing doublet *together* which causes the crowd's amazement because the healing in 9:27–34 is certainly not the first time when Jesus exorcises demons (cf. 4:24; 8:16).

142. Nolland comments that Son of David in Matthew is a royal messianic designation, *Matthew*, 400; also, Basser says that the title Son of David is another title for Messiah in rabbinic Judaism (*Mind behind the Gospels*, 300). Luz goes further and purports that "There is little to be gained from inquiring into the roots of the 'Son of David' title in religious history. Matthew makes plain his own understanding of this expression through his story," *Theology*, 71.

143. See above footnote 123 on the discussion of ἔφθασεν. See also Cope's discussion in *Scribe Trained for Kingdom*, 38.

144. Verse 11:5 alludes to Isa 35:5–6 in which the theme is the arrival of the messianic age and the day of the Lord. Also, as Lybaek argues, 12:18–21 "continues the Christological theme of the immediate context as well as that introduced in Matt 11:3–5," *New and Old*, 100.

145. The wording of 12:18a, ὁ ἀγαπητός μου εἰς ὃν εὐδόκησεν ἡ ψυχή μου, corresponds more to 3:17 ("This is my beloved son with whom I am well pleased") rather than to the MT or LXX of Isaiah 42:1a. Especially, Matthew's use of ὁ ἀγαπητός leads some scholars to suspect that Matthew redacts Isaiah 42:1a intentionally to remind his audience of 3:17; see Krister Stendahl,

to the reader that Jesus is indeed ὁ ἐρχόμενος in the answer to John the Baptist (11:3–5), the author arranges the narrative in order to "show" the messianic identity of Jesus through the authoritative Scripture as well as the reversal of blind and deaf miracles in 12:17–37. If, as is likely, Matthew's reader is familiar with the Hebrew Scripture, they would not miss that Matthew intends to paint this character of Jesus with the image of a Messiah filled with God's spirit.

The second goal the author attempts to achieve by arranging the current conflict story immediately following the Isaiah quotation in 12:17–37 is equally important. It is to commence a transitional section in the Matthean narrative that shifts Jesus's mission from primarily toward the Jews to the Gentiles as the due consequence of Jewish leaders' rejection.[146] Such an understanding can be supported by the following analysis: (1) Jesus as the coming Messiah will bring justice – a characteristic of the messianic age – to the Gentiles; meanwhile, he will bring judgment to the Jewish leaders. One of the key themes running through the whole passage is κρίσις, which appears three times in 12:17–37.[147] More specifically, κρίσις is not only central to this longest Scripture quotation in Matthew, but, as Barth argues, ἕως ἂν ἐκβάλῃ εἰς νῖκος τὴν κρίσιν (12:20c) is the governing statement of 12:18–21 that expresses "the proper and decisive vocation of the servant of God."[148] The understanding of κρίσις here should encompass the English gloss of both justice and judgment because the narrative surrounding the Isaiah quotation (i.e. 12:1–16[149]

The School of St. Matthew, and Its Use of the Old Testament, 2nd ed. (Philadelphia: Fortress, 1968), 109–111; also Kingsbury, *Matthew: Structure, Christology, Kingdom* (Philadelphia: Fortress, 1975), 95. Many other imageries, such as "brood of vipers," good/evil trees/fruits also clearly tie 12:17–37 back to Matt 3 (e.g. 3:10 and 12:33; 3:7 and 12:34), although they are not exactly of messianic nature.

146. A similar point is made by Luz in passing, "... Matthew wanted to use this long and important formula quotation here in the middle of his gospel and *at the point in his narrative where the separation from Israel begins . . .*," but he does not elaborate nor does he substantiate this assertion. Luz, *Matthew 8–20*, 191, italics added.

147. The three times are 12:18, 20, 36 plus a closely associated word κριτής in 12:27. Also cf. 12:41, 42.

148. Especially, as Barth points out, 12:20c as an important redaction for the author is more likely a theological interpretation; "Matthew's Understanding of the Law," 141. Similarly, Lybaek states that the whole Isaiah quotation in Matt 12 "is not meant simply as a reciting of Scripture word for word, but is in itself both an interpretation of Scripture as well as an interpretation of the ministry of Jesus," *New and Old*, 100.

149. The argument that the preceding context (11:28–12:16) to the Isaiah quotation in Matt 12 warrants "justice" (but perhaps not excluding "judgment") as the English gloss for

and 12:22–50[150]) properly reflects the two meanings. On the one hand, the judgment of Jesus on the Pharisees' action can be shown by the logic of his argument, which clearly and progressively establishes their guilt and leads to his final condemnation that "by your words you will be condemned" (v. 37b).[151] On the other hand, the final tone of the Isaiah quotation is indeed positive (12:21: καὶ τῷ ὀνόματι αὐτοῦ ἔθνη ἐλπιοῦσιν).[152] Therefore, it necessitates a neutral, if not equally positive, interpretation for the first κρίσις in 12:18d. In both 12:18d and 12:21, Gentiles are mentioned regarding their relationship to the servant, neither of which seems negative. (2) However, nothing in the current conflict story (or the previous narrative) really fulfils the Isaianic prophecy that Jesus will bring the messianic age to the Gentiles. It then leaves a possible expectation for the reader that a shift in Jesus's mission from primarily toward the Jews to the Gentiles will soon happen in the following narrative. The reading of Matthew 13–15 proves this point to be true and will be discussed further in the next chapter. Suffice it to say that, the third conflict story in Matthew 12, combined with the Isaianic quotation, indeed "endorses a servant of God whose mission is the institution of the universal just rule of God."[153]

3.1.3.4 Summary of 12:22–37 in Its Immediate Narrative and Rhetorical Context (11:2–12:50)

The third conflict story in Matthew 12 starts with a brief miracle of Jesus's healing the blind and mute man followed by the accusation of the Pharisees that Jesus acts in the power of Satan. It is Jesus's response following the

---

κρίσις in 12:18–21 is offered by Beaton, "Messiah and Justice: A Key to Matthew's Use of Isaiah 42:1–4?" *JSNT* 75 (1999): 17–22.

150. The later part of Matt 12 has two more occurrences of κρίσις in 12:41, 42, which will be discussed in the next conflict story. Suffice it to say that κρίσις in both verses clearly refers to "judgment."

151. Jesus first demonstrates the Beelzebub charge is logically faulty (vv. 25–29), he then states a general rule (v. 31) followed by an application on the Pharisees (v. 32). Finally, the author has Jesus recall the imagery of good/bad trees/fruits and call the Pharisees "brood of vipers" (vv. 33–37), echoing the harsh judgment of John the Baptist (3:7–12). Also see discussion on the establishment of Pharisees' guilt in Cope, *Scribe Trained for Kingdom*, 38–39.

152. However, one must notice the qualification of the personal pronoun, αὐτοῦ, which is correctly translated/interpreted as Gentiles by many versions of English Bible.

153. Beaton, *Isaiah's Christ*, 172. More so, Cope believes that the whole of Matt 12 is constructed on the basis of the Isaiah citation, *Scribe Trained for Kingdom*, 34–36.

Pharisees' accusation that features significantly in the author's composition. Jesus's healing miracle effectively functions as a restatement of a previous story (9:27–34) but with more poignant nuances because the crowds become more aware of Jesus's messianic identity as the Son of David. The context (the conflicts in 12:1–8 and 12:9–14) poignantly shows a Jesus as one who has divine status; therefore, it is no surprise for the Matthean audience to understand Jesus acting *in the place of* God who will bring justice to all. What is surprising, however, is that the opponents in this story still denounce Jesus of his authority which leads to the major part of the conflict – Jesus's long refutation to his opponents.

The foregoing analysis shows that the story of 12:22–37 is closely connected to its preceding context, the quotation of Isaiah 42:1–4 in Matthew 12:18–21. The meaning of κρίσις in 12:18 and verse 20 should encompass both justice and judgment. Multiple themes and imageries, such as the chosen servant, spirit-filled, the Son of David, good/bad trees/fruits link 12:17–37 back to the messianic theme in 11:3–5 and Matthew 3. Interpreting the conflict story through the lenses of the Isaiah quotation, it seems that the author places a sharper focus on the identity of Jesus as the Messiah. Moreover, the entire passage of 12:17–37 commences a transitional watershed section in the Matthean narrative plot that shifts Jesus's mission from primarily toward the Jews to the Gentiles as the due consequence of Jewish leaders' rejection. In other words, the fact that such shift will begin is the judgment the Jews (represented by Pharisees) duly deserve. The audience should expect such a shift in Jesus's mission in the later narrative.

3.1.4 Matthew 12:38–45

3.1.4.1 The Setting of the Story

This conflict story includes Jesus's refusal to give a "sign from heaven" and it appears in all Synoptic Gospels. Matthew's version, however, is unique in that he narrates two such similar reports (12:38–42; 16:1–4) and the current conflict story has the most complex and developed form.[154]

Because a simple τότε connects the current conflict scene with the last story, the two stories likely share the same narrative setting. That is, Jesus

---

154. Edwards, *The Sign of Jonah: In the Theology of the Evangelists and Q* (London: SCM Press, 1971), 96.

healed the dumb and mute man (12:22), which causes the crowds to wonder at his messianic identity (12:23). However, just before the current conflict scene, Jesus finishes a tirade of refutation that not only overthrows the Pharisees' challenge but also warns them of the final judgment. From the narrative point of view, therefore, it can be seen that the entire story in 12:22–37 functions to provide a certain mood for the reader to encounter this current conflict (12:38–45). This mood has already prepared for the reader's recognition of the irony that the Pharisees are blind, yet they still ask to *see* signs from Jesus.

3.1.4.2 Matthew 12:38–45: The Conflict Scene Proper and the Interpretive Role of Matthew 12:18–21/Isaiah 42:1–4

This is the second time the scribes appear as Jesus's opponents in a conflict story,[155] joining the Pharisees to challenge Jesus to show a sign from heaven. In the previous conflict Pharisees are the targets of Jesus's condemnation. Therefore, the grouping of the scribes with the Pharisees inevitably extends Jesus's opponents to a wider range of Jewish leaders. The author is likely preparing the reader's mind for the saying γενεὰ πονηρὰ καὶ μοιχαλὶς (12:39).

Through the previous conflict (12:22–37), the reader has already gained an impression that the Pharisees are *blind* to Jesus's messianic identity. This story continues such an impression. The earlier miracle points to Jesus's messiahship because even the crowds wonder at the miracle as to whether Jesus acts as the Messiah, Son of David (12:23).[156] However, Jesus's condemnation of the scribes and Pharisees[157] logically implies that they are completely *blind* to what that miracle signifies.[158] Consequently, except that Jesus calls them to see (ἰδοὺ) "the one is greater than Jonah/Solomon" (v. 41c, v. 42c), there will be no signs given to them until τὸ σημεῖον Ἰωνᾶ τοῦ προφήτου is given to them in the future (v. 39, δοθήσεται).

Similarly, the author also gives the audience an impression that the scribes and the Pharisees are *deaf*. This is because despite "hearing" Jesus's defence of

---

155. The first time the scribes act as Jesus's opponents is in the first conflict story (9:1–8).

156. Cope, *Scribe Trained for Kingdom*, 40.

157. The text in 16:3 makes the point more explicitly to show the leaders fail to interpret the miracle as an eschatological sign but here the point is implicit.

158. Malina and Neyrey argues slightly differently, though along the similar line, that Jesus's "casting out of a demon must logically be construed as a sign that 'the kingdom of God has come among you,'" *Calling Jesus Names*, 64.

working under the Holy Spirit and the warning that the Pharisees' blasphemous words will bring them fitting judgment (12:25–37), they still wish to see a sign (ἰδεῖν) from him (12:38). Jesus responds to their request by giving two examples of those Gentiles who had "heard" and repented or understood (12:41–42).[159] This is in opposition to the scribes and the Pharisees. Such a contrast between the Jewish leaders and the Gentiles fits the expectation of the audience brought by previous conflict which indicates a shift in Jesus's mission from toward the Jews to toward the Gentiles.

The implication of the scribes and the Pharisees as blind and deaf in this conflict story reflects a significant point in Isaiah 42 (especially 42:18–20).[160] This is because in Isaiah 42, Israel as God's servant is portrayed as blind and deaf. By showing the reader how the Jewish leaders are completely blind and deaf to the fact that Jesus is the Messiah and initiates the dawn of a new age, Matthew provides the evidence for their judgment. Consequently, Jesus's role as the divine agent of justice is highlighted in this story, echoing his polemic comments in the previous conflict (12:22–37). It is no surprise then that in 12:41 and 42 the word κρίσις appears in Jesus's response again. As Neyrey correctly observes, the repetition of κρίσις constitutes another point of contact between the Isaiah quotation in 12:18–21 and the remaining narrative of Matthew 12 (cf. 11: 20–24).[161]

It is against this background that one can begin to interpret τὸ σημεῖον Ἰωνᾶ (12:39; 16:2; Luke 11:16; Mark 8:11). Scholars have offered a plethora of meanings to τὸ σημεῖον[162] Ἰωνᾶ,[163] ranging from, for example, God's great pow-

---

159. "Hearing" is implied by the fact that Nineveh repented at Jonah's "preaching" (v. 41) and the Queen of the South endured hardship to come in order that she might "hear" the wisdom of Solomon (v. 42, ἀκοῦσαι).

160. As mentioned above, the whole passage of Isaiah 42 is the context of Matthew's citation of Isa 42:1–4 (Matt 12:18–21).

161. See the seventh point of Neyrey's eight points of contact, judgment upon unbelievers, "Thematic Use of Isaiah 42:1–4," 472.

162. The meaning of σημεῖον in Greek possibly encompasses both miraculous and natural things; see "σημεῖον" in *BDAG*, 920, which lists Matt 12:38f under the category of "an event that is an indication or confirmation of intervention by transcendent powers"; also see discussion by Hans Bayer, *Jesus' Predictions of Vindication and Resurrection* (Tübingen: Mohr, 1986), 111–112.

163. See the more detailed survey by Chow, *Sign of Jonah Reconsidered: A Study of Its Meaning in the Gospel Traditions* (Stockholm: Almqvist & Wiksell, 1995), 15–18.

er to rescue Jonah from the sea,[164] Jonah's or Jesus's preaching of repentance,[165] Jesus's death and resurrection,[166] John the Baptist,[167] the dove,[168] to Jonah or Jesus himself.[169] The great variety of interpretation is a reflection of the number of possible parallels between Jesus and Jonah: (1) the role as Israel's prophet, (2) preaching of the impending judgment, (3) God's miraculous rescue of them from death, and (4) mission to the Gentiles. In this Matthean conflict story, however, which one (or more) of these shared characteristics is (or are) stressed by the author for his narrative purposes?

Because of its reappearance in Matthew 16:1–4, a full understanding cannot be achieved until both of the "sign of Jonah" sayings are taken into account. However, a close reading of the conflict story within its narrative context recognizes the following five reasons. They support the interpretation that the sign points to the death and resurrection of Jesus.

---

164. Jeremias argues that the sign "consist[s] in the authorization of the divine messenger by deliverance from death," assuming that the Ninevites knew that Jonah had been delivered and the Son of Man returning from the dead will in fact renew the sign of Jonah, "Ἰωνᾶς," *TDNT* 3: 409–410; Rebecca Denova argues this point for Luke's account, *The Things Accomplished among Us: Prophetic Tradition in the Structural Pattern of Luke-Acts* (Sheffield: Sheffield Academic Press, 1997), 109; Bayer, *Jesus' Predictions*, 138.

165. Manson, *The Sayings of Jesus*, 90–91, 382; John S. Kloppenborg, *The Formation of Q: Trajectories in Ancient Wisdom Collections* (Philadelphia: Fortress, 1987), 132–133; S. Schulz, *Q, Die Spruchquelle der Evangelisen* (Zürich: Theologischer Verlag, 1972), 255–256. Luz, *Matthew 8–20*, 219. Landes also holds the sign as Jesus's preaching not of repentance but of the divine liberation from death; George M. Landes, "Matthew 12:40 as an Interpretation of 'The Sign of Jonah' against Its Biblical Background," in *The Word of the Lord Shall Go Forth: Essays in Honor of David Noel Freedman in Celebration of His Sixtieth Birthday*, eds. Carol Meyers, Michael P. O'Connor and David Noel Freedman (Winona Park: Eisenbrauns, 1983), 676.

166. See, for example, Edwards, *Sign of Jonah*, 98; Garland, *Reading Matthew*, 142; Chow, *Sign of Jonah Reconsidered*, 211; Repschinski, *Controversy*, 137.

167. Bacon believes that the name Ἰωνᾶς is either a corruption of the name "Johanon" or a pun so the sign refers to the preaching of repentance of both John the Baptist and Jesus himself; "What Was the Sign of Jonah?" *Biblical World* 20 (1902): 99–112. Also, Hugh Michael, "The Sign of Jonah," *JTS* 21 (1920): 151.

168. For example, John Howton, "The Sign of Jonah," *SJT* 15 (1962): 288–304. He argues that the dove (or Jonah) was the sign to the Gentiles. In this case, it is not Jonah's name but the dove which is a symbol of the Spirit. The dove was the sign for Israel of whom the Son of Man was conceived as a remnant, he and Israel are both sons of God, although in different sense; the sign to this generation is again the sonship, represented by the dove; and so we have the comparison between the Son of Man and the sign of Jonah or the dove – conclusion in p. 304.

169. Bultmann, *History*, 117–118.

First, the text of 12:40 as an entire Matthean insertion[170] is significant for interpreting "the sign of Jonah." It specifies the connection between the person of Jonah and Jesus;[171] therefore, 12:40 can be argued as the author's own explanation of the sign of Jonah.[172] Matthew draws attention to the parallel characteristics between Jonah and Jesus by repeating the phrase τρεῖς ἡμέρας καὶ τρεῖς νύκτας,[173] which may possibly have been a passion kerygma already established at the time of Matthew's gospel.[174] The use of two conjunctions, ὥσπερ γὰρ indicates that the author's view of the most prominent commonality between John and Jesus is . . . τρεῖς ἡμέρας καὶ τρεῖς νύκτας. That is to say, the author sees their miraculous rescue from death by God as the key link between the two. As a result, τὸ σημεῖον Ἰωνᾶ seems most likely to refer to the death and resurrection of Jesus.

Second, in the Matthean account, the scribes' and the Pharisees' challenge clearly revolves around the person of Jesus. Therefore, it is unlikely that τὸ σημεῖον focuses on others than on Jesus himself. This can be seen from the unique wording of the question in Matthew: <u>θέλομεν ἀπὸ σοῦ</u> σημεῖον ἰδεῖν (12:38).[175] The response of Jesus that emphasizes "the one greater than Jonah/Solomon" also addresses the challenge directly. Furthermore, the irony in 12:39 is established precisely because in the immediate context the challengers could not see the miracle/sign concerning Jesus's messianic identity (12:22–23). Therefore, the text and its context determine that τὸ σημεῖον Ἰωνα in Jesus's answer cannot refer to anything/anyone else (such as John the Baptist, Jonah's preaching, or the dove) except the person of Jesus.

Third, since the author inserts 12:40 before the mention of Ninevites and the Queen of the South, how exactly does he intend to interpret "the sign of Jonah" in light of the passages in 12:41–42? Besides the obvious fact that Matthew intends to follow his sources, the question may be answered by the comparison between the structure of 12:41 and verse 42:

---

170. Repschinski, *Controversy*, 135. The insertion is a direct quotation from the LXX of Jonah 2:1, καὶ ἦν Ἰωνᾶς ἐν τῇ κοιλίᾳ τοῦ κήτους τρεῖς ἡμέρας καὶ τρεῖς νύκτας.

171. The sentence begins with the conjunction ὥσπερ to mark the similarity between two events or states, see entry for ὥσπερ; *BDAG*, 1106.

172. Edwards, *Sign of Jonah*, 97.

173. Though scholars argue that the phrase points more to the state of interment and less on the return to life of both; see Nolland, *Matthew*, 511, footnote 107.

174. See elaboration on this point by Edwards, *Sign of Jonah*, 99.

175. Davies and Allison, *Matthew 8–18*, 354.

41a. ἄνδρες Νινευῖται ἀναστήσονται
ἐν τῇ κρίσει μετὰ τῆς γενεᾶς ταύτης καὶ
κατακρινοῦσιν αὐτήν

42a. βασίλισσα νότου ἐγερθήσεται
ἐν τῇ κρίσει μετὰ τῆς γενεᾶς ταύτης καὶ κατακρινεῖ αὐτήν

41b. ὅτι μετενόησαν εἰς τὸ κήρυγμα Ἰωνᾶ,
42b. ὅτι ἦλθεν ἐκ τῶν περάτων τῆς γῆς ἀκοῦσαι τὴν σοφίαν Σολομῶνος,

41c. καὶ ἰδοὺ πλεῖον Ἰωνᾶ ὧδε.
42c. καὶ ἰδοὺ πλεῖον Σολομῶνος ὧδε.

It must be noted that while reproducing his sources, the author changes the order slightly.[176] As shown above, Matthew's redaction results in a meticulous parallel between the structures of two passages. It seems to suggest that such a parallelism is used as a literary device to convey the same point, which is highlighted by the last phrase (v. 41c, 42c) in each example: ἰδοὺ πλεῖον ... ὧδε (behold, something greater...is here). It is plausible that the author is inviting the reader to recall a similar saying τοῦ ἱεροῦ μεῖζόν ἐστιν ὧδε preceding this conflict story in the context (12:6).[177] Therefore, as far as the two passages of 12:41-42 are concerned, the focus still remains christological and it excludes the possibility that τὸ σημεῖον Ἰωνα refers to anything or anyone else (e.g. John the Baptist, Jonah's preaching, or the dove).

Fourth, the reason the sign of Jonah in Matthew points to the death and resurrection of Jesus is suggested by the use of the future tense of two verbs

---

176. Cf. Q 11:31-32; most commentators believe that Matthew changed the order of Q in order to bring the sayings concerning Jonah into a closer a unit; for example, see Davies and Allison, *Matthew 8-18*, 357; also Repschinski argues that this change of order in turns provides an opportunity for Matthew to explicate more nuance on his rendering of the sign, *Controversy*, 137.

177. Even though the adjective here is slightly different than 12:6, the basic point remains the same. Moreover, Edwards argues for another link between Jesus and the temple saying because of the kerygma of "three days," *Sign of Jonah*, 100.

δοθήσεται (12:39) and ἔσται (12:40).[178] In both uses, Jesus refers to future events in the story time. Thus, it renders the interpretations as Jonah's/Jesus's preaching of repentance or the person of Jonah/Jesus improbable as the meaning of the sign of Jonah.

Last but not least, in the early Jewish tradition Jonah is seen as an example of God's saving his people because the highlight is on Jonah's miraculous rescue from the sea monster.[179] While it is true that according to the Book of Jonah, the Ninevites could nowhere have known of Jonah's miraculous rescue,[180] this early Jewish tradition regarding Jonah – which Matthew's implied reader should be familiar with – supports Matthew's interpretation.

After finding a solution for the key interpretive puzzle τὸ σημεῖον Ἰωνα, it is now possible to determine the author's second and more important narrative purpose through this fourth conflict story of Matthew 12. That is, the story is to *continue* the transitional watershed section in the Matthean narrative, which starts from 12:17–37, shifting Jesus's mission focus from primarily on the Jews to the Gentiles as the due consequence of the Jewish leaders' rejection. The text and the context of the conflict story provide the following indications preparing the reader for this inevitable shift.

The first indication of a focus on a mission is that the story presents two Gentiles who heard and repented/believed God's message (12:41–42).[181] Their action serves as a testimony against Israel's unbelief.[182] The schism

---

178. Davies and Allison, *Matthew 8-18*, 352. More detailed survey and discussion that favors a future use of the verb is in Bayer, *Jesus' Predictions*, 121–124, particularly footnote 89. Though others argue against the future use in both δοθήσεται (Luke 11:29/Matt 12:39) and ἔσται (Luke 11:30) as being gnomic, Luz, *Matthew 8-20*, 218. The same future verbs are also used in Q 11:29–30 without specific reference to τρεῖς ἡμέρας καὶ τρεῖς νύκτας, it does not preclude this fourth point.

179. For example, see 3 Macc 6:8, Jos. *Ant 9:205-214*; Chow suggests that "Jewish writers in the first century and earlier tend to focus on Jonah's miraculous saving from the belly of the fish," although he finds that there is a variety of characterization of the figure of Jonah in the tradition, *Sign of Jonah Reconsidered*, 42; see more discussions of Jonah in Jewish literature in pp. 27–44.

180. This could be a counter-argument for the parallel between Jonah's deliverance and Jesus's resurrection; Davies and Allison, *Matthew 8-18*, 353, footnote 84.

181. Two might be necessary to establish a legitimate testimony in Jewish tradition, though Luz also argues that they function as "a double 'signal' to the church's future gentile mission after Easter." Luz, *Matthew 8-20*, 220.

182. Luz sees this fact alone already "signals in advance this great turning of God's way from Israel to the Gentiles," *Matthew 8-20*, 218. Also as Paul Meyer states, the faith of certain

among seers/hearers follows a previous similar schism (12:22–24),[183] continuing the motif of contrasting beliefs developed most evidently from 12:18ff.[184] According to Jesus's words, the reason that the Ninevites and the Queen of the South are able to rise up and judge this generation is because, even though being Gentiles, they still repented and obeyed the truth proclaimed to them. Therefore, the Ninevites and the Queen of the South can be seen as the prototype of Gentiles who are accepted by God. The implication, connecting to the author's previous citation of Isaiah, is that Jesus will similarly proclaim justice to the Gentiles and they will put their hope in his name (cf. 12:19–21).[185]

The second indication is Jesus's "calling their [the scribes and Pharisees] name" as an evil and adulterous generation.[186] The implication cannot be overlooked because now the scribes and Pharisees seem to have become the representatives of this generation as the judgment is also extended to the whole generation (vv. 41 and 42, κατακρινοῦσιν / κατακρινεῖ αὐτήν).[187] This is the first time Jesus addresses his opponents in such broad terms in conflict stories but certainly it is not the last time (cf. 16:4). Therefore, just as in the days of Jonah, the Gentiles repent at the message of the kingdom; however, "this generation" remains impenitent and thereby brings judgment upon itself.[188] Such a result reflects what the author believes about Jesus in the prophecy of Isaiah, "he will lead justice to victory" (12:20/Isa 42:3).

How then does the sign of Jonah fit within the whole picture? Because the narrative reports Jesus's words, "there will not be any sign given to them

---

Gentiles will serve ... to condemn impenitent Israel." Paul Meyer, "Gentile Mission in Q," *JBL* 89 (1970): 407.

183. The term is coined by Hare, who argues it as "the rejection motif," *Jewish Persecution of Christians*, 134–137.

184. Neyrey amends Hare's idea to contrasting reaction motifs and not just rejection, "Thematic Use of Isaiah 42:1–4," 461, footnote 12. See also Hummel, *Die Auseinandersetzung*, 118–119, 23–25.

185. Davies and Allison, *Matthew 8–18*, 357–359.

186. According to Malina and Neyrey, condemning the condemners is a common strategy to react against deviance labeling which is the case in the previous conflict where the Pharisees negatively labeled Jesus (12:24). Malina and Neyrey, *Calling Jesus Names*, 63–64.

187. At this point of the narrative, whether it is targeted toward the entire nation of Israel is unclear; Luz, *Matthew 8–20*, 217; what can be inferred though is that the focus is no longer on the leading group, but they may undertake a more corporate role for Israel. See more discussion on the 'evil generation' in Davies and Allison, *Matthew 8–18*, 260, 355.

188. Meyer, "Gentile Mission in Q," 405–408.

until the sign of Jonah (i.e. the only one in the future)," it prepares the reader for the Jewish leaders' consistent obduracy toward Jesus and his ministry. In other words, in the ensuing narrative the audience should expect to hear the Jewish leaders (together with "this generation") continue acting in complete blindness towards Jesus's words and deeds until Jesus's death and resurrection. Such an understanding of the role "the sign of Jonah" for the conflict corresponds to Verseput's comment, "[t]o the scribes and Pharisees' request for a sign, Jesus has harshly replied that the only sign to be given will be the reversal of Israel's murderous rejection of Jesus in the resurrection. This, as we have seen, is not a sign to evoke faith, but a confirmation of God's wrath upon a chosen people who had decisively opposed themselves to their Messiah."[189]

The third indication that Jesus's mission shifts away from the Jews can be discerned from the parable of the seven evil spirits (12:43–45) and the story immediately following the conflict (12:46–50). The author's redactional hands are evident in the arrangement of these two passages in relation to the saying of "the sign of Jonah."[190]

Matthew	Mark	Q/Luke	
12:22–30	Beelzebul Conflict	3:22–27	11:14ff, 17–23
12:31–37	Sin against the Holy Spirit	3:28–30	12:10; 6:43–45
12:38–42	Sign of Jonah	8:11–13	11:16, 29–32
12:43–45	Return of the Evil Spirit		11:24–26
12:46–50	Jesus' True Family	3:31–35	8:19–21

The author uses the parable of the evil spirit to conclude the conflict of "the sign of Jonah" instead of retaining its original location following Jesus's exorcism conflict (Q 11:24–26). In addition to other minor changes, the most prominent is the fact that the entire sentence οὕτως ἔσται καὶ τῇ γενεᾷ ταύτῃ τῇ πονηρᾷ (12:45d) is inserted in order to tie it closely with Jesus's previous answer (12:39–42). Therefore, regardless of the exact meaning of the parable,[191]

---

189. Verseput, *Rejection of the Humble King*, 276; cf. Luz, *Matthew 8–20*, 218.

190. The composition of two conflict stories in Matthew and their context in comparison to the ordering in Mark and Q/Luke; reproduced with slight change from Edwards, *Sign of Jonah*, 101.

191. Davies and Allison list six interpretive options for this parable; see *Matthew 8–18*, 359. Cf. Repschinski, *Controversy*, 139–140.

as far as the Matthean narrative is concerned, the message of the parable is to be understood as a prophetic illustration either in terms of a prediction or a stern warning against Jesus's opponents. Even though such an answer is in the same vein as Jesus's words in the previous conflict (esp. 12:33–37), in this conflict the tone is more harsh because of its sure implication for the future (12:45: . . . τὰ ἔσχατα . . . ἔσται . . .):[192] this evil generation will live in a gloomy and dreadful state at the end times.

The author places Jesus's saying regarding his true family immediately following the conflict (12:46–50). It is not only echoing the message in a previous conflict that shows Jesus's willingness to call sinners (9:9–13) to establish a new community, but more importantly, the saying defines the boundaries for the family of God in relation to Jesus himself (12:50). Therefore, Jesus's saying in 12:46–50 presses further to specifically set the only criterion for dividing those within God's kingdom from those without: ὅστις γὰρ ἂν ποιήσῃ τὸ θέλημα τοῦ πατρός μου τοῦ ἐν οὐρανοῖς. The implication of such a criterion for the reader is indeed radical. The author leads the reader to expect that, in the future, Jesus's family (i.e. the kingdom of God) is no longer restricted to "the lost sheep of Israel" (cf. 10:5–6). It is open to all who obey the will of the God,[193] even possible for the Gentiles, whereas "this generation" may face the final judgment. Such an understanding of the context confirms to the previous analysis that the conflict story continues the transition of Matthean narrative that Jesus's mission is shifting to the Gentiles.

3.1.4.3 Summary of 12:38–45 in Its Immediate Narrative and Rhetorical Context (11:2–12:50)

In this conflict story, the author continues to impress the image on the reader that the Jewish leaders are completely blind and deaf toward the person Jesus. Following Jesus's healing miracle to restore a demon-possessed man to sound and sight (12:22–24), the Jewish leaders still request to see a sign. Jesus refuses them except for offering "the sign of Jonah" in the future, which points to the death and resurrection of himself. The description of the two Gentiles who heard and repented/believed God's message serves as a testimony against

---

192. The sure implication for the future can also be confirmed by the repetition of future tense verbs: δοθήσεται (12:39), ἔσται (v. 40), ἀναστήσονται (v. 41), ἐγερθήσεται (v. 42).

193. Cf. Hagner, *Matthew 1–13*, 360.

the unbelief of "this evil generation." In addition, the Matthean Jesus uses a parable to illustrate the dreadful fate of "this generation" in the end times. Therefore, Jesus's rebuke to the opponents appears to be more polemic than his earlier warning (12:25–37).

For the purpose of the plot development in Matthew, the story functions to continue the transition section that shifts Jesus's mission focus from primarily on the Jews to the Gentiles as the inevitable consequence of the Jewish leaders' rejection. It essentially prepares for the realization of Isaiah's prophecy that Gentiles will have hope in Jesus's name (12:20–21). The new community of God can be expected to include Gentiles and is only defined in relation to the person of Jesus.

3.2 Conflict Stories in Context

Each of the four conflict stories in Matthew 12 has been examined individually as well as within its context. It is also important to consider their links within the larger narrative. The fact that the author arranges all four in close connection with each other compels the analysis to go further to investigate the function of the four stories as a group and the role the group plays in the author's literary composition.

The first two conflicts (12:1–8, 9–14) in Matthew 12 are tied together by their shared subject matter, the Sabbath observance. The other two (12:22–37, 38–45) are connected closely in that both are triggered by issues of "seeing/not seeing and hearing/not hearing." As demonstrated in the previous section, while the summary statement (12:15–17) and the quotation of Isaiah 42:1–4 in 12:18–21 as the author's insertion seem to separate the two sets of conflicts, in reality the two passages function to provide a framework for the rest of Matthew 12. In addition to many points of contact between the Isaiah quotation and the text of conflict stories,[194] there arises the following most noticeable themes:

(1) Christological focus: the author refines his portrayal of Jesus to be not only the Davidic Messiah but also the one who enjoys the same divine status as God (12:6, 8, 12, 18, 23, 28, 32, 41, 42).

---

194. See Neyrey's example, "Thematic Use of Isaiah 42:1–4," 472.

(2) Preparation for the mission to the Gentiles: even though nothing in the context narrates Jesus's ministry to the Gentiles, nonetheless, the text prepares the reader for the drift of Jesus's mission to the Gentiles in later narrative. This can be seen by Matthean Jesus's redefinition of Sabbath based on "mercy" (12:7–8), the insertion of the Isaiah quote which prophesied that "he will proclaim justice to the nations (ἔθνεσιν) . . . in his name the nations (ἔθνη) will put their hope" (12:18, 21), and the Gentiles were able to repent and be deemed righteous by God when justice prevails (12:41–42).

(3) Jesus will bring justice to victory: there are frequent appearances of legal vocabularies such as "it is lawful . . .," "innocent," "condemn," "forgive," "justify," "justice," "last," "wicked," and "the day of judgment" frequently appear in the context (12:2, 4, 5, 7, 10, 12, 18, 20, 27, 31, 32, 36, 37, 39, 41, 42, 45).

Whereas the conflict stories in Matthew 12 continue the christological focus set out by the previous conflicts, Jesus's polemic against the Jewish leaders is heightened, and in particular the day of Judgment is in view. Inevitably, the Jewish leaders resort to a murderous plot against Jesus (12:14). Therefore, it is obvious that the author portrays a much deeper schism between Jesus and the Jewish leaders. Distinctive also is the author's reference to several repentant Gentiles. Their role will be reversed at the end times not only to judge the "blind and deaf" opponents of Jesus, but the judgment encompasses "this generation." The Gentiles' relationship to Jesus is foreshadowed by Matthew's unique insertion of Isaiah 42:1–4 in the midst of the conflict sequence. Therefore, when the four conflicts in Matthew 12 are viewed as a group, they function to move the Matthean plot forward by preparing the reader for the shift of Jesus's mission focus from primarily on the Jews to the Gentiles as the due consequence of Jewish rejection. With this in view, the fact that Gentiles will be part of God's kingdom should not be a surprise to the audience (cf. 12:48–50) as later narratives of Matthew make clear. This point will be discussed in the next chapter of this study.

CHAPTER 4

Conflict Stories in Matthew 13, 15, 16 and 19
The Parting of the Ways

Unlike other conflict stories that appear in clusters, there are four conflict stories scattered over four different chapters of the Matthean narrative (Matt 13, 15, 16, and 19). Each conflict involves a rather distinct issue of contention; however, they are collected together in this chapter for the purpose of structuring this study proportionally to its pages and not due to their literary affinity. It is curious how Matthew spreads out these conflicts in comparison to his earlier concentration of conflict stories. This discussion will seek to assess Matthew's narrative purpose in such an arrangement and continues seeking answers for these questions: How do these conflict stories contribute to the plot development of the author? What are the author's purposes of dispersing these conflict stories within a large span of narrative complexes in Matthew 13–20? And how does the author achieve these purposes? In this chapter, I will first analyze each conflict story as well as its relationship with its narrative context. At the end of the chapter, a synthesis will be provided to answer the above questions.

4.1 Analysis of Individual Pericopea: Matthew 13:53–58; 15:1–9; 16:1–4; 19:1–9

4.1.1 Matthew 13:53–58

4.1.1.1 Matthew 13:53–54a: The Setting of the Story

Matthew 13:53 is a transitional summary. It ends the parable discourse and shifts the narrative from discourse (13:1–52) to a new narrative context, both in terms of geographical location and the form of the narrative. In Matthew's gospel, here in 13:54a is the last mention of Jesus's teaching in συναγωγῇ αὐτῶν.[1] Though the word "Nazareth" is not mentioned, it is very likely that πατρίδα αὐτοῦ refers to Nazareth.[2]

4.1.1.2 Matthew 13:54b–58: The Conflict Scene Proper

Differing slightly from Luz who suggests that the entire structure of the conflict story is chiastic,[3] this study considers that the text narrating the opponents' words and deeds is more clearly structured as a chiasm. To this extent, the conflict scene can be seen as composed of two parts: the opponents' challenge focusing on Jesus's origin which takes up more narration (13:55–56a), and Jesus's reaction in his words (13:57c) and deeds (13:58).

In comparison with other conflict stories, this conflict appears to have two peculiar characteristics: (1) in this story, Jesus's opponents as a character group[4] now include the people from his hometown. However, in the Matthean narrative they do not appear anywhere else except in this story;[5] (2) this story does not seem to have an obvious coherent relationship with its narrative context; that is, it appears to be an isolated event between the parable discourse and the death of John the Baptist. Therefore, the question remains: what is the author's intention to arrange such a conflict story within his narrative?

This study considers that the transition section in Matthew's narrative begins with Matthew 11 and continues through to Matthew 13. In this section, Jesus's mission shifts from being directed primarily toward the Jews to new foci.[6] Appearing at the end of Matthew 13, the current conflict story

---

1. France, *Matthew*, 547.

2. Cf. Matt 2:23; 4:13. See, for example, Richard Sturch, "The '*PATRIE*' of Jesus," *JTS* 1 (April 1977): 94–96. Against this view, for example, see Frans van Segbroeck who believes that πατρίδα refers to Galilee as a whole, "Jèsus rejeté par sa patrie (Mt 13:5–58)," *Bib* 49 (1968): 171–179.

3. Luz, *Matthew 8–20*, 301, 303; cf. Davies and Allison, *Matthew 8–18*, 451.

4. In fact, as a group the opponents of Jesus function as a single character, see Powell, *What Is Narrative Criticism?*, 51.

5. Repschinski, *Controversy*, 146.

6. In Matthew's narrative, Jesus's early ministry seems to be focusing on the people of Israel, as revealed by Jesus's own teaching (10:5–6). But the mission focus begins to change from Matt 11 onward and the whole of Matt 11–13 can be seen as a transition section. This is because (1) after Jesus's discourse to the disciples, Matthew narrates "a juxtaposition of

therefore plays a key role. The following analysis will demonstrate that the conflict story not only concludes the transition section, but also commences another narrative section where Jesus focuses on discipling his followers and his mission to the Gentiles. Three main reasons support such an understanding. Meanwhile, the above two peculiarities of the story will be dealt with in the process of the analysis.

First of all, the rejection from the people of Jesus's hometown seems to complete the puzzle of the Jewish rejection of Jesus. It is likely that the author intends to align the characterization of Jesus's townsmen to that of the religious leaders because this story has many points of contact with the last conflict in 12:38–45 (the sign of Jonah). As a result, they become part of the negative characters portrayed in Matthew. The similarity between this conflict and the conflict in 12:38–45 is evident: both stories employ *irony* as a primary literary device.[7] In the eyes of the audience, just like the religious leaders who are blind to recognize Jesus's miracle as a messianic sign (12:22–23), the people from Jesus's hometown are also blind and fail to recognize him as more than a man who grew up in their midst (13:55–57a), even though they feel utterly astonished at the reality of Jesus's wisdom and power (13:54b, c). There are other parallels which contribute to the similarity between two stories. For example, the words "wisdom" and "prophet" are mentioned in

---

opposites; the Galilean cities upon whom Jesus pronounced the judgment of destruction and the 'simple people' to whom the Father will reveal the things he withholds from the mighty," Luz, *Theology of Matthew*, 81; (2) stories and parables in Matt 12 and 13 reflect such opposites; (3) especially toward the end of Matt 13, Jesus begins to withdraw into his circle of disciples (13:36) and eventually ceases doing miracles in his home town (13:58). From Matt 13 onward in Matthew's narrative, not only Jesus's instructions are increasingly given to the disciples (Luz, *Theology of Matthew*, 85), but more gentile believers are introduced.

7. Here irony is understood more as a "dramatic irony," which according to Muecke, refers to an observer's knowledge of what the "victim" is yet to find out; *The Compass of Irony* (London: Methuen & Co., 1969), 99–115. More specifically, the irony shown by these two conflict stories fits more of the setting of a theatre, where, in Muecke's words, "the audience already knows the outcome or the true state of affairs . . . the irony is a true spectacle of blindness." *Irony and the Ironic*, The Critical Idiom 13, 2nd ed. of Irony (New York: Methuen & Co., 1982), 54. Repschinski's redactional analysis of this story also detects the irony, *Controversy*, 154. See also the Oxford English Dictionary, "A condition of affairs or events of a character opposite to what was, or might naturally be, expected; a contradictory outcome of events as if in mockery of the promise and fitness of things," 12 vols. and supplement (London: OUP, 1933), 5:484. Eleanor Hutchens in her article defines irony as "the sport of bringing about a conclusion by indicating its opposite"; "The Identification of Irony," *English Literary History* 27, no. 4 (Dec. 1960): 358.

both stories (12:42/13:54; 12:39/13:57).[8] The challenge recorded in the current conflict is against the origin of Jesus's miraculous powers,[9] which echoes the challenges in the last two conflicts (12:22–37, 38–45).

Furthermore, the character group of Jesus's townsmen is portrayed in a generalized fashion to represent a wider Jewish opposition to Jesus. This characterization is quite puzzling given the fact that they never appear before or after this conflict story in the whole Matthean narrative. Compared to the Markan account (Mark 6:1), it seems that Matthew omits "the disciples" from this story in order to underline the role of the people from Jesus's hometown. One would wonder what the author's purpose is in introducing this character group. To be sure, they are already portrayed in a light of "otherness" (if not all negative) in the setting of the story by the Matthean redaction of ἐδίδασκεν αὐτοὺς ἐν τῇ συναγωγῇ αὐτῶν (13:54a).[10] More importantly, the identity of Jesus's addressees becomes more generalized in this Matthean version. The author omits Mark's qualifying phrase πολλοὶ ἀκούοντες (Mark 6:2) and simply uses αὐτοὺς (13:54). While it is possible that such generalization[11] is due to Matthew's intention to focus on the teaching of Jesus,[12] it is equally possible that this character group is deliberately generalized to lead the audience to fuse this character group with all other opponents who are blind within the context of 13:53–58. That is, they reject Jesus upon hearing or seeing his teaching or miracles. These blind opponents include, for example, the Pharisees in 12:22–37, the scribes and Pharisees in 12:38–45; and the crowds in 13:1–52.[13]

---

8. Especially because the word "prophet" is inserted by Matthew in 12:39, see Davies and Allison, *Matthew 8–18*, 355.

9. The reason that the scribes and the Pharisees ask Jesus to show a sign is because they do not believe the authority or identity of Jesus has anything to do with God, rather than genuinely request to see an authentication of a prophet; Luz, *Matthew 8–10*, 216, pace Davies and Allison, *Matthew 8–18*, 354. The current story tells the reader that Jesus's townsmen also "recognise the force of Jesus' wisdom and mighty works, but not their origin"; Cousland, *Crowds in Matthew*, 127.

10. Regardless of different explanation on συναγωγῇ αὐτῶν, most scholars agree that the term is used by Matthew to distinguish them from Jesus's group in the story. See detailed discussion on "their synagogue" in Davies and Allison, *Matthew 1–7*, 413–414.

11. Matthew does sometimes generalize the addressees of the Jesus saying in his episodal comments; Byrskog, *Jesus the Only Teacher*, 373.

12. Repschinski, *Controversy*, 147–148.

13. While it is debatable whether the crowds in Matthew are portrayed overall negatively, in Matt 13 they are clearly a negative character group; see more discussion in Cousland, *Crowds in Matthew*, 241–262.

The generalization of Jesus's reply also indicates Matthew's depiction of a wider Jewish opposition within the transition section of Matthew 11–13. The saying (13:57), according to many scholars, resembles popular proverbial sayings paralleling with contemporary non-Christian tradition.[14] Therefore, the abbreviated version in 13:57 is more like a general comment than a refutation of the opponents in this specific situation.[15] Such a generalization, in Bultmann's words, expresses "... a truth in some metaphorical sort of situation which, by reason of wider reference, gives the apophthegms their symbolic character."[16] It is no surprise then for Bultmann to consider the story as one of the "ideal" biographical apophthegms. Whether in a story the symbolic character necessitates an absence of historicity is certainly debatable,[17] nonetheless, Bultmann is probably right in discerning the representative aspect of this conflict story. That is, the generality produces an interesting literary effect on the audience. It enables this conflict story to go beyond the immediate narrative flow and to be associated with other rejections. In the mind of the audience then, Jesus's townsmen are easily identified in their outlook with the scribes and the Pharisees, thus becoming "many other Jews" who oppose Jesus. This factor provides an additional evidence for a wider Jewish opposition to Jesus.

Second, seen in the light of its context, this conflict stirs up the memory of the audience regarding the rejection of prophets in the Jewish tradition. There are many prophets rejected by disobedient Israel in the Hebrew Scripture. In this conflict story, the author includes a specific evocation of the motif of a rejected prophet in characterizing Jesus, which should not be strange to a Jewish ear. The most obvious one coming to the reader's mind is probably Jeremiah because he was also a prophet rejected by the people from his hometown (cf. Jer 1:1; 11:21; 12:6). Such a saying even leads some to consider it as an evidence for the prophetic self-consciousness of Jesus.[18]

---

14. Davies and Allison, *Matthew 8–18*, 459–460; Repschinski, *Controversy*, 151, footnote 22; Luz, *Matthew 8–20*, 302–303, also footnote 16.

15. Different reasons were offered to this redaction; see Davies and Allison, *Matthew 8–18*, 459; Repschinski, *Controversy*, 150.

16. Bultmann, *History*, 56–57.

17. Bultmann may press the symbolism too far to attribute any historicity to these biographical apophthegms; *History*, 57.

18. For example, McNeil writes that "the Lord accepts his popular reputation as a prophet"; *St. Matthew*, 207. Also, Davies and Allison, *Matthew 8–18*, 460; some other Matthean passages

However, the self-consciousness of Jesus as a "prophet" is not the same as the prophet in the Hebrew Bible because there are ample passages in the first gospel particularly pointing to the inadequacy of such a perception.[19] In fact, the prophetic self-consciousness of Jesus is consistently qualified by a rejection even to death. For example, the reader frequently encounters the gloomy reality of prophets being rejected or killed either in Jesus's sayings or parables.[20] If Jesus is any way aligned with Israel's prophets, it is more likely, as Fuller rightly claims, that such a prophetic role is ". . . in so far as it involved rejection and martyrdom."[21] In the development of the narrative, this conflict story is the only place where the motif of "a rejected prophet" is plainly merged with the person of Jesus (13:57);[22] however, the author places the story of Herod killing John the Baptist immediately after the story, in case the reader fails to see his intention. Therefore, even though there appears to be an interruption to the narrative time causing disjunction between 13:53–58 and 14:1–12, what connects the two pericopae is the image of a rejected prophet, with the death of John the Baptist foreshadowing the fate of Jesus.[23]

Third, the reason that this conflict concludes the transition section of Matthew can be derived from its context. The transition shifts the mission of Jesus from primarily toward the Jews to the Gentiles (Matt 11–13). Such a shift is both illustrated by two key themes of the parable discourse and reflected

---

may also support such a view, e.g. 23:26–27.

19. The most significant passage is probably 16:14–17, where Peter discredits calling Jesus a prophet and instead identifies him as the Christ, Son of God. Others include the crowds' inadequate understanding of Jesus in 21:11, 46. Even John the Baptist is considered as more than a prophet, 11:9; Repschinski, *Controversy*, 151; Luz, *Matthew 8–20*, 302.

20. Passages regarding prophets being rejected or killed: Matt 5:11–12; 11:18–19; 12:14; 13:57; 16:21; 17:12, 22–23; 20:17–19; 21:35–36; 22:6; 23:29–32, 34–37.

21. Fuller, *Foundation*, 127. Michael Knowles similarly points out that in 16:13–14, John the Baptist, Elijah and Jeremiah are all suffering prototypes of Jesus, representing this approximation of Jesus's identity. Knowles, *Jeremiah in Matthew's Gospel: The Rejected-Prophet Motif in Matthean Redaction* (Sheffield: Sheffield Academic Press, 1993), 153.

22. Previously the author has included only a few passages implicitly alluding to Jesus's own persecution or death, some of which in the context of the persecution of prophets (5:11; 11:19; 12:14).

23. This is another example of parallels between Jesus and John the Baptist, both of whom are rejected by Israel and martyred as end-time prophets; Meier, "John the Baptist in Matthew's Gospel," *JBL* 99 (1980): 399ff. Similarly, Edwards observes that the link between the two pericopae is the death of John the Baptist and Herod's being "manipulated by the opinions of others"; Edwards, *Matthew's Story*, 52. In Matthew, this point is further supported by the comparison between John and Jesus in the Transfiguration narrative, 17:12–13.

by the conflict. The conflict between Jesus and people from his hometown immediately follows the parable discourse, connected by a transitional summary signified by these actions: ... ὅτε ἐτέλεσεν ... τὰς παραβολὰς ταύτας, μετῆρεν ἐκεῖθεν καὶ ἐλθὼν εἰς τὴν πατρίδα αὐτοῦ ... (13:53–54a). But the puzzling question is: how is the conflict between Jesus and the people of his hometown related to the teaching on kingdom parables? The answer can be found from the overarching theological dimension of the parable discourse,[24] which has been largely neglected. This is probably due to the fact that most of the scholarly attention has been upon either the interpretation or synoptic tradition of individual parables.[25] Although much can be said in this regard, for the purpose of relating to the conflict story, it will suffice to underline two key themes in the parable discourse of Matthew 13.

In Matthew 13, the first one among the seven parables[26] – the parable of the sower – reveals the theme of obduracy.[27] According to Matthew, this first theme is the reason for Jesus's speaking in parables.[28] The remaining six parables are composed of two sets of twin parables enclosed by the parable of weeds and the net, both of which convey the inevitable eschatological consequence – the great division between the sons of the kingdom[29] and

---

24. Hill, in passing, acknowledges that Matt 13 does form a distinct block in Matthew's mind; *Matthew*, 241.

25. Among many, for example, see Klyne Snodgrass, *Stories with Intent: A Comprehensive Guide to the Parables of Jesus* (Grand Rapids: Eerdmans, 2008); Hultgren, *The Parables of Jesus: A Commentary* (Grand Rapids: Eerdmans, 2000); Jeremias, *Parables of Jesus*; Ivor Harond Jones, *The Matthean Parables: A Literary and Historical Commentary*, NovTSup 80 (Leiden: Brill, 1995); Dodd, *Parables*; Dan O. Via, Jr., "Matthew on the Understandability of the Parables," *JBL* 84 (1965): 430–432; M. Hunter Archibald, *Interpreting the Parables* (London: SCM Press, 1960); Eta Linnemann, *The Parables of Jesus: Introduction and Exposition* (London: SPCK, 1966); Via, *The Parables: Their Literary and Existential Dimension* (Philadelphia: Fortress, 1967). A slight exception is perhaps Kingsbury's study, *The Parables of Jesus in Matthew 13: A Study in Redaction-Criticism* (London: SPCK, 1969). However, he still focuses on the Matthean redactional feature of parables in comparison with Mark or Q.

26. Most scholars exclude 13:51-52 as a parable, though Mark Bailey includes it as a parable of the householder; "The Parable of the Sower and the Soils," *BiblSac* 155 (1998): 173.

27. See detailed discussion of the theme of obduracy in Craig Evans, *To See and Not Perceive: Isaiah 6:9-10 in Early Jewish and Christian Interpretation*, JSNT S 64 (Sheffield: Sheffield Academic Press, 1989), 108–113. He particularly points out that Matthew views the opponents of Jesus as obdurate, "especially the Pharisees (and so deserving of parabolic teaching only), but the responsibility of this obduracy lies wholly with them"; *To See and Not Perceive*, 113.

28. Davies and Allison, *Matthew 8–18*, 460; also, Evans, *To See and Not Perceive*, 110.

29. Refers to the righteous, defined by their relationship to the Son of Man, 13:37.

the sons of the evil one.[30] The following table illustrates the six parables in relation to each other:

Kingdom Parables	Key Issue of the Parables
Weeds	Sowing and division in the harvest time
Mustard seeds	Nature of the kingdom[31]
Leaven	
Weeds (interpretation)	Sowing and division in the harvest
Hidden treasure	Value of the kingdom
Pearls	
Net	Division in the harvest time

As can be seen from the above table, the six parables of the kingdom reveal the second significant theme in Matthew 13. That is, there will be a great division between two types of people in the end times,[32] depending on their relationship with the Son of Man (cf. 12:30, 46–50).

Interestingly, both themes of obduracy and the great division are reflected in the current conflict. Three factors support such an interpretation. First, the rejection by the townsmen of Jesus's authority comes from their intimate knowledge of his blood relationship, that is, the humanity of Jesus.[33] This is shown by the chiastic structure in Matthew's narration. However, such an intimate knowledge of Jesus inadvertently prevents them from changing their views and thus makes their obduracy a continuing condition. The comment of Jesus comparing himself to a rejected prophet further manifests their obduracy (13:57). Second, the great division at the end times is now

---

30. Refers to the wicked, defined by their relationship to the devil, 13:39.

31. Garland correctly encapsulates the common theme between the parable of mustard seeds and the leaven: the inglorious nature of the advent of the kingdom; see his discussion in *Reading Matthew*, 150–151.

32. Cf. Bailey, "The Parable of the Sower and the Soils," 173.

33. Though focusing on the Markan pericope, Erich Grässer's comment that the Nazarenes' familiarity with Jesus's blood relationship becomes an argument against his divine authority can be applied to the Matthean account as well. Grässer, "Jesus in Nazareth (Mark 6:1–6a)," *NTS* 16 (1970): 20.

anticipated by the fact that the rejection of Jesus has secured their fate of being rejected by him (13:58). Matthew's redaction of Mark here highlights the initiative of Jesus to reject.[34] Third, the proverbial saying (13:57) echoes Jesus's saying regarding his family boundary, which immediately precedes the parable discourse (12:49–50).[35] There, similarly, depending on one's relationship to Jesus, the inclusion into or exclusion from his family is made plain. Furthermore, the objective attitude καὶ ἐσκανδαλίζοντο ἐν αὐτῷ (13:57a) can be considered as a reverse echo to καὶ μακάριός ἐστιν ὃς ἐὰν μὴ σκανδαλισθῇ ἐν ἐμοί (11:6). The saying in 11:6 commends those who accept Jesus's messianic identity when they see the reality of his teaching and miracles. In contrast, the people of Jesus's hometown see the same events (13:54c) yet their rejection has resulted in losing that blessing.

4.1.1.3 Summary of 13:53–58 in Its Immediate Narrative and Rhetorical Context (Matt 11–13)

The conflict story of 13:53–58 contributes to the Matthean plot development in such a way that it both ends the transition section of Matthew 11–13 and begins a new narrative section. The transition section in the Matthean narrative prepares the reader for the shift in Jesus's mission from primarily toward the Jews to the Gentiles. The new narrative will focus on Jesus's mission to the Gentiles[36] and his circle of disciples (Matt 14–20).[37] The analysis of the conflict story leads to four specific observations identifying the authorial intent of the transition section: (1) Following the negative portrayal of Jewish religious leaders (Matt 9, 12), and the crowds (Matt 13),[38] now the people of Jesus's hometown are also characterized unfavorably and in all probability are aligned with the scribes and the Pharisees. Such a negative characterization

---

34. Matthew changes Markan's οὐκ ἐδύνατο ἐκεῖ ποιῆσαι οὐδεμίαν δύναμιν to Jesus taking the initiative to reject (οὐκ ἐποίησεν).

35. Edwards, *Matthew's Story*, 51.

36. See passages such as 15:16–20, 21–28, 29–39; 16:24–25; 17:20–21; 18:10–14, 15–17; 19:13–15; 20:1–16.

37. See passages such as 15:1–20; 16:5–28; 17:9–13, 19–20, 22–23; 17:25–18:35; 19:10–12; 19:23–20:16; 20:20–28.

38. Especially their portrayal in Matt 13 is negative and is clearly distinguished from the disciples. Even though the crowds are not characterized so negatively in the previous conflict stories, because Matt 13:1–52 is the immediate context of the current story, it leaves a more direct literary impact in the reader's mind.

of all of them together implies a message that Jesus meets with rejection "by all segments of Israel" which may be extended to "this evil and adulterous generation" (cf. 12:39).[39] (2) It appears that Matthew intentionally characterizes Jesus's townsmen in a generalized fashion to represent wider Jewish opposition to Jesus. The author's ambiguous mention of them and the general nature of Jesus's response to the rejection support this claim. (3) Through the conflict story and its immediate context (14:1–12), the author includes the motif of rejected prophets, which not only draws upon the disobedience of Israel in the Hebrew Bible, but further anticipates the ominous fate of Jesus. (4) The conflict story reflects two key themes of the parable discourse: obduracy and great division at the end times. These themes link the story closely with its preceding context. The rejected prophet motif also enables the story to be connected smoothly with the following story of the death of John the Baptist.

It is worth noting that while it is true that Jesus's townsmen may not represent the whole of Israel,[40] the author does depict a generalized identification of the opponents. In addition, the image of rejected prophet is evoked and the story is placed within a continuation of the contrast between understanding and blindness,[41] believing and faithlessness. These literary arrangements compel the reader to anticipate and prepare for a wider scale of Jewish rejection of Jesus,[42] just as Israel did to their prophets of the old. Hagner may have gone too far by arguing for the kingdom shift in this conflict story;[43] however it is not going too far to speculate that Matthew's intention is to complete the justification of the parting of ways from both sides of the fence.[44]

---

39. Bauer, *Structure of Matthew*, 93.

40. Repschinski, *Controversy*, 152, footnote 24.

41. Gundry, *Matthew*, 282.

42. Similarly Luz writes, "Thus the Nazarenes anticipate what will later prove true of the entire people – their no to Jesus, their unbelief. Our story thus has the character of a signal for what is to come"; *Matthew 8–20*, 303.

43. Hagner, *Matthew 1–13*, 406.

44. Cousland also notices the rejection on Jesus's part through his withdrawal from the crowds; *Crowds in Matthew*, 107.

4.1.2 Matthew 15:1–9

4.1.2.1 Matthew 15:1: The Setting of the Story

In the Matthean narrative, this story has the first reference to Jesus's opponents coming from Jerusalem. Scholars have offered much speculation on the significance of this Jerusalem origin.[45] However, from the angle of a literary analysis of the text, the significance should not be over emphasized. It simply points to a possible escalation of the conflict, as Jesus's opponents are now associated with the Jewish authorities in Jerusalem.

4.1.2.2 Matthew 15:2–9: The Conflict Scene Proper

From the outset, it needs to be noted that the Matthean account of 15:1–20 forms a coherent literary unit.[46] Although there are three separate scenes, each of which consists of a dialogue between Jesus and a different party (15:1–9, 10–11, 12–20), three factors indicate their literary unity: (1) the phrases οὐ γὰρ νίπτονται τὰς χεῖρας ... ἐσθίωσιν in 15:2 and ἀνίπτοις χερσὶν φαγεῖν in 15:20 bracket all three scenes together.[47] (2) The key issue of food-related defilement in verse 11 and the Pharisees' offence in verse 12 ties both scenes (vv. 10–11, 12–20) back to the conflict story (vv. 1–9).[48] There the Pharisees (and the scribes) are the opponents raising the issue of ritual defilement against Jesus. (3) According to Daube, the overall structure of 15:1–20 resembles a typical Rabbinic form – public retort and private explanation.[49]

Therefore, even though this analysis will focus on the conflict scene (15:1–9), the coherent literary structure of 15:1–20 compels the following discussion to take into account 15:10–20 when it helps to illuminate the functions of the conflict story. Within the literary unit of 15:1–20, this conflict story can be seen as a prelude to Jesus's teaching on true defilement, as verse 11 is Jesus's

---

45. For example, Luz speculates it may signify the coming of Jesus's passion; *Matthew 8–20*, 329; though commenting on the Markan parallel (Mark 7:1) of Matt 15:1, Stephen Westerholm believes that it shows "the zeal of Pharisaic leaders in attempting to spread their influence and ideas over all Israel"; *Scribal Authority* (Lund: CWK Gleerup, 1978), 72. Similarly, Hagner thinks they are a delegation from Jerusalem for inquiring into Jesus's legal views; *Matthew 14–28*, 430; also Hill, *Matthew*, 250.

46. Commentators agree on the unity of 15:1–20, although they view the "knot" holding the three scenes together slightly differently; among others see Davies and Allison, *Matthew 8–18*, 516; Luz, *Matthew 8–20*, 325; Gnilka, *Matthäus II*, 18.

47. Luz, *Matthew 8–20*, 325.

48. Gnilka, *Matthäus II*, 18.

49. See detailed discussions of the examples in Daube, *Rabbinic Judaism*, 141–142.

opinion to the public in relation to the challenge of the opponents,[50] and the section of verses 16–20 is a fuller explanation of verse 11 to the disciples.[51]

At the rhetorical level, Matthew closely follows Mark's narrative order. In both gospels, this conflict story follows the miracle of Jesus's walking on the water and precedes Jesus's healing of the daughter of the Canaanite/Syrophenician woman. Because the conflict addresses a rather isolated legal issue concerning a ritual defilement caused by eating with unwashed hands, on the surface it appears to be disjointed within its narrative context.[52] However, close investigation of the story in its context as well as Matthean redactional features demonstrate that the story contributes to the Matthean plot in two ways.

First, Matthew uses this conflict to provide an introduction for preparing the reader for the exclusion of Jewish leaders from God's kingdom, a point less readily discernible in Mark 7:1–23. This can be seen from textual evidences in the conflict scene proper. Matthew extensively redacts the Markan account (Mark 7:1–13) which results in intensifying the opposition between the Jewish leaders and Jesus.[53] This feature is typical of Matthew and consistent with other Matthean redactional characteristics in previous conflict stories such as 9:9–13; 12:1–8, 9–14, 22–37. What is distinctive, however, is that Matthew also ties the subsequent sections – Jesus's instructions to the crowd and disciples (15:10–11, 12–20) – so closely with the conflict that the latter two scenes cannot stand alone but arise from the conflict narrative. As a result, the conflict becomes a trigger for Jesus's prophecy on the Pharisees' doomed fate of being "uprooted and discarded."[54] For example, Matthew connects the

---

50. Daube, 142.

51. Cope, *Scribe Trained for the Kingdom*, 61; similarly, Davies and Allison believe that vv. 12–20 is in fact a commentary on vv. 10–11; *Matthew 8–18*, 516.

52. As Cope suggests, this story has no logical connection to either the preceding or to the following text; *Scribe Trained for the Kingdom*, 53.

53. In 15:1–9, Matthew clarifies the contrast between the understanding disciples (and the crowds) on the one hand, and the opposing Jewish leaders on the other. Matthew heightens the contrasting nature of the opposition to Jesus by restricting it entirely to the Pharisees and eliminating the Markan theme of the lack of understanding among the disciples. For more detailed discussion on the Matthean redactional feature, see Repschinski, *Controversy*, 155–156, 307.

54. Although in Jer 45:4 and Isa 5:4–7 it is not specifically the leaders of Israel but the entire nation of Israel that is being uprooted; see the detailed survey on the theme of God's planting and uprooting Israel in Blaine Charette, *The Theme of Recompense in Matthew's Gospel* (Sheffield: Sheffield Academic Press, 1992), 44–48. Knowles particularly points out that 15:13

dialogue between Jesus and the disciples back to the conflict scene (15:12) and inserts Jesus's polemic comment against the Pharisees (15:13–14). On such an occasion (15:12–14), knowing the Pharisees are being offended, Jesus neither offers any defence, nor does he extend the attack on their tradition to respond to the challenge concerning the disciples' violation, as one would expect. Instead, Jesus evokes the image of God's eradicating plants (φυτεία[55]) and calls the Pharisees "blind guides." Interestingly, in the Hebrew Bible it is Israel that is commonly referred to as God's plant which symbolizes its privileged status of being elected by God for salvation.[56] However, in 15:13 Matthew uses the image of God's plant in quite a reversed manner (πᾶσα φυτεία ἣν οὐκ ἐφύτευσεν ὁ πατήρ μου ὁ οὐράνιος ἐκριζωθήσεται). It especially resembles the images depicted in Jeremiah 45:4[57] and Isaiah 5:4–7.[58] In the words of Jesus, now God destroys the plants – the Pharisees – because they no longer belong to God.

That this conflict provides an introduction preparing the reader for the exclusion of Jewish leaders from God's kingdom can also be seen from multiple textual echoes between Matthew 12–13 and 15:1–20. They are listed in sequence to suggest their cumulative effect:[59]

a. The blindness (of the Pharisees), a major character trait for the leaders,[60] echoes a key theme of "not seeing" in Matthew 13 (cf. 13:13–15). Among different groups of Jewish religious leadership in the first century Palestine, Pharisees have a special concern for

---

does not actually identify Pharisees as φυτεία, but the focus is on the consequence of their being uprooted; *Jeremiah in Matthew*, 190.

55. The word itself is a New Testament *hapax legomenon*; Davies and Allison, *Matthew 8–18*, 532; it is also found in Ezek 17:7 in the Hebrew Bible, cf. *Pss. Sol.* 14:4. Its literal meaning is used in Mic 1:6; for more discussion see Knowles, *Jeremiah in Matthew*, 190.

56. The image of φυτεία is used as a self-designation for Israel, see Isa 5:1–2; 17:10; 60:21; 61:3; Ezek 17:7; Pss 1:3; 7:34; 21:24; it is also used for particular groups identifying themselves as true Israel, e.g. *Ps. Sol.* 14:3–4; Jub 1:16; 1QS 8:5; 11:8; 1QH 6:15–17; 7:10, 18–19; 8:4–27; 10:31; CD 1:7; 1 *Enoch* 10:16; Gnilka, *Matthäus II*, 25. See other Second Temple texts e.g. *Wis* 4:3–5.

57. Luz, *Matthew 8–20*, 333, footnote 62.

58. Gundry, *Matthew*, 307.

59. Textual echoes here include primarily verbal repetition, analogous images/pictures and themes. See detailed discussion on the significance and functions of verbal repetition particularly in Anderson, *Matthew's Narrative Web*, 43–45.

60. This epithet of "blind guide" is repeated many times in Matthew (cf. 15:14; 23:16, 17, 19, 24, 26) therefore it is an important characterization of the Jewish leaders, especially the Pharisees.

ritual observances in order to "guard" the Torah. The Matthean text suggests the contrary: Jesus calls them τυφλοί εἰσιν ὁδηγοὶ [τυφλῶν] (15:14), because their insistence on ritual observances "conceal(s) the actual will of God" and makes them in effect far away from God (15:3, 8).[61] In both Matthew 13 and 15:14, the blindness is caused by the hardened hearts which prevent truthful perception (cf. 13:15 and 15:8).[62]

b. The division of "inclusion and exclusion" in the kingdom of God is another key theme of the parable discourse in Matthew 13. There, people will be divided into two groups – those who will be included in the kingdom, and those excluded (parables of the weeds and the net). The parable of the weeds, for example, twice has the image of plants (weeds) being uprooted and destroyed (13:29–30, 40–42), symbolizing those who are excluded from the kingdom. Together with the destruction of plants and trees, such images are consistently applied to the Jewish leaders in Matthew (cf. 3:10; 7:19). The image of "uprooting a plant" (15:13) clearly echoes this theme and should remind the reader of the parables in Matthew 13.[63]

c. The word τὴν παραβολὴν is specifically used in the disciples' question (15:15). Even though Matthew follows Mark here (cf. Mark 7:17), it is highlighted by the form of a question and likely reminds the reader of many parables in its proximate context of Matthew 13.

d. There is a period of tolerance expressed by the phrase ἄφετε αὐτούς (15:14). This is similar to the period indicated in the parables of the weeds and the net (13:24–30, 36–43, 47–50).[64]

---

61. Held, "Matthew's Understanding of the Law," 88.

62. Cf. Wesley Olmstead who also notices this link; *Matthew's Trilogy of Parables: the Nation, the Nations and the Reader in Matthew 21:28–22:14* (Cambridge: Cambridge University Press, 2003), 55.

63. Many commentators see this connection. For example, Cope states that "the use of the metaphor of intruding plants is exactly the same as the use in the interpretation of the parable of the Tares"; *Scribe Trained for Kingdom*, 58; also Olmstead sees the leaders as the planting work of the enemy, *Matthew's Trilogy*, 66.

64. Harington, *Matthew*, 230.

e. Matthew redacts Mark's vice list so that sins of the tongue and thoughts are at the centre of attention (15:19).[65] It reminds the reader of the condemnation of Jesus in a previous conflict story where on the judgment day the Pharisees will give account for the evil words spoken out of their evil hearts (12:34-37).

The second function of this story is that the author intends to provide an occasion to pave the way for Gentile inclusion in Jesus's mission.[66] While in Jewish tradition, defilement is one of the key criteria for excluding Gentiles from becoming accepted in God's eyes, this story introduces an occasion where one of the cardinal tenets of the oral Torah – the boundary of defilement – is invalidated by Jesus's teaching on true defilement. Within the conflict scene, the citation of Isaiah 29:13 leads the repudiation of both the Pharisaic authority and their tradition to a climax. Instead of placing the citation in the beginning of Jesus's response as in Mark (Mark 7:6-7), Matthew moves it to the end of the conflict scene, creating an emphatic effect for the conflict.[67] The quotation text follows the Septuagint text[68] which omits the phrase "[this people] draw near with their mouth (יַעַן כִּי נִגַּשׁ הָעָם הַזֶּה בְּפִיו)" in the MT.[69] Consequently, the concept τίμα in the quotation is highlighted in correspondence with the two contrasting ways of τίμα in 15:4 and 15:6:[70]

---

65. Luz, *Matthew 8-18*, 334.

66. This point is already present in the Markan account. Because the overarching reason for this claim is that, particularly regarding Mark 6:14-8:21, Matthew retains most of the material and the ordering of the Markan text (from Matt 14 onward). Moreover, it is generally assumed that Matthew at large embraces Mark's theological ideas by reproducing 80 percent of Mark's gospel in his own account; see Luz, *Studies in Matthew* (Grand Rapids: Eerdmans, 2005), 24, 28, 35; *Matthew 1-7*, 50; Hagner, *Matthew 1-13*, lx; Beaton, "How Matthew Writes," in *The Written Gospel*, eds. Markus Bockmuehl and Donald Hagner (Cambridge: Cambridge University Press, 2005), 120; Meier, "Antioch," in *Antioch and Rome: New Testament Cradles of Catholic Christianity*, Raymond E. Brown and John P. Meier (London: G. Chapman, 1983), 51-52. However, for opposing arguments, among others see Stanton, "The Fourfold Gospel," *NTS* 43 (1997): 341; Bauckham, "For Whom Were the Gospels Written?," 13; Sim, "Matthew's Use of Mark: Did Matthew Intend to Supplement or to Replace His Primary Source?," *NTS* 57 (2011): 178-188.

67. Gundry, *Matthew*, 305.

68. Not only Matthew, but Mark 7:6, 1 Clem 15:2 and Justin Martyrs's *Dial.* 78:11 all follow the LXX form. Cope suggests that the shorter form may be widely known to the early Christians; *Scribe Trained for Kingdom*, 55. Even so, the literary impact of the omission remains the same, that is, the concept of τίμα receives more emphasis.

69. Gundry, *Matthew*, 305.

70. Gundry, 305.

God's command to honour one's parents in contrast to their refusal to do so. The quotation points to the contradiction between the Jewish leaders' outward appearance of worshipping God and their hardened hearts against God. Through applying Isaiah's criticism of Israel to the Pharisees and scribes,[71] Jesus also invalidates the authority from which "their tradition" (τὴν παράδοσιν ὑμῶν) of defilement is derived.[72]

Once the authority of Jewish leaders and their boundary demarcating purity from defilement is renounced, Jesus redraws the boundary – he elaborates on the teaching of true defilement (15:11) by offering a vice list.[73] To this extent, Matthew generally follows Mark's narration.[74] But Matthew notably redacts Mark to make the list shorter and arranges the items in a different order with omissions and additions. The Matthean list of vices is shaped into a more biblical fashion, resembling the sixth to ninth commandments (15:19).[75] In this way Matthew places Jesus's principle of defilement within the framework of the Decalogue, but at the same time redraws the boundary appealing to the divine intention behind the law.[76] Its effect is radical. The Matthean Jesus essentially expresses what God intends for the inner heart, rather than outward/ritual formalities determining true purity or defilement.

Moreover, the conflict story is situated within a context which provides examples which illustrate that Gentiles are included in Jesus's mission. Immediately following Jesus's teaching on new boundaries of defilement (15:1–20) is the healing of the daughter of the Canaanite woman (15:21–28). One should wonder how the two events are related to each other. It is likely that Jesus's acceptance of the Canaanite woman is an application of what he

---

71. Within the context of Isa 29, 29:13 fits neatly into one of the underlined themes of rejection and obduracy on Israel's part. The citation shows that it is not by adhering to the halakhic tradition that the leaders have an inaccurate understanding of God's law, but that in their heart the leaders reject God already, which is, in Jesus's mind, comparable to Israel's rejection of God during Isaiah's time.

72. Saunders, "No One Dared," 286.

73. The significance is the same as in Mark that the parable in 15:11 is the "kernel" of the entire section of 15:1–20; cf. Charles E. Carlston, "Things That Defile (Mark 7:14) and the Law in Matthew and Mark," *NTS* 15 (1968): 94.

74. Though Mark lacks a specific attack on the Pharisees as in Matt 15:12–14.

75. Davies and Allison, *Matthew 8–20*, 535–536; Carlston, "Things That Defile," 82, 90, though he mistakenly says the list consists of the fifth to the eighth commandments.

76. Luz similarly states, "... the Decalogue is for him [Matthew] the basic expression of God's will. Thus, in our text he is not concerned with the abolition of the law but with its fulfillment and at the same time with its new evaluation"; *Matthew 8–20*, 334.

teaches in 15:10–20, "purity is *primarily* a purity of heart."⁷⁷ The Pharisaic boundary of purity/defilement entails "separation from all that was unclean, including Gentiles and many Gentile practices,"⁷⁸ which is likely the *a priori* conviction of the Matthean audience. In the healing miracle, the emphasis is on the laboured plea of the Canaanite woman, who may be seen as a "prototype of the Gentiles."⁷⁹ Intriguingly, Jesus's initial answer to the woman is redacted by Matthew to be even more negative and harsh than Mark (7:27).⁸⁰ It makes the woman's plea seem more adamant; therefore, "her eventual triumph is more emphatic."⁸¹ In this case, regardless of her gentile identity, the faith of the woman in her heart determines the outcome of receiving Jesus's blessing. Additionally, the feeding of the four thousand is likely referring to the feeding of the Gentiles, or at least Gentiles are included in the crowds.⁸² It is the second example of inclusion of Gentiles in the immediate context of the conflict and Jesus's teaching on the new boundary of defilement.

---

77. Luz, 334.

78. Borg, *Conflict, Holiness and Politics*, 74.

79. This is a comment by Gnilka on the Syrophoenician woman, which I believe is also appropriate for the Canaanite woman in Matthew. Gnilka, *Das Evangelium nach Markus I*, 2 vols. (Zürich: Benziger; Neukirchen-Vluyn: Neukirchener Verlag, 1978–1979), 293; especially with the name "Tyre and Sidon" introduced in the setting of the healing story.

80. France, *Matthew*, 590.

81. France, 590.

82. Even though this analysis recognizes that although the feeding of the four thousand in Matthew refers to Gentiles is highly debated, it embraces a gentile interpretation for these reasons: (1) The story of healing of the Canaanite woman immediately precedes the healing summary, signifying a movement in Jesus's ministry from focusing only on Israel to the Gentiles. This point can be further supported by the preceding conflict story regarding purity, which has "radical implications for Jew-Gentile relationships." France, *Matthew*, 600–601. (2) Matthew's insertion of "Jesus's sitting on the mountain" frames the narrative of both healing (15:30–31) and feeding (15:32–39). It is probable that Matthew is alluding to Isa 25:6, which clearly has a universalistic focus; see Hagner, *Matthew 14–28*, 451–452. (3) In comparison to 9:8, the designation of "God of Israel" in 15:31 possibly implies the presence of Gentiles. (4) The unusual use of the plural form of ὄχλοις may imply a multiple composition of the crowds; Cousland, *Crowds in Matthew*, 37; also 35, footnote 19. (5) The argument that the context determines a gentile feeding was also held by early church fathers such as Hilary of Poitiers (Manlio Simonetti, ed. *Matthew: 14–28*, Ancient Christian Commentary Series, New Testament Ib [Downers Grove: InterVarsity Press, 2002], 33). For a contrary argument, see, e.g. Cousland, "The Feeding of the Four Thousand *Gentiles* in Matthew? Matthew 15:29–39 as a Test Case," *NovT* 41 (1999): 1–23; Davies and Allison, *Matthew: 8–18*, 569. However, even though Cousland argues for a Jewish feeding in 15:32–39, the fact that he also sees Isa 25:6 behind the feeding story (*Crowds in Matthew*, 119) seems to be self-contradictory because the messianic banquet in Isaiah 25:6 has a universalistic focus.

Having established Matthew's two ecclesiological intentions for the conflict story within its context (i.e. Jewish leaders will be excluded whereas Gentiles will be included in God's kingdom), it seems necessary also to discuss why in 15:1–20 the concern for the law and its interpretations should not be considered as the primary focus.[83] Even though the legal dispute as a topic within the conflict story ostensibly gives rise to the conflict, textual evidences seem to suggest the focus of the story is otherwise. For example, the *inclusio* formed by the phrases οὐ γὰρ νίπτονται τὰς χεῖρας . . . ἐσθίωσινin 15:2 and ἀνίπτοις χερσὶν φαγεῖν in 15:20 suggests a structural unity for the section of 15:1–20, but does not necessitate that the hand-washing tradition is the focus of the discussion. The insertion of 15:12–14 also suggests that the blindness of Pharisees and their exclusion from God's kingdom is important for the Matthean agenda.[84] In this conflict, the epithet ὑποκριταί is used for the first time by Matthew and is a crucial theme for the first gospel as a specific reference to the Jewish leaders (15:7).[85] Therefore, although the content of the debate between Jesus and the Jewish leaders is about legal interpretation, for the author the purpose of telling such a story is clearly something else. The author's intent is seen also from his editorial hand. In Matthew, the citation of Isaiah 29:13 is moved to the end of the conflict to emphasize the hypocritical character of the Pharisees.[86] The insertion of 15:12–14 further comments on the Isaiah citation (15:8–9). Together they denote that at the centre of Jesus's refutation is the faithless heart of Jewish leaders against God rather than their inaccurate understanding of the law.[87]

---

83. *Pace* Hultgren, who specifically argues, in analyzing Mark 7:5–8, that the purpose for which the conflict story was composed is as "an apologetic text to defend the church against Jewish criticism"; *Adversaries*, 118. As the evidence from this study shows, while the apologetic purpose is possible, it is not the primary purpose for the overall narrative even in the Markan account, less so in Matthew.

84. Cf. Saunders, "No One Dared," 286.

85. Cf. 22:18; 23:13, 15, 23, 25, 27, 29; 24:51. See detailed discussion on the repetition of this epithet in Anderson, *Matthew's Narrative Web*, 103–105.

86. Hagner, *Matthew 14–28*, 432.

87. George Kilpatrick, *The Origins of the Gospel According to St. Matthew* (Oxford: Clarendon, 1946), 108. *Pace* Hultgren, *Adversaries*, 118.

4.1.2.3 Summary of 15:1-9 in Its Immediate Narrative and Rhetorical Context (Matt 13-16:12)

The first impression of the conflict in 15:1–9 seems to be a discussion of defilement according to the oral Torah. However, a close investigation of the conflict story within its context provides different insights into the authorial intention. Matthew arranges and redacts the story in such a way that the conflict contributes to the narrative in two ways. First, it provides an introduction for predisposing the reader to the exclusion of Jewish leaders from God's kingdom. Second, it provides an occasion to pave the way for Gentile inclusion in Jesus's mission.

This conflict story shares several similarities with two previous conflicts in 12:1–8 and 12:9–13. The structure of all these conflicts is composed of an opening section, which includes a question and a counter-question.[88] Moreover, in each of them the ostensible legal dispute in fact elicits the author's deeper theological considerations. However, compared to the previous ones, this conflict has several unique features. First, the two conflicts of 12:1–8 and 12:9–13 clearly have a christological focus where the authority of Jesus is challenged but clarified. The current conflict focuses on an ecclesiological matter and displays a higher intensity in Jesus's refutation/judgment against the Jewish leaders. Second, the authority of Jesus at this point of the narrative seems to be an established reality for the reader. Because there is no more justification given for the disciples (hence for Jesus), instead, the negative characterization of the Pharisees dominates the conflict scene. It continues to be in step with the overall development of the Matthean plot in that the conflict between Jesus and the opponents becomes more intense. This story also has many points of literary contact with its preceding context (Matt 13) and is closely linked to the following context (Matt 15:21–16:12). Additionally, because of the ecclesiological intention of this conflict, it not only echoes but more importantly fine tunes the idea from 9:9–13 about the new community of Jesus. Who will and will not be considered as true people of God is only dependent on one's inward nature in relation to God, not on one's outward righteous appearance.

---

88. Cope, *Scribe Trained for Kingdom*, 53.

4.1.3 Matthew 16:1–4

4.1.3.1 The Setting of the Story

After the feeding of the four thousand, there is a change of geographical location with Jesus's sailing to Magadan (15:39). One can assume that this second sign of Jonah story takes place in Magadan as well.[89]

4.1.3.2 Matthew 16:1–4: The Conflict Scene Proper

From the outset, because a number of early manuscripts do not include 16:2b–3,[90] the passage poses a significant problem in terms of textual criticism.[91] This discussion, however, chooses to analyze the longer reading of the story for two reasons. First, the external evidence for inclusion or omission of the passage seems to weigh equally.[92] Therefore, the inclusion of 16:2b–3 as the original text remains a possibility. Its omission, as argued by scholars, is because those copyists in Egypt perceived that it did not suit the weather climate there.[93] Another reason for its omission, for example, is due to the effort to harmonize with its Markan parallel (cf. Mark 8:11–13).[94]

---

[89]. There is much ambiguity surrounding the Matthean redaction of Mark's location in Dalmanutha (Mark 8:10) because both Magadan and Dalmanutha are unclear; see discussion in Gundry, *Matthew*, 322.

[90]. Including some of the best witnesses, such as א B V X G f¹³ syr^{c,s} sa, etc.; see Nestle-Arland, *Novum Testamentum Graece*, 27th ed., 44; Bruce M. Metzger, *A Textual Commentary on the Greek New Testament* (London: United Bible Societies, 1971), 41; also see Toshio Hirunuma, "Matthew 16:2b–3," in *New Testament Textual Criticism: Its Significance for Exegesis*, eds. Eldon J. Epp and Gordon D. Fee (Oxford: Oxford University Press, 1981), 36.

[91]. Manuscripts that include 16:2b–3 are, for example, C D K L (N) W A Q II f¹ 33 565 700 892 1071 1241 syr^{p.h}; manuscripts that omit 16:2b–3 are, for example, א B V X G f¹³ 157 267 472 1216 1573 2430 syr^{c,s}; for more discussion, see Hirunuma, "Matthew 16:2b–3," 36.

[92]. Hirunuma, 44. The witnesses that include 16:2b–3 are predominantly in the West whereas the shorter readings are predominantly known in Egypt. Those who opt for the shorter reading primarily base this on the possibility of Lucan/Q influence. That is, the early interpolation of the text may have come from efforts to harmonize with the Lucan parallel or from a common origin in Q. For similar reasons Hirunuma prefers the omission of the passage, though many scholars offer strong refutation to this argument, among them, see Repschinski, *Controversy*, 168–169; Christopher Tuckett, *Q and the History of Early Christianity: Studies on Q* (Peabody: Hendrickson, 1996), 158; Davies and Allison, *Matthew: 8–18*, 577–578.

[93]. F. H. A. Scrivener and Edward Miller, *A Plain Introduction to the Criticism of the New Testament for the Use of Biblical Students II*, 2 vols. (Eugene: Wipf & Stock, 1894, 1997), 326–327; M. J. Lagrange, *Evangile selon Saint Matthieu*, 3rd ed. (Paris: Gabalda, 1927), 315; also Metzger, *Textual Commentary*, 41; Gundry, *Matthew*, 323; Hagner, *Matthew 14–28*, 453.

[94]. Gundry, *Matthew*, 323. Hagner, *Matthew 14–28*, 453.

Second, the internal evidence suggests the likelihood of the original inclusion of 16:2b–3:[95]

a. Because the first evangelist displays a habit of using proverbial sayings elsewhere,[96] the fact that 16:2b–3 parallels popular proverbial sayings in antiquity should support the longer reading, rather than be against it.[97]
b. The plural and eschatological τῶν καιρῶν, which is peculiar to Matthew,[98] calls attention to the eschatological events narrated in preceding stories.[99] Therefore, the presence of 16:2b–3 enables the conflict story to smoothly follow the previous narrative, in addition to retaining the overall thrust of Jesus's response in the story.[100] The short reading, however, leads the conflict story to appear abruptly in the narrative and be a simplified repetition of 12:38–42.

---

95. Two main reasons against the longer text include: (1) the weather signs may not hold true for a Palestinian or Syrian region (Repschinski, *Controversy*, 170); and (2) Rabbinical weather sayings usually are concern with cloud and wind, as in Luke, but not with the color of the sky; Manson, *Sayings*, 201; cf. Str-B, 1:727–728. But neither reason is decisive for the omission of the text; Gnilka, *Matthäus II*, 40.

96. For example, two proverbial sayings appear in conflicts stories (9:12; 13:57); the third one is a Matthean redaction (11:17).

97. Contrary to Luz's argument that the saying corresponding to a widespread popular weather rule speaks against the longer reading, *Matthew 8–20*, 347. Others who argue for the shorter reading and give the reason that it was added later to imitate the Lukan parallel or Q (e.g. McNeile, *Matthew*, 235; W. C. Allen, *A Critical and Exegetical Commentary on the Gospel According to St. Matthew*, 3rd ed. ICC [Edinburgh: T & T Clark, 1912], 173) fail to account for the gross differences between the two texts; cf. Davies and Allison, *Matthew: 8–18*, 577.

98. While the singular form of καιρός appears frequently in all Synoptic Gospels, only Matthew uses the plural of καιρός. The other occurrence is in 21:41, which is Matthew's redaction. Both interestingly refer to eschatological times. Cf. Davies and Allison, *Matthew: 8–18*, 581, see point (iv) within footnote 12. Van Tilborg also contends that the use of καιρός appropriately suits its use elsewhere in Matthew, so the original inclusion of the passage is likely; *Jewish Leaders*, 36, footnote 1.

99. As a proverbial phrase, "the signs of the times" refers to eschatological expectation and is used for events that are already here for all to see; France, *Matthew*, 606. The preceding context contains two miracles highlighted by an eschatological focus. The healing of the lame, dumb and mute in 15:30–31 echoes Isa 29:18–19, 23; 35:5–6; France, *Matthew*, 598; Hagner, *Matthew 14–28*, 446. The feeding of the four thousand likely echoes Isa 25:6, the eschatological gathering of the people and messianic banquet; Hagner, *Matthew 14–28*, 445. Though it may not specifically point to Zion eschatology as Terence Donaldson argues, *Jesus on the Mountain: A Study in Matthean Theology* (Sheffield: Sheffield Academic Press, 1985), 130–131.

100. In Hirunuma's words, the text 16:2b–3 "accurately responded to the question"; "Matthew 16:2b–3," 45. Also Edwards, *Sign of Jonah*, 105.

c. The saying displays some parallelism typical of Matthew's literary style (16:2b//16:3a):[101]

Ὀψίας γενομένης λέγετε. Εὐδία, πυρράζει γὰρ ὁ οὐρανός·
πρωΐ. Σήμερον χειμών, πυρράζει γὰρ στυγνάζων ὁ οὐρανός.

Having argued for the greater likelihood of the longer reading of 16:1–4, we can now move to examine the function of the story in its context. The conflict starts with the Pharisees and the Sadducees initiating a challenge to see a sign from heaven. This story and the one in 12:38–45 are the only doublets within all the conflict stories in Matthew. In contrast to the first doublet, except for the insertion of 16:2b–3, this one follows the Markan account more closely in its wording and sequence in the narrative.[102] Its function, however, is similar to that of 12:38–45 in that the story is also tied closely with its preceding narrative and moves the Matthean plot forward. This suggestion can be unpacked by the following two observations.

First, this story mirrors the conflict between Jesus and Satan (4:1–7), marking the first of a string of conflict stories that have a cosmic connotation in their nature. In contrast to Mark 8:11, Matthew moves the verb πειράζω to the start of the sentence so that the evil motives behind the leaders' request are emphasised. In Matthew, the word πειράζω is applied only to two characters in Matthew: Satan (4:1, 3) and the religious leaders (16:1; 19:3; 22:18, 35). Here is the first of four conflict stories where the word πειράζω is used to characterize Jesus's opponents (cf. 19:3–9; 22:15–22, 34–40). In particular, this conflict resembles the first Temptation story (4:1–4). Like ὁ πειράζων (4:3), the Pharisees and the Sadducees request Jesus perform some kind of miracle (cf. 12:38), rather than challenging him with questions as in most other conflicts. In addition, the word πειράζω (16:1) is placed within the context of feeding and bread (cf. 15:32–38; 16:5–12). It corresponds especially to the first Temptation story concerning feeding on bread.[103] Besides parallels in content, there is also a parallel in vocabulary. In 16:1, one reads προσελθόντες . . . πειράζοντες, which echoes the phrase προσελθὼν ὁ πειράζων in 4:3. It is reasonable to conclude that Matthew's characterization of the

---

101. Davies and Allison, *Matthew 8–18*, 581, see point (iii) within footnote 12; cf. *Matthew 1–7*, 94.

102. Davies and Allison, 578.

103. Patte, *Matthew*, 229, footnote 37.

Jewish leaders now aligns them with Satan.[104] What is ironic is that, contrary to their accusation of Jesus (cf. 9:34; 12:34), the leaders now become representatives of Satan.[105]

Second, the story is the key connection point upon which the preceding context and its following narrative are tied together. The conflict and its context where Jesus warns against the teaching of the Pharisees and the Sadducees (16:5–12) anticipate the first passion/resurrection prediction (16:21). This claim can be derived from Matthew's structuring of the narrative within 15:29–16:28 as well as the reader's *a priori* understanding of the Sadducees.

Although the Sadducees are infrequently mentioned in Matthew,[106] their occurrences are most concentrated in 16:1–12. They are mentioned four times here, all of which derive from Matthew's redactional hand. The insertion of Σαδδουκαῖοι in 16:1 suggests the author's intention to connect the conflict closely with the following teaching of Jesus against the Pharisees and the Sadducees.[107] This context determines that the teaching of the Pharisees and the Sadducees is to be understood in relation to their failure to understand the σημεῖα τῶν καιρῶν, that is, signs indicating the messianic nature of the authority and ministry of Jesus.[108]

---

104. Patte, 225.

105. Or, as Keener suggests, they are "the devil's mouthpiece" and "the devil is their theological source"; Keener, *Matthew*, 420; cf. Anderson, *Matthew's Narrative Web*, 117. This finding corresponds to Powell's thesis that the clash between Jesus and the religious leaders serves as a subplot to the main plot in Matthew, namely, God's plan and Satan's challenge; "The Plot and Subplots of Matthew's Gospel," *NTS* 38 (1992): 199–201. Jesus's final action of καταλιπὼν αὐτούς (which Matthew redacts from Mark's ἀφεὶς αὐτούς) also carries "the connotation of judgmental abandonment"; Gundry, *Matthew*, 324. The word καταλέιπω is used only four times in Matthew, three times referring to Jesus's activity (4:13; 16:4 and 21:17). The fourth time is in Jesus's words quoting Gen 1:27 (19:5). Its use in 4:13 has an implication of finality and the three other uses all convey the idea of "abandonment and leaving behind"; *BDAG*, 520.

106. Matt 3:7; 16:1, 6, 11, 12; 22:23, 34.

107. So far in Matthew, the Sadducees occur only one other time in 3:7 (where Matthew also inserts the Sadducees), but these two groups are certainly not natural teammates; Davies and Allison, *Matthew 8–18*, 579; Hagner, *Matthew 14–28*, 457.

108. Hagner, *Matthew 14–28*, 455. This argument remains valid even if 16:2b–3 is not part of the original text, because the preceding context (i.e. Jesus's healing of the blind and deaf as well as the feeding of the four thousand [15:29–39]), supplies an abundance of evidence showing the messianic nature and ministry of Jesus. Yet, the Pharisees and Sadducees are not able to understand it by asking for more signs from heaven (16:1), thus the request is refused again. To this extent, the story and its context plainly parallels with its doublet in 12:38–45 and the context (12:22–37).

Interestingly, the messianic intention of the author is supported by Peter's confession in 16:13–16. It immediately follows 16:1–12 and is the most explicit statement identifying Jesus as the Messiah in the Matthean narrative. Most of the previous conflict stories display the Pharisees' opposition to Jesus's messianic identity and authority (e.g. 9:1–8, 9–13, 14–17; 12:1–8, 9–14, 22:37, 38–45). This conflict reinforces the blindness of the Pharisees (and Sadducees) in the reader's eyes (i.e. they are not able to see messianic signs [16:1–4] in contrast to the Canaanite woman and "the crowds who marvel at Jesus' healing power").[109] Therefore, it is very likely that the leaven in 16:5–12 relates to the Jewish leaders' rejection of Jesus's messiahship.[110] Matthew places side by side the blindness of the leaders and the warning against their leaven (16:5–12). Then the two pericopae are immediately followed by Peter's confession (16:13–16). Such an arrangement is intended to anticipate and forestall the reader's (residual) doubt concerning Jesus's messiahship.

But the question remains, what do the Sadducees have to do with the story? Historically the Sadducees and the Pharisees were two rival groups prior to the fall of Jerusalem.[111] Within the leadership of Judaism, their teachings and doctrines differed in several important points.[112] What then motivated Matthew to insert the Sadducees side by side with the Pharisees (cf. Mark 8:11–12)? Some scholars speculate that Matthew is ignorant of their differences.[113] It is more likely, however, that Matthew inserts the Sadducees in 16:1–12 for a specific purpose. The answer lies in the *a priori* knowledge of the reader regarding the Sadducees.

The key characteristic that the New Testament portrays about the Sadducees being the opponents of Jesus and the church is their rejection

---

109. Anderson, *Matthew's Narrative Web*, 123.

110. McKnight also suggests that Matthew's polemic against the Pharisees representing a particular form of Judaism (non-messianic Judaism) is due to their rejection of Jesus as the Messiah, "Loyal Critic," 61.

111. John Bowker, *Jesus and the Pharisees* (Cambridge: Cambridge University Press, 1973), 10.

112. Jos. *Ant.* 13 §297–298; see more discussion on the pairing of the Pharisees and Sadducees in Davies and Allison, *Matthew 1–7*, 301–304.

113. For example, based on these facts Meier argues for a gentile authorship of Matthew; Meier, *Law and History in Matthew's Gospel: A Redactional Study of Mt. 5:17–48* (Rome: Biblical Institute Press, 1976), 16–20.

of resurrection.[114] This characteristic was also confirmed by Josephus.[115] Therefore, the implied reader of the first gospel must have had this preconception of the Sadducees already in mind. Matthew presents a warning against their teaching ahead of Jesus's prediction of passion and resurrection (16:21) to pre-empt the reader accepting any of their influence concerning the resurrection.[116] The redactional emphasis of τὸ σημεῖον Ἰωνᾶ also points to the possibility that the author is preparing the reader's mind against any denial of resurrection. There are ample speculations on whether τὸ σημεῖον Ἰωνᾶ here in 16:4 is a result of Matthew's redacting Mark 8:11–13,[117] or of Matthew's dependence on Q (cf. Luke 11:29–32).[118] However, here it is suffice to show that Matthew inserts[119] Ἰωνᾶ in 16:4 even though he is fully aware of the Markan account.[120] The analysis of 12:38–45 in the previous chapter has shown that, for Matthew, the meaning of the sign of Jonah points to the passion and resurrection of Jesus (see previous discussion on pp. 109–119). Moreover, following the conflict, Peter's recognition of Jesus – σὺ εἶ ὁ χριστὸς ὁ υἱὸς τοῦ θεοῦ τοῦ ζῶντος – is immediately qualified by Jesus's following comment (16:21–23). As a result, together with 16:1–20, Jesus's view of the messiahship is made plain: it cannot be fully established without his death and resurrection (16:21–23). Seen in its context, therefore, the conflict story prepares the reader to recognize the inability of the Pharisees and the Sadducees to understand the sign of the end time. Consequently, their teaching against Jesus's messiahship and resurrection becomes unacceptable.

---

114. Matt 22:23, par. Mark 12:18; Luke 20:27; Acts 4:1; 23:6–8.

115. For example, Jos. *Ant.* 18 §11, 16; also Saldarini, *Pharisees, Scribes and Sadducees in Palestinian Society* (Edinburgh: T & T Clark, 1988), 304. New Testament authors also point out this feature of the Sadducees; see Matt 22:23//Mark 12:18; Luke 20:27; Acts 4:1; 23:6–8.

116. Hagner touches on the point by pointing out that here Matthew speaks against a teaching held in common by both the Pharisees and the Sadducees, that is, it has something to do with "a preconception of the nature of the Messiah and messianic fulfillment." But his speculation on the preconception being a national-political understanding of the Messiah seems to be over-stretched. *Matthew 14–28*, 460.

117. For example, Luz, *Matthew 8–20*, 347; Chow, *Sign of Jonah*, 92.

118. For example, Bayer, *Jesus' Predictions*, 115. Davies and Allison, *Matthew 8–18*, 577.

119. Or "retains" if he follows adopts Q, it still shows his redaction from Mark in the overall context.

120. Because from Matt 14 onwards, the author follows Mark 6:14ff closely at both narrative and rhetoric levels; cf. Davies and Allison, *Matthew 8–18*, 578.

4.1.3.3 Summary of 16:1–4 in Its Immediate Narrative and Rhetorical Context (Matt 14–18)

Because 16:1–4 is the second and a shorter doublet of the saying "the sign of Jonah" in Matthew, and because of the textual critical problem of 16:2b–3, scholars tend to discuss the story briefly. Others try to focus primarily on its relation to 12:38–45 or its Markan/Lukan/Q parallels. An unfortunate result is that they largely fail to explain the function and significance of 16:1–4 in its own right.[121]

The above analysis first presents three internal points of evidence for the longer reading of the text. It also argues that the conflict story aligns the religious leaders with Satan and ties the following narrative closely to the preceding context. A close investigation of the story within its context then reveals several interesting findings. For example, the insertion of Sadducees (in 16:1, 6, 11 and 12) helps to construct 16:1–4 and verses 5–12 as a tight unit. It places the "teaching of the Pharisees and Sadducees" in light of their failure to understand "the signs of the times." The *a priori* understanding of the reader regarding the Sadducees is that they dogmatically denied the resurrection of the dead.[122] However, the analysis of this conflict finds that the author is likely to highlight the death and resurrection of Jesus by inserting the "sign of Jonah" in the story. The fact that the Sadducees are placed side by side with the Pharisees, with the blindness of both implied by the conflict (16:1–4), leads to the warning against the teaching of both (16:5–12). Such a narrative arrangement anticipates and forestalls for the reader any incorrect understanding of the messiahship of Jesus, which is the focus of the next passage (16:13–28).

The main task of the analysis is to seek the authorial intention for the conflict story. Together with 16:5–12, it anticipates and prepares the reader for the teaching on Jesus's messiahship (16:13–19, 21). That is, Jesus's messianic role cannot be fulfilled without his death and resurrection. It

---

121. For example, van Tilborg suggests that 16:1–4 offers little for readers; *Jewish Leaders*, 36. Chow devotes an entire book to the "sign of Jonah" but only gives two pages to Matt 16:1–4 as an excursus; *Sign of Jonah*, 92–93. Repschinski's four brief observations fail to offer any insights on the literary function of the story; *Controversy*, 172.

122. See above footnote 117.

particularly sheds light on the puzzling appearance of the Sadducees in the story.¹²³ Historically the Pharisees and the Sadducees were rival groups prior to the fall of Jerusalem.¹²⁴ Yet Matthew seems to align the Sadducees' together with the Pharisees (cf. 16:12: τῆς διδαχῆς τῶν Φαρισαίων καὶ Σαδδουκαίων). While it is possible, as some scholars would argue, that the author may seek to present a "united front" of the Pharisees and Sadducees as Jewish leaders against Jesus,¹²⁵ the above observations demonstrate that the author is more likely to have arranged the conflict story in such a way as to pave the way for the qualification of the messiahship (i.e. it cannot be completed without the death and resurrection of Jesus [16:16, 20–21]).

4.1.4 Matthew 19:1–9

4.1.4.1 Matthew 19:1-2: *The Setting of the Story*

Matthew 19:1-2 is the last summary statement of Jesus's public ministry. Seen within the overall narrative structure of Matthew, 19:1 summarizes Jesus's teaching on humility and forgiveness in the church (ἐτέλεσεν ὁ Ἰησοῦς τοὺς λόγους τούτους). It also inaugurates Jesus's journey to Jerusalem (ἦλθεν εἰς τὰ ὅρια τῆς Ἰουδαίας πέραν τοῦ Ἰορδάνου).¹²⁶ The discussion in the next section will elaborate more on the significance of this summary passage.

It is worth noting that Matthew replaces Mark's ὡς εἰώθει πάλιν ἐδίδασκεν αὐτούς (Mark 10:1) with ἐθεράπευσεν αὐτοὺς ἐκεῖ (19:2b), similar to the redaction in Matthew 14:14 (cf. Mark 6:34). While one needs be cautious and not make too much theological inference from this redaction, it is plausible at least to conclude that Jesus continues to have great compassion¹²⁷ on the

---

123. In commenting on 16:5–12 especially, commentators cannot explain why Matthew replaces Mark's "leaven of Herod" with "of the Sadducees" hence consider the story enigmatic; H. B. Green, *The Gospel According to Matthew* (Oxford: Oxford University Press, 1975), 148.

124. See detailed discussion on the Sadducees from the socio-historical perspective by Saldarini, *Pharisees, Scribes and Sadducees*, 298–308.

125. Hagner, *Matthew 14-28*, 460. Cf. Bultmann, *History*, 53. Though Davies and Allison disagree, *Matthew 1-7*, 303.

126. Bauer, *Structure of Matthew's Gospel*, 23; cf. Hagner, *Matthew 14-28*, 543; William Farmer, *Jesus and the Gospel: Tradition, Scripture, and Canon* (Philadelphia: Fortress, 1982), 138–140. It is also likely, as Davies and Allison suggest, that this geographic marker echoes the beginning of Jesus's ministry so that "the places around which the action centered at the beginning (2:3; 3:1; 4:25) will be the focus of activity at the end," *Matthew 19-28*, 7.

127. Lidija Novakovic, *Messiah, the Healer of the Sick*, 143.

suffering crowd on his way to Jerusalem[128] – a place where Jesus himself will suffer many things and eventually die (cf. 16:21).[129] The conflict formally ends at 19:9; however, the dialogue between Jesus and the disciples (vv. 10–12) concerns the issue which ensued from the contention in the conflict story. Therefore, the following analysis will incorporate the discussion of 19:10–12 when it helps to illuminate the understanding of the function of 19:1–9.

4.1.4.2 Matthew 19:3–9: The Conflict Scene Proper

This is the last conflict before Jesus enters Jerusalem. Among all conflict stories in Matthew, it is the first of the four stories in which the opponents speak twice. The other three conflicts all occur in Jerusalem (21:23–27; 22:15–22; 22:41–46). Because this story deals with the question of marriage and divorce, which is of great consequence to church practice, much attention has been paid to the exegesis of Matthew 19:9 – the Matthean "exception clause." It is not surprising that the passage of 19:1–9, particularly 19:9, is considered by scholars a *crux interpretum* in regards to Jesus's (or the church's) teaching on divorce and remarriage.[130] To borrow Bockmuehl's question, "With so much scholarship on these passages already in print, what can possibly be the justification of yet another attempt at explanation?"[131]

What is surprisingly lacking, however, is an investigation into the relationship of this story with its surrounding narrative context. Why does the author place Jesus's teaching on marriage and divorce as the first story of Jesus on the way to Jerusalem? How does the conflict function in its context? These are the questions this analysis attempts to unravel, so that frustrations, such as in the words of Sigal, "we have no way of knowing what the relevance of the *perushim*'s [the Pharisees'] question was at the moment," can finally be dealt with.[132]

---

128. Patte, *Matthew*, 261.

129. Luz suggests that the readers are reminded of the "impending major conflict in Jerusalem"; *Matthew 8–20*, 488.

130. Bruce Vawter, "The Divorce Clauses in Mat 5,32 and 19,9," *CBQ* 16 (1954): 155; Witherington, "Matthew 5.32 and 19.9," 571.

131. Marcus Bockmuehl, "Matthew 5.32; 19.9 in the Light of Pre-rabbinic Halakhah," *NTS* 35 (1989): 291.

132. Sigal, *Halakhah of Jesus*, 113.

The function of this story within its context, as seen from the following analysis, is operating at two levels: narrative and rhetorical. At the narrative level, the story continues to contrast the character of the opponents to that of Jesus. It continues emphasizing the superiority of Jesus. This feature is consistent with other conflict stories. For instance, the author continues the negative characterization of the Pharisees as this is the second conflict story in Matthew where the word πειράζω is used to characterize the evil intent of Jesus's opponents (cf. 16:1). Although it is already present in Mark 10:2, Matthew moves πειράζοντες αὐτὸν forward to the beginning of the sentence to draw the attention of the reader (19:3).

Also, the Pharisees are presented as having a faulty understanding of God because of their hardness of heart, because Matthew changes the order of the argument and inserts οὐκ ἀνέγνωτε to begin the counter-argument.[133] If historically the Pharisees were presumed to be well-versed in the Scriptures, then the phrase again brings out the irony of their consistent ignorance of the Scriptures (cf. 12:3, 5). The author advances the Genesis principle, which establishes the indissolubility of marriage (19:4). In this way, the author demonstrates that by asking for a legitimate reason for divorce (19:3: . . . κατὰ πᾶσαν αἰτίαν), the Pharisees have already departed from the creation will of God.[134] As Matthew makes it clear, the Pharisees are concerned with the legality of the law but Jesus seeks after the will of God. Matthew changes Mark's κτίσεως (Mark 10:6) to ὁ κτίσας to highlight the Creator (19:4).[135] Additionally, their second question (19:7) seems to be based on a "contradiction" found in Jesus's first answer to the Mosaic tradition (19:4–6). However, it is precisely where the Pharisees misunderstand God's will. The change from ἐνετείλατο (19:7) to ἐπέτρεψεν (19:8) is not a simple switch of verbs.[136] Rather, Matthew

---

133. The phrase οὐκ ἀνέγνωτε only appears in the conflict story in Matthew (12:3, 5; 19:4; 21:16, 42; 22:31), Repschinski, *Controversy*, 173. Half of its occurrences are Matthew's redaction; 12:5; 19:4; 21:16.

134. Cf. Repschinski, *Controversy*, 175.

135. Gundry, *Matthew*, 378. The subject of καὶ εἶπεν before the quotation of Gen 2:24 (Matt 19:5) is also likely referring to God, which reinforces the previous use of ὁ κτίσας; cf. Davies and Allison, *Matthew 19–28*, 11; Hagner, *Matthew 14–28*, 548.

136. As Banks rightly suggests, ". . . Matthew has sharpened Jesus' response, portraying his expression as a deliberate correction of the Pharisaic terminology"; *Jesus and the Law*, 151, also footnote 2.

indicates that the opponents misread Moses's concession to the hardness of heart as a command to divorce.[137]

Another feature that is consistent with other conflict stories is that, in contrast to the opponents, Jesus is in charge of the conversation. In both answers, Jesus does not answer the opponents' question directly. Rather, he extricates himself from an apparent contradiction and uses it as an occasion to point out the spiritual deficiency of the opponents – τὴν σκληροκαρδίαν (19:8). Furthermore, the superior status of Jesus over against the Pharisees is evidenced by Matthew's insertion of the phrase λέγω δὲ ὑμῖν (19:9; cf. 12:6) because "the expression is used only by one whose social status is superior to the individual or group being addressed."[138] The insertion, according to Davies and Allison, "reflects at least Jesus' implicit claim to be God's prophetic spokesman, and one should compare the OT legitimation formula, 'Thus says Yahweh.'"[139]

At the rhetorical level, this story deepens the polarization between the kingdom Jesus is ushering in and the opponents, which foreshadows more fierce opposition to come in Jerusalem. To unpack this idea, we need to begin with the overall picture of the narrative in 19:1–12. Though dealing with the specific issues of marriage and divorce, the story essentially reflects the radical nature of the kingdom of heaven. The "private" teaching of Jesus to the disciples (19:10–12) proceeds from Jesus's answer to the Pharisees and it explicitly mentions that διὰ τὴν βασιλείαν τῶν οὐρανῶν one can choose not to (re)marry (19:12).[140] In the world of first-century Palestine, a society where marriage and procreation are seen to be compulsory for men, this teaching

---

137. The intention of Moses behind the command in Deut 24:1 is to "minimise its [divorce's] gross abuse by granting some protection to woman"; Banks, *Jesus and the Law*, 149.

138. This is the second usage of the phrase in the conflict stories. The first is in 12:6. Aune observes that this expression "I say to you," "whether directed to an individual or to a group, has a consistent social function wherever it occurs in early Jewish, early Christian, and (very rarely) Greco-Roman sources: the expression is used only by one whose social status is superior to the individual or group being addressed." Aune, *Prophecy in Early Christianity and the Ancient Mediterranean World* (Grand Rapids: Eerdmans, 1983), 164–165.

139. Davies and Allison, *Matthew 1–7*, 490; cf. Manson, *The Teaching of Jesus: Studies of Its Form and Content* (Cambridge: Cambridge University Press, 1963), 207.

140. In the context of divorce and remarriage, it is probably after divorcing his/her immoral partner. Though there exists a variety of interpretations, this follows Gundry's suggestion that 19:10–12 "portrays the single life of Christian men who have not remarried after divorcing their immoral wives as an act of discipleship"; *Matthew*, 383.

of the kingdom of heaven is unconventional.[141] However, this seems to be exactly what Jesus conveys.

First of all, the surrounding context with which 19:1–12 is closely linked focuses on the kingdom of heaven (16:13–20:28).[142] The significance of the kingdom theme is seen in the author's interest in either the word βασιλεία or kingdom-related issues.[143] A more explicit evidence can be seen from the use of the motif τὰ παιδία / τῶν μικρῶν. It forms an *inclusio* between Matthew 18:1 and 19:15 and suggests a literary unity for the passage. Within this *inclusio*, the little ones are to be received (18:5), imitated (18:3, 4), and blessed (19:15), not despised (18:10), because theirs is the kingdom of heaven (19:14).[144] Within the context of kingdom teaching (16:13–20:28), there is a repeated emphasis on the radicalization or reversal of human relationships in the teaching of Jesus (e.g. 16:24–25; 18:2–4, 8–9, 12–14, 15–17, 21–35; 19:1–12, 14, 21–23, 30; 20:1–16).

Second, marriage and divorce as the topic of the conflict also reflect this focus on the kingdom of heaven. Through the conflict, the author insists that marriage is in line with God's original intent for human beings (19:4–5; cf. Gen 1:27). Such is not the case for divorce (19:8). However, in first-century Palestine, especially within Jewish communities, a husband has the sole right to initiate a divorce, often based on any reason.[145] In other words, the *a priori*

---

141. Cf. Ben Witherington III, *Matthew* (Macon: Smyth & Helwys, 2006), 383.

142. The kingdom of heaven, a theme prominent in the third discourse of Matthew's gospel (Matt 13) becomes conspicuously absent in its following narrative (Matt 13:53–16:12). It is so much so that Mark Saucy comments, "a turning point has taken place in the parables of 'the kingdom' in Matthew 13"; "The Kingdom-of-God Sayings in Matthew," *BiblSac* 151 (1994): 196. However, the kingdom of heaven reappears as a key theme during the narrative of Jesus's three passion predictions (16:13–20:28) – the surrounding narrative context where the current conflict is situated.

143. The word βασιλεία is explicitly mentioned in 16:19, 28; 18:3–4, 23; 19:12, 14, 23; 20:1. For example, Jesus's duty to the temple tax is compared to the duty of the king's son to their country's tax (17:25–26). In Jesus's teaching discourse (Matt 18), values and relationships in the kingdom for its members are the focus of all pericopae (18:1–6, 10–14, 15–20, 21–35). In the passage where Jesus blesses the little children and encounters the rich young man, one's relationship with the kingdom of heaven is clearly the primary concern (19:13–15, 16–26). The teaching on reward in heaven then immediately follows (19:27–30; 20:1–16). In addition to these examples, the kingdom of heaven is also implied by the analogy of the mustard seed (17:20, cf. 13:31–32) and the throne scene of the Son of Man with his disciples.

144. Cf. Garland, *Reading Matthew*, 204.

145. Hence, we hear of the rabbinic debate between the schools of Shammai and Hillel regarding valid grounds for divorce; Gundry, *Matthew*, 377; also Green, *Matthew*, 167–168. Davies and Allison, *Matthew 19–28*, 9. However, Sigal argues against this view: Jesus agrees

reality for Matthew's reader is that men hold the power in a marriage/divorce relationship. When Jesus's answer in 19:8–9 is understood against this backdrop, his teaching is indeed radical because it clearly curbs the rights of a husband:[146] divorce and remarriage are against the intention of God's creation, therefore are considered adultery.[147] In this conflict, Jesus reiterates a similar

---

with neither (*Halakhah of Jesus*, 114–115); and Sigal again says that, what the Matthean Jesus is saying is that if one follows either the Hillelite or the Shammaite position, he is guilty of adultery (*Halakhah of Jesus*, 123). Jesus argues that neither one of them is close enough to what Moses intended. The question εἰ ἔξεστιν ἀνθρώπῳ ἀπολῦσαι τὴν γυναῖκα αὐτοῦ κατὰ πᾶσαν αἰτίαν that the Pharisees bring up to Jesus also reflect this presumption (19:3).

146. Even though Jesus starts the answer with an appeal to Genesis 1 and 2, the use of these Scriptures is really "stepping stones in the construction of the pericope for an argument"; Cope, *Scribe Trained for the Kingdom*, 84.

147. I must point out that the statement here is understood in its most general sense. I recognize that the interpretation of 19:9 is highly debated because of the ambiguity of the exceptional clause inserted by Matthew: μὴ ἐπὶ πορνείᾳ (19:9). However, for the purpose of this analysis, suffice it here to summarize the two most probable options: (1) The exception μὴ ἐπὶ πορνείᾳ qualifies both divorce and remarriage. This means 19:9 should be understood as, *if anyone who divorces his wife and marries another woman, except on the grounds of sexual unfaithfulness, commits adultery himself*. This view has dominated Protestant tradition for centuries, although the view was raised first by non-Protestant Christian humanists such as More and Erasmus. At the time they were both reacting against the Roman Catholic position of total prohibition of divorce and remarriage. More believes that the marriage bond can be broken not only by an unfaithful spouse but also by mutual consent or intolerable behavior, and remarriage naturally follows (Valerian Paget, *More's Millennium: Being the Utopia of Sir Thomas More Rendered into Modern English* [New York, John McBride, 1908], 185, 188, 197). Erasmus also holds that Jesus allows divorce and remarriage on the ground of adultery. Similar to More, he includes other causes such as cruelty or mutual hatred as valid ground for divorce and remarriage ("Marriage," in *The Colloquies of Erasmus*, trans. Craig R. Thompson [Chicago: University of Chicago Press, 1965]). Although modern scholars vary as to how to understand πορνείᾳ, they generally have a consensus on permitting remarriage after divorce in the case of adultery. Scholars upholding this position include, among others, Wiebe (P. H. Wiebe, "Jesus Divorce Exception," *JETS* 32 [1989]: 327–333), Instone-Brewer (*Divorce and Remarriage in the Bible: The Social and Literary Context* [Grand Rapids: Eerdmans, 2002]), Keener (*... And Marries Another: Divorce and Remarriage in the Teaching of the New Testament* [Peabody: Hendrickson, 1991]); Carson (Don A. Carson, *Matthew 13–28*, The Expositor's Bible Commentary with the NIV [Grand Rapids: Zondervan, 1995], 408–419); Sigal (*Halakhah of Jesus*, 105–143); Fitzmeyer ("Matthean Divorce Texts and Some New Palestinian Evidence," *Theological Studies* 37 [1976]: 197–226); and Witherington ("Matthew 5:32 and 19:9 – Exception or Exceptional Situation?," *NTS* 31 [1985]: 571–576); or (2) the exception μὴ ἐπὶ πορνείᾳ qualifies only divorce but not remarriage. This means 19:9 should be understood as, *if anyone who divorces his wife, except on the grounds of sexual unfaithfulness, commits adultery; and if he marries another woman then he commits adultery*. Scholars supporting this view are, for example, Gordon Wenham ("Matthew and Divorce: An Old Crux Revisited," *JSNT* 22 [1984]: 95–107); Q. Quesnell ("Made Themselves Eunuchs of the Kingdom of Heaven (Mt 19:12)," *CBQ* 30 [1968]: 335–358); J. Dupont (*Mariage et divorce dans l'Évangile: Matthew 19,3–12 et parallels* [Bruges: Addaye de Saint-André & Desclée de Brouwer, 1959]); W. A. Heth (and Gordon Wenham, *Jesus and Divorce* [Nashville: Nelson, 1985]), and Hagner (*Matthew 14–28*, 549–550).

teaching on divorce and adultery to the one in the Sermon on the Mount (Matt 5:31-32),[148] which is consistent with the teaching of kingdom ethics. As Allison rightly points out, "the Sermon presents the perfect, unadulterated will of God, the will of God in its nakedness, because it proclaims the will of God is it should be lived in the kingdom, when God's will is done on earth as in heaven."[149]

Third, the polarization between the kingdom Jesus proclaims and the paradigm that the opponents represent is deepened because of the author's emphasis on each end of the pole in the conflict.

On the one end of the pole, the kingdom of heaven is where the will of God is fully realized. The repetition of the phrase ἀπ' ἀρχῆς (19:4, 8), both of which belong to Matthew's redaction,[150] alludes to Gen 1:1. The citation of Gen 1:27 and 2:24 together with the phrase ἀπ' ἀρχῆς is likely to remind the reader of the creation order in the Garden of Eden (19:4-6). Within the context where the kingdom of heaven is the ongoing theme (16:13-20:28), the author's repeated appeal to the creation story (cf. Gen 1:27 and 2:24) deserves attention. It is likely that at least in this story the kingdom is intended to reflect 'a restored perfection,' where the will of God is fully carried out and only existed in the Garden of Eden before the Fall (aÓpΔ aÓrchvß).[151]

---

148. Garland, *Reading Matthew*, 202. Allison, *The Sermon on the Mount: Inspiring the Moral Imagination* (New York: Crossroad, 1999), 9-10.

149. This is why Allison argues that one cannot correctly understand the Sermon on the Mount without recognizing its eschatological orientation, as he writes, "The Sermon may address ordinary circumstances, but it sees all through the eyes of eternity. It does not so much look forward, from the present to the consummation, as it looks backwards, from the consummation to the present ... This explains why it is seemingly heedless of all earthly contingencies, why it is so radical ... The Sermon is not primarily concerned with what is practical or possible in the here and now but with the unobstructed, perfect will of God"; *Sermon on the Mount*, 12-13.

150. Matthew redacts Mark (Mark 3-6) so that Jesus's answer begins with ... ἀπ' ἀρχῆς (19:4) as a refutation to the Pharisees' first question of valid grounds for divorce. He inserts the phrase to support Jesus's refutation to the Pharisees' second question (19:8).

151. Or as Hagner expresses, "The kingdom of God brought by Jesus is ultimately to involve the restoration of the perfection of the pre-fall creation ... As God intended no divorce for the garden of Eden, so divorce is not to be allowed in the new era of the kingdom of God"; *Matthew 14-28*, 550. Paul also appeals to the same Genesis passage (Gen 2:24) to refer to "becoming one flesh" in regards to the ideal relationship between Jesus and the church in 1 Cor 6:16 and Eph 5:31. Dahl suggests that there the eschatological use of Gen 2:24 implies a sense of "*Urzeit = Endzeit*"; Nils Dahl, *Jesus in the Memory of the Early Church* (Minneapolis: Augsburg, 1976), 136. I think this nuance is present in Jesus's appeal to the creation story in teaching about the kingdom of heaven.

Yet on the other hand, the hardness of heart separates one from the kingdom of heaven. The second use of the phrase ἀπ' ἀρχῆς is followed by δὲ in order to bring out what is in contrast to the beginning: the practice of divorce as an expression of hardness of heart (19:8). The predicament of one's heart in Matthew is further emphasized. For example, the word σκληροκαρδίαν is only used to describe Jesus's opponents in Matthew (19:8), unlike Mark (Mark 16:14; cf. Mark 6:52; 8:17).[152] Moreover, the fact that the negative condition of one's heart is related to one's standing regarding the kingdom of heaven is featured in Matthew 13 (vv. 15 and 19) and the context leading up to Matthew 19 (15:8, 18, 19; 18:35). If, as is likely, Matthew 13 is a critical turning point in Matthew's presentation of Jesus's ministry,[153] along the development of the narrative plot until Matthew 19, the Pharisees are presently standing outside of the kingdom of God.

4.1.4.3 Summary of 19:1–9 in Its Narrative and Rhetorical Context (16:13–20:28)

The function of this conflict at the narrative level is consistent with previous conflicts. That is, it contrasts the character of the opponents to that of Jesus, but focuses on the superiority of Jesus. A more specific function, however, is at the rhetoric level. It advances Matthew's narrative plot by showing the deepened polarization between Jesus and his opponents and by preparing the reader for later Jerusalem conflicts.

The polarization between Jesus and the Jewish leaders starts with the first conflict story where the author presents the authority of Jesus as superior to the one upheld by the opponents (9:1–8). As the narrative unfolds, the reader encounters a series of conflict stories (9:9–13, 14–17; 12:1–8, 9–14, 22–37, 38–45; 13:53–58; 15:1–9; 16:1–4). Now at this juncture, when Jesus begins the last phase of his journey before entering Jerusalem, the audience encounters the conflict within a context where the author concentrates on many aspects of the horizontal dimension of relationships in Jesus's teaching of the kingdom. They include humility, compassion, mercy, forgiveness,

---

152. In Mark, the disciples are characterized as καρδία πεπωρωμένη (6:52)/ πεπωρωμένην ἔχετε τὴν καρδίαν ὑμῶν (8:17) even though the specific word σκληροκαρδίαν is not used.

153. Kingsbury, *Parables of Jesus*, 31; Rudolf Schnackenburg, *God's Rule and Kingdom* (Freiburg: Herder, 1963), 188.

unity and patience (16:13–20:28).[154] The kingdom, exemplified by the life in the community, requires an utter reversal of hardness of heart. Together with the other three conflicts narrated following the turning point of Matthew 13 (i.e. 13:53–58; 15:1–9; 16:1–4), they deepen and widen the rift between Jesus and the Jewish leaders, which will come to its climax in the conflicts in Jerusalem (Matt 21–22).

4.2 Conflict Stories in Context Matthew 13–20

Unlike the other three groups of conflict stories knitted together by the author in close proximity with each other (Matt 9, 12, 21–22), these four conflicts are scattered across the span of seven chapters in the Matthean narrative (Matt 13–19). Each seems to have a slightly different function as the author presents; however, seen from the overall structure of the narrative, they also share some similarities.

In the Matthean narrative, passages beginning from 12:15 to chapter 13 mark a watershed section between two stages of Jesus's mission. If in the beginning of his ministry, Jesus's salvific effort is toward the "lost sheep of Israel" in order to "save his people from their sins" (1:21; 10:5–6), then, starting from Matthew 13, there is a distinct shift in Jesus's mission from toward the Jews to the Gentiles, as a response to the persistent rejection from his own people (e.g. 13:57–58). The conflict in 15:1–9 has an appearance of legal debates between Jesus and the Jewish leaders. However, our analysis of the conflict within its context shows that it in fact provides an introduction for the exclusion of Jewish leaders from God's kingdom and provides an occasion to pave the way for gentile inclusion in Jesus's mission. The focus of the story is clearly ecclesiological. It highlights a higher intensity in Jesus's judgment against the Jewish leaders whereas the authority of Jesus seems to be an established reality. The ecclesiological intention of this conflict, not only echoes

---

154. Forgiveness based on mercy is particularly highlighted in the context immediately preceding the conflict story. This can be seen from Matthew's redaction to the Markan narrative. Even though in this section Matthew largely follows Mark in terms of event order (between Jesus's second and third passion predictions, Matt 17:24–20:16/Mark 9:33–10:31), there are several additions of both narratives and parables. Among those additions, 18:15–35 is the context immediately preceding the conflict.

but more importantly fine tunes the idea from 9:9–13. The kingdom of God is only defined by one's inward nature in relation to Jesus as a new community.

As the plot continues to develop, the conflict of 16:1–4 now aligns the religious leaders with Satan. The Sadducees make an interesting appearance here to help the author tie the story with its context which anticipates and prepares the reader for the teaching on Jesus's messiahship (16:13–19, 21). That is, Jesus's messianic role cannot be fulfilled without his death and resurrection. Like the conflict in 15:1–9, the one in 19:1–9 also has an appearance of a legal debate. However, the author arranges this story as the last conflict before Jesus's final journey and entering Jerusalem. The primary intention, as is likely, is to deepen the polarization between Jesus and his opponents and to prepare the reader for the climax in the conflicts in Jerusalem.

Though the author presents each conflict with a slightly different purpose, seen together within the wider narrative context of Matthew 13–20, there are two most distinctive similarities shared by all four conflict stories. First, the divine status of Jesus and his superiority seems to be an established factor in these stories. In other words, the christological focus in these stories seems to be less prominent than in the previous seven conflicts and the authority of Jesus is less challenged than in previous stories. What has become prominent is the focus on the obduracy of the Jewish people, and Jesus's stern judgment upon them. Second, the message the author conveys through these conflicts within their context is more ecclesiological: the new community of Jesus as the kingdom of God on earth is both divisive and encompassing at the same time. It is divisive because there can be only two types of people, those who will be included and those who will be excluded (cf. 12:30). It is also encompassing in that, not only descendants of Abraham but Gentiles will now have equal footing in entering the kingdom of God. This is because the boundary is no longer according to the observance of the Torah, but about one's heart in relation to Jesus the Messiah.

CHAPTER 5

The Jerusalem Conflict Stories
Whose Son Is the Christ?

These six conflicts, Matthew 21:14–17, 23–27, 22:15–22, 23–33, 34–40, and 22:41–46, are grouped as the Jerusalem conflict stories in this chapter because they all occur in Jerusalem during the final days of Jesus. Here the intensity of the conflict stories reaches a climax. This can be seen from the fact that all conflict stories, except for the first one, are narrated without the interruption of any story-time gap between them. In other words, except for the first temple conflict, all the remaining conflicts seem to occur consecutively on the same day. As a result, such a narrative arrangement brings out the impact of a cumulative intensity on the audience.

This chapter continues to seek answers to these questions: how do these conflict stories contribute to the Matthean plot development? What are the author's purposes in arranging these conflict stories within such a short span of time and space? And how does the author achieve these purposes? In this chapter, each conflict story as well as the relationship with its narrative context will first be examined. Then a brief summary will be provided at the end of each section.

5.1 Analysis of Individual Pericopea: Matthew 21:14–17, 23–27; 22:15–22, 23–33, 34–40, 41–46

5.1.1 Matthew 21:14–17
5.1.1.1 Matthew 21:14: The Setting of the Story
This story is the only conflict peculiar to Matthew and is often deemed by

scholars as an entirely Matthean insertion.¹ Interestingly, however, the repeated phrase ἐν τῷ ἱερῷ (21:12, 14 and 15) indicates that even as an insertion, the author intends to tie it closely to Jesus's temple cleansing given the proximity of the two events. Moreover, in contrast to Mark's chronology that arranges the Jerusalem entry of Jesus and his temple cleansing into two consecutive days, Matthew redacts the story time into seemingly the same day event so that the temple cleansing is also closely connected to the Jerusalem entry narrative.² Therefore, this conflict will be discussed in light of its preceding narrative of both the Jerusalem entry (21:1–11) and the temple cleansing (21:12–13).

The setting of this story displays three parallels with two previous passages in the Matthean narrative – one is the double healing in 9:27–34 and the other is the conflict story in 12:22–37: (1) all these healing occasions mention that Jesus heals specific infirmities (e.g. blind and dumb/deaf in both 9:27–34 and 12:22, and lame in 21:14).³ (2) The reversal of these specified infirmities allude to the Isaianic imagery that the messianic age is dawning (esp. Isa 29:18–20; 35:5–6; cf. Matt 11:5). (3) The healing activity of Jesus gives rise to public comment on his identity, which results in the anger or hostility of the Jewish leaders toward Jesus.⁴ Despite these parallels to previous stories, this conflict displays a notable progress in the plot development which will be discussed in the next section.

---

1. Repschinski, *Controversy*, 187; Luz, *Matthew 21–28*, 6; Gnilka, *Matthäus II*, 207. Gundry's suggestion that here Matthew revises some tradition kept by Luke 19:39–44 is less convincing; *Matthew*, 414. Byrskog also raises objection to Gundry's suggestion in that "the opponents' identity and the utterance are totally different in two versions (*Jesus the Only Teacher*, 390, footnote 3). Another possibility could be, as Davies and Allison agree with Schweizer, that this story may share a common origin of an independent objection story in which the Jerusalem leaders oppose Jesus's accepting people's praises (*Matthew 8–18*, 133; cf. Schweizer, *Matthew*, 407), though this fact does not contradict the possibility that Matthew inserts the conflict story after the temple cleansing.

2. Dennis Duling, "The Therapeutic Son of David: An Element in Matthew's Christological Apologetic," *NTS* 24 (1978): 405.

3. The setting is also parallel to that of the conflict story in 19:1–9, but the healing mentioned in 19:2 is more of a summary rather than specific infirmities; therefore, it is of less relevance to this conflict, except for the fact that both conflicts begin with Jesus's compassion (exemplified by his healing activities) for the poor and needy.

4. Novakovic notices that "it appears that only the public application of the title 'Son of David' to Jesus provokes the objection of Jesus' opponents, whereas their reaction to its individual usage is not reported"; *Messiah, the Healer of the Sick*, 90. However, because this conflict is closely connected to the preceding temple cleansing, it is possible that the precedent for τὰ θαυμάσια also includes Jesus's cleaning the temple; Repschinski, *Controversy*, 189–190.

5.1.1.2 Matthew 21:15-17: The Conflict Scene Proper

At first, it is worth noting the opponents of Jesus in this story. The regular opponents, the Pharisees, are now replaced by another group, οἱ ἀρχιερεῖς καὶ οἱ γραμματεῖς. Historically they were the authorities in the setting of the Jerusalem temple. However, this group of Jewish leaders is not new for the Matthean audience. In fact, they appear very early in the narrative as co-conspirators with king Herod in Jerusalem. Together they sought to kill the infant Jesus (2:4).[5] Then οἱ ἀρχιερεῖς καὶ οἱ γραμματεῖς are mentioned again twice in Jesus's passion prediction as both persecutors and murderers (together with τῶν πρεσβυτέρων in 16:21; 20:18). After this conflict, they will appear again (with πρεσβυτέρων) for the last time in the Matthean narrative as the main characters mocking the crucified Jesus (27:41–44). Therefore, the author has consistently associated this group not only with Jerusalem, but also with the murder plot against Jesus. Although here is the first time οἱ ἀρχιερεῖς καὶ οἱ γραμματεῖς appear in a conflict story, the literary impact on the reader is plain through such a characterization: as soon as he enters the city of Jerusalem, Jesus comes face to face with his mortal enemies.

A literary critical investigation of this succinct conflict story demonstrates three key functions for the development of the Matthean narrative. They will be discussed in the following order according to their significance.

First, as is apparent from the context, what is being suggested here is that the conflict story confirms Jesus's identity not only as the Davidic Messiah, but he also assumes the divine status of God. Their four observations serve to substantiate the argument cumulatively. This function is most salient because it has several lasting consequences that will be played out in the rest of the conflict stories.

1. The narration of the healing activity points to the dawning of the messianic age ushered in by the person of Jesus. The reader at this point is already familiar with the author's interest in grouping specific infirmities including blindness and lameness (e.g. 9:27–33; 11:3–5; 12:22–24; 15:30–31).[6] By associating Jesus's healing

---

5. Davies and Allison suggest that their first appearance in fact foreshadows their murderous role at the end of Matthew's story, *Matthew 1–7*, 240.

6. This cataloging is especially highlighted by the healing list in 11:3–5, which qualifies ὁ ἐρχόμενος as a messianic designation. Interestingly, ὁ ἐρχόμενος also occurs together with the title ὁ υἱὸς Δαυίδ as the object of the crowd's praise (21:9). As Davies and Allison rightly

(or reversal) of these particular infirmities with the framework detailed by Isaiah regarding the messianic age (cf. Isa 29:18–20; 35:5–6), the author clearly intends to depict Jesus's healing as messianic deeds.[7]

2. The author provides a further scriptural basis for Jesus as the Davidic Messiah who assumes the divine status of God in the temple. Jesus's answer ναί refutes his opponents' challenge. He further affirms the children's praise by quoting Psalm 8:3 (LXX)[8] as a scriptural justification.[9] Seen from the perspective of speech-act theory, by quoting the Hebrew Scripture as a confirmation to the challenge of the opponents, Jesus is performing an assertive speech-act which defends the appropriateness of the children's praise.[10] But how is it appropriate, if on the one hand the infants in the Psalm praise God, whilst on the other hand it is Jesus that the children praise in the temple? The Matthean narrative context where Psalm 8:3 LXX is quoted (21:1–17)[11] has many points of

---

suggest, "Jesus is the Coming One of John's preaching, the Messiah of prophecy who, through his proclamation to the poor and his miraculous and compassionate deeds, brings to fulfillment the messianic oracles uttered so long ago by Isaiah the prophet"; *Matthew 8–18*, 242. See also A. Strobel, *Untersuchungen zum eschatologischen Verzögerungsproblem auf Grund der spätjüdisch-urchristlichen Geschichte von Habakuk 2,2ff.* (Leiden/Köln: E.J. Brill, 1961), 274. Gundry, on other hand, proposes an antithetic typology between Jesus and David because the infirmities (the blind and lame of 21:14) can also allude to 2 Sam 5:8 where David "hates" the blind and lame. Gundry, *Use of the Old Testament*, 140, also *Matthew*, 413; cf. Green, *Matthew*, 177.

7. See Novakovic's comprehensive discussion linking Jesus's healing activities with the messianic deeds; *Messiah, the Healer of the Sick*, 152–184.

8. The Matthean quotation agrees with LXX Ps 8:3 in verbatim; Hagner, *Matthew 14–28*, 602. Therefore, the Greek αἶνον renders the Hebrew עז of MT as "praise" which is more fitting in the context of 21:14–17; France, *Jesus and the Old Testament: His Application of Old Testament Passages to Himself and His Mission* (London: Tyndale Press, 1971), 251. Gundry proposes that עז in MT meaning "strength" was to "emphasise Yahweh's might working through the weakness of children"; *Use of the Old Testament*, 121.

9. Byrskog, *Jesus the Only Teacher*, 390.

10. See detailed definition of "assertive" speech-act in previous discussion; see also Searle, *Expression and Meaning*, 3, 12.

11. Matt 21:1–7 is deemed as the narrative context for the quotation of Ps 8:3 LXX because of Matthew's redaction of the Markan account. This conflict story is not only closely connected with Jesus's temple cleansing, but also with the Jerusalem entry because Matthew changes Mark's chronology by placing the two events within the same day, and "this juxtaposition permits a closer link between the Entry cry and the children's cry in the temple"; Duling, "Therapeutic Son of David," 405. Therefore, Matthew constructs a unity from all three narrative accounts of 21:1–11, 12–13 and 14–17.

contact with its scriptural context.¹² This arrangement shows a deliberate parallel between Jesus and God so that the Matthean Jesus in effect takes upon himself what the Psalmist says about God.¹³ Therefore, it leaves this literary impact on the reader. That is, it is only by bestowing on Jesus this divine status that Psalm 8:3 LXX can be said to justify the children's praise.¹⁴ Consequently, the Psalm quotation here can be seen as an emphatic qualification on ὁ υἱὸς Δαυίδ.¹⁵

3. The children's praise highlights Jesus's identity as the Son of David. As mentioned above, the fact that Jesus's healing activity gives rise to the public comment on his identity is one of the three parallels shared by 9:27–34, 12:22–37 and 21:14–17. Yet, there appears to be a steady progress in the public recognition of Jesus as Son of David. In the first incident (9:27–34), the crowd simply marvels: Οὐδέποτε ἐφάνη οὕτως ἐν τῷ Ἰσραήλ (9:33). They are

---

12. There are four points of contact between the context of Ps 8:3 LXX and that of Matt 21:16 which indicate the author's intention to parallel Jesus with God: (1) the word θαυμαστός appears in both contexts (LXX Ps 8:2, 10; Matt 21:15) and points to the wonderful things God and Jesus have just done to trigger the praise; (2) both contexts include exalting the majestic name of the Lord (LXX Ps 8:2, 10; Matt 21:9), Gundry, *Matthew*, 414–415; (3) both praises come from the mouths of babies/children; (4) the praise is uttered in the presence of the enemies in both accounts. In addition to Matthew, other New Testament writers also interpret Ps 8 christologically (cf. 1 Cor 15:27; Eph 1:22 and Heb 2:6). It shows that such hermeneutics belonged to early Christian tradition; cf. Davies and Allison, *Matthew 19–28*, 142; Hill, *Matthew*, 294.

13. France specifically lists 21:16 under the premise of "the Assumption of the Role of Yahweh"; *Jesus and the Old Testament*, 151. *Pace* Repschinski and Davies and Allison. Repschinski suggests that Ps 8:3 shows Jesus is the Son of David endorsed by God himself; *Controversy*, 191; this suggestion is insufficient to explain the parallel between two contexts. Davies and Allison's proposal of the Moses typology, though sound, is contradicted by the Matthean transfiguration account where Jesus is clearly greater than Moses; *Matthew 19–28*, 142, 144. The suggestion by Carson and Beale is more plausible and the logic of their argument can be modified: in Ps 8 the infants praise God, here in Matthew the children praise Jesus; *New Testament Use of the Old Testament*, 70. The fact that Matthew uses Ps 8 to justify 21:15 is appropriate and can be sustained on the ground that Jesus actually equals the God of the Scripture.

14. Even though it is Jesus who speaks of Ps 8:3 LXX, the historical present λέγει (21:16) aligns the narrator/author and Jesus on the same phraseological plane; Anderson, *Matthew's Narrative Web*, 61–62. As France puts it correctly, "Unless he [Jesus] is here setting himself in the place of Yahweh, the argument is a *non sequitur*"; *Jesus and the Old Testament*, 152.

15. It is also possible that through this qualification the author intends to distinguish the children's praise from the crowd's earlier praise Ὡσαννὰ τῷ υἱῷ Δαυίδ which leads to the not-so-accurate conclusion ὁ προφήτης Ἰησοῦς (21:9).

too amazed to postulate a precise question[16] but the Pharisees' comment confirms that their bafflement concerns the identity of Jesus.[17] In the second incident (12:22–37), the author bestows the crowd with a little more insight so that their question μήτι οὗτός ἐστιν ὁ υἱὸς Δαυίδ calls for an association between Jesus and a specific messianic title ὁ υἱὸς Δαυίδ. Finally, in this conflict, the crowd is replaced by the children who give an unequivocal praise to Jesus, Ὡσαννὰ τῷ υἱῷ Δαυίδ, which repeats and emphasizes the same praise by the crowd during Jesus's entry to Jerusalem (21:9). Unlike the crowd, however, the children as a character (group) are portrayed positively in Matthew. They are given God's hidden things (11:25–26),[18] entrusted with the kingdom of heaven (18:2; 19:14), and receptive to the wonders of God's universe (21:16; cf. Ps 8:2). Therefore, in the reader's eyes they are a reliable character in Matthew's gospel. Such a characterization of the children gives a compelling credibility to the praise and thus confirms Jesus's identity as ὁ υἱὸς Δαυίδ.

(4) The author's rhetoric in redacting the conflict within its context also shows his intention to identify Jesus as the Davidic Messiah who assumes the divine status of God. Mark encloses the temple cleansing with the cursing of the fig tree so that the destruction of the temple as the coming judgment is in focus (Mark 12:12–21).[19] Matthew, however, seems to have something else in mind. The story of temple cleansing is separated from the cursing of the fig tree in Matthew, but it is juxtaposed with the conflict story where Jesus performs messianic healing and receives praise

---

16. The crowd's comment is more of an exclamation of astonishment than of fact because they have seen Jesus's exorcism and healing before (cf. Matt 8–9).

17. Hence Davies and Allison correctly notice that 9:33 sets the stage for 9:35ff where the crowd as the lost sheep of Israel is the mission target, *Matthew 8–18*, 141.

18. Matthew's use of νήπιοι only occur here (11:25) and in 21:16. In fact, the children's high praise of Jesus is in contrast with the leaders' anger, which creates an irony echoing back to Jesus's saying in 11:25: you have hidden these things from the wise and learned and revealed them to little children.

19. Sanders, *Jesus and Judaism*, 75. Evans, *Mark 8:27–16:20*, WBC 34B (Nashville: Thomas Nelson, 2001), 182.

from the children, both of which also occur in the temple.[20] One needs to be reminded that the *a priori* understanding of the Jerusalem temple in the mind of the Matthean audience is that it is the physical centre of the Jewish faith. There can be no higher authority than God himself in the temple.[21] Despite this, the Matthean Jesus goes straight to the temple[22] and acts as one with authority (21:12–14, 16),[23] while the cursing of the fig tree is left as an event for the next day. Matthew's focus seems to shift from the destruction of the temple to Jesus's messianic authority in the temple.[24] Furthermore, in Matthew, Jesus is already said to be greater than the temple (12:6) and more than a prophet (12:41; cf. 16:14–16).[25] Therefore, it is likely that the author intends to highlight Jesus's messianic identity through this conflict.[26]

Relating closely to the first one, the second function of the story is that, as the climax of Jesus's triumphal entry into Jerusalem,[27] it foreshadows the final conflict story where the Pharisees could no longer answer Jesus's question regarding the lordship of the Son of David (22:41–46). In fact, through

---

20. Note the repetition of ἐν τῷ ἱερῷ in this story (21:14 and 15).

21. The theological importance of the Jerusalem temple is evident in the Hebrew Scripture and the early Jewish tradition. The temple is where God (or his *shekinah*) is present; see, for example, 1 Kgs 8:10–11; 2 Chr 5:14; 7:1–2; Ps 26:8; Ezek 43:4–7; 44:4; Zech 2:10–11; 11QTemple 46:12.

22. Cf. Hagner, *Matthew 14–28*, 602.

23. Despite the fact that God is the highest authority in the temple, what Jesus did and said in the temple (21:12–16) shows that he "was implicitly claiming *to do and be what the Temple was and did*" because he himself now is the dwelling-place of the living God: Wright, "Jerusalem in the New Testament," in *Jerusalem: Past and Present in the Purposes of God*, ed. Peter W. L. Walker (Grand Rapids: Baker Books, 1994), 58, 66. Similarly, Peter Walker suggests that, "Matthew has a quite distinctive way, unparalleled in Mark, of teaching this truth about Jesus as the new Temple: Jesus is himself the *shekinah* presence of God"; *Jesus and the Holy City: New Testament Perspectives on Jerusalem* (Grand Rapids: Eerdmans, 1996), 30.

24. The cursing of the fig tree for Matthew is then linked more with the power of prayer and less with the temple incident; Walker, *Jesus and the Holy City*, 28–29.

25. Hence Harrington's explanation that "Jesus' action is best seen as a symbolic action in keeping with the prophets' symbolic actions" is not sufficient especially in the light of 12:41 as well as 17:1–5; *Matthew*, 295.

26. Or in Carson and Beale's words, "one cannot help but wonder if a more indirect claim of Jesus acting as God was not in mind at least by the time Matthew compiled his Gospel"; *New Testament Use of the Old Testament*, 70.

27. It is the climax because it is the last and most affirmative pericope to identify who Jesus is within the unity of 21:1–17.

this story, the answer is given to the audience. In the discussion of the last conflict story this function will be raised again in further detail. Suffice it here to say that at the beginning of the Jerusalem conflicts, the author has made one point clearly to the reader. That is, the hero of his narrative, Jesus, is the Davidic Messiah. Yet, he is more than the Messiah of Israel.[28] He is also the Lord of David who assumes the divine status of God according to the Jewish Scripture. However, in both the first and the last Jerusalem conflicts the religious leaders refuse to recognize the identity of Jesus.

Third, placed in the beginning of the Jerusalem conflicts narrative, this story prescribes the thematic tone for the nature of the remaining conflict stories. That is, what stands at the centre of the Jerusalem conflicts is the identity of Jesus.[29] But at this point of the Matthean narrative, it is more than showing the audience who Jesus is. This "kernel event"[30] (21:14–17) seriously challenges the Jerusalem authorities and leads to the next conflict in which the leaders ask Jesus to show them the origin of his authority.[31] The irony is that, the more clearly the supremacy of Jesus is displayed, the more fierce the objection becomes. Eventually their rejection of Jesus's identity brings him to the cross. To be sure, this function will be seen more clearly as we finish the analysis of the rest of the Jerusalem conflicts. At this stage, it is important to recognize that Jesus's action (both healing of the blind/lame and rebuke of the leaders) serves as a powerful ironic commentary on the wilful blindness of the opponents.[32]

---

28. Luz suggests that this point is part of the "entire Matthean Christology" and that Jesus's Davidic sonship should be understood in this larger horizon; *Matthew 21–28*, 90–91.

29. Harrington, *Matthew*, 296.

30. Matera includes this larger pericope of 21:1–17 as one of the kernel events of Matthew's plot. He follows Chatman's definition of a "kernel" which (1) advances the plot, (2) occasions a puzzling or difficult problem (crux) in the narrative, (3) cannot be deleted without destroying the logic of the plot, and (4) calls for the completion of another kernel and so kernels form a sequence of action; Chatman, *Story and Discourse*, 53–56; cf. Matera, "The Plot of Matthew's Gospel," 237–239.

31. Hagner, *Matthew 14–28*, 609.

32. Saunders, "No One Dared," 333.

5.1.1.3 Summary of 21:14-17 in Its Immediate Narrative and Rhetorical Context (Matt 20-22)

In this conflict story, the author mentions Jesus's healing of the lame and the blind for the last time in his narrative. The healing triggers the public (children's) praise of Jesus as the Son of David, which leads to the objection of the Jerusalem authorities. The fact that the chief priests and the scribes are angry at both Jesus's healing act, as well as the children's praise (21:15) inadvertently serves as a crucial evidence – it *is* Jesus's identity as the Davidic Messiah that is at the centre of contention. The above analysis draws three conclusions regarding the function of this conflict story. The first function is of primary importance: it confirms Jesus's identity as the Davidic Messiah who assumes the role of God.

The other two functions are that it foreshadows the final conflict story and prescribes the thematic tone for the nature of the remaining conflict stories which will be brought to a full light when the rest of the conflict stories are unfolded later. The abrupt ending of the story without any further description of the opponents gives an uneasy suspense to the reader: what will they do next?

5.1.2 Matthew 21:23-27
5.1.2.1 Matthew 21:23a: The Setting of the Story

The spatial setting in this conflict is significant because it once more places Jesus in the temple. The next indication of the temple is in 24:1, ἐξελθὼν ὁ Ἰησοῦς ἀπὸ τοῦ ἱεροῦ, therefore, it can be assumed that the teaching and the rest of the conflict stories all occur on the premises of the Jerusalem temple.[33] Even though Mark has a similar spatial setting for the conflict, Matthew redacts Mark by only mentioning Jesus in the scene.[34] He also adds that the activity of Jesus in the temple is teaching, which again demonstrates the authority of Jesus. Through such redaction the author maintains and sharpens the tension between Jesus and the temple authority, the chief priests and the elders of the people.[35]

---

33. Luz, *Matthew 21-28*, 29. This includes all parables following this conflict story as well as the polemic teaching in Matt 23.

34. So καὶ ἔρχονται πάλιν εἰς Ἱεροσόλυμα in Mark (Mark 11.27a) becomes ἐλθόντος αὐτοῦ (Matt 21:23a).

35. Repschinski, *Controversy*, 195-196.

5.1.2.2 Matthew 21:23b–27: The Conflict Scene Proper

21:26	ἐὰν δὲ εἴπωμεν· Ἐξ ἀνθρώπων, φοβούμεθα τὸν ὄχλον, πάντες γὰρ ὡς προφήτην ἔχουσιν τὸν Ἰωάννην.
21:27	καὶ ἀποκριθέντες τῷ Ἰησοῦ εἶπαν.
	Οὐκ οἴδαμεν.
	ἔφη αὐτοῖς καὶ αὐτός.
	Οὐδὲ ἐγὼ λέγω ὑμῖν ἐν ποίᾳ ἐξουσίᾳ ταῦτα ποιῶ.

In this conflict, Jesus and his opponents exchange dialogues twice, which is rare in the conflict stories.[36] What is unique about the story is that it functions as a mutual rejection to the most intense extent in all seventeen conflict stories narrated in the Gospel of Matthew. This means that in this story the author arrives at the climax in his composition of a conflict series.

This can be seen, first, by the fact that the author portrays the rejection by the Jerusalem leaders reaching its most inexcusable extent. The mutual rejection is also demonstrated, on the other hand, by the fact that Jesus denies the Jewish leaders an opportunity to discover his divinity. The following observations will unpack these two aspects.

First of all, how does the author present to the reader that the Jerusalem leaders' rejection of the divine authority of Jesus is to the most inexcusable extent? The clearest evidence suggesting the leaders are inexcusable is shown by their own words. The leaders' initial question seems to be slightly more genuine than a usual challenge. For instance, it is no longer a question of εἰ ἔξεστιν (e.g.12:2, 10), or breaking some tradition or taboo (e.g. 9:11; 15:2). Rather, among all conflict stories, the leaders here cast the most direct inquiry into Jesus's authority: Ἐν ποίᾳ ἐξουσίᾳ . . . τίς σοι ἔδωκεν τὴν ἐξουσίαν ταύτην (21:23).[37] Here the author inserts no description of any evil intent on their part by asking such a question. Unfortunately, however, their scheming among themselves reveals that they would reject the truth just like they did to John

---

36. Altogether there are three conflicts including multiple exchanges of dialogues between Jesus and his opponents, 19:1–9; 21:23–27 and 22:15–22.

37. Daube proposes that this story may bear the earliest tradition referring to Jesus's authority as "divine" or "almighty" and is more than "rabbinic authority" occurring earlier in the narrative (cf. 7:29); *New Testament and Rabbinic Judaism*, 217–218.

the Baptist (21:25-26). The author here takes up an omniscient role and lays out the thought process of the leaders,[38] which is known only to the reader of the gospel. The intriguing shift from an editorial comment ἐφοβοῦντο τὸν ὄχλον (Mark 11:32) to direct speech φοβούμεθα τὸν ὄχλον (21:26) displays the leaders' own awareness of their culpability.[39] It is clear from the leaders' thoughts that they know the right answer to Jesus's question, yet, "they cannot say it without exposing themselves."[40] The leaders finally choose not to answer Jesus's question by pretending to be ignorant and refusing to acknowledge the truth (21:27). As a result, in the reader's eyes, the Jerusalem leaders' own words unwittingly testify that their rejection of John is inexcusable (cf. 21:41).

Additionally, the Matthean narrative so far has made it clear that John the Baptist acts as the prophet Elijah (esp. 3:4; 17:10-13).[41] Therefore, in the mind of the reader, the leaders' rejection of John (hence of Jesus) cannot be sustained without denying the undeniable prophetic tradition (21:27). The condition set by Jesus and his question to the Jewish leaders (21:24-25a) indicate that the reader is led to see Jesus's authority in relation to the authority of John's baptism.[42] But how does Matthew persuade the reader to agree with this premise that John's authority was from God? To be sure, all three Synoptic Gospels share the characteristics of paralleling Jesus with John the Baptist.[43] Matthew, however, is unique in his presentation of John. Not only

---

38. Gundry suggests that ἐν ἑαυταῖς suggests private reflection rather than an open discussion among each other, in contrast to πρὸς ἑαυτοὺς in Mark (Mark 11:31) and Luke (Luke 20:5); *Matthew*, 420.

39. Gundry, *Matthew*, 420. It is the author's technique of "showing" instead of "telling" in characterizing the Jewish leaders.

40. Luz, *Matthew 21-28*, 29-30. As France rightly points out, the leaders' rejection of John is well-known, cf. 21:32; France, *Matthew*, 799.

41. John the Baptist appears or is mentioned in these passages: 3:1-7; 4:12; 9:14; 11:2-11; 14:1-13; 16:13-20; 17:10-13; 21:23-32.

42. Kingsbury suggests that "the counter-question of Jesus functions in the debate to identify Jesus with John in a manner that permits what is said of John to be accounted as applicable also to Jesus"; *Matthew: Structure, Christology*, 59.

43. Mark's John the Baptist is an Elijah *incognito* who prepares the way for a secret Messiah; Walter Wink, *John the Baptist in the Gospel Tradition* (Cambridge: Cambridge University Press, 1968), 17. Luke also portrays a parallel between Jesus and John the Baptist by including two annunciations and two birth narratives; Raymond E. Brown, *The Birth of the Messiah: A Commentary on the Infancy Narratives in the Gospels of Matthew and Luke* (New York: Associated Sulpicians of the US, 1977, 1993), 241-243.

is the parallel of the two men most pronounced in Matthew,[44] but the author most explicitly presents John as Elijah who ushers in the eschaton.[45] Therefore, John the Baptist seems to have a more elevated role in Matthew than in Mark and Luke. The implication is clear: if the one who prepares the way for Jesus has the authority from heaven, how much more is the authority of Jesus?

But what does the reader know about "John's baptism" that can be linked to the origin of Jesus's authority (21:24–25)? Or is it simply a verbal trick to cast opponents into a dilemma?[46] John's baptism is specifically mentioned in two pericopae in Matthew (3:1–12, 13–17). In both places the author portrays John as someone endowed with a divinely sanctioned authority. Yet, John's baptism is clearly inferior to that of Jesus. In the first appearance where John offers a baptism of repentance accompanied by polemical preaching (3:1–12), Matthew portrayed John as the Elijah of the last days.[47] However, in John's

---

44. Matthew develops the characterization of Jesus alongside that of John the Baptist. This observation can be shown through one of Matthew's literary characteristics – verbal repetition. That is, Matthew uses similar or same motifs in the portrayal of Jesus and John the Baptist. For example, the verb παραγίνεται is used to introduce John's appearance on the scene (3:1), and it is again used for Jesus's appearance in 3:13. This verb is only used here in Matt 3 and one other place for the coming of the Magi (2:1). Only Matthew sums up the preaching of John and of Jesus in similar expressions (3:2, 4:17 and 10:7). For other examples, see 3:7 and 12:34; 23:33; 3:8, 10 and 7:16–20/12:33–35; 3:10 and 13:42, 50; 3:12 and 13:30; 4:12 and 14:13; 14:1–2 and 16:14; 14:5 and 21:26, 46. Moreover, the narratives regarding John constitute a subplot that is analogous to the main plot of Jesus; see detailed discussions on the character and plot development of John the Baptist in comparison to Jesus in Anderson, *Matthew's Narrative Web*, 83–90, 172–174. Therefore, as Meier points out, "The tendency to parallel the two figures could be seen simply as a natural thrust of Christian faith as it developed and reflected further on key figures in the gospel story. Yet this tendency to parallel appears with great clarity only in Matthew . . ."; "John the Baptist in Matthew," 401–402.

45. Matthew's insertion of 17:13 gives the clearest comment to the reader linking John the Baptist with Elijah, which can be seen particularly by comparing Matt 11:14–15 to Luke 16:16, and Matt 17:10–13 to Mark 9:11–13. The eschatological tone is not only shown through John's identification with the prophet Elijah who prepares for the way of the Lord (3:3), but also through his message to proclaim that the kingdom is dawning and the judgment is coming (3:2, 7, 9, 12). Furthermore, the author reports that John lives in the wilderness and quotes the words of Isaiah (3:3//Isa 40:3). This peculiar location associates John with the eschatological prophet because for the Jewish mind, ". . . the desert is the place with which Israel's expectations of the end were associated" and it is a place to receive the final revelation of God; Bornkamm, *Jesus of Nazareth* (London: Hodder & Stoughton, 1960), 45. For arguments against Elijah as the forerunner of the Messiah before the beginning of Christianity, see James Robinson, "Elijah, John and Jesus: An Essay in Detection," NTS 4 (1958): 34ff.

46. This seems to be Gundry's suggestion; Gundry, *Mark: A Commentary on His Apology for the Cross* (Grand Rapids: Eerdmans, 1993), 667.

47. The expression οὗτος γάρ ἐστιν ὁ (3:3a) is clearest among synoptic accounts (cf. Mark 1:4; Luke 3:3–4) to identify John with "the preparer of the Lord's way" according to Isaiah 40:3.

own words, his baptism is inferior to that of Jesus which comes from πνεύματι ἁγίῳ καὶ πυρί (3:11–12). Because if such a mightier baptism is associated with God (πνεύματι ἁγίῳ),[48] then the authority of the person who performs such a baptism must be of divine nature. The anticipation of the divine origin of Jesus is immediately confirmed by the story following the appearance of John – Jesus's baptism by John (3:13–17). John's objection (3:13), his plea to be baptized by Jesus (3:14), the Spirit of God descending on Jesus (3:16) and the Scripture allusions (cf. Gen 22:2; Ps 2:7 and Isa 42:1)[49] all point to the superiority of Jesus and his divine origin as God's beloved Son (3:17; cf. 17:5).[50] Therefore, as far as the reader is aware, the divinely sanctioned authority of John entails a higher authority status that belongs to Jesus. The immediate context of the conflict also informs the reader of Jesus's divine authority.[51] As argued in the previous section (5.1.1 on Matt 21:12–17), the author demonstrates Jesus's authority status by his assuming the role of God

---

Combined with John's peculiar attire and diet, John is alluded to the prophet Elijah (2 Kgs 1:8) hence he bears divine-sanctioned authority; Bornkamm, *Jesus of Nazareth*, 45.

48. A strong case for this claim is put forward by Hughes, "John the Baptist: The Forerunner of God Himself," *NovT* 14 (1972): 192–201; cf. CD 4:20–21.

49. It is significant that Matthew redacts Mark's σὺ εἶ ὁ υἱός μου to οὗτός ἐστιν ὁ υἱός μου, which, as Meier correctly points out, suggests a public theophany and testimony to Jesus; Meier, *The Vision of Matthew: Christ, Church, and Morality in the First Gospel* (New York: Crossroad, 1979, 1991), 58.

50. Here is one of the only two places in Matthew that the author reports God's direct intervention in the narrative (cf. 17:5), which suggests the author's intention to associate Jesus's status directly to God; Keener, *Matthew*, 134. Jesus's divine sonship is captured by Kingsbury, *Matthew: Structure, Christology*, 40–83, especially 59; and France, *Matthew: Evangelist and Teacher*, 292–297. I am aware that the Christology regarding the Matthean Son of God title receives heated debates. There is a large body of literature discussing the issue: among others, see for example, Verseput, "The Role and Meaning of the 'Son of God' Title in Matthew's Gospel," *NTS* 33 (1987): 532–556; Kingsbury, "The Title 'Son of God' in Matthew's Gospel," *BTB* 5 (1975): 3–31. It is beyond the scope of this analysis to settle the debate in one way or another. Suffice it to say that it is highly unlikely that the "my son" refers to Israel, as Gibbs argues ("Israel Standing with Israel: The Baptism of Jesus in Matthew's Gospel," *CBQ* 64 [2002]: 511–526), because the preceding context refers to an individual who will baptize people with the Holy Spirit and fire.

51. Because when the chief priests and elders ask for Jesus's authority in doing ταῦτα, the reader likely understands it to refer to the actions not only of his teaching in the temple, but also those of the preceding day – the clearing of the temple and the healings, and possibly cursing of the fig tree; McNeile, *St. Matthew*, 304; Lohmeyer, *Matthäus*, 305, footnote 1; John Fenton, *The Gospel of Saint Matthew* (Baltimore: Penguin, 1963), 338; Hill, *Matthew*, 296; Beare, *Matthew*, 422–423; Hagner, *Matthew 14–28*, 609. However, there are scholars who disagree with this view; see Gundry, *Matthew*, 419; Alexander Sand, *Das Evangelium Nach Matthäus* (Regensburg: Verlag Friedrich Pustet, 1986), 427–428; Josef Schmid, *Das Evangelium Nach Matthäus* (Regensburge: 1965), 302; Schweizer, *Matthew*, 409.

in the temple through the conflict.⁵² The cursing of the fig tree, moreover, displays Jesus's prophetic act of judgment (21:19).⁵³

The second aspect of the function of this conflict story as the climax of all conflict stories is that Jesus denies the Jerusalem leaders any further chance to know the truth about his authority. The two responses of Jesus are unusual for conflict stories. Instead of a refutation (e.g. 9:4, 15; 12:3, 5; 15:3; 21:16), the initial response agrees to answer the leaders' question but with a condition: ἐὰν εἴπητέ μοι κἀγὼ ὑμῖν ἐρῶ (21:24). In the second response, however, instead of a statement of truth claims (e.g. 9:6, 13, 16; 12:6–8, 45; 15:7; 16:4; 19:8–9), Jesus refuses to reveal the right answer to the leaders (21:27).⁵⁴ Although the reader may anticipate the right answer to be "from God," the leaders deliberate rejection of Jesus's authority renders them unworthy to receive the truth. As a result, Jesus in this story shows a rather unusual attitude because he no longer provides any more explanation, nor does he address his own authority. His final response ends with a plain οὐδὲ ἐγὼ λέγω ὑμῖν (21:27).

The context following the conflict story serves as an illustration of the message of mutual rejection conveyed by the conflict. That is, the Jerusalem leaders' rejection of Jesus leads to God's rejection of them. The three parables following the conflict form a larger literary unit with the conflict story. The conflict formally only includes 21:23–27, but Matthew uses literary markers to tie the following parables closely to the conflict story.⁵⁵ In the conflict, the author provides details of how the Jerusalem leaders decide to reject John the

---

52. Jesus's temple cleansing is also related to the eschatological warnings issued by John the Baptist, as an act of judgment upon the temple leadership; see discussions in G. S. Shae, "The Question on the Authority of Jesus," *NovT* 16 (1974): 28.

53. However, it is still debatable whether the judgment is directed against the temple cult, or Israel as a whole; see Repschinski, *Controversy*, 312, also footnote 57; Davies and Allison, *Matthew 19–28*, 153.

54. As Luz puts it, "with v. 27 a preliminary conclusion is achieved, yet the dialogue remains strange"; *Matthew 21–28*, 26.

55. These literary markers include: (1) the beginning of the first parable is Jesus's direct speech immediately following his final answer in the conflict (21:28), Luz, *Matthew 21–28*, 26; (2) the next two parables include Matthew's redactional introduction, Ἄλλην παραβολὴν ἀκούσατε, in 21:33 and a Matthean characteristic of πάλιν εἶπεν ἐν παραβολαῖς αὐτοῖς in 22:1; see detailed discussion of Matthew's redaction of these introduction clauses in Olmstead, *Matthew's Trilogy*, 40–46; (3) there is no change of audience, France, *Evangelist and Teacher*, 223; (4) the conflict and the parable of two sons share a common motif that the leaders did not believe John the Baptist (21:25, 32); and (5) the parable of the wicked tenants repeats the leaders' reaction of fearing the people in the conflict (21:26, 46). All these markers suggest that the three parables follow the conflict closely to form a large literary unit.

Baptist and hence miss the opportunity to believe in Jesus, whereas Jesus's refusal to answer their question seems simply because the leaders fail to meet the condition (ἐὰν εἴπητέ μοι κἀγὼ ὑμῖν ἐρῶ). Yet, the refusal is firm and formidable because it is reinforced by what follows. In each of the three parables, the message is precisely that the disbelief or disobedience of the characters to a higher authority brings disastrous consequences upon themselves.[56]

The author's interesting qualifier λαός for οἱ ἀρχιερεῖς καὶ οἱ πρεσβύτεροι (21:23) elevates the degree of conflict between the leaders and Jesus to a new level of intensity and scale. In Matthew, whenever λαού is combined with οἱ ἀρχιερεῖς καὶ οἱ πρεσβύτεροι, it is due to the insertion of the author (21:23; also cf. 26:3, 47; 27:1). On most occasions, they are consistently characterized as those who explicitly press for the death of Jesus.[57] Interestingly, although this story is the only occasion among all conflict stories where the author introduces the opponents qualified by τοῦ λαοῦ,[58] and although the story does not explicitly narrate the leaders' pursuit for the death of Jesus, it is located within the illustration of the conflict story where death occurs for both opposing characters (21:39, 41, 44; 22:6, 7, 13). If Cousland is correct to suggest that λαού as a qualifier for the leaders often has an ethnic connotation, that is, it refers to Israel,[59] then the opponents of Jesus are no longer leaders of an isolated location but the ruling elite of Israel.[60] As a result, in this story the reader may see the beginning of clashes between Jesus and Israel, which is represented by οἱ ἀρχιερεῖς καὶ οἱ πρεσβύτεροι τοῦ λαοῦ.[61]

---

56. Green maintains that Matthew adds two more parables to Mark and puts the three parables in an ascending order: the first parable speaks of Israel during Jesus's days, the second one points to the destruction of Jerusalem, and the third one represents God's eschatological judgment; Green, *Matthew*, 178. It is difficult to agree with all that Green suggests; however, all three parables do display a common warning, that is, the leaders' rejection of John and Jesus thus rendering them to be excluded from God's kingdom.

57. Cf. Matt 26:3, 47 and 27:1; Repschinski, *Controversy*, 194, footnote 31; cf. Gnilka, *Matthäus II*, 216. The word πρεσβύτερος appears many more times without the λαός, but it is probably implied in the context, 16:21; 27:3, 12, 20, 41; 28:12.

58. Matt 21:23: οἱ ἀρχιερεῖς καὶ οἱ πρεσβύτεροι τοῦ λαοῦ.

59. Cousland believes that it is because these leaders are the ruling elite of Israel rather than local leaders; *Crowds in Matthew*, 77–78.

60. The opponents being the ruling elite of the nation may already be present in the first temple conflict (21:15: οἱ ἀρχιερεῖς καὶ οἱ γραμματεῖς), but their identity as being the leaders of the nation of Israel is furthermore emphasized by the qualifier τοῦ λαοῦ here (21:23).

61. So far Matthew's narrative does maintain a clear distinction between the leaders and the people/crowds; Olmstead, *Matthew's Trilogy*, 58. However, here the addition of λαός is likely

The references to John and his baptism (21:25-26, 32) remind the reader of John's warning to the descendants of Abraham (3:8-9). Within the Matthean narrative, the baptism and message of John are related to fruit bearing, repentance and judgment (3:2, 7-12). If this is what the reader has in mind, then the references to John here are likely to help the reader in making connections between the message of John and the themes occurring in the context of this conflict, namely, fruit/fruitless (21:19-20), repentance/unrepentance (21:25, 28-32, 35-39; 22:3, 5-6, 11-12, 45-46) and the judgment upon the fruitless/unrepentant (21:41, 43-44; 22:7, 13). Moreover, it needs to be noted that John's warning is addressed to all descendants of Abraham that do not produce good fruit (3:8-10, especially with the expression: πᾶν οὖν δένδρον μὴ ποιοῦν καρπὸν καλόν, even though the characters mentioned in the narrative are the Pharisees and the Sadducees (3:7)). It is likely that Matthew 21 brings those themes to a final conclusion of warning of judgment not just against the leaders of Israel but also all who follow them (cf. 21:43).[62]

5.1.2.3 Summary of 21:23-27 in Its Immediate Narrative and Rhetorical Context (Matthew 20-22)

This story is the only conflict where Jesus's authority is explicitly mentioned and challenged. Interestingly, however, the story does not offer any new information about Jesus's authority.[63] It differs from all other conflicts because the story does not include a dominical saying, nor does it have a clearly debated issue.[64] It is indeed a story of mutual rejection between Jesus and the opponents to the most intense extent. Therefore, this story is the climax in the author's composition of conflict series. There will be more conflicts in the temple, but as far as the Jewish leaders are concerned in the narrative, their hardness of heart has led them to the point of no return in their path to destruction.

---

pointing to its future use in the narrative which results in both the leaders and the people having joined responsibilities to plot and kill Jesus.

62. Cf. Charette who maintains that the warning is against the nation of Israel; *Recompense in Matthew*, 135. While such claim is possible because the scriptural background of the cursing of the fig tree – Isa 34:4; Jer 8:13 and Hos 2:12; 9:10 – all point to the nation of Israel, whether it is Matthew's intention in 21:18-20 is not certain.

63. Hagner, *Matthew 14-28*, WBC, 610.

64. Hultgren, *Adversaries*, 73-75.

The above analysis demonstrates that this story is not only another demonstration of the divine authority of Jesus but also a verdict on the culpable party, namely, all descendants of Israel who oppose Jesus. The conflict story connects with its wider narrative context, which links the origin of the authority and baptism of Jesus with that of John. Various explanations have been asserted to probe Matthew's theological intention for the parallel placement of Jesus and John.[65] From the perspective of literary analysis, however, the most plausible idea is: if the forerunner already enjoys an highly exalted status and fulfils the expected role of Elijah,[66] then how much more exalted is the status of ὁ ἐρχόμενος who is ushered in by the forerunner?[67] To put it more plainly in Wright's words, "If John is Elijah, this means, without question, that Jesus is the Messiah. Therefore, the whole discussion of John turns out to be a veiled discussion of Jesus himself."[68] This story shows that the Jerusalem leaders, who represent all descendants of God, know the origin of John's baptism as evidenced in their own words. However, by rejecting John the Baptist, they also intentionally reject Jesus. In return, Jesus refuses to further reveal the truth to the Jerusalem leaders that will eventually lead them to be excluded from the kingdom of God.

5.1.3 Matthew 22:15-22

5.1.3.1 Matthew 22:15: *The Setting of the Story*

The temple continues to be the venue for this conflict regarding paying tax to Caesar. By narrating ὅπως αὐτὸν παγιδεύσωσιν ἐν λόγῳ, the author provides the reader an inside view of the evil intent of the opponents. This is the second reference to the Pharisees since Jesus entered Jerusalem. It continues the course established in the first reference where the Pharisees (together

---

65. Following Trilling ("Täufertradition," *BZ* 3 [1959]: 288–289). Wink also provides a helpful survey on various explanations; *John the Baptist*, 40–41.

66. Anderson, *Matthew's Narrative Web*, 172–174, 190.

67. In this sense, Yamasaki is quite right to point out that John's primary significance in the first gospel is to "influence the way in which the narratee experiences the narrative" and that the character of John the Baptist functions mainly at the level of Matthew's rhetoric (discourse level). However, I find it questionable, as Yamasaki suggests, that John's story makes no contribution at the story level apart from John's baptism of Jesus; *John the Baptist in Life and Death*, 148.

68. Wright, *Jesus and the Victory of God* (Minneapolis: Fortress, 1996), 496.

with the chief priests) intend to arrest Jesus (21:45).⁶⁹ The following conflict scene commences a description of how they attempt to carry out the scheme. There are two points worth noting in the setting, and their significance will be discussed in the next section:

1. Instead of following Mark's account (Mark 12:13: ἀγρεύσωσιν), the author uses an unusual word συμβούλιον to describe the Pharisees' intention.⁷⁰
2. The phrase συμβούλιον ἔλαβον is a repeated motif in Matthew, describing the Jewish leaders' murderous action against Jesus (cf. 12:14; 22:15; 27:1,7; 28:12).

5.1.3.2 Matthew 22:16-22: The Conflict Scene Proper

The conflict is the first of the last four conflict stories connected uninterruptedly in the Matthean narrative (cf. 22:23–33, 34–40, 41–46). Although following Mark's order of events, the author alters two stories in Mark (Mark 12:28–34, 35–40) into the form of conflicts.⁷¹ The four conflicts are redacted in such a way that they form a literary unit,⁷² which implies that this conflict shares similar functions and contributes to similar authorial purposes with the other three conflicts.

This conflict scene consists of several dialogue exchanges, similar to the stories in 19:1–9 and 21:23–27. As mentioned in the previous sections (4.1.4 and 5.1.2), the first question in the scene (ἔξεστιν δοῦναι κῆνσον Καίσαρι ἢ οὔ) is suspended and addressed only after the subsequent parenthetical exchange is dealt with. What is distinctive of this story, however, is that it contains

---

69. Although both "the chief priests" and "the Pharisees" are inserted (cf. Mark 12:12), the mention of the Pharisees in 21:45 deserves particular attention because their presence cannot be assumed from the context, unlike the chief priests (21:23); therefore, the author's insertion has to be an intentional addition to the characters.

70. It is unusual because the Greek word παγιδεύω is a NT *hapax legomenon*; Davies and Allison, *Matthew 19-28*, 212.

71. It is likely, as Daube suggests, that the grouping of these four stories represent "a fourfold scheme with which the first-century Rabbis were familiar. More precisely, he [the author] regarded these questions as representative of four different types of question distinguished by the early Rabbis." See more discussion on the four types of question in Daube, *New Testament and Rabbinic Judaism*, 158–163.

72. Van Tilborg argues for this unity in *Jewish Leaders*, 49–50. His reason rests primarily on the fact that "the Pharisees of 22:15 are structurally connected with those of 22:34 and 22:41"; 50.

elaborate praises to Jesus from the Jewish leaders,[73] which occur nowhere else in Matthew's narrative. The distinction contributes to the author's intention to emphasize the hypocrisy of the Pharisees and draws the reader's attention back to them after a series of conflicts between Jesus and the temple authorities in Jerusalem. The function of this conflict can be viewed in two facets.

First, it functions to advance the Matthean plot in anticipation of the distinctive features of Matthew 23, where the Pharisees are the main target of Jesus's indictment. Such a function can be detected from the author's particular highlight on the hypocrisy and evil of the Pharisees. Through the eyes of the reliable character, Jesus, the author tells the reader explicitly about the πονηρίαν of the Pharisees and them being ὑποκριταί (22:18).[74] It anticipates Matthew 23 where the word ὑποκριταί occurs frequently as a key characteristic of the Jewish leaders (23:23, 15, 23, 25, 27, 29).[75] Even though the Pharisees also appear in Mark's account (Mark 12:13), Matthew makes it more explicit by moving it forward and using a nominative form of Φαρισαῖοι (22:15). It calls attention to the Pharisees who are really the opponents of Jesus behind the trapping plot.[76] This is in contrast to Mark's account where the opponents are the members of the Sanhedrin (Mark 12:13; cf. 11:27).[77] Furthermore, the Pharisees are characterized as "tempting/testing" Jesus (22:18).[78] This characterization echoes the temptation account (4:1–11). Not only does the word πειράζω occur in both stories (22:18; cf. 4:1, 3), they also share a similar ending with the challenger leaving Jesus (ἀψίημι αὐτὸν in both 4:11 and 22:22).

Other Matthean redactional features further exemplify the author's focus on the Pharisees being evil. Within the context of the conflict – the parable of

---

73. The intention could be a mock of praise, or part of an entrapment through flattery. However, the words themselves use the language of praise, which only occurs in this conflict.

74. This disposition of the Pharisees is a common motif in Matthew; see, for example, 12:34–35, 39, 45; 13:38–39; 16:4.

75. As Anderson points out, the word ὑποκριταί is an epithet used by Matthew for the Jewish leaders. It first occurs in the context of the Sermon on the Mount but without specific characters attached. It is not until 15:7 that the word is applied to the scribes and the Pharisees. However, the occurrence here in 22:18 is the most relevant context for ch. 23; see Anderson, *Matthew's Narrative Web*, 103–105.

76. Luz, *Matthew 21–28*, 62; Davies and Allison, *Matthew 19–28*, 212.

77. Repschinski, *Controversy*, 199.

78. Even though Jesus's questioners are the disciples of Pharisees and the Herodians (22:16), as shown above, Matthew's redaction in the setting of the story (22:15) clearly shows that the Pharisees are the key characters in the story. This claim can be further supported by the frequent occurrences in the later conflict stories (cf. 22:34, 41).

wicked tenants (21:45), in a similar fashion,[79] the author inserts οἱ Φαρισαῖοι (together with οἱ ἀρχιερεῖς) as the recipients of the polemic parable (21:33–44). In the setting of the story (22:15), the evilness of the opponents is shown by Matthew's insertion of the phrase συμβούλιον λαμβάνειν in 22:15. This is a motif repeated in Matthew, which occurs five times. The phrase is first used at the end of the Sabbath controversy to describe the Pharisees' murderous plot against Jesus (12:14). After this conflict, the phrase is used three more times, solely designating those plots as of a deathly nature (see 27:1, 7; 28:12; also cf. the verb συνεβουλεύσαντο in 26:4[80]). The evilness of the opponents is also shown by Matthew's redaction of Mark's ἀγρεύσωσιν (Mark 12:13) to παγιδεύσωσιν, a word which only occurs here in the New Testament.[81] Both words are used figuratively in the text: ἀγρεύσωσιν means "to catch unguarded,"[82] and παγιδεύσωσιν means "to set a snare/trap."[83] However, Matthew's παγιδεύσωσιν is more intense and thus serves to heighten the evilness of Pharisees. The word is usually used metaphorically as a hunting term;[84] therefore, Jesus in this story seems to have become the "prey" of the opponents.

Furthermore, the hypocrisy and evil of the Pharisees is shown by their own words.[85] Despite previous encounters between Jesus and the Jewish leaders that are hostile in nature,[86] this conflict story contains the only praise of Jesus by the opponents. However, it is shown to be a false flattery because the author has already given such a clue to the reader in the setting of the story: it is intended to "ensnare" Jesus (22:15). The three-tiered effusive praises underline

---

79. Similar to the redaction in 22:15, Matthew inserts οἱ ἀρχιερεῖς καὶ οἱ Φαρισαῖοι instead of maintaining a general "they" implied by the verb ἐζήτουν which points to the chief priest, teachers of the law and the elders in Mark 11:27.

80. The verb is a counterpart to the phrase συμβούλιον λαμβάνειν; Anderson, *Matthew's Narrative Web*, 115–116.

81. It is a NT *hapax legomenon*; cf. footnote 70.

82. *BDAG*, 15.

83. *BDAG*, 747.

84. Though rare in the New Testament, this word occurs frequently in the LXX, e.g. Deut 7:25; 12:30; 1 Sam 28:9; Prov 6:2; Eccl 9:12, *BDAG*, 747; Gundry, *Matthew*, 441; cf. McNeile, *Matthew*, 318.

85. The word ἀποστέλλουσιν allows the assumption that the following words delivered by the disciples of Pharisees and the Herodians are in fact representing the Pharisees' view.

86. So far in the Matthean narrative there are thirteen conflict stories: 9:1–8, 9–13, 14–17; 12:1–8, 9–14, 22–37, 38–45; 13:53–58; 15:1–9; 16:1–4; 19:3–9; 21:14–17, 23–27.

their deceitfulness.[87] In fact, the Jewish leaders' behavior in previous conflicts exhibits exactly the opposite of these praises: they are not true (21:27); they do not teach the way of God truthfully (21:25, 32); their opinions depend on the view of others (21:25-27). Following the praise, the author redacts Mark's question (12:14) to an imperative εἰπὲ οὖν ἡμῖν τί σοι δοκεῖ. As a result, it lays bare the intent of the praise – to place Jesus's honour in focus and to force him to answer the question.[88] In the end, the praise is proven to be false by Jesus's own comment (22:18).

The hypocrisy and evil of the Pharisees can also be seen from their pairing up with Herodians. This conflict has the only occurrence of τῶν Ἡρῳδιανῶν in Matthew.[89] Even if historically the Pharisees and the Herodians both paid Roman tax, they were unlikely allies according to the reader's *a priori* knowledge, because the Herodians were politically and theologically against the Pharisees.[90] What is more intriguing is that, instead of following Mark's account where the chief priests and the elders pair the two groups together,[91] Matthew has the Pharisees initiating it.[92] This strange cooperation displays the Pharisees' determination to corner Jesus because each group favors either a yes or a no answer,[93] either of which is enough to fatally trap Jesus. The fact that the opponents have a Roman coin in their possession may also

---

87. The three-tiered praises contain: (1) Jesus's attribute – being true, (2) Jesus's action – teaching God's way truthfully, (3) Jesus's further attribute – not partial to anyone. Donahue suggests that (1) and (3) are often used to describe the attributes of God, see Lev 19:15; 1 Sam 16:7; Acts 10:34; Rom 2:11; Eph 6:9; Col 3:2; Jas 2:9; "A Neglected Factor in the Theology of Mark," *JBL* (1982): 572-573, also note 33. Cf. Davies and Allison, *Matthew 19-28*, 213-214.

88. It shows that the opponents are not interested in what the law says (ἔζεστιν) but what Jesus thinks; Davies and Allison, *Matthew 19-28*, 214.

89. See a helpful survey of scholarly debates regarding their identity in Meier, "Historical Jesus and Historical Herodians," *JBL* 119 (2000): 741. Who the Herodians are exactly is beside the point of this analysis; suffice it to say that they are likely in favor of the Roman rule and thus would take a "no" answer as offensive.

90. See Hoehner, "Herodian Dynasty" in *DJG*, 325.

91. Mark 12:13 records that the Herodians are sent by the chief priests and the elders.

92. The subject is the Pharisees: ἀποστέλλουσιν αὐτῷ τοὺς μαθητὰς αὐτῶν μετὰ τῶν Ἡρῳδιανῶν . . .

93. Herodians would be more willing to pay than Pharisees who are more reluctant; Hill, *Matthew*, 303; Meier, *The Vision of Matthew*, 155; Gundry, *Matthew*, 442; Lohmeyer, *Matthäus*, 324; McNeile, *Matthew*, 318; and Pierre Bonnard, *L'évangile selon Saint Matthieu* (Neuchâtel: Delachaux & Niestlé, 1963), 322. Pace Patte, *Matthew*, 310; Klaus Wengst, *Pax Romana and the Peace of Jesus Christ*, trans. John Bowden (Philadelphia: Fortress, 1987), 58, 195. Wengst's reason is that nothing in the text indicates that the two groups held differing positions on the issue. However, silence from the text does not prove anything and we need to resort to historical

be an indication of their hypocrisy. Historically, the image-bearing coin was considered blasphemous by many of Jesus's contemporaries so much so that they would refuse to carry it.[94] Therefore, as Giblin suggests, "... Jesus points out the hypocrisy of his questioners by having them produce a coin, which shows in effect their allegiance to Caesar ..."[95]

The second aspect of the function of this conflict is that it begins a series of conflicts culminating in Jesus's unequivocal victory over his opponents. It serves as a step building up toward Jesus's superiority over the opponents because the scheme to trap Jesus in his words is quickly thwarted.[96] Even though the opponents seem to create a well-planned dilemma for Jesus, the narrative makes plain to the reader that in fact Jesus is in charge of the conversation. The author arranges a rebuke (22:18), a counter-question (22:20), and two commands as Jesus's response (22:19, 21). The rebuke of Jesus exposes their evil nature to the reader (22:18). Then, instead of responding to the question, Jesus returns with a command (22:19). Following the command, Jesus still does not answer the question but asks the opponents another question (22:20). All of Jesus's questions and commands are responded to by the opponents' compliance. Finally, instead of arresting Jesus, the opponents left him, showing their defeat in this conflict. Interestingly, the phrase ἀψέντες αὐτὸν echoes the ending of the temptation story in 4:11 where the devil's scheme is also thwarted.[97] At the end of the conflict, the attitude of the opponents changes from malicious tempting to being amazed (ἐθαύμασαν in 22:22). It does not necessarily mean that they turn to admire Jesus or his

---

studies to determine the Herodians' attitude. Though others hold that the identity of Herodians is simply ambiguous, e.g. see France, *Matthew*, 832.

94. Hipp. *Refut*. 9:21 (of some Essenes); also see discussion on means of payment and customs by Zeev Safrai, *The Economy of Roman Palestine* (New York: Routledge, 1994), 171–177.

95. As Charles H. Giblin suggests, "The first counter-question makes a special point of the questioners' hypocrisy by immediately unmasking it. Accordingly, Jesus' next statement (in Matthew and Mark) can be taken as bringing them to supply the proof"; "The 'Things of God' in the Question Concerning Tribute to Caesar: (Lk 20.25, Mk 12.17, Mt 22.21)," *CBQ* 33 (1971): 526; also Davies and Allison, *Matthew 19–28*, 215.

96. This function is the first step because all last four conflicts share this function and the intensity only increases with the superiority of Jesus being repeated over and over again.

97. Luz, *Matthew 21–28*, 67.

answer;[98] however, it does reveal to the reader that they finally admit Jesus's victory in this conflict.[99]

5.1.3.3 Summary of 22:15-22 in Its Immediate Narrative and Rhetorical Context (Matthew 20-22)

The conflict story begins a series of final four conflicts following the Matthean trilogy of parables (21:28-32, 33-46; 22:1-14).[100] Beginning here, throughout the rest of the conflict stories Jesus's opponents no longer challenge the authority of Jesus, nor question his identity. This is likely because each side has reached their final rejection in the previous conflict (21:23-27). Instead, the final four conflicts then bear witness to the Jewish leaders' vicious acts toward Jesus, that is, their attempts to either humiliate Jesus or trap him in a murderous plot.[101] Meanwhile, they also function to demonstrate Jesus's unequivocal superiority over his opponents culminating in the conflicts. These two functions are significant for advancing the Matthean plot because they enable the author to intensify the ironic contrast between the superiority of Jesus in the conflict stories and his Jerusalem trial leading to the crucifixion.

It is within this wider context that the conflict stands. This story in particular shows the Pharisees' hypocrisy and evil, but at the same time Jesus's superiority is made plain to the reader. The narrative of the leaders' hypocrisy anticipates Matthew's polemic discourse in Matthew 23 where the Jewish

---

98. Pace Hagner's claims that here the word ἐθαύμασαν is used positively to show the opponents' admiration of Jesus because the context is unclear about admiration; *Matthew 14-28*, 636.

99. The word ἐθαύμασαν expresses a sense of astonishment and the word itself is neutral. Only the context of this word determines whether it is used positively or negatively; *BDAG*, 444; cf. Luz, *Matthew 21-28*, 67. It is used by Matthew for expressing amazement of different characters, including Jesus, the disciples, the crowds, Jesus's opponents and Pontius Pilate, 8:10, 27; 9:33; 15:31; 21:20; 22:22; 27:14.

100. The term "trilogy" is adopted from Olmstead's work, *Matthew's Trilogy*, 20.

101. This point is in line with Schweizer's proposal for a trial schema for the overall structure of Matt 21-25 although it seems more appropriate to consider Schweizer's schema as an analogy rather than a well-planned structure of Matthew. Schweizer suggests that 22:15-46 contains a trial of Israel where the leaders are unable to answer Jesus's counter-questions. Then the verdict is given in 23:1-32 – guilty. He further identifies 23:33-36 as the sentence – the punishment for the murder of all righteous blood will fall upon this generation. The "execution of the sentence" is carried out in 23:37-24:2 with God himself (Jesus) leaving the temple, followed by the prediction of its destruction. However, all these are only the introduction to the main concern of Matthew, the warning to the community which begins in 24:3ff; Schweizer, *Matthäus und Seine Gemeinde* (Stuttgart: KBW Verlag, 1974), 116-125.

leaders are condemned for their failing characters, some of which are already being exhibited in the story. Namely, the Jewish leaders are hypocrites who refuse the truth (21:27), they do not teach the way of God truthfully (21:25, 32) and they are easily swayed by the view of others (21:25–27).

5.1.4 Matthew 22:23–33

5.1.4.1 Matthew 22:23a-b: The Setting of the Story

The author intends to closely link this conflict with the previous one (22:15–22) by inserting the phrase ἐν ἐκείνῃ τῇ ἡμέρᾳ in the setting of the story.[102] This is the third time the Sadducees appear in the Matthean narrative (cf. 3:7 and 16:1–12). But unlike the previous two appearances where the Sadducees are mentioned together with the Pharisees, here the Sadducees come onto the stage by themselves.

5.1.4.2 Matthew 22:23c–33: The Conflict Scene Proper

This pericope, recorded by all Synoptic Gospels, features a challenge posed by the Sadducees, which appropriately depicts their belief – the denial of the resurrection of the dead:[103] λέγοντες μὴ εἶναι ἀνάστασιν. This story is similar in form to the majority of conflict stories, which comprise only one exchange of dialogue (9:1–8, 9–13, 14–17; 12:1–8, 9–14, 22–37, 38–45; 13:53–58; 15:1–9; 16:1–4; 21:14–17).

Additionally, like many other conflict stories (cf. 9:14–17; 12:1–8, 9–14; 15:1–9; 19:3–9), the story appears to address doctrinal concerns, in this case, the resurrection of the dead and/or marriage in the afterlife.[104] However, a literary analysis of the story demonstrates that this view is insufficient for several reasons. First of all, it does not account for the author's decision to

---

102. The phrase is missing in both Mark (12:18) and Luke (20:27). France comments that the phrase is an editorial connection holding "together the series of disparate debating topics as part of a single complex"; *Matthew*, 837; similarly, Hagner believes this is "a way of linking similar passages rather than a strictly chronological note"; *Matthew 14–28*, 640.

103. Cf. Acts 23:8; Jos. *War* 2:164–165; *Ant.* 13:278–279; 18:16–17. Furthermore, apparently Sadducees often pose challenges to the idea of resurrection, especially to the Pharisees; E. Ellis, *The Gospel of Luke* (Grand Rapids: Eerdmans, 1981), 236.

104. This view mainly derives from the assumption that Jesus's dominical saying is independent of the narrative context in its original form. Not surprisingly this view is mostly upheld by scholars of source or form criticism who believe that this story is created to meet doctrinal concerns within the Christian community; Hultgren, *Adversaries*, 129–130; Bultmannn, *History*, 36.

situate this story in this part of the narrative. Moreover, the view of a simple doctrinal concern is inadequate because Jesus's answer seems to focus equally (if not more) on the nature of God, not simply on the doctrinal issues of whether there is marriage in afterlife.

A close literary reading of the story finds that the function of this conflict resembles the previous story of paying tax to Caesar (22:15–22), even though the challenge in this story concerns a completely different matter. The function of the story includes two aspects.

First, this story is intended to show the insincerity and foolishness of the Sadducees and to anticipate Jesus's indictment of the Jewish leaders in Matthew 23. Even though the word πειάζω is not specifically mentioned here, the conflict is another "testing/tempting" story, which aligns the Sadducees' moral status with that of the Pharisees.[105] Here, these Jewish leaders are (again) characterized to be on the same side with the "tempter" Satan (cf. 4:1, 3). The editorial comment, λέγοντες μὴ εἶναι ἀνάστασιν,[106] is the most explicit characterization of the Sadducees in Matthew. Yet, by revealing to the reader this belief of the Sadducees, the author sets out an irony because the subsequent challenge arises precisely from an assumed reality of afterlife.[107] The irony[108] of the story of seven brothers leads scholars to correctly suggest that on this occasion the Sadducees "test" Jesus and aim to ridicule his idea

---

105. As Hagner rightly puts, "... it is clear that the Sadducees, like the Pharisees, have come to 'test' Jesus as a teacher"; *Matthew 14–28*, 640.

106. The Matthean redaction of Mark's οἵτινες λέγουσιν (12:18) to λέγοντες leads to textual variations as well as some scholarly debates. Some early manuscripts, such as a² K L Q *f*¹³, include οἱ before λέγοντες, probably due to the assimilation of the parallels (Mark 12:18; Luke 20:27); Metzger, *Textual Commentary*, 58. This analysis considers λέγοντες as a participle referring to a relative clause (who are saying ...) rather than a direct discourse. The main reason is that the dialogue seems to begin with the main verb ἐπηρώτησαν and the second λέγοντες (22:24), otherwise the double use to introduce an utterance made by the same subject in such a short distance from each other seems redundant. Yet, however the conclusion is, it does not change the fact that this is the editorial comment of the author to characterize the Sadducees.

107. However, this irony is not unique to Matthew but is retained by all synoptic authors because all three include the comment on the Sadducees' belief; cf. Mark 12:18; Luke 20:27.

108. Irony in this case is understood as something that occurs "when the reverse of an expected course of action takes place, or when an effect or paradox or contrast is introduced"; Werner Kelber, *The Oral and Written Gospel: The Hermeneutics of Speaking and Writing in the Synoptic Tradition, Mark, Paul and Q* (Bloomington: Indiana University Press, 1983, 1997), 123. Also, see discussion of irony in the previous chapters, especially under the heading 4.1.1.2.

of resurrection.[109] Instead of telling the reader of their testing, the author shows such a picture of the Sadducees through their own words. They raise a scenario of a woman marrying seven brothers in the afterlife, which is only possible under the levirate marriage law (Deut 25:5–6; cf. Gen 38:8). It is intended to make the idea of resurrection absurd, because ". . . the woman is destined to spend eternity as the wife of seven men at once, and polyandry is not acceptable in Jewish culture."[110]

Moreover, the Sadducees already appeared as tempters in a previous conflict story (16:1). Such a characterization is likely to be remembered by the reader at this point of the narrative. The insincerity and foolishness of the Sadducees is exposed by the reliable character Jesus. The response of Jesus does not begin with any answer to the question. Instead, it begins with a negative appraisal of the character of the Sadducees: Πλανᾶσθε μὴ εἰδότες τὰς γραφὰς μηδὲ τὴν δύναμιν τοῦ θεοῦ (22:29).[111] The word πλανάω here refers to "proceed without a sense of proper direction."[112] It is often used for those who wander like sheep without a shepherd (cf. 9:36).[113] One needs to bear in mind that the Sadducees are part of the ruling class in Jewish society, particularly in Jerusalem.[114] As leaders, they are supposed to know their Scripture and God's power. Therefore, the fact that such a description applied to the Sadducees who are supposed to be the leaders of the people produces an ironic effect and discredits them in the eyes of the reader. In this story, Jesus also comments twice that the Sadducees do not know the Scripture (22:29, 31). Matthew particularly highlights the Sadducees' guilt by replacing οὐκ ἀνέγνωτε . . . πῶς εἶπεν αὐτῷ ὁ θεός (Mark 12:26) with οὐκ ἀνέγνωτε τὸ ῥηθὲν ὑμῖν ὑπὸ τοῦ θεοῦ λέγοντος.[115] As a result, the Sadducees are aligned as guilty

---

109. Garland, *Matthew*, 227; all the Synoptic Gospels record that Jesus believes in resurrection after death, particularly his own (cf. *par* Matt 16:21; 17:23; 20:19; Luke 14:14; 16:19–31; 23:43).

110. France calls it a *reductio ad absurdum*, *Matthew*, 838; cf. Repschinski, *Controversy*, 210.

111. Luz says here Jesus "turns immediately to a frontal attack"; *Matthew 21–28*, 70.

112. BDAG, "πλανάω", 821.

113. See Herbert M. Braun, "πλανάω, κτλ.," *TDNT* 6:242ff.

114. Günther Baumbach suggests that the Sadducees belong to those who are regulars of the higher Jerusalem priesthood; *Jesus von Nazareth im Lichte der jüdischen Gruppenbildung* (Berlin: Evangelische Verlaganstalt, 1971), 51; Saldarini, *Pharisees, Scribes and Sadducees*, 298.

115. Gundry, *Matthew*, 446; here is the only occasion in Matthew where he inserts ὑμῖν in the scriptural quotation; however, I find the text does not warrant a claim of "to the Jewish people" here as Hagner suggests; *Matthew 14–28*, 642. Instead, ὑμῖν is used intentionally to

as the Pharisees for their ignorance of the Scripture in the Matthean narrative (cf. 9:13; 12:3, 5, 7; 15:3; 19:4; 21:42).

Other textual evidences showing the evilness of the Sadducees include, for instance, the phrase παρ' ἡμῖν (22:25) in the Sadducees' words exposing their deceitfulness. Even though Matthew largely follows Mark's account in this conflict, he inserts παρ' ἡμῖν to show the reader that the Sadducees endeavor to make the scenario sound as a true event, whereas the context of "testing" Jesus indicates to the reader that in reality it is fictitious.[116] In addition, the Sadducees' address of Jesus as Διδάσκαλε is ironical.[117] They are hypocritical just like the Pharisees, because this address is not out of respect for Jesus, but for the sole purpose of introducing their ridicule of him with a sarcastic tone.

The second aspect of the function of this story is that it is intended to show the supremacy of Jesus over his opponents and to prepare for the polemic force of his indictment on the leaders in Matthew 23. This is demonstrated by the manner with which he responds to the challenge. As in many other conflict stories, Jesus does not answer the question asked by the opponents. This way, Jesus switches the power in the exchange to his hands. Jesus first gives the audience a negative evaluation of his opponents (22:29).[118] By pointing out that the Sadducees know neither the Scripture nor the power of God, Jesus essentially is saying they do not know their God. This way, the opponents' question, τίνος τῶν ἑπτὰ ἔσται γυνή, is never directly answered

---

express an irony: the Sadducees, being the descendants of the patriarchs, do not understand the Scripture.

116. As Repschinski rightly suggests, "With this brief insertion Matthew treats the Sadducees with irony. The preposterous case that the Sadducees propose makes them preposterous as well, since it supposedly occurred among them"; *Controversy*, 210. Pace Hagner, *Matthew 14–28*, 641, and Gundry, *Matthew*, 445. However, I find it very unlikely that Matthew intends to show the Sadducees presenting a true scenario by inserting παρ' ἡμῖν.

117. France, *Matthew*, 837. In Matthew, the title διδάσκαλε is never used by the disciples, but only used by strangers or opponents; France, *Evangelist and Teacher*, 257; cf. Günther Bornkamm, "End-Expectation and Church in Matthew," in *Tradition and Interpretation*, eds. Günther Bornkamm, Gerhard Barth, and Heinz Joachim Held (London: SCM Press, 1963), 41. For the title of διδάσκαλε, see Kingsbury, "On Following Jesus: The 'Eager' Scribe and the 'Reluctant' Disciple (Matthew 8:18–22)," *NTS* 34 (1988): 48–49. For a full discussion on Jesus as διδάσκαλε, see Byrskog, *Jesus the Only Teacher*, 200–220, who does not agree with France's notion that the title is used negatively.

118. Although in this story Matthew follows Mark (12:24) closely, Matthew redacts Jesus's rhetorical question into a statement as if "he renders a verdict on the Sadducees," therefore the Matthean Jesus appears to be more forceful; Repschinski, *Controversy*, 210; Gundry, *Matthew*, 446.

because Jesus firstly invalidates their assumption: ἐν γὰρ τῇ ἀναστάσει οὔτε γαμοῦσιν οὔτε γαμίζονται ... (22:30).[119]

The supremacy of Jesus is also demonstrated by his understanding of the Scripture in terms of the power of God in the resurrection.[120] The purpose of Jesus's answer is neither to explain marriage in the afterlife, nor to defend resurrection.[121] Instead, he intends to expound on the nature of God manifest by the Scripture.[122] Jesus's response alludes to several Exodus passages (22:32; cf. Exod 3:6, 15, 16) which serve as the rationale for the conclusion, οὐκ ἔστιν [ὁ] θεὸς νεκρῶν ἀλλὰ ζώντων.[123] It is worth noting that both the rationale and the conclusion focus on the nature of God.[124]

But how does the God of the patriarchs relate to the God of the living (22:31–32)?[125] And how do all these statements relate back to the power of God (cf. 22:29b)? Apparently, Jesus is not unique in his statements (22:29b,

---

119. Luz, *Matthew 21–28*, 70.

120. Repschinski believes that the Scripture allusion verse serves as a proof for the existence of resurrection and shows that Jesus is superior in knowledge of the Scripture. However, he does not provide a detailed explanation; *Controversy*, 210–211.

121. Luz, *Matthew 21–28*, 73–74; on this point, Kegel's comment concerning Mark's version of this story is applicable to Matthew as well: "Ein theologisches Interesse an der Auferstehungsfrage ist hier bei ihm nicht zu spüren. Er hat das Streitgespräch so gut wie unverändert übernommen und zusammen mit anderen zu einer eindrucksvollen Demonstration der Überlegenheit Jesu gestaltet" ["There is no theological interest in the resurrection issue here. He took over the argument almost unchanged and, together with others, made it an impressive demonstration of Jesu' superiority"]; Günter Kegel, *Auferstehung Jesu-Auferstehung Der Toten* (Gütersloh: Gütersloher Verlagshaus Gerd Mohn, 1970), 70.

122. As F. G. Downing observes, "Jesus' reply by-passes the details of the query and is addressed to what seems to underlie"; "Resurrection of the Dead: Jesus and Philo," *JSNT* 15 (1982): 45.

123. Though some scholars see 22:32b as rather a complementary premise than a conclusion; Luz, *Matthew 21–28*, 72; I think it is necessary to consider it a conclusive statement to Jesus's response; also Davies and Allison, *Matthew 19–28*, 231, footnote 76.

124. This claim is similar to Donahue's suggestion in regards to the Markan account of the story: "The saying of Jesus in 12:26–27 also touches on the nature of God"; "A Neglected Factor," 577. Although it seems to me that Jesus's saying not just "touches on," but in fact focuses on, God's nature.

125. This is a highly debated question among scholars. Davies and Allison summarize the explanation in seven options; *Matthew 19–28*, 231–232. The core disagreement essentially lies between whether either the patriarchs are still alive after death, e.g. Hagner, *Matthew 14–28*, 642; Meier, *Matthew*, 255; or how they will be raised up in the resurrection because "the living God would not define himself in terms of the dead"; Fenton, *St. Matthew*, 356. However, the former option seems to be more metaphorical rather than actual therefore cannot be argued from a linguistic point of view; *pace* Gundry, *Matthew*, 446. Because it poses several interpretative difficulties (it either renders Jesus's argument to rabbinic style or it calls for clarification of bodily resurrection; see discussion in McNeile, *Matthew*, 322), the latter option is more likely;

31–32). Scholars have observed that these words reflect a well-known Jewish prayer contemporary to Jesus's time. In the first and second *berakah* of the Eighteen Benedictions, there is such a prayer, ". . . our God and God of our fathers; God of Abraham, God of Isaac and God of Jacob . . . You are powerful . . . sustain the living, reviving the dead."[126] Such text witnesses to the Jewish understanding that the power of God is evidenced in his ability to sustain the living and revive the dead. If this is indeed the logic at work in Jesus's response, then God can only be acknowledged as the God of living. Moreover, what relates the living God with the patriarchs is in fact dependent on the nature of covenant made between them. That is, the covenant is perpetual and lasts beyond their death.[127] The Sadducees unfortunately missed precisely this aspect of the patriarchs' relationship with God.[128] Matthew inserts the ending of the story: the crowds were astonished (22:33: ἐκπλήσσω).[129] Of all four times this word is used in Matthew (cf. 7:28; 13:54; 19:25), the context is

---

pace Hagner (yet he recognizes the patriarchs only "are alive in God" after they died; *Matthew 14–28*, 642).

126. The Eighteen Benedictions, according to Instone-Brewer, was dated pre-70 CE; *Traditions of the Rabbis from the Era of the New Testament, Vol. 1: Prayer and Agriculture* (Grand Rapids: Eerdmans, 2004); see the text of the Eighteen Benedictions on 98; also cf. 115–116.

127. There are two aspects derived from this perpetual covenantal relationship: (1) as France notes, the living God identifies himself with the patriarchs, therefore "the covenant by which he [God] binds himself to them [the patriarchs] is too strong to be terminated by their death . . . and therefore they must be alive with him after their earthly life is finished"; France, *Matthew*, 840–841; also "The God of the patriarchs is for Israel the covenant God who accompanies and will redeem Israel"; Luz, *Matthew 21–28*, 72; cf. François Dreyfus, "L'argument scripturaire de Jésus en faveur de la résurrection des morts: Marc 12:26–27," *RB* 66 (1959): 213–224; (2) the power of God surpasses the need to perpetuate one's name through biological heirs. The result is that when God accepts one into a covenantal relationship with him, the question of continuing the name – the test case raised by the Sadducees (22:25–28) – becomes irrelevant; Downing, "Resurrection of the Dead," 45–46; cf. J. G. Janzen, "Resurrection and Hermeneutics: On Exodus 3:6 in Mark 12:26," *JSNT* 23 (1985): 49–52, 54–56. Option (2) is further supported by Patte's suggestion that there is a word play between ἀναστήσει (22:24c) and ἀναστάσεως; in his words, "the raising of the dead (cf. 22:31a) performed by God is taking the place of the raising up of the children for a dead man performed by a man"; *Matthew*, 312–313.

128. Hence Matthew redacts Jesus's words to underline the irony, οὐκ ἀνέγνωτε τὸ ῥηθὲν ὑμῖν ὑπὸ τοῦ θεοῦ.

129. The word ἐκπλήσσω is defined as the state of mind that is "filled with amazement to the point of being overwhelmed"; *BDAG*, 308.

consistently related to Jesus's teaching and emphasizes his superior authority.[130] Here Jesus is shown to have defeated his opponents again.[131]

5.1.4.3 Summary 22:23–33 in Its Immediate Narrative and Rhetorical Context (Matt 20–22)

This conflict story is the second of the final four conflicts in the Matthean narrative. These four conflicts are closely connected by the author, both in terms of the rhetoric and narrative order. In this conflict, the Sadducees alone as Jesus's opponents, attempt to ridicule the idea of resurrection which is a belief held by Jesus.[132] Again, Jesus refutes them successfully. The story in appearance seems to address the question whether there are marriages in the afterlife, or to show the reader a Jesus who defends the resurrection. However, a close literary reading of the story paints a different picture.

The function of the story, evidenced from the above analysis, is very similar to the previous story (i.e. paying tax to Caesar in 22:15–22). On the one hand it bears witness to the vicious acts of the Jewish leaders toward Jesus. More specifically, this conflict reveals to the reader the hypocrisy and absurdity of the Sadducees. Together with the other three conflicts within its context (22:15–22, 34–40, 41–46), it anticipates Jesus's indictment of the Jewish leaders in Matthew 23. On the other hand, it functions to demonstrate Jesus's unequivocal superiority over his opponents. These two functions converge within the same story to continue to advance the Matthean plot. The irony in the story is expressed when the Sadducees not only fail to achieve their purpose to ridicule Jesus, but their challenge inadvertently leads to the exposure of their ignorance of the Scripture. It foreshadows the more pointed irony elaborated in Matthew 23 which, through the rebuke of Jesus, demonstrates vivid inconsistency and contrast between the words and deeds

---

130. Timothy Dwyer, *The Motif of Wonder in the Gospel of Mark* (Sheffield: Sheffield Academic Press, 1996), 20–21; Davies and Allison, *Matthew 19–28*, 233.

131. Even though it does not necessarily mean that the crowd has decided to follow Jesus; Luz, *Matthew 21–28*, 73; Hagner, *Matthew 14–28*, 642. The defeat of the Sadducees is confirmed by the beginning of the next conflict that they were ἐφίμωσεν (22:34a).

132. Daube suggests that the four conflicts in Matt 22 represent four types of questions in early rabbinic debates. This conflict, then, resembles the question of *boruth*, namely, they are "mocking questions designed to ridicule a belief of the Rabbi. And they are all directed against the same belief, namely, belief in resurrection." Daube, *New Testament and Rabbinic Judaism*, 158–159; cf. Hill, *Matthew*, 305.

of the religious leaders (e.g. 23:3–4, 13, 15, 23–32).[133] Furthermore, the two functions contribute to the greater irony in the passion story where a person of divine identity and authority (demonstrated by a series of conflict stories) will be put to death on the cross.

5.1.5 Matthew 22:34–40

5.1.5.1 Matthew 22:34: The Setting of the Story

After the conflict between the Sadducees and Jesus (22:23–33), the spotlight turns back to the Pharisees. The setting of this conflict exhibits a similar feature with the setting in the previous story. That is, as the author's redaction,[134] it closely ties the story to its previous context by providing an ending: ἐφίμωσεν τοὺς Σαδδουκαίους. In addition, compared to Mark's account (Mark 12:35), Matthew identifies the opponents of Jesus as οἱ Φαρισαῖοι explicitly and adds a phrase συνήχθησαν ἐπὶ τὸ αὐτό. The significance of the redaction will be discussed in the next section in relation to the literary function of this conflict.

5.1.5.2 Matthew 22:35–40: The Conflict Scene Proper

Although this story is the penultimate within the whole series of conflict stories, it is the last confrontation initiated by the opponents of Jesus. In the Matthean narrative context, this story presumably still occurs in the temple[135] as part of Jesus's teaching activities.[136] Because the centre of the teaching is on the double commandment of love, it is not surprising then that most scholarly comments focus on the interpretation of such commandments. While it is necessary to seek appropriate understanding of Jesus's teaching, the literary function of the story remains unanswered. For example, why does the author place the teaching on the great commandment at this juncture of the narrative? What purpose does the author intend to achieve by turning

---

133. As Samuel MacComb correctly observes, Matthew 23 "contains one of the most cutting and searching pieces of irony in literature"; "The Irony of Christ," *Biblical World* 23, no. 2 (1904): 106.

134. Except for the word ἀκούσαντες, as Repschinski writes, "the setting owes almost nothing to Mk 12.28"; *Controversy*, 216; Hagner, *Matthew 14–28*, 645.

135. Between ἐλθόντος αὐτοῦ εἰς τὸ ἱερόν (21:23) ἐξελθὼν ὁ Ἰησοῦς ἀπὸ τοῦ ἱεροῦ (24:1), there is neither a new venue nor a change of venue mentioned in the narrative.

136. It is implied by the insertion of διδάσκοντι in 21:23 and continues in Jesus's long discourse in ch. 23–25:46; cf. van Tilborg, *Jewish Leaders*, 49.

a 'scholastic dialogue'[137] into a conflict story?[138] How does this conflict story function to advance the Matthean narrative plot? The following analysis is an attempt to address these questions.

The literary analysis of the story displays an interesting factor. That is, the function of this story is consistent with its preceding context. Just like the story of paying tax to Caesar (22:15–22) and the question of resurrection (22:23–33), it continues to anticipate the crescendo of the denunciation of Jewish leaders in Matthew 23. Furthermore, it paves the way for the further ironic contrast between Jesus's supreme role and his trial and death in chapters 26–27. This general observation can be unpacked into two points.

First, this story continues to show the deceitfulness and hostility of the Pharisees and it anticipates Jesus's indictment of the Jewish leaders, especially the Pharisees, in Matthew 23. Mark's account mentions only εἷς τῶν γραμματέων whose exact identity is ambiguous (Mark 12:28),[139] but Matthew highlights the opponents as the Pharisees by redacting Mark and mentions οἱ Φαρισαῖοι explicitly (22:34). The emphasis on the Pharisees is consistent with Matthew's redaction in 21:45 and 22:15 (see discussion in 5.1.3.2). It anticipates the condemnation of Jesus particularly on the Pharisees in Matthew 23 (23:2, 13, 15, 23, 25, 27, cf. 23:16, 33). The deceitfulness of the Pharisees is also exposed by the author's redactional emphasis of πειράζων αὐτόν (22:35). This word is the most explicit indicator for the question (ποία ἐντολὴ μεγάλη ἐν τῷ νόμῳ) to be considered as a trap, unlike the genuine question in Mark's account.[140] In Matthew, this word πειράζω is only used to characterize the

---

137. Bultmann categorizes Mark 12:28–34 as a scholastic dialogue, which is defined as "in the scholastic dialogues it is not necessary to have some particular action as the starting-point but for the most part the Master is simply questioned by someone seeking knowledge." However, Bultmann also notes a close relationship between the controversy and scholastic dialogues; *History*, 54–55.

138. Similarly, Hagner comments that "Matthew has turned Mark's didactic story (*Schulgespräch*) into a conflict story (*Streitgespräch*)," *Matthew 14–28*, 645. However, there are scholars who reject the question of the Pharisees as a challenge and conclude that the story is not a conflict, such as Abrahams, although he seems to have confused Matthew's account with Mark's by mentioning the scribes and the Pharisees in the same context; *Studies in Pharisaism and the Gospels*, 18.

139. Schweizer suggests that the scribe/teacher of the Law in Mark 12:28 "need not have been one of the Pharisees"; *Matthew*, 424.

140. Green observes that "the purpose of the question is to 'tempt' Jesus, i.e. to trap him into an answer which could be used against him"; *Matthew*, 184. The question, according to Garland, is presumably intended to expose Jesus's lack of mastery of the law; *Matthew*, 228. Admittedly, without the word πειράζω and based on the question only, it is difficult to conclude

Jewish leaders (cf. 16:1; 19:3; 22:18) and one other character, Satan (4:1, 3). It is likely, therefore, that the author intends these "testing" stories (16:1-4; 19:3-9; 22:15-22, 34-40; cf. 22:23-33) to mirror the cosmic warfare between God and Satan.[141]

Furthermore, the author shows the reader the hostility of the Pharisees in the setting of the story (22:34). Mark's version has no commendation for the interlocutors (Mark 12:28, 32, 34), whereas Matthew adds a phrase συνήχθησαν ἐπὶ τὸ αὐτό. It is likely, as many commentators observe, that it alludes to the LXX Psalm 2:2,[142] in which the context describes the hostility of the rulers against God and his anointed one.[143] The phrase συνήχθησαν ἐπὶ τὸ αὐτό itself seems redundant,[144] yet it agrees with the LXX text verbatim (Ps 2:2: καὶ οἱ ἄρχοντες συνήχθησαν ἐπὶ τὸ αὐτό κατὰ τοῦ κυρίου καὶ κατὰ τοῦ χριστοῦ αὐτοῦ). In addition, the verb συνάγω is used again to describe the Pharisees (22:41) in the context of a question περὶ τοῦ χριστοῦ in 22:42.[145]

The setting tells the reader that the cross-examination by Jewish leaders of Jesus continues. The author constructs this story closely with the previous conflict by concluding that the Sadducees are silenced. Instead of sending their disciples to trap Jesus (22:15), now the Pharisees themselves try their turn.[146] The Pharisees address Jesus as διδάσκαλε, which is insincere and

---

whether it has a malicious intent or not; Luz, *Matthew 21-28*, 81; this is because the question itself was hotly debated among Jewish rabbis; Carson, *Matthew II*, 646. The question alone could be taken as either finding faults in the answer to trap Jesus, or it is equally possible that the Pharisees seek an answer that they do not really know themselves.

141. See Powell's argument that the conflict between Jesus and the Jewish leaders constitutes a subplot for the main plot of conflict between God and Satan; "The Plot and Subplots," 199-201.

142. Gundry, *Matthew*, 447, and *The Use of the Old Testament*, 141; Repschinski, *Controversy*, 216; Hagner, *Matthew 14-28*, 646; France, *Matthew*, 844; McNeile, *St. Matthew*, 324; Gnilka, *Matthäus II*, 258-259. Davies and Allison suggest other parallel texts as well, e.g. LXX Neh 4:8; 6:2; Ps 101:23; cf. Acts 4:26; 1 Clem 34:7; *Matthew 19-28*, 239. However, Luz says the appearance of ἐπὶ τὸ αὐτό together with συνήχθησαν might be a coincidence; *Matthew 21-28*, 75, note 4.

143. Even though the rulers and kings in the Psalm text may refer to the Gentiles, it does not necessarily negate the possible link between the two texts.

144. Especially συνήχθησαν already means "to be brought together," and then it is added with ἐπὶ τὸ αὐτό (in the same place); France, *Matthew*, 841, footnote 1.

145. Gnilka believes that it further shows Matthew's intention to allude to Ps 2:2; *Matthäus II*, 259.

146. France, *Matthew*, 844. Despite the difference between the Pharisees and the Sadducees in the story world, at least for Matthew's reader, it is not surprising that the two groups come together to oppose Jesus (16:1, 6, 11-12; cf. 3:6).

ironical (22:36). The author's insertion here is to conform to previous two conflicts (22:15–22, 23–33).[147] Just as in the previous two, the author creates an ironic contrast where the opponents seemingly pay respect to Jesus while it is the opposite feeling in their hearts.[148]

Second, in this story, Jesus's superiority over his opponents is demonstrated through the nuanced messianic role of Jesus in relation to the Scripture. It foreshadows the focal point of the next (and final) conflict story where the author concludes the temple conflicts with Jesus as the Lord and the Messiah (22:41–46; cf. 21:14–17). It is worth noting that Jesus answers the test by first quoting the Scripture (22:37/Deut 6:5; 22:38/Lev 19:18).[149] Such a manner is similar to way he responds to Satan's testing questions earlier in the gospel (4:4, 7, 10). Just like his answer to the Sadducees' question regarding the resurrection, here again Jesus's answer does not conform to the assumptions of the opponents. The question, ποία ἐντολὴ μεγάλη ἐν τῷ νόμῳ, assumes the disparity of the law.[150] However, the Jewish tradition is not consistent in whether to emphasize the equality or the disparity of the law.[151] Interestingly,

---

147. As discussed in 5.3 and 5.4, the title διδάσκαλος is only used by strangers or opponents in Matthew; France, *Matthew, Evangelist and Teacher*, 257.

148. This feature is a classic feature of an irony, "a contrast of appearance and reality"; D.C. Muecke, *Irony: The Critical Idiom* (London: Methuen, 1970), 35.

149. The joining of "loving God" with "loving one's neighbor" is not Jesus's own invention; see for example, in Luke 10:27 it is attributed to Jesus's questioner. It is likely to have existed in pre-Christian Judaism, see e.g. *Test. of Iss.* 5:2, 7:6; *Gen. Rab* 14 [16b]; Mic 6:8; Philo, *Decal.* 22:108–110, *Sifra Lev* 19:18; cf. Daube, *Rabbinic Judaism and the New Testament*, 247. Here Matthew omits Mark's opening of the *Shema*, "Hear O Israel . . ." (Mark 12:29), which was usually recited twice daily by pious Jews in Jesus's day. However, see Foster's challenge on the uniformity of the wording of the *Shema* in the first century; "Why Did Matthew Get the *Shema* Wrong?: A Study of Matthew 22:37," *JBL* 122 (2003): 321-333.

150. It is generally agreed that μεγάλη is superlative as "the greatest" because it is a Semitic locution; James H. Moulton and N. Turner, *A Grammar of New Testament Greek*, vol. 3 (Edinburgh: T & T Clark, 1906-1976), 31; also cf. France, *Matthew*, 844; Hagner, *Matthew 14–28*, 646; Klaus Berger, *Die Gesetzesauslegung Jesu: Ihr historischer Hintergrund im Judentum und im Alten Testament* (Neukirchen-Vluyn: Neukirchener Verlag, 1972), 203.

151. On the one hand, there is evidence showing that all the laws are of equal weight and importance. Daube observes that, "though by the time of Jesus most Rabbis held that the entire religion was implied in a small number of first principles, or even in a single one, yet they never ceased to insist on the absolute and independent validity of each particular commandment"; *Rabbinic Judaism and the New Testament*, 251. For example, *Mek. Ex.* 6 and *Sifra Deut.* 12:8, 19:11; cf. Str-B 1: 902ff. On the other hand, there are also rabbinic discussions involving questions concerning the most important commandment. For example, a famous "golden rule" (what is hateful to you, do not to your neighbour) given by Hillel is said to be the "whole Torah, while the rest is commentary" (*b. Shab* 31a); *Test. Iss.* 6 gives certain Scriptures as the epitome of the law; cf. Hagner, *Matthew 14–28*, 646; Luz, *Matthew 21–28*, 81.

Jesus's answer seems to affirm the equality of the commandments as much as their disparity (αὕτη ἐστὶν ἡ μεγάλη καὶ πρώτη ἐντολή. Δευτέρα δὲ ὁμοία αὐτῇ . . .).[152]

The personal authority of Jesus related to ὁ νόμος . . . καὶ οἱ προφῆται, which is most salient in the first gospel also demonstrates the superiority of Jesus (cf. 5:17; 7:12; 11:13). In this story, Jesus proposes a specific relationship between the whole scriptural tradition and the two commandments of love:[153] ἐν ταύταις ταῖς δυσὶν ἐντολαῖς ὅλος ὁ νόμος κρέμαται καὶ οἱ προφῆται. The key word here is κρεμάννυμι, which is used figuratively in Matthew to refer to "hang/depend on," like "a door hangs on its hinges."[154] Among various nuances offered by scholars,[155] the two commandments of love may be best described as the fundamental hermeneutical principle through which all laws must be interpreted.[156] By describing such a relationship between the commandments

---

152. Matthew not only omits Mark's qualification of other commandments being less than these two, μείζων τούτων ἄλλη ἐντολὴ οὐκ ἔστιν, he also adds δευτέρα δὲ ὁμοία αὐτῇ to emphasize the equality even though the latter is called "the second"; the commandment "to love one's neighbor is no longer, as in Mark, subordinated to the commandment to love God"; Repschinski, *Controversy*, 219. The Pharisees probably would agree with its importance but dispute the degree; Hagner, *Matthew 14–28*, 647.

153. As an entirely Matthean redaction, "this statement is peculiar to Matthew"; Hultgren, *Adversaries*, 48; cf. Gundry, *Matthew*, 449; Repschinski, *Controversy*, 219; Davies and Allison, *Matthew 19–28*, 245.

154. Most commentators agree on this semantic meaning, e.g. Georg Bertram, "κρεμάννυμι," *TDNT* 3:919–21; *BDAG*, 566; France, *Matthew*, 847.

155. Scores of studies are devoted to interpreting the saying revolving around κρεμάννυμι; see, for example, Moo's succinct summary of different understanding of the relationship implied by κρεμάννυμι into three categories ("Jesus and the Mosaic Law," 6–7). In addition to the alternative adopted by this analysis, the other two are: (1) as a general principle, the double commandment of love is to be set apart from the rest of the law, which can be derived from the double commandment – this is a scholastic exercise not applicable to the New Testament usage; cf. Carson who argues that because the law and the Prophets cannot be simply deduced from these two commandments, κρεμάννυμι does not imply "derivation"; *Matthew 13–28*, 465; (2) the double commandment of love is isolated from the rest of the Scriptures, yet does not eliminate the validity of the latter; cf. Banks, *Jesus and the Law*, 169. On the parallel between Matthew's and the rabbinic usage of the word κρεμάννυμι as a technical term in Jewish exegesis, scholars seem to reach a better agreement; Donaldson, "The Law That 'Hangs' (Mt 22.40): Rabbinic Formulation and Matthean Social World," *SBL 1990 Seminar Papers*, ed. David J. Lull (Atlanta: Scholars Press, 1990), 15; cf. Daube, *Rabbinic Judaism and the New Testament*, 250. Rabbinic evidence can be seen, for example, *b. Shab* 31a; *Sifra Lev* §195 (on Lev 19:1–4), §200 (on Lev 15–20); *Exod. Rab.* 30:19, "The whole Torah rests on justice" (comments on Exod 21:1); *m. Ḥag.* 1.8, "they are the essentials of the law."

156. This is the second alternative of nuances summarized by Moo, "Jesus and the Mosaic Law," 7; cf. Barth, "Matthew's Understanding of the Law," 78–85; Victor P. Furnish, *The Love Command in the New Testament* (London: SCM Press, 1973), 74; Hagner's comment is also

of love and the phrase ὁ νόμος καὶ οἱ προφῆται, which encompasses the whole scriptural tradition (cf. 5:17; 7:12; 11:13),[157] the Matthean Jesus here essentially is interpreting the Torah based on his own supreme authority.

The phrase ὁ νόμος κρέμαται καὶ οἱ προφῆται is not new for the Matthean reader. This is because Matthew uses it repeatedly (5:17; 7:12; 11:13; 22:40) more than other evangelists (cf. Luke 16:16; Acts 13:15).[158] Furthermore, the phrase ὁ νόμος καὶ οἱ προφῆται appears only in the pronouncements of Jesus in Matthew (cf. Rom 3:21).[159] It is likely that Matthew intends to bind the authority of ὁ νόμος καὶ οἱ προφῆται with the person of Jesus. Such an intention can also be discerned from the first appearance of the phrase (5:17).[160] Therefore, for Matthew, ὁ νόμος καὶ οἱ προφῆται are no longer a set of impersonal rules;[161] instead, Jesus becomes the "fulfilment" of the law and the prophets (οὐκ ἦλθον καταλῦσαι ἀλλὰ πληρῶσαι, 5:17b).[162] Such a personal

---

very similar to this nuance and perhaps captures both the ambiguity and the general sense of the interpretation: "the commandments of the law and the teaching of the prophets cannot be fulfilled apart from the twofold love commandment"; *Matthew 14–28*, 647.

157. The phrase ὁ νόμος καὶ οἱ προφῆται is not a common term in Jewish literature. Evidence includes, for example, 2 Macc 15:9; 4 Macc 18:10; cf. Str-B 1:240. The New Testament evidence emphasizes the unity of the whole scriptural tradition: Sand, *Das Gesetz und die Propheten: Untersuchungen zur Theologie des Evangeliums nach Matthäus* (Regensburg: Pustet, 1974), 192; Hubert Frankemölle, *Jahwebund und Kirche Christi: Studien zur Form- und Traditionsgeschichte des Evangeliums nach Matthäus* (Münster: Aschendorff, 1974), 298ff; Grundmann, *Matthäus*, 478. Therefore, in Matthew the phrase is most likely to signify the whole Scripture (cf. 5:17; 7:12; 11:13). Berger adds the need to include explicit references to the Scripture in the context, *Die Gesetzesauslegung Jesu*, 224; cf. Davies and Allison, *Matthew 1–7*, 484.

158. Variations of the phrase elsewhere in the New Testament either have the name Moses attached to the law, e.g. Luke 24:44 (τῷ νόμῳ Μωϋσέως καὶ τοις προφήταις καὶ ψαλμοῖς); Acts 28:23 (τοῦ νόμου Μωϋσέως καὶ τῶν προφητῶν); or they communicate an action related to the law and the prophets, e.g. John 1:45 (τῷ νόμῳ καὶ οἱ προφῆται εὑρήκαμεν); Acts 24:14 (τοῖς κατὰ τὸν νόμον καὶ τοῖς ἐν τοῖς προφήταις γεγραμμένοις).

159. Among the use of the phrase and its variation by other New Testament writers (cf. Luke 16:16; 24:44; Acts 13:15; 24:14; 28:23; Rom 3:21), they appear only twice in the pronouncements of Jesus in Luke (Luke 16:16 and 24:44).

160. Cf. Foster, *Community, Law and Mission*, 185–186.

161. As used in 2 Macc 15:9; 4 Macc 18:10; also see discussion above in note 157.

162. This feature is distinctive to Matthew to the extent that he includes the most explicit statement on the 'fulfilment' relationship (5:17b). However, this aspect of 'fulfilment' is also implied by other New Testament texts, for example, Luke 24:44; John 1:45; Acts 24:14; Rom 3:21. There is a large body of literature on how to interpret plhrow. See discussions and helpful summaries of different alternatives in, for example, Davies and Allison, *Matthew 1–7*, 485–487; Luz, *Matthew 1–7*, 214–215; Hagner, *Matthew 1–13*, 105; Foster, *Community, Law and Mission*, 185–186.

aspect of Jesus attached to ὁ νόμος καὶ οἱ προφῆται also displays his superiority which cannot be matched by his opponents.

5.1.5.3 Summary of 22:34–40 in Its Immediate Narrative and Rhetorical Context (Matt 20–23)

This conflict story is the third of the final four conflicts in the Matthean narrative. These four conflicts are closely linked to each other by the author, both in terms of the rhetoric and narrative order.

The function of this story in the narrative, evidenced from the above analysis, is very similar to the previous two stories (i.e. paying tax to Caesar and the question on the resurrection, 22:15–22, 23–33). On the one hand it continues to bear witness to the vicious acts of the Jewish leaders toward Jesus. The author's redactional hands clearly show the reader the deceitfulness and hostility of the Pharisees. It prepares for the fifth discourse in the following context where Jesus pronounces his unabating judgment on the Jewish leaders (Matt 23). On the other hand, the conflict functions to demonstrate the superiority of Jesus over the opponents. This story echoes the teaching of Jesus in the first discourse where Jesus claims to "fulfil" the law and the prophets. In a real sense, at this point of the Matthean narrative, in the reader's eyes the person of Jesus *is* the fulfilment. These two functions again converge within the same story and continue to highlight the unequivocal supremacy of Jesus in the face of the opponents' repetitive attempts to trap him. Together with the other three conflicts within its context (22:15–22, 23–33, 41–46), they advance the Matthean plot by anticipating the crescendo of Jesus's indictment of the Jewish leaders in Matthew 23, where the Pharisees appear as their representative.[163]

---

163. Cf. Carson, *Matthew 13–28*, 465. The message of Matt 23 is appropriately captured by Garland's comment, "Matthew recalled and spliced together the earlier traditions of Jesus' encounters with these contentious leaders in order to form the montage we have in chap. 23. This served to illustrate how the Jewish leaders, here represented by the scribes and Pharisees, had failed in vital matters, most notably in their interpretation of the law, so that they stood in direct opposition to God's will and ultimately shut men out of the kingdom of heaven." Garland, *Intention of Matthew 23*, 213.

5.1.6 Matthew 22:41–46

5.1.6.1 Matthew 22:41a: The Setting of the Story

This is the final of the six temple conflicts as well as the last conflict story in the whole gospel. The setting of the story is succinct. Yet the author repeats the verb συνηγμένων and its subject τῶν Φαρισαίων, both of which are also featured in the setting of the previous conflict (22:34–40). The significance of the repetition will be discussed in the next section, suffice it to mention three characteristics: (1) the repetition reinforces the author's allusion to Psalm 2.[164] (2) It closely ties this conflict to the previous one, which renders the four conflicts in Matthew 22 into a literary unit. (3) The author changes Jesus's audience from the general public to his usual opponents,[165] the Pharisees, and thus redacts the story into a conflict.[166]

5.1.6.2 Matthew 22:41b–46: The Conflict Scene Proper

As the last conflict story in the gospel, the issue in contention is evidently christological, echoing that of the first conflict in Matthew 9:1–8. However, it does not simply address the question of the Son of David. Instead, as will be shown in the following, the story is concerned with the nexus between the Son of David and David's Lord, the God of Israel. This nexus of the two ultimately defines the Messiah in Matthew. Literary analysis suggests that this story functions at two levels.

At the narrative level, the story maintains the contrast between the superiority of Jesus over the opponents and the incompetence of the Jewish leaders. This function is consistent with that of all other temple conflicts (cf. 21:14–17, 23–27; 22:15–22, 23–33, 34–40). The incompetence of the Pharisees as Jewish leaders is shown in their inability to answer Jesus's question, that is, they could not comprehend the divine status of the Messiah. As far as verbal conflict is concerned, they are no longer able to challenge Jesus (22:46). The emphasis of the narrative, however, rests on the unanswered question of Jesus, which is intended to elicit the reply of the readers.[167] The dialogue

---

164. I agree with Gundry who suggests that συνηγμένων is a "Mattheanism" echoing Ps 2:2, *Matthew*, 450; cf. Davies and Allison, *Matthew 19–28*, 251.

165. This can be inferred from Mark 12:35, 37.

166. Bultmann *History*, 51; cf. Repschinski, *Controversy*, 225.

167. Or as Davies puts it, "the readers of the narrative had been prepared from its beginning to answer this question. Jesus is understood to be the Christ, and the messianic

scene shows that Jesus is in charge of the conversation just like in all the other conflicts. However, unlike all other stories in the conflict series, this final story has a distinctive feature. That is, this is the only occasion where Jesus takes on the role of a challenger and poses a dilemma to the opponents. They respond with an answer to the first question without any deflection, but they are silenced by the second question (22:46). So, what is so difficult about the second question of Jesus for the leaders?

Jesus's reasoning and questions ultimately intend to elicit an answer to affirm the divinity of the Davidic Messiah.[168] The first question is concerned with the relationship between the Christ and the Son of David. The opponents affirm Jesus's implication that the Son of David is the Messiah (22:42). However, Jesus's second question implies that Messiah is also the Lord of David, which is supported by the citation of Psalm 110 (22:43-44). Therefore, the key issue really lies in the second question where the divinity of David's Lord is in view (22:43, 45).[169]

The context in the Matthean narrative already demonstrates that Jesus is the Christ in the line of David. Although the title τος χριστος is addressed in the third person in Jesus's question (22:42), up to this point of the narrative the reader has already been shown the messiahship of Jesus.[170] Moreover,

---

descendant of David"; Margaret Davies, *Matthew*, 2nd ed. (Sheffield: Sheffield Phoenix Press, 2009), 178.

168. Regarding the relationship between the Son of David and David's Lord, scholars divide over the implicit answer as to whether it is a denial of the Messiah being the Son of David. For example, commenting on Mark 12:35-37, William Wrede believes that the question implies that Jesus is not David's son but God's; *Vorträge und Studien* (Tübingen: Mohr, 1907), 174; Burger argues for a direct polemic against "Son of David" as a title in this passage in Mark 12:35; *Jesus als Davidssohn: Eine traditionsgeschichtliche Untersuchung* (Göttingen: Vandenhoeck & Ruprecht, 1970), 52ff. Others argue for a radical interpretation of the relationship between the two, or an affirmation of the divine status of the Messiah, e.g. Hultgren, *Adversaries*, 45; Kingsbury, "The Title 'Son of David' in Matthew's Gospel," *JBL* 95 (1976): 595-596.

169. There are only two alternatives to this question. Either, Jesus is denying the fact that the Messiah can be the Son of David; however, this position contradicts both what Matthew has presented in the gospel that Jesus as the Messiah is the Son of David (1:1, 16, 17, 20; 9:27; 12:23; 15:22; 20:30-31; 21:9, 15) as well as the common knowledge in Jewish tradition that the Messiah comes from the Davidic lineage (e.g. 2 Sam 7:12-13; Ps 89:4; Ps of Sol 17:21); or, Jesus is affirming that the Messiah is both David's son and David's Lord. Duling rightly suggests that the Matthean Jesus is in effect asking the Pharisees to ponder in what ways the Messiah can be both David's son and David's Lord; "Therapeutic Son of David," 406; cf. Brian Nolan, *The Royal Son of God: The Christology of Matthew 1-2 in the Setting of the Gospel* (Fribourg: Editions Universitaires Fribourg Suisse, 1979), 182.

170. So far, the key evidence from the Matthean text includes: (1) the prologue of the gospel as the authorial commentary repeatedly affirms that Jesus is the Christ (1:1, 16, 17,

even though Jesus never addresses himself as the "Son of David," it is used by the author (1:1, 20[171]) as well as the supplicants to address Jesus and is a title Jesus willingly accepts (9:27; 12:23; 15:22; 20:30–31; 21:9, 14).[172] Therefore, as far as Matthew intends to show to the reader, Jesus takes on the role of the Davidic Messiah.[173]

However, the author intends more significance for Jesus's messiahship than simply the descendant of David. He uses the quotation of Psalm 110:1 to provide a scriptural basis for a Messiah who assumes a divine status.[174] Psalm 110:1 contains three themes, namely, the Messiah's enthronement by God (κάθου ἐκ δεξιῶν μου), the defeat of his enemies as promised by God, and the title κύριος.[175] The enthronement theme, being the most significant

---

18); (2) as the reliable character in the gospel, Jesus implicitly accepts the Messiah as his title (16:16, 20); cf. Repschinski, *Controversy*, 226. There are also many texts where Jesus is implied as the Messiah from the author's use of the Scripture, e.g. 1:23/Isa 7:14; 3:3/Isa 40:3; 4:14–15/Isa 9:1–2; 8:17/Isa 53:4; 11:10/Mal 3:1; 12:18–21/Isa 42:1–4; cf. Donald Juel's discussion on the messianic interpretation of servant passages in Isaiah; *Messianic Exegesis: Christological Interpretation of the Old Testament in Early Christianity* (Philadelphia: Fortress, 1988), 128–131. Therefore, the reader is more informed on Jesus being the Christ in Matthew's narrative; Luz, *Matthew 21–28*, 89.

171. Even though in 1:20 the title "Son of David" is addressed to Joseph through the voice of an angel, in effect it still points to the Davidic lineage of Jesus.

172. It needs to be noted that Matthew is the only evangelist who explicitly addresses Jesus as "the Son of David"; cf. David Hay, *Glory at the Right Hand: Psalm 110 in Early Christianity* (New York: Abingdon, 1973), 116; cf. Duling, "Therapeutic Son of David," 405–406; Nolan, *Royal Son of God*, 183.

173. The notion of the Davidic Messiah is widely accepted in Judaism, not only in the New Testament: the Christ comes from the lineage of David; Géza Vermès, *Jesus the Jew*, 130–140. However, Marinus de Jonge offers a different opinion. He suggests that the term anointed does not designate any specific person, nor does the expectation of an anointed form an essential part of Jewish eschatological thinking; see "The Use of the Word 'Anointed' in the Time of Jesus," *NovT* 8 (1966): 132–148.

174. Even though Ps 110 is regarded as a Royal Psalm (France, *Jesus and the Old Testament*, 165), it is likely that the figure enthroned in Ps 110 is messianic such as the one mentioned in Dan 7:9, possibly through the bridge of Ps 80:18: Let your hand be upon the man of your right hand, and the son of man whom you have made strong for yourself; Hay, *Glory at the Right Hand*, 26, also note 32; also cf. France, *Jesus and the Old Testament*, 164–165. Moreover, the assumption that Ps 110 refers to the Messiah is the basis upon which the two dialogue parties can carry out their conversation; cf. Novakovic, *Messiah, the Healer of the Sick*, 55.

175. Ferdinand Hahn, *The Title of Jesus in Christology: Their History in Early Christianity* (London: Lutterworth, 1969), 129–130; cf. Martin Hengel, *Studies in Early Christology* (Edinburgh: T & T Clark, 1995), 135. However, Hay suggests four themes in Ps 110:1 with the fourth one being "intercession or priesthood of Jesus," whereas the other three are essentially the same with Hahn's category; Hay, *Glory at the Right Hand*, 45. This analysis, however, considers Hay's fourth category as secondary, therefore, it is omitted in the listing. This is because compared to the first three themes explicit in the text of Ps 110:1, the fourth theme is

one among the three,[176] is typically used by New Testament writers to refer to the exalted status of Jesus after his resurrection or in his heavenly reign (e.g. 26:64; Act 2:34–35; Rom 8:34; 1 Cor 15:25; Eph 1:20; Col 3:1; Heb 1:3, 13; 8:1; 10:12–13).[177] Yet in this pre-Easter story, the Psalm is quoted to solve the "riddle"[178] of how David's Son (i.e. the Messiah) can be David's Lord at the same time. It seems, therefore, at least for Matthew, this Psalm is intended to define the exact status of the Messiah.[179] As far as the narrative indicates, the exalted status is applied to the Messiah as a general quality rather than only a temporal-limited attribute. It shows that the author attempts to establish the divinity of the Messiah over against the mere human designation of "Son of David" as upheld by the Pharisees.[180]

The interpretation of Psalm 110 which includes the divine sonship of the Messiah finds witnesses in the LXX and later Jewish literature. The Greek translation of Psalm 110:3 (LXX Ps 109:3) "distinctly describes the birth of a

---

in fact most salient in Ps 110:4. The usage such as in Rom 8:34; Heb 8:1; 10:12–13 (as cited by Hay as examples of the fourth theme) is likely implied from the context of Ps 110:1. Among the three themes, the title κύριος seems to be the focus in Jesus's question (22:43, 45). Loader rightly points out that here the focus on the title κύριος is different from the majority usage of Ps 110:1 in Christian tradition: "Christ at the Right Hand – Ps.CX.1 in the New Testament," *NTS* 24 (1978): 214. However, because the three themes form a meaningful unity (Hengel, *Studies in Early Christology*, 135), and because all three are present in the quotation of this Psalm in Jesus's reasoning for his second question (22:45), they need to be interpreted as a whole to determine the function of Ps 110:1 in this story.

176. Hahn, *Title of Jesus*, 130; cf. Hengel, *Studies in Early Christology*, 135–136. The throne itself relates to the image in Dan 7:9, another Scripture passage that bears the possible divine characteristic of a Messiah; Alan Segal, *Two Powers in Heaven: Early Rabbinic Reports about Christianity and Gnosticism* (Leiden: Brill, 1977), 47–49.

177. According to Hay, "the right-hand position certainly symbolizes highest honour and closeness to Yahweh"; *Glory at the Right Hand*, 20, 59; cf. Hagner, *Matthew 14–28*, 650.

178. The term is borrowed from Wright's "Royal Riddles," *Jesus and the Victory of God*, 493, 510.

179. Cf. Carson, *Matthew 13–28*, 466–467. In this sense, although Kingsbury is right to point out the divinity of the sonship in this story, Jesus's sonship as the Son of God is not so much a salient point of focus as the identity of the Messiah defined by his highly exalted status. Kingsbury argues that in understanding this story, the sonship is more important than lordship in that Son of God surpasses the Son of David; "The Title 'Son of David,'" 596. The context of Ps 110:1 also points to a messianic figure that assumes the prerogative of God, such as in v. 6: the Messiah judges the whole earth and crushes the rulers of the whole earth.

180. This statement essentially agrees with Loader's comment on Mark 12:35ff. Leaving aside Loader's quest for earlier or later dating of this christological reflection, his view is probable that here is "an understanding which saw in the exchange an expression of the inadequacy of the simple human designation 'Son of David' to express the full significance of the messiahship of Jesus, who is Son of God and Lord . . ."; "Christ at the Right Hand," 215.

divine child."[181] Moreover, there are several Jewish texts from the second half of the third century CE which also witness to the messianic interpretation of the psalm.[182] Moreover, the larger context within the Matthean narrative compels the reader to link the Son of David with David's Lord beyond a mere human level of affairs. This is due to another title of Jesus, "Son of God," which is always accompanied by divine connotation in Matthew (e.g. 1:18, 20, 21, 23; 3:16–17; 4:3–10; 8:29; 14:33; 16:16–17; cf. 26:63–64). So far Matthew presents Jesus as Son of God who has divine status just like God, and now Jesus as the Son of David who is also David's Lord; therefore, for these to be true, the messianic identity has to be consistent with Jesus's divine sonship.[183] The mentioning of ἐν πνεύματι (22:43) affirms that the lordship of the Messiah to David is true, to the extent that one "takes into account the involvement of the divine in human affairs."[184]

Additionally, the setting of the conflict scene confirms Jesus's status as the Messiah. The author repeats the subject (the Pharisees)[185] and the verb συνάγω in genitive absolute form (22:41) in order to link the story to the preceding conflict (cf. 22:34). There, as discussed in the previous section (5.1.5.2), the author is alluding to Psalm 2. If such a scriptural context still resonates in the

---

181. Hay, *Glory at the Right Hand*, 21–22. The text of LXX Psalm 109:3: μετὰ σοῦ ἡ ἀρχὴ ἐν ἡμέρᾳ τῆς δυνάμεώς σου ἐν ταῖς λαμπρότησιν τῶν ἁγίων ἐκ γαστρὸς πρὸ ἑωσφόρου ἐξεγέννησά σε. Justin Martyr also considers the divine sonship of the Christ in this verse, *Dial.* 63. Cf. Davies and Allison, *Matthew 19–28*, 253; Davies suggests that the LXX translation of Ps 110:3 implies a messianic interpretation; *Paul and Rabbinic Judaism: Some Rabbinic Elements in Pauline Theology* (London: SPCK, 1955), 161.

182. For example, see *Gen. Rab.* 85:9, see Str-B 4:457f; and Hay, *Glory at the Right Hand*, 28, also footnote 44. For detailed discussion on different Jewish witnesses, see Hay, *Glory at the Right Hand*, 23–33.

183. As Davies and Allison suggest, "Although the question [22:42] is designed to draw forth a conventional answer, 'Son of David,' it simultaneously hints at another title, 'Son of God.'" Davies and Allison, *Matthew 19–28*, 251–252. For a full discussion on "the Son of God," see Verseput, "Role and Meaning of the 'Son of God,'" 532–536; Kingsbury, "The Figure of Jesus in Matthew's Story," *JSNT* 21 (1984): 3–36; *Matthew: Structure, Christology, Kingdom*, especially 40–83; Rudolf Schnackenburg, *Jesus in the Gospels: A Biblical Christology* (Louisville: Westminster John Knox, 1995), 74–130.

184. Patte, *Matthew*, 316. The link between the Davidic Messiah and the Son of God can be further attested by Qumran text 4Q174 (the Florilegium) which interprets 2 Sam 7:14 and explicitly identifies the Branch of David as the Son of God; Collins, *The Scepter and the Star: Messianism in Light of the Dead Sea Scrolls*, 2nd ed. (Grand Rapids: Eerdmans, 1995), 184–185; Pace Fitzmyer, *The Gospel According to Luke (I–IX)* (New York: Doubleday, 1981), 206.

185. The insertion of τῶν Φαρισαίων is a Matthean redaction, which also reinforces the connection to the previous conflict; Repschinski, *Controversy*, 226.

author's mind (and probably in the reader's mind as well), then the connotation of Psalm 2 is also appropriate for this story, especially because here Jesus as the Messiah is also facing the opposition of the leaders of Israel. Nolan, for example, concisely expresses such an understanding:

> Since the Pharisees cannot explain how the Christ is both David's son and David's Lord, they are reduced to silence, as intimated in the unspoken continuation of Psalm 8:2 cited by Jesus in 21:16 ... He has cited his forefather's songs in 21:16, 42, and 22:44. If it be granted that the gathering together (συνηγμένων, 22:41) of the Pharisees colours the whole scene with the second psalm, several of the latter's phrases become active. For example, "The rulers take counsel (συνήχθησαν) together against the *Lord* and his *Christ* ... I have set my *king on Zion* ... You are *my son*" (Psalm 2:2, 6, 7). The Davidid (*sic*) is here asserting his royal authority.[186]

The function of this story also operates at the rhetorical level. That is, the author employs the story as the ending to all the conflict stories as well as a transition to the last discourse of Jesus before the passion narrative. More specifically, this conflict not only concludes the verbal conflicts of Jesus with the Jewish leaders; it also anticipates the judgment of Jesus on God's enemies and the temple cult (Matt 23–25). Instead of being the climax,[187] this story serves as an emphatic conclusion to the preceding temple conflicts.[188] It echoes the first temple conflict in that both imply the identity of Jesus as the Davidic Messiah who assumes the role of God.[189] But it is more than a simple echo – it explains and justifies Jesus's temple actions (21:12–16) and parabolic teaching

---

186. Nolan, *Royal Son of God*, 182–183.

187. Pace Hagner, *Matthew 14–28*, 649; Luz, *Matthew 21–28*, 88.

188. Luz believes all conflicts reach both a climax and conclusion here; *Matthew 21–28*, 88. However, while it is clearly the ending of all conflicts, this study argues that the climax of conflicts is the question on Jesus's authority in 21:23–27 where both sides completely reject each other (see discussion under 5.1.2).

189. See detailed discussion in 5.1.1. Suffice it to list three point of contacts here between the two stories: (1) Jesus is compared to the Son of David in both stories; (2) the author's allusion/quotation to Psalms (Ps 8 and 110) provide a scriptural basis for associating the mentioned Son of David with God/Yahweh; (3) Psalm 8 and 110 share an important theme: under the feet (of the messianic figure), so much so that scholars see a possible influence of Ps 8:6 (LXX Ps 8:7) on the Greek wording of Ps 110:1; Davies and Allison, *Matthew 19–28*, 253; Luz, *Matthew 21–28*, 89; Davies, *Matthew*, 178.

(21:18–22:40). According to Psalm 110, the Messiah's enthronement also includes his promised role as the high priest in the order of Melchizedek (Ps 110:4). This is the context of Psalm 110:1 and needs to be considered in the interpretation of the story. The significance of Psalm 110:4 is that because the office of the king and the high priest are combined,[190] when interpreting the use of the Psalm in this story, it is plausible to conceive that Jesus the Messiah is presented to replace the temple.[191] As Wright argues, "If a would-be king acted in the Temple in such a way as to precipitate a confrontation with the present priestly regime, Ps 110 was exactly the right text with which to claim legitimacy for such an action."[192]

This story also provides an ending to all conflict stories because no one dares to verbally challenge him *again* in public (22:46). As the ending, it resonates with the theme underlined by the first conflict between Jesus and opponents (9:1–8). There, the conflict is intended by the author to establish Jesus's divine status as an alternative authority, which is different from the one upheld by the Jewish leaders.[193] Similarly, this story confirms the divine status of Jesus, who is greater than the Jewish understanding of the Davidic Messiah.[194]

The function of this story as a transition is to anticipate the judgment discourse of Jesus (Matt 23–25). Interestingly, being the final conflict, this is the only occasion where Jesus takes up the role of a challenger by Matthew's redaction.[195] However, it is not so much a contest of authority per se[196] as a display of Jesus's superiority because his opponents are not up to the challenge

---

190. See discussion on Ps 110:4 by Hay, *Glory at the Right Hand*, 20; also, France, *Jesus and the Old Testament*, 102.

191. Wright, *Jesus and the Victory of God*, 509, 511; cf. his supporting argument that "Temple and battle were thus central symbols of a royal vocation . . . within some, the central symbols and the royal praxis were expressed in terms of scriptural prophecy," 485ff.

192. Wright, 509.

193. See full discussion of Matt 9:1–8 in previous section 2.1.1.

194. *Pace* Luz, *Matthew 21–28*, 89, footnote 10; 91.

195. Therefore, the story is redacted into a conflict story rather than part of Jesus's teaching to the crowd.

196. *Pace* Rollin Grams who suggests 22:41–46 is another contest over authority just like 21:23–27; "Temple Conflict Scene: A Rhetorical Analysis of Matthew 21–23," in *Persuasive Artistry: Studies in New Testament Rhetoric in Honor of George A. Kennedy*, ed. Duane F. Waston (Sheffield: Sheffield Academic Press, 1991), 51.

(οὐδὲ ἐτόλμησέν).¹⁹⁷ Still there is another conflict embedded within the story – the conflict between the royal Messiah and God's enemies in Psalm 110:1–2. The conflict in Matthew mirrors the one in the Psalm, which should compel the reader to reflect on the influence one has on the other: how to understand the conflict between Jesus and the leaders in light of the Psalm, one of an eschatological nature?¹⁹⁸

The context of the conflict – the polemic discourse of Jesus, which comprises eschatological warnings and judgment (Matt 23–25) – seems to answer this question. In other words, the conflict and its ramification foreshadow what is to come. After the temple conflicts, the narrative time slows down dramatically to record Jesus's sayings word by word, ranging from polemical statements (Matt 23–24:41) to parables (Matt 24:42–25).¹⁹⁹ The content of these sayings focus on warnings and future judgment, resembling an "eschatological court scene,"²⁰⁰ but these words also present a Jesus "speaking in a majestic, powerful, and completely authoritative stature" (e.g. 23:39; 24:30–31, 35; 25:31),²⁰¹ consistent with the portrayal of Jesus in this final conflict. To this extent, the following context elaborates what the reader has already encountered in the conflict story.

---

197. The temporal reference to τις ἀπ' ἐκείνης τῆς ἡμέρας not only brings a closure to the temple conflicts (Davies and Allison, *Matthew 19–28*, 256), but also enables this narrative referent to extend to the implied reader.

198. Such an arrangement in effect implies that "the messiah's kingdom will not be a mere renewal of David's" and the elicited answer entails "a deliberate rejection of the mundane interpretation of Ps 110"; Hay, *Glory at the Right Hand*, 111.

199. There, woeful judgments are expanded from targeting the Pharisees (23:13–32) to "this generation" (23:33–36), Jerusalem (23:37–39) and the temple (24:2); cf. Wright, *Jesus and the Victory of God*, 509. The woeful warnings to the disciples are interwoven with the judgment on the last day (24:4–8, 9–28, 29–31). These warnings and judgments are further complemented by parables of eschaton (Matt 25).

200. Scenes like "coming on the clouds of heaven" are also part of messianic enthronement and "an eschatological event"; Hahn, *Title of Jesus*, 130; also, Wright, *Jesus and the Victory of God*, 511.

201. Larry Hurtado, *Lord Jesus Christ: Devotion to Jesus in Earliest Christianity* (Grand Rapids: Eerdmans, 2003), 337; also see Hurtado's discussion on the divine capacities of Jesus in 336; cf. Luz, *Matthew 21–28*, 90–91.

5.1.6.3 Summary of 22:41–46 in Its Immediate Narrative and Rhetorical Context (Matt 20–22)

This story, being the final one in all the conflict story series, plays an indispensable role in Matthew's story. It is the only conflict where Jesus poses the challenge and gives a dilemma to the opponents to respond. What is consistent with other conflict stories is that Jesus is in complete control of the conversation whereas the opponents are unable to give an answer. This feature continues the contrast between the superiority of Jesus over the Jewish leaders.

At the core of this conflict is a christological issue, which is also present in most of the conflict stories (9:1–8, 9–13, 14–17; 12:1–8, 9–13, 14–17; 21:14–17, 23–27, 15–22, 23–33, 34–40). The story is arranged as such that even though the opponents could not answer Jesus's question, the reader should supply an affirmative conclusion regarding the divine status of the Davidic Messiah. As the ending to all conflicts, this story seems to have the most obvious display of the nexus between the Son of David and David's Lord, the God of Israel. This nexus of the two fundamentally defines the Messiah in Matthew. Therefore, the narrative function of this conflict story is to continue the contrast between Jesus's superior authority and the utter hypocrisy and foolishness of the Jewish leaders.

However, more important significance remains with the rhetorical function of the story. As discussed above, the story encompasses a compound allusion to two Psalms. The allusion to Psalm 110 is more obvious because of the direct quotation of Psalm 110:1 in Jesus's words. Interpreting the conflict within the entire context of Psalm 110, then the offices of the king and of the high priest can be seen as converging on the person of Jesus. Another layer of allusion to Psalm 110 lies within the conflict between the royal Messiah and God's enemies and where the fate of the enemies is sealed by God's own action in the eschaton (Ps 110:1–2). Less obvious, but equally significant, is the allusion to Psalm 2. The antagonistic image of the royal Messiah and the leaders of the world in Psalm 2 is likely singing in the author's mind when he presents this conflict between Jesus as the Messiah. What is the purpose then? The answer is, the author intends for the conflict to not only draw an end to the conflict series, but also to provide a transition in that it heralds the author's presentation of Jesus's eschatological judgment (Matt 23–25).

5.2 Conflict Stories in the Context of Matthew 21–25

The text between Matthew 21 and 25 can be seen as the last block of material for the author to compose or edit before the Passion narrative. These six conflicts – Matthew 21:14–17, 23–27, 22:15–22, 23–33, 34–40, and 22:41–46 – are grouped as the Jerusalem conflict stories in this chapter because they all occur in Jerusalem during the final days of Jesus. Here the intensity of the conflict stories reaches a climax. This can be seen from the fact that all conflict stories, except for the first one, are narrated without the interruption of any story-time gap between them. In other words, except for the first temple conflict, all the remaining conflicts seem to occur consecutively in the same day. As a result, such a narrative arrangement brings out an impact of a cumulative intensity on the audience.

In the last conflict story, the author intertwines the hero Jesus with a Jewish understanding of the Son of David, Messiah and the divine Lord of David. As a result, the reader is persuaded to "elevate the concept of Messiah from that of a special human being to one who uniquely manifests the presence of God – and thus one whom David has also to address as his Lord,"[202] and thereby to stand in opposition to the Pharisees.[203] The victorious tone in the story prepares the reader for Jesus's long discourse of judgment, and is instrumental in the building up of great irony because "Jesus will face a violent and humiliating death at the hands of his enemies" in the passion narrative (Matt 26–27).[204] However, the crucifixion of this Messiah will eventually and ironically fulfil God's salvation plan for the world (Matt 28).

---

202. Hagner, *Matthew 14–28*, 651.

203. The Pharisees understand the Messiah only in human terms as descended from David, but the title κύριος (22:43, 44) is meant to refer to the "*divinity of Christ, his divine nature*, by virtue of which he is differentiated from the human sphere"; Bultmann, *Theology of the New Testament I*, 128–129.

204. Hurtado, *Lord Jesus Christ*, 337.

CHAPTER 6

Summary and Conclusions

The purpose of this study is to explore the significance of conflict stories in the Gospel of Matthew from a literary-critical perspective. The key research question this study has attempted to answer is: what functions do conflict stories play in Matthew's narrative? There are previous studies attempting a similar pursuit; however, because their interest is often limited to the *Sitz im Leben* behind the Matthean text, those studies have treated the Matthean text as a window through which historical circumstances received the primary attention. As a result, conflict stories are viewed as providing insights into Matthew's polemical program against the Jews or Judaism, be it of *intra* or *extra muros* nature. For example, Hultgren suggests,

> What is most characteristic about the conflict stories in Matthew is that they portray Jesus as interpreter of the law for the church ... Matthew makes use of conflict stories to draw out important insights and teachings for his reader. They are used in the service of presenting Jesus as Teacher to the church in which Matthew worked, a church which had to develop its own doctrinal self-consciousness apart from the contemporary rabbinate.[1]

Repschinski's summary of the function of conflict stories is in a similar vein:

> Throughout his gospel Matthew uses the controversy stories to develop a narrative contrast between Jesus' powerful deeds and

---

1. Hultgren, *Jesus and His Adversaries*, 187.

teaching and the reaction of his opponents to them . . . Matthew takes great care to set the controversy stories with in [*sic*] the framework of Jesus' inner-Jewish ministry.[2]

While these previous studies provide helpful ways to understand the text, they neglect what is perhaps the more central concern of the author. That is, besides Matthew's desire to reflect or preserve the contemporary situation of his community, the author is more interested in arousing or affirming the readers' faith by telling the story of Jesus. It is Jesus to whom faith is directed in the first gospel and this is an inseparable part of the author's theological program which he expounds in the narrative form. How exactly then has his literary work achieved this purpose? In order to fill the gap created by previous form and source redaction studies, this study has taken up the task of focusing on the literary function of the conflict stories in the gospel. Recognizing the literary unity of the Matthean text, this study has treated the text more as a mirror rather than a window and explored literary nuances reflected by the textual "surface." Under such a premise, this narrative analysis has highlighted three foci which will be included by the following summary of findings:

1. The connection which each conflict makes with its narrative and rhetorical context;
2. How the Hebrew Scripture interacts with the author's composition or redaction of the stories; and
3. The literary impact these stories have on the implied reader (or the audience).

6.1 Conclusion and Findings

This study selects a total of seventeen conflict stories in Matthew (9:1–8, 9–13, 14–17; 12:1–8, 9–14, 22–37, 38–45; 13:53–58; 15:1–9; 16:1–4; 19:1–9; 21:14–17, 23–27; 22:15–22, 23–33, 34–40, 41–46) based on three criteria:

1. The presence of an *attitude* of hostility or challenge at the outset of the narrative (either explicit or implied);
2. The presence of a question or an accusation or a challenge; and

---

2. Repschinski, *Controversy*, 320–321.

3. The question or the accusation is usually followed by a reply from Jesus.

Each story, though addressing various issues of contention, presents a stark contrast between Jesus and his opponents but the progression of conflicts throughout the gospel displays an escalating rejection of Jesus by the opponents.

The study recognizes that the conflict stories as a whole serve as the prelude to the Passion narrative in Matthew,[3] therefore, the literary analysis in this study finds two key functions of Matthean conflict stories which will be discussed in the following summary of chapters 2 to 5 of this analysis.

1. Conflict stories function, either individually or in clusters, as kernels of the Matthean plot to advance the narrative in order to reach its climax in the Passion narrative.
2. The christological focus in conflict stories, when present, is consistently concerned not only with the superiority of Jesus over the opponents, but more importantly with the nexus between the divine status of Jesus and him being the messianic figure.[4]

In the Matthean narrative there are many short stories, either in the words of Jesus or in the words of the author, to exhibit the life of Jesus and his mission to Israel and beyond. For example, in addition to conflict stories, there are another thirty-five dialogue stories found in the first gospel (see appendix 1 for the full account of fifty-one dialogue stories). Moreover, other short narratives include, for instance, the parable stories in Matthew 13, 18, 20, 21, 22, 24, 25, several miracle stories in Matthew 8–9, the appearance and the death of John the Baptist (3:1–12; 14:1–12), the two feeding stories (14:13–21; 15:32–39), and numerous stories involving other characters in the Passion

---

3. Or, in Powell's description, the Passion "represents the goal and purpose of the entire narrative"; "The Plots and Subplots of Matthew's Gospel," *New Testament Studies* 38 (1992): 198. This is also true for all Synoptic Gospels. Also cf. Hultgren, although he suggests that "the conflict stories in Matthew serve the structure of the gospel narrative as preludes to the Passion narrative less than in Mark"; *Jesus and His Adversaries*, 189.

4. Twelve out of seventeen conflict stories show a clear christological concern at the narrative level of the story: 9:1–8, 9–13, 14–17; 12:1–8, 9–14, 22–37; 21:14–17, 23–27, 22:15–22, 23–33, 34–40, 41–46.

narrative (Matt 26–27).[5] While the fact that the author includes, redacts or composes these stories within the narrative shows their importance for the overall story of Jesus, not all should be considered as being kernels of the plot.

This is because, according to Chatman, in order for stories to be kernel events, they have to "give rise to cruxes in the direction taken by events. They are nodes or hinges in the structure, branching points which force a movement into one of two (or more) possible paths."[6] The importance of kernel events is shown most importantly by their location in the narrative arrangement, which cannot be changed without interrupting the intention of the author to deliver the message to his reader. As will be shown in the following summary, conflict stories serve as turning points, climaxes, hinges and joints in the narrative flow upon which the plot takes a turn or moves forward. To this extent, they are "intentional, goal-oriented and forward-moving" to bring about the climax of the first gospel.[7]

Before summarizing findings from the analysis of individual conflict stories, it is necessary to recapitulate both of what the meta-narrative frame of Matthew is and of what the Matthean plot development is nuanced in comparison to Mark and Luke as discussed in chapter 1 of this study. The meta-narrative plot frame of Matthew is: God sent Jesus as the Messiah to save his people (e.g. 1:1, 17, 20–25), Jesus's ministry leads many people to be his disciples (e.g. 4:12–25; 9:35–10:4), yet the leaders of Israel reject Jesus as the Messiah by killing him (e.g. 9:1–17, 34; 12:1–14, 24, 13:54–58; 15:1–2; 21:14–15, 23–27, 45–46; 22:15–17, 23–24, 34–36; chs. 26–27). However, the death and subsequent resurrection of Jesus as the climax of the plot paradoxically fulfils God's salvific plan for all the nations (Matt 27–28).[8]

---

5. For example, Judas betraying Jesus (26:14–16), Peter denying Jesus (26:69–75), Judas hanging himself (27:1–10).

6. Chatman, *Story and Discourse*, 53. This definition is in the similar vein with Culler's suggestion: "If kernels are to be units of the plot we must accept that we recognize kernels only when we identify the role of an action in the plot, or put in another way, promote an action to a constituent of the plot"; Jonathan Culler, "Defining Narrative Units," in *Style and Structure in Literature: Essays in the New Stylistics*, ed. Roger Fowler (Oxford: Blackwell, 1975), 135. Rhoads, Dewey and Michie, however, use "key events" instead to the same effect; *Mark as Story*, 73.

7. Cf. Brooks, *Reading for the Plot*, 12.

8. This summary is similar to Matera's description of Matthew's plot: "In the appearance of Jesus the Messiah, God fulfills his promises to Israel. But Israel refuses to accept Jesus as the Messiah. Consequently, the Gospel passes to the nations"; Frank J. Matera, "The Plot of Matthew's Gospel," *CBQ* 49 (1987): 243.

The plot development distinct to Matthew is that the author seems to arrange a watershed section in Matthew 12–13 dividing the narrative prior to the Passion narrative into two parts. The narrative part before Matthew 12–13 focuses on the continuity of Jesus's ministry with Judaism in that the life of Jesus and his mission are squarely situated within the Jewish tradition. However, the narrative part after Matthew 13 no longer has such a focus. Instead, it highlights the discontinuity by demonstrating the polarization of Jesus and his Jewish opponents and the author's ecclesiological concern of gentile inclusion in Jesus's ministry.

Following the introductory chapter, chapters 2 to 5 of this study divide the seventeen conflict stories into four groups. Chapters 2, 3 and 5 each contain a group of conflict stories according to their narrative interconnection. By contrast, chapter 4 includes four conflict stories scattered throughout a large body of text (Matt 13–20).

Chapter 2 covers the first three conflict stories (9:1–8, 9–13, 14–17). As the first group of conflict stories, they are placed within a cluster of miracle stories (Matt 8–9) in Matthew's narrative. The three conflicts are closely connected with each other. At the narrative level, the christological themes are most prominent because all three stories unfold key aspects of the identity of Jesus through his authoritative pronouncements.[9] Moreover, the close narrative structure of this group of conflicts determines that the christological focus of the author needs to be discerned from how the stories together reflect such a focus. For example, Matthew 9:1–8 tells the reader that Jesus assumes God's authority to forgive sins. The story of 9:9–13 shows the reader that God's mercy is epitomised in Jesus's mission to save sinners. Jesus's conflict with the disciples of John the Baptist (9:14–17) highlights the eschatological significance of Jesus's presence as the expected Messiah. More than repeating the christological theme in 1:20–23 where the divine commission of Jesus is to show God's presence and save sinners, the focus here (9:1–17) seems to merge the messianic identity of Jesus as the saviour together with a divine status – Jesus acts in the place of God. Interestingly, in the discussion of other conflict stories, such a concern of the author for the nexus between the divine status of Jesus and him being the messianic figure will appear again.

---

9. *Pace* Luz, who suggests that in Matthew 8–9, the author only tells stories but does not present themes; *Matthew 8–20*, 1.

At the rhetorical level, the first three conflict stories play a crucial role for the Matthean plot. Their literary function is foundational not only for all conflict stories, but also in their own right for the entire Matthean narrative. This is because these conflicts are placed in strategic locations within Matthew's narrative sequence. This provides the opportunity for the author to progressively fine tune his christological message.

In the initial four chapters of Matthew, two important aspects of Jesus's identity emerge: the Davidic Messiah-King (e.g. 1:1–17) and the Son of God (e.g. 3:13–17; 4:1–11).[10] The next section of Matthew 5–9 consists of Jesus's teaching as well as healing miracles, and both types of activities are already anticipated by the summary statement in 4:23–25. However, the teaching discourse and miracle narratives cannot be seen simply as examples of Jesus being the Davidic Messiah-King or the Son of God.[11] More significantly, the author uses these materials to qualify the identity of Jesus with new dimensions. It is precisely in this aspect of introducing new dimensions that the first three conflicts contribute most in qualifying the identity of Jesus.

The new dimension, first of all, is presented in the first conflict (9:1–9). It demonstrates that Jesus assumes God's prerogative on earth (9:3, 6).[12] The fact that such an important christological aspect is introduced in a conflict context is not coincidental. Rather, it seems that the author intends to use the conflict to echo and elaborate what has been hinted at by the summary of Jesus's teaching discourse: because he taught as one who had authority and not as their teachers of the law (7:29). Although this is not the first schism occurring between Jesus and Israel's leaders in Matthew (cf. 2:16), it is certainly the first rupture Jesus himself actively engages in. In such an initial clash, the fact that Jesus enjoys divine status becomes immediately significant.

The next two conflicts (9:9–13, 14–17), being arranged close to the first one progressively reveal new dimensions of Jesus's identity. As a result, the identity of Jesus as the one who assumes God's prerogative is further complemented by the two conflicts (9:9–13, 14–17). Because Jesus has authority to forgive sins on earth, it becomes possible for him to gather the sinners (9:13) and fulfil his divine commission (1:21). Even though the recipients of Jesus's

---

10. Kingsbury, *Matthew as Story*, 43–58.
11. *Pace* Kingsbury, "Observations," 572.
12. See discussion of section 9.1.1 in chapter 2.

calling in the second conflict seem to be ambiguous (9:12–13), the context points to those whom the religious leaders would naturally exclude from their midst (hence their objection). In effect, the call of Jesus here redefines the boundary of God's people and extends God's mercy to all sinners (9:13). The location of this story is not random because it echoes a previous healing story in its context where Jesus predicts the presence of Gentiles at the eschatological banquet in view of the centurion's faith in him, whereas the "sons of the kingdom" will be excluded (8:11–12). It seems that, in light of both accounts (i.e. Jesus calling the sinners and healing the centurion's servant), the boundary of the people of God is drawn only according to their relationship with Jesus.

The third conflict, which shares the same setting with Jesus eating with tax collectors and sinners, contributes to an eschatological aspect of Jesus's identity as the Messiah. This is because in this story the author conveys an implicit christological connection between Jesus and the bridegroom of the messianic banquet. With the presence of Jesus, a new age is coming upon the earth. What is more important, however, is the qualification of this new age: it is entirely incompatible with the old one. Once again, the new or old age is no longer determined by the simple chronological time frame but by the presence or absence of the person Jesus.

In Matthew's plot development, the first round of clashes between Jesus and the Jewish leaders (9:1–8, 9–13, 14–17) has set the tone for the remaining long strand of conflicts between Jesus and the Jewish leaders. Jesus represents a superior authority, and it is incompatible with the old Israel of the Jewish leaders. Their presence in the midst of miracle stories functions to specify for the reader not only that Jesus has miraculous power, but also that such a power entails grave consequence to the existing establishment represented by the Jewish leaders.

The four conflict stories in Matthew 12 are analyzed in chapter 3. The first two conflicts are closely linked together (12:1–8, 9–14), as are the latter two (12:22–37, 38–45). At the narrative level, the two pairs do not appear to be closely connected with each other because they are separated by a summary statement followed by the quotation of Isaiah 42:1–4 (12:15–21) and the two pairs appear to address different issues. However, the four conflicts are closely joined with each other at the level of rhetoric. That such a cluster of four conflicts is separated by a summary statement and the quotation of Isaiah 42:1–4 is not due to the random arrangement of the author (12:15–21). On the contrary, the Isaiah quotation, which is entirely a Matthean insertion, has many points of thematic contact with the rest of Matthew 12. Consequently, the Isaianic prophecy informs the overarching program for Matthew 12 by which the two apparent disjunctive pairs of conflicts are joined closely together as the fulfilment of the Isaianic prophecy. Such an arrangement enables the author to mould this chapter into the beginning of the turning point in the narrative, preparing to move Jesus's mission to the Jews outward to the Gentiles.

The first pair of conflicts in Matthew 12 (12:1–8, 9–14) deals with the response of Jesus to the challenge of the opponents regarding Sabbath law. The shared issue of contention connects two conflicts closely with the preceding context (11:25–30), which presents Jesus as the one providing true rest. Then in 12:1–8 the author explicitly establishes Jesus's authority as the Lord of Sabbath who is greater than the temple. The consequence of such an authoritative status is shown by the next conflict where Jesus shows mercy in restoring a withered hand (12:11–13), which is in contrast to the Pharisees' plot to destroy life (12:14). To a certain extent, this pattern of authority-consequence is similar to the first two conflicts in Matthew 9 (9:1–8, 9–13).

Following a summary statement and the quotation of Isaiah 42:1–4 (12:15–21), the narrative introduces another conflict (12:22–37). On the surface it seems to repeat the healing account in 9:27–34. But the extended rebuke from Jesus certainly marks the distinction of this conflict. The rebuke is filled with fiery language of condemnation and a warning of judgment (12:25–37). Jesus's response in the fourth conflict in Matthew 12 is of a similar polemical nature but contains a different emphasis. It describes a picture of the positive response of the Gentiles in comparison to the Jewish rejection (12:41–42) and ends with cryptic language of judgment on "this evil generation" (12:43–45).

That the four conflict stories framed by Isaiah 42:1–4 advance Matthew's plot can be shown by three factors. First of all, even though some of the tension is similar to previous conflicts, this becomes much more intense in terms of its severity. For example, the coupling of Jesus's identity and its ensuing impact is already present in conflict stories in Matthew 9 (9:1–8, 9–13). In Matthew 12, the author restates the new dimension of his Christology through the conflict stories. That is, Jesus assumes the prerogative of God (12:1–8, 9–14), in addition to the affirmation of Jesus's identity as the Son of God (11:25–27) and the Davidic Messiah (12:13, 22–23).

Moreover, the author's concern for connecting the messianic identity of Jesus with his divine status in these conflict stories needs to be noted again, similar to the christological focus of the author in the first group of conflicts (9:1–8, 9–13, 14–17). What is different, however, is that the christological claim is made much more explicit and appears more frequently (12:6, 8, 28, 41, 42). As a consequence, the hostility of the opponents has become intensified so much that they seek to murder Jesus (12:14). But Jesus also changes from the one who, in previous conflicts, explains and defends his action (9:1–8, 9–13, 14–17) to the one who lashes out with prophetic warnings and eschatological judgment on the opponents (12:3–8, 25–37, 39–45).[13] At this point of the narrative, both sides in the conflicts evidently have become much more aggressive toward each other than in previous conflicts.

Second, the conflict stories in Matthew 12 move the plot forward by expanding the scale of the schism between Jesus and the opponents. The clash is not only confined to one between Jesus and the specific group of the Pharisees and the scribes. More people as Jesus's opponents are implicated in the conflicts. The incompatibility of two parties revealed in a previous conflict (e.g. 9:14–17) is now elaborated by polemical expressions such as "the kingdom of God has come upon you" (12:28), "anyone who speaks against the Holy Spirit will not be forgiven either in this age or in the age to come" (12:32), or "by your words you will be condemned" (12:37). For example, in Jesus's response to the opponents, impersonal pronouns, such as ὁ or οἱ ἄνθρωποι (12:30–32, 35, 36) and inclusive phrases, such as γενεὰ πονηρὰ καὶ μοιχαλίς begin to emerge (12:39, 41, 42, 45). These expressions indicate that the warnings and the condemnation are extended to whoever is qualified as such within the story world and beyond, and are no longer limited to the immediate dialogue partners.[14]

---

13. This observation is in line with Neyrey's general statement that Matthew's intent in Matt 12 "lies in the direction of presenting an extensive conflict between Jesus and the Pharisees, a full airing of the polemical charges, and an apologetic answer, which includes strong judgment"; "Thematic Use of Isa 42.1–4," 471.

14. Howell suggests the use of impersonal or inclusive expressions is to evoke the implied reader's response and therefore has a discipleship focus; *Matthew's Inclusive Story*, 221. Cf. Evald Lövestam's argument for a typological interpretation of ἡ γενεὰ αὕτη in Mark 13:30 parr, "The ἡ γενεὰ αὕτη Eschatology in Mk 13.30 parr," in *L'Apocalypse Johannique et l'Apocalyptique dans le Nouveau Testament*, ed. Jan Lambrecht (Gembloux, Belgique: J.Duculot, 1980), 403–413.

Third, Matthew's plot is moved along by the conflicts in Matthew 12 because they illustrate the Isaianic prophecy of the Messiah's justice. Through the conflict stories, the reader encounters both Jesus's judgment on those who reject him and an anticipation of the Gentiles' positive responses in juxtaposition with negative portrayal of this γενεά.[15] Up to here in the Matthean narrative (Matt 12), the reader has encountered repeated opposition to Jesus, to the point of plotting to kill him (12:14). The author then uses Jesus's awareness of the murder plot and subsequent withdrawal to introduce the prophecy of Isaiah 42:1–4, which contains an important theme of justice (12:18, 20, 21). In what follows, Jesus as the servant of God fulfils the mission by bringing judgement to all who reject him (12:28, 30, 32, 34–37, 39, 41, 42, 45) and justice to all who acknowledge him (12:41, 42).[16] Among the latter, the Gentiles of the past are particularly mentioned in contrast to this unrepentant γενεά, even though actual examples of faithful Gentiles do not appear in the narrative until later (15:21–31).[17] Therefore, together with Isaiah 42:1–4, the conflicts in Matthew 12 begin the transition in Matthew's plot to look forward to Jesus's mission to the Gentiles.

Contrary to Saunders's broad statement that "[t]he controversy stories in Matthew have a consistently christological focus,"[18] this study discovers that not every conflict story is primarily preoccupied with a christological concern. As will be shown in the following discussion, seven conflicts are such examples and four of them are addressed in chapter 4 (13:53–58; 15:1–9; 16:14; 19:1–9).[19] At the narrative level, although the superiority of Jesus can still be seen in each conflict, all four stories seem to deal mainly with the rejection of Jesus and its subsequent consequences. That is to say, they demonstrate the author's ecclesiological concern in the narrative. The four conflicts are scattered across seven chapters in Matthew and none of them follows each

---

15. Even though the positive response of the Gentiles is first mentioned in the story of Jesus's healing of the centurion's servant, the focus there is Jesus's astonishment over the fact that his authority is highly esteemed by a Gentile (8:10–11).

16. The repetition of the word κρίσις in Matt 12 is a textual evidence. It bears two aspects of the meaning of the English word "justice": judgment (negative) and justice (positive).

17. With the exception of the gentile centurion in 8:5–13.

18. Saunders, "No One Dared," 465.

19. The remaining three examples, 22:15–22, 23–33, and 22:34–40, are discussed in chapter 5.

other closely. However, each story plays an important role within its own context in order to move the plot along.

The conflict between Jesus and the people of his hometown (13:53–58) is narrated following Matthew's third discourse (13:1–52). Instead of conveying a christological message to the reader, the story highlights the objection of both parties of the dialogue. The listing of Jesus's family members (13:55–56) echoes the one immediately preceding the discourse where Jesus redefines his family (12:49–50).[20] In effect, the parable discourse (13:1–52) is bracketed by the two narratives concerning the "family" of Jesus (12:46–50; 13:53–58). Such arrangement of the material is deliberate. So far in the narrative, the author has established Jesus's identity as not only the Davidic Messiah and the Son of God but also with a striking qualification. That is, Jesus assumes the authority of God on earth. However, this identity of Jesus ensures grave consequences in the face of an increasing opposition not only from the Jewish leaders but also from "this generation." Several stories and parables following the conflicts of Matthew 12 reflect these consequences. For example, according to one's relationship with him, Jesus redefines the boundary of his family (12:46–50) (cf. 11:27; 12:30, 50). The conflict of 13:53–58 also indicates an unambiguous division between the people of his hometown and Jesus (13:58). Similarly, the parable discourse sandwiched between the two stories contains two main themes: the theme of obduracy and of the great divide between those who are in the kingdom and those who are outside. Interestingly, as the ending of Matthew 13, the conflict of 13:53–58 concludes the parable discourse by echoing both themes. At this juncture of the narrative, the reader begins to witness the split between Jesus and those who reject him, including people other than the Jewish leaders. Through this conflict, the author finishes the transition section of Matthew 11–13 and prepares for a new narrative section which focuses on Jesus's ministry to his inner circle of disciples and to the Gentiles (Matt 14–20). There is an additional point indicating that this conflict (13:53–58) moves the plot along: it contains an important motif of rejected prophets. The motif draws upon the disobedience of Israel in the Hebrew Scripture and forewarns the ominous fate of "the prophet" Jesus. That the author moves on to narrate the death of John the Baptist immediately

---

20. Cf. Luz, *Matthew 8–20*, 301.

after the conflict only seems logical: it is to anticipate the similar fate of Jesus in the Passion narrative (cf. 14:5 and 21:46).[21]

The story in 15:1–9 at the narrative level is a conflict over Jewish purity practices. The issue of contention, the hand-washing custom, represents the wider Jewish tradition of purity laws. At the rhetorical level, however, the story forms a literary unity with two following dialogues (15:10–14, 15–20). They together advance the Matthean plot in two aspects. First, the conflict is used to prepare for the exclusion of Jewish leaders and their followers from God's kingdom. The divisive nature of God's kingdom on earth and the dreadful fate of the leaders – being cast out of the kingdom – are brought into a sharp focus in 15:1–20 to the extent that many topics in the previous narrative of Matthew 12–13 are compressed into 15:1–20. They include, for example, the image of a hardened heart and blind guides (15:8, 14; cf. 13:13–15), sins of the tongue and of the thoughts (15:18–19; cf. 12:34–37), and the theme of inclusion/exclusion in God's kingdom (15:9, 13–14; cf. 13:24–30, 36–43, 47–50).

Second, the conflict functions to introduce justification for the inclusion of Gentiles in the kingdom of heaven. The refutation of Jesus begins with pointing out the hypocrisy of the opponents. The author uses the quotation of Isaiah 29:13 to conclude the refutation which invalidates the legitimacy of the opponents to draw a boundary between purity and defilement (15:7–9). The boundary is then redefined so that being clean and unclean is only determined by one's inward quality (15:16–20). The redefined boundary for purity and defilement has a radical implication: Jesus points out that God seeks devotion from one's heart but not outward formalities. The new boundary now permits Gentiles to be able to come to God simply based on their inward qualification. Such a function of the conflict is substantiated by the following narratives where Gentiles are accepted by Jesus (15:21–39).

Though these two conflict stories (13:53–58 and 15:1–9) are arranged apart from each other within the Matthew narrative flow, interrupted by the death of John the Baptist and Jesus's miracles, there is a distinctive similarity between the two. It is the author's ecclesiological concern for the "family" of Jesus and the kingdom of God. But they are more than similar to each other: the latter conflict accentuates the ecclesiological point in the former much

---

21. Cf. Luz, 305.

more. While the conflict in 13:53–58 and its context demonstrate to the reader the new boundary drawn between those who are within Jesus's family and those who are without, the conflict in 15:1–9 and its context demonstrate that those who are excluded will have the perilous consequence whereas the formerly excluded Gentiles can be included within the kingdom of God.

Two other conflict stories included in the analysis of chapter 4 are 16:1–4 and 19:1–9. At the narrative level, the issue of contention in the conflict of 16:1–4 seems to repeat an earlier story in 12:38–45: the opponents ask to see a sign from heaven. Besides the authoritative response of Jesus, this conflict does not reveal to the reader anything about the identity of Jesus. However, at the rhetorical level this conflict has two functions for the Matthean plot development. First, it heightens the intensity of the ongoing clash between Jesus and the Jewish leaders to a new level in the narrative. This story not only characterises the Jewish leaders as similar to Satan but the narrative itself resonates with the temptation stories (4:1–7) in several aspects. To a certain extent, therefore, this story raises the contention between Jesus and the leaders to the level of cosmic conflict. Second, it prepares for the appearance of the first Passion prediction in the plot development. The phrase "the sign of Jonah," as the author's insertion, refers to the death and resurrection of Jesus and is consistent with its interpretation in 12:38–45. The author's painstaking redaction of the Sadducees (16:1) in the story as well as in the following context (16:6, 11, 12) also forewarns the reader of the Sadducees' denial of resurrection. Their denial is specifically mentioned in the later narrative (cf. 22:23), but it may have been an *a priori* knowledge of the implied reader.[22] Such an arrangement advances Matthew's plot because it anticipates Jesus's pivotal qualification of Peter's confession (16:16). That is, the messiahship cannot be fully realized without the death and resurrection of Jesus (16:21–28).

The issue of the conflict in 19:1–9, (re)marriage and divorce, has caused ample scholarly and pastoral debates throughout the centuries. An unfortunate consequence is that the function of this conflict within its context has been largely ignored. At the narrative level, similar to previous stories (13:53–58; 15:1–9; 16:1–4), the christological issue regarding Jesus is not the primary concern, except that the author continues demonstrating the superiority of the Jesus over the opponents. At the rhetorical level, however, this

---

22. Cf. Jos. *Ant* 18 §11, 16.

analysis finds that the story continues the contrast between the kingdom Jesus proclaims and the paradigm the opponents represent, echoing an ongoing theme in the conflict narrative.

More importantly, the conflict characterizes the opponents in such a way that it continues to align them with Satan and therefore place them in absolute opposition to Jesus. The contrast between the natures of two paradigms is in sharp focus. On the one hand, the conflict emphasizes the fact that the reality of God's kingdom should exemplify God's original intent for the creation of man as in the beginning (19:4, 8). On the other hand, it points out that the reason separating one from the kingdom is one's hardness of heart (19:8; cf. 13:13–15; 15:8). Because the surrounding context clarifies the nature of God's kingdom (Matt 16:24–20:28), the story contributes to the plot by deepening the polarization between the two opposing parties (i.e. Jesus and the Jewish leaders) that was set out by the first set of conflicts (9:1–17) and prepares the reader for the climax of conflicts in Jerusalem.

Within the wider narrative context of Matthew 13–20, the author makes a clear shift from focusing on the identity and authority of Jesus to more ecclesiological concerns. In each of the conflicts, Jesus's superior status is a confirmed but more emphasised is his highly polemical response to the opponents. The message seems to be, when the kingdom of God arrives with the presence of Jesus, it brings out a sharp division among all who encounter Jesus. There is no longer segregation between the Jews and Gentiles according to the old paradigm of ritual observance of the law, but only the segregation between those who accept Jesus and those who reject him. Therefore, a natural implication of these stories for the reader is that Gentiles will be included when their relationship with Jesus is set right (e.g. 15:21–28; 19:13–15, 16–30; 20:1–16).

Chapter 5 analyzes six conflict stories because they all happen inside the temple area and are structured close together within the narrative. The first temple conflict (21:14–17) is a Matthean insertion and is composed as such that it is tied to both the narrative of Jesus's entry to Jerusalem (21:1–11) and cleansing the temple (21:12–14). The function of the first temple conflict cannot be overemphasized because of its pivotal role in this series of conflict stories. First, as a Matthean compositional arrangement, it ties temple conflicts back to the beginning of the conflict narratives. The christological concern of the author is again back in focus as this story echoes the theme of the first set of conflicts (9:1–8, 9–13, 14–17) by confirming the identity of Jesus as the Messiah who assumes the divine status of God.[23] However, Matthew develops the theme further by the reference to Psalm 8 by Jesus himself, which unambiguously praises the God of Israel. Second, it sets the thematic tone for the rest of the temple conflicts. That is, Jesus's identity is the stumbling block for the opponents and their rejection of Jesus renders the clash between them irreconcilable. Third, the conflict foreshadows the final conflict (22:41-46) by answering its question for the reader, which the opponents could not do. The context of Psalm 8:3 LXX quoted in the conflict also prefigures the silence of the opponents as God's enemy (cf. Ps 8:3b LXX).

In the conflict of 21:23-27 where the leaders question the origin of Jesus's authority, the author presents the climax of his composition of the conflict series. It is considered the climax because of two factors. First, the leaders' rejection of the divine authority of Jesus is shown to be so calculated that it is utterly inexcusable (21:24-26). Second, as much as Jesus's mission on earth is intended to 'save his people from their sins' (cf. 1:21), he rejects the Jewish leaders by refusing to reveal any further truth about his authority (21:27b). The context in addition serves to support the climax of rejection in the conflict. This is because, the conflict follows the prophetic act of judgment of Jesus (i.e. cursing the fig tree in 21:18-22). Then it is followed by the three parables to illustrate the theme of rejection and judgment (21:28-32, 33-44; 22:1-14). In other words, the context helps to clarify the message which is already evident in the conflict story: that the leaders' rejection of Jesus results in their own rejected status in the view of God (cf. 21:31, 43-44; 22:7, 13). To this extent, the conflict narrative is the driving force for further development of the plot.

Meanwhile, the christological focus of the conflict is clearly in view in the conflict of 21:23-27. By comparing Jesus to John and Baptist (21:24-25), the author affirms both the divine origin of Jesus's authority and his messianic identity. In Matthew, the author specifically tells the reader that John the Baptist is the anticipated Elijah who is endowed with a divinely sanctioned authority (3:1-12; 11:9-11, 14; 17:10-13; cf. 21:25). Even so, the baptism of John is still inferior to that of Jesus (3:13-17). Although the opponents refuse

---

23. Within the series of conflict stories, this identify is first established by Jesus's authority to forgive sins (9:6) and then reinforced by Jesus's lordship of the Sabbath (12:8) which is greater than the temple (12:6).

to accept such a message (21:27), it is made plain to the reader: if the forerunner of Jesus the Messiah (3:3/Isa 40:3, 3:11; 11:10/Mal 3:1) has a divinely ordained authority, how much more is the authority of Jesus?

Following the trilogy of parables (21:28–22:14), the remaining four conflict stories are narrated without any interruption by story time. The redaction of the author renders three conflicts into a group of testing/tempting stories (22:15–12, 23–33, 34–40). The final conflict is the only one where Jesus initiates the challenge (22:41–46). Even though each story at the narrative level addresses a different issue, the author ties all four conflicts closely together so that they advance the plot accumulatively. More specifically, such an arrangement not only develops the crescendo of contrast between Jesus's supremacy and the hypocrisy or ignorance of the opponents, but also anticipates the polemic verdict of the Jewish leaders in Matthew 23. There are two features common to all four stories. First, the challenge in each story comprises some sort of dilemma. In the first three stories, Jesus successfully solves the dilemma. However, in the last story the only dilemma Jesus poses to the opponents completely silences them. Second, the author no longer ventures to establish Jesus's authority as he does in the earlier conflicts (e.g. 9:1–8, 9–13; 12:1–8, 9–14). Instead, Jesus's authority seems to be a default in the story and the story focuses on the contrasting dialogue between the two parties. The christological concern in the three stories in 22:15–22, 22:23–33 and 22:34–40 is displayed in so far as the supremacy of Jesus contrasts with the opponents' incompetence and obduracy. It is in the final conflict where the identity of Jesus (22:41–46) alone is under the spotlight without much distraction in the narrative. In this respect, it echoes the christological focus of the first temple conflict (21:14–17). In this story, the relationship between David's Lord and the Son of David is posed by Jesus as a question to the opponents (22:43). Even though the author does not attempt to verify the answer positively, the quotation of Psalm 110:1 seems to serve as the key to solve such a dilemma. It is precisely this seemingly cryptic nexus between David's Lord and the Son of David that has become the stumbling block for the opponents. That the intensifying contrast between Jesus and the opponents is combined with the final display of Jesus's superior authority in the last conflict (22:41–46) provides a perfect stage for the Matthean Jesus to launch a bitter tirade at the Jewish leaders in the immediately following context of Matthew 23.

The foregoing analysis helps the reader to gain appreciation of the conflict stories from a literary perspective. Individual or clusters of conflicts play vital roles within their context. More importantly, the conflict stories as a whole serve as the driving force in the narrative to reach its climax in that they demonstrate the logic and mechanism that lead to Jesus being nailed on the cross.[24] The identity and authority of Jesus is posed as such a threat to the "reality" the leaders endeavour to uphold that the rift becomes irreconcilable following the final conflict. Therefore, in order to terminate the conflict, the leaders must seek to put the earthly life of Jesus to an end. However, the irony is that, it is precisely through the death and resurrection of Jesus that the ultimate solution to the conflict can be reached.

6.2 Summary

The literary-critical approach adopted in this analysis focuses on the Matthean text as the final form and permits the research to steer away from speculating on the *Sitz im Leben* behind the text. To this extent, this study not only investigates Matthew's redaction of his sources but more importantly, it explores the author's overall rhetorical strategies to shape the gospel into its final literary unity. Seen from this perspective, the conflict stories are no longer the mere products of the author's repeated effort to portray Jesus's doctrinal teachings,[25] nor his attempt to construct the polemic environment encountered by his own church.[26] Rather, a literary-critical approach brings to light how conflict stories in their own right contribute to Matthew's composition of the whole gospel. Through conflict stories, various aspects of the author's Christology are placed under sharp focus. In addition, conflict stories are the main catalyst for Matthean narrative plot to develop because the rupture between Jesus and the religious leaders and between the paradigms represented by each side becomes deeper in every conflict encounter.

The analysis of the conflict stories has attempted to explain their functions within the Matthean narrative. If the climax and purpose of the whole

---

24. Cf. Saunders, "No One Dared," 466.
25. For example, as Hultgren believes, *Jesus and His Adversaries*, 187–190.
26. For example, as Bultmann suggests, *History*, 39–41; Repschinski, *Controversy*, 321.

narrative of Matthew is Jesus's Passion and resurrection,[27] then the conflict stories, as this study has demonstrated, are the kernels to Matthew's plot, advancing the storyline either in clusters or individually. Because they echo events that happened before them, connect different events or foreshadow future events still to happen, the plot depends on conflict stories to move forward. Even though all the conflict stories display the superiority of Jesus over the opponents, not all focus on the identity/authority of Jesus. Some conflicts are concerned with the consequence of such authority such as the objective of Jesus's mission or the irreconcilable nature between the kingdom of God and the opponents. However, they all share one thing in common, that is, the plot advances when conflict stories develop from one to another. In the beginning of Jesus's ministry, he receives a positive response from the crowd but the leaders are suspicious and antagonistic, but only to the extent of which they would probably be toward any other rival rabbis of their time. Then, as the divine messianic status of Jesus is revealed further, the Jewish leaders came to realize the significance of such a threat and sought to kill him. When the superiority of Jesus becomes indisputable, especially through the temple conflicts, the murderous intent of leaders become more evident. The final conflict story silences the leaders in public only to compel them to attempt the killing plot in secret (cf. 26:3–4, 14–16), which eventually leads to the crucifixion of Jesus. Seen from the perspective of the author's rhetoric strategy, these conflict stories are not simply a reflection of the contrast between Jesus's words and deeds and those of his opponents.[28] Rather, more than some other narratives in the gospel, they are indeed the kernels of the Matthean plot because none of the conflicts can be deleted without in one way or another disrupting the flow of the narrative.

It has also become apparent, from the analysis of all the conflict stories, that Matthew endeavours to defend his conviction that Jesus is both the Davidic Messiah and the possessor of divine status. In other words, Jesus is the expected Messiah, but one who also assumes the prerogatives of God. However, for Jewish-Christians of the first century, this proposal entails a

---

27. In Powell's description, the passion "represents the goal and purpose of the entire narrative"; "Plots and Subplots," 198.

28. *Pace* Repschinski, who suggests that the key function of conflict stories is to "develop a narrative contrast between Jesus' powerful deeds and teaching and the reaction of his opponents to them"; *Controversy*, 320.

serious dilemma: on the one hand, early Jewish-Christians believed in the God of the Hebrew Scripture who is incomparable to any other deities. On the other hand, they became overwhelmingly convinced that Jesus as the Christ enjoys a divinity equivalent to God. To deal with this dilemma, early Christians were compelled to "either soften their emphasis upon the heavenly glory of Jesus or to justify more fully and firmly their conviction about his significance." [29] As far as conflict stories are concerned, Matthew seems to have taken the latter course of action.

---

29. Hurtado, *One God, One Lord: Early Christian Devotion and Ancient Jewish Monotheism* (Philadelphia: Fortress, 1988), 122–123.

APPENDIX 1

Jesus in Dialogue with Other Characters in the Gospel of Matthew

Dialogue Stories	Verses	Characters									Attitudes	
		John the Baptist	The Devil	The Disciples	Spirits	Sick/Poor/Needy	Jewish Leaders	John's Disciples	(Member of) the Crowd	Pilate	Attitudes toward Jesus	Jesus's Attitude
1. Baptism of Jesus	3:13–15	√									Reverent	Neutral
2. Temptation of Jesus	4:1–11		√								Hostile	Hostile
3. Healing the Leper	8:1–4					√					Reverent	Merciful
4. Faith of the Centurion	8:5–13					√					Reverent	Surprised, merciful
5. Cost of Following Jesus #1	8:18–20						√				Reverent	Neutral
6. Cost of Following Jesus #2	8:21–22			√							Neutral	Neutral
7. Jesus Calms the Storm	8:22–27			√							Reverent	Disappointed

Dialogue Stories	Verses	John the Baptist	The Devil	The Disciples	Spirits	Sick/Poor/Needy	Jewish Leaders	John's Disciples	(Member of) the Crowd	Pilate	Attitudes toward Jesus	Jesus's Attitude
8. Healing of Two Demon-Possessed Men	8:28–34				√						Reverent	Hostile
9. Healing the Paralytic	9:1–8					√					Hostile	Hostile
10. Eating with Tax Collectors and Sinners	9:9–13						√				Hostile	(Slightly) Hostile
11. Question about Fasting	9:14–17							√			Hostile	(Slightly) Hostile
12. Healing the Blind	9:27–31					√					Reverent	Merciful
13. Speaking to John's Disciples	11:2–6							√			Inquiring	Neutral
14. Plucking the Grain on Sabbath	12:1–8						√				Hostile	Hostile
15. Healing on Sabbath	12:9–14						√				Hostile	Hostile
16. The Beelzebub Controversy	12:22–37						√				Hostile	Hostile
17. Asking Signs from Heaven	12:38–45						√				Hostile	Hostile
18. Jesus's Mother and Brothers	12:46–50								√		Neutral	(Slightly) Hostile
19. Parable of the Sower and More*	13:1–52			√								
20. A Prophet without Honor	13:53–58								√		Hostile	Hostile
21. Feeding the Five Thousand	14:13–21			√							Neutral	Neutral
22. Walking on the Water	14:22–36			√							Doubting Reverent	Assuring Disappointed

Jesus in Dialogue with Other Characters

Dialogue Stories	Verses	Characters									Attitudes	
		John the Baptist	The Devil	The Disciples	Spirits	Sick/Poor/Needy	Jewish Leaders	John's Disciples	(Member of) the Crowd	Pilate	Attitudes toward Jesus	Jesus's Attitude
23. Hand Washing Tradition	15:1–9						√				Hostile	Hostile
24. Teaching on Clean and Unclean	15:10–20			√							Neutral	Disappointed
25. The Faith of the Canaanite Woman	15:21–28					√					Reverent	Merciful
26. Feeding the Four Thousand	15:29–39			√							Neutral	Neutral
27. Asking Signs from Heaven	16:1–4						√				Hostile	Hostile
28. Yeast of the Pharisees and Sadducees	16:5–12			√							Inquiring	Disappointed
29. Peter's Confession	16:13–20			√							Reverent	Praising
30. Jesus Predicts His Death	16:21–28			√							Reverent	Hostile
31. The Transfiguration	17:1–13			√							Reverent	Assuring
32. The Healing of a Boy Possessed by a Demon	17:14–18					√					Reverent	Merciful
33. The Disciples Failing to Heal the Boy	17:19–23			√							Inquiring	Disappointed
34. Paying the Temple Tax	17:24–26			√							Neutral	Neutral

Dialogue Stories	Verses	Characters									Attitudes	
		John the Baptist	The Devil	The Disciples	Spirits	Sick/Poor/Needy	Jewish Leaders	John's Disciples	(Member of) the Crowd	Pilate	Attitudes toward Jesus	Jesus's Attitude
35. Greatest in Kingdom of Heaven and More*	18:1–35			√								
36. Question on Divorce°	19:3–12			√			√				Hostile	Hostile
37. The Rich Young Man	19:16–20:16			√					√		Reverent Inquiring	Neutral
38. Jesus again Predicts His Death	20:17–28			√							Reverent Inquiring	Neutral
39. Two Blind Men Receive Sight	20:29–34					√					Reverent	Merciful
40. Jesus at the Temple	21:12–17						√				Hostile	Hostile
41. The Fig Tree Withers	21:18–22			√							Reverent Inquiring	Assuring
42. Question about Authority	21:23–22:14						√				Hostile	Hostile
43. Paying Taxes to Caesar	22:15–22						√				Hostile	Hostile
44. Question on Resurrection	22:22–33						√				Hostile	Hostile
45. Question on the Greatest Commandment	22:34–40						√				Hostile	Hostile
46. Whose Son Is the Christ	22:41–46						√				Hostile	Hostile
47. Signs of the End of the Age*	24:1–25:46			√								

Dialogue Stories	Verses	Characters									Attitudes	
		John the Baptist	The Devil	The Disciples	Spirits	Sick/Poor/Needy	Jewish Leaders	John's Disciples	(Member of) the Crowd	Pilate	Attitudes toward Jesus	Jesus's Attitude
48. Jesus Anointed at Bethany	26:6–13			√							Disagreeing Inquiring	Neutral
49. The Lord's Supper	26:17–30			√							Inquiring	Assuring
50. Peter's Denial of Jesus	26:31–35			√							Reverent	Neutral
51. Before the Sanhedrin	26:57–64						√				Hostile	Hostile
52. Jesus before Pilate	27:11–14									√	Hostile	Hostile

º Dialogues involves multiparty in which disciples only play a secondary role to other characters as dialogue partners of Jesus; attitude toward Jesus will be categorized according to the primary speaker.

*Dialogues embedded within Jesus's teaching monologue, therefore "attitude" category does not apply.

Bibliography

Abrahams, Israel. *Studies in Pharisaism and the Gospels*, Vol. 1. Cambridge: Cambridge University Press, 1917.

Abrams, M. H. *A Glossary of Literary Terms*. 7th edition. Boston, MA: Heinle & Heinle, 1999.

———. *The Mirror and the Lamp: Romantic Theory and the Critical Tradition*. New York: W. W. Norton, 1953.

Albertz, Martin. *Die synoptishen Streitgespräche: Ein Beitrag zur Formgeschichte des Urchristentums*. Berlin: Trowitzsch, 1921.

Allen, W. C. *A Critical and Exegetical Commentary on the Gospel According to St. Matthew*. 3rd edition. ICC. Edinburgh: T & T Clark, 1912.

Allison, Dale C. *Constructing Jesus: Memory, Imagination, and History*. Grand Rapids: Baker Academic, 2010.

———. *The Sermon on the Mount: Inspiring the Moral Imagination*. New York: Crossroad, 1999.

Alter, Robert. *The Art of Biblical Narrative*. New York: Basic Books, 1981.

Anderson, Janice Capel. *Matthew's Narrative Web: Over, and Over, and Over Again*. JSNTSup 91. Sheffield: Sheffield Academic Press. 1994.

Archibald, M. Hunter. *Interpreting the Parables*. London: SCM Press, 1960.

Aune, David E., ed. *The Gospel of Matthew in Current Study*. Grand Rapids: Eerdmans, 2001.

———. *The New Testament in Its Literary Environment*. Philadelphia, PA: Westminster Press, 1987.

———. *Prophecy in Early Christianity and the Ancient Mediterranean World*. Grand Rapids: Eerdmans, 1983.

Austin, John L. *How to Do Things with Words*. 2nd edition. Oxford: Clarendon Press, 1975.

Bacon, Benjamin W. "What Was the Sign of Jonah?" *Biblical World* 20 (1902): 99–112.

Bailey, Mark L. "The Parable of the Sower and the Soils." *Bibliotheca Sacra* 155 (1998): 172–188.

Bal, Mieke. *Narratology: Introduction to the Theory of Narrative.* 2nd edition. Toronto: University of Toronto Press, 1997.

Balch, D. L., ed. *Social History of the Matthean Community: Cross-Disciplinary Approaches.* Minneapolis: Fortress, 1991.

Banks, Robert. *Jesus and the Law in the Synoptic Tradition.* Cambridge: Cambridge University Press, 1975.

Bar-Efrat, Shimon. *Narrative Art in the Bible.* JSOTSup 70. Sheffield: Almond Press, 1989.

Barth, Gerhard. "Matthew's Understanding of the Law." In *Tradition and Interpretation*, edited by Günther Bornkamm, Gerhard Barth, and Heinz Joachim Held, 58–164. London: SCM Press, 1963.

Basser, Herbert. *The Mind behind the Gospels: A Commentary to Matthew 1–14.* Boston: Academic Studies Press, 2009.

Bauckham, Richard. "For Whom Were Gospels Written?" In *The Gospels for All Christians: Rethinking the Gospel Audiences*, edited by Richard Bauckham, 9–48. Grand Rapids: Eerdmans, 1998.

Bauer, R. David. *The Structure of Matthew's Gospel: A Study in Literary Design.* JSNTSup 31. Sheffield: Almond Press, 1989.

Baumbach, Günther. *Jesus von Nazareth im Lichte der jüdischen Gruppenbildung.* Berlin: Evangelische Verlaganstalt, 1971.

Bayer, Hans. *Jesus' Predictions of Vindication and Resurrection.* Tübingen: Mohr, 1986.

Beale, G. K., and Don A. Carson. *Commentary on the New Testament Use of the Old Testament.* Grand Rapids: Baker Academic, 2007.

Beare, F. W. *The Gospel According to Matthew.* Oxford: Basil Blackwell, 1981.

Beaton, Richard C. "How Matthew Writes." In *The Written Gospel*, edited by Markus Bockmuehl and Donald Hagner, 116–134. Cambridge: Cambridge University Press, 2005.

———. *Isaiah's Christ in Matthew's Gospel.* Cambridge: Cambridge University Press, 2002.

———. "Messiah and Justice: A Key to Matthew's Use of Isaiah 42:1–4?" *Journal for the Study of the New Testament* 75 (1999): 5–23.

Berger, Klaus. *Die Gesetzesauslegung Jesu: Ihr historischer Hintergrund im Judentum und im Alten Testament.* Neukirchen-Vluyn: Neukirchener Verlag, 1972.

Bertram, Georg. "κρεμάννυμι." In *Theological Dictionary of the New Testament*, vol. 3, edited by Gerhard Kittel and Gerhard Friedrich; translated by Geoffrey W. Bromiley, 914–921. Grand Rapids: Eerdmans, 1964.

Blomberg, Craig. "The Structure of 2 Corinthians 1–7." *Criswell Theological Review* 4, no. 1 (1989): 3–20.

Bockmuehl, Marcus. "Matthew 5:32; 19:9 in the Light of Pre-rabbinic Halakhah." *New Testament Studies* 35 (1989): 291–295.

Bonnard, Pierre. *L'évangile selon Saint Matthieu*. Neuchâtel: Delachaux & Niestlé, 1963.

Booth, Wayne. *Critical Understanding*. Chicago: University of Chicago Press, 1979.

———. *The Rhetoric of Fiction*. Chicago: University of Chicago Press. 1961.

Borg, Marcus J. *Conflict, Holiness, and Politics in the Teaching of Jesus*. New York: E. Mellen, 1984.

Bornkamm, Günther. "End-Expectation and Church in Matthew." In *Tradition and Interpretation*, edited by Günther Bornkamm, Gerhard Barth, and Heinz Joachim Held, 15–51. London: SCM Press, 1963.

———. *Jesus of Nazareth*. London: Hodder & Stoughton, 1960.

Bowker, John. *Jesus and the Pharisees*. Cambridge: Cambridge University Press, 1973.

Braun, Herbert M. "πλανάω." In *Theological Dictionary of the New Testament*, vol. 6, edited by Gerhard Kittel and Gerhard Friedrich; translated by Geoffrey W. Bromiley, 656–716. Grand Rapids: Eerdmans, 1964.

Briscoe, Peter. "Faith Confirmed through Conflict – The Matthean Redaction of Mark 2:1–3:6." In *Back to the Sources: Biblical and Near Eastern Studies in Honor of Dermot Ryan*, edited by Kevin J. Cathcart and John F. Healey, 104–118. Dublin: Glendale, 1989.

Brooks, Peter. *Reading for the Plot: Design and Intention in Narrative*. Cambridge, MA: Harvard University Press, 1984.

Brown, Raymond E. *The Birth of the Messiah: A Commentary on the Infancy Narratives in the Gospels of Matthew and Luke*. New updated edition. New York: Associated Sulpicians of the US, 1977, 1993.

Buchanan, George W. *The Gospel of Matthew*. 2 vols. Lewiston, NY: Mellen Biblical Press, 1996.

Bultmann, Rudolf. *The History of the Synoptic Tradition*. 2nd edition. Translated by John Marsh. New York: Harper, 1968.

———. *Theology of the New Testament*. Vol. 1. London: SCM Press, 1952.

Burger, Christopher. "Jesu Taten nach Matthäus 8 und 9." *Zeitschrift für Katholische Theologie* 70 (1973): 272–287.

———. *Jesus als Davidssohn: Eine traditionsgeschichtliche Untersuchung*. FRLANT 98. Göttingen: Vandenhoeck & Ruprecht, 1970.

Burnett, Fred W. "Characterization and Reader Construction of Characters in the Gospels." *Semeia* 63 (1993): 3–78.

Burridge, Richard. *What Are the Gospels?: A Comparison with Graeco-Roman Biography*. 2nd edition. Grand Rapids: Eerdmans, 2004.

Byrskog, Samuel. *Jesus the Only Teacher: Didactic Authority and Transmission in Ancient Israel, Ancient Judaism and the Matthean Community*. Stockholm: Almqvist & Wiksell, 1994.

Camery-Hoggatt, Jerry. *Irony in Mark's Gospel: Text and Subtext*. Cambridge: Cambridge University Press, 1992.

Carlston, Charles E. "Things That Defile (Mark 7:14) and the Law in Matthew and Mark." *New Testament Studies* 15 (1968): 75–96.

Carson, Don A. *Matthew 13–28*. The Expositor's Bible Commentary with the NIV. Grand Rapids: Zondervan, 1995.

Carter, Warren. "Jesus' 'I Have Come' Sayings in Matthew's Gospel." *Catholic Biblical Quarterly* 60 (1998): 44–62.

———. *Matthew and the Margins: A Socio-Political and Religious Reading*. JSNTSup 204. Sheffield: Sheffield Academic Press, 2000.

Charette, Blaine. *The Theme of Recompense in Matthew's Gospel*. JSNTSup 79. Sheffield: Sheffield Academic Press, 1992.

Chatman, Seymour. *Story and Discourse: Narrative Structure in Fiction and Film*. Ithaca: Cornell University Press, 1978.

Chilton, Bruce. *The Isaiah Targum: Introduction, Translation, Apparatus and Notes*. Wilmington: M. Glazier, 1987.

Chilton, Bruce, and Jacob Neusner. *Judaism in the New Testament: Practices and Beliefs*. London: Routledge, 1995.

Chow, Simon. *Sign of Jonah Reconsidered: A Study of Its Meaning in the Gospel Traditions*. Stockholm: Almqvist & Wiksell International, 1995.

Clarke, Howard W. *The Gospel of Matthew and Its Readers: A Historical Introduction to the First Gospel*. Bloomington: Indiana University Press, 2003.

Cohn-Sherbok, D. M. "An Analysis of Jesus' Arguments Concerning the Plucking of Grain on the Sabbath." *Journal for the Study of the New Testament* 2 (1979): 31–41.

Collins, John J. *The Scepter and the Star: Messianism in Light of the Dead Sea Scrolls*. 2nd edition. Grand Rapids: Eerdmans, 1995.

Comber, Joseph A. "Jesus and the Jews in Matthew 11 and 12." PhD diss., University of Chicago, 1975.

Cope, O. Lamar. *Matthew: A Scribe Trained for the Kingdom of Heaven*. CBQMS 5. Washington, DC: Catholic Biblical Association of America, 1976.

Cousland, J. R. C. *The Crowds in the Gospel of Matthew*. Leiden: Brill, 2002.

———. "The Feeding of the Four Thousand *Gentiles* in Matthew? Matthew 15:29–39 as a Test Case." *Novum Testamentum* 41 (1999): 1–23.

Culler, Jonathan. "Defining Narrative Units." In *Style and Structure in Literature: Essays in the New Stylistics*, edited by Roger Fowler, 123–142. Oxford: Blackwell, 1975.

Culpepper, R. Alan. *Anatomy of the Fourth Gospel: A Study in Literary Design*. Philadelphia: Fortress, 1983.

Dahl, Nils A. *Jesus in the Memory of Early Church*. Minneapolis: Augsburg, 1976.

Dahrendorf, R. *Class and Class Conflict in Industrial Society.* Stanford: Stanford University Press, 1959.
Daube, David. *The New Testament and Rabbinic Judaism.* London: Athlone Press, 1956.
Davies, Margaret. *Matthew.* 2nd edition. Sheffield: Sheffield Phoenix Press, 2009.
Davies, William D. *Paul and Rabbinic Judaism: Some Rabbinic Elements in Pauline Theology.* London: SPCK, 1955.
———. *The Setting of the Sermon on the Mount.* Cambridge: Cambridge University Press, 1966.
Davies, William D., and Dale C. Allison. *A Critical and Exegetical Commentary on the Gospel According to Saint Matthew.* 3 vols. ICC. Edinburgh: T & T Clark, 1988–1997.
de Jonge, Marinus. "The Use of the Word 'Anointed' in the Time of Jesus." *Novum Testamentum* 8 (1966): 132–148.
Denova, Rebecca I. *The Things Accomplished Among Us: Prophetic Tradition in the Structural Pattern of Luke-Acts.* JSNTSup 141. Sheffield: Sheffield Academic Press, 1997.
Dibelius, Martin. *From Tradition to Gospel.* New York: Scribners, 1934. Translated by Bertram L. Woolf in collaboration with the author. London: Ivor Nicholson & Watson, 1934. Translation of *Die Formgeschichte des Evangeliums.* 2nd edition. Tübingen: Mohr Siebeck, 1933.
Dodd, C. H. *The Parables of the Kingdom.* Revised edition. London: Fontana Books, 1961.
Doeve, J. W. *Jewish Hermeneutics in the Synoptic Gospels and Acts.* Assen: Van Gorcum, 1954.
Donahue, John R. "A Neglected Factor in the Theology of Mark." *Journal of Biblical Literature* 4 (1982): 562–594.
———. "Tax Collector." In *The Anchor Yale Bible Dictionary*, vol. 6, edited by David Noel Freedman et al., 337–338. New Haven: Yale University Press, 1992.
———. "Tax Collectors and Sinners: An Attempt at Identification." *Catholic Biblical Quarterly* 33 (1971): 39–61.
Donaldson, Terence L. *Jesus on the Mountain: A Study in Matthean Theology.* Sheffield: Sheffield Academic Press, 1985.
———. "The Law that 'Hangs' (Mt 22:40): Rabbinic Formulation and Matthean Social World." In *SBL 1990 Seminar Papers*, edited by David J. Lull, 14–33. Atlanta: Scholars Press, 1990.
Downing, F. Gerald. "Resurrection of the Dead: Jesus and Philo." *Journal for the Study of the New Testament* 15 (1982): 42–50.
Dreyfus, François G. "L'argument scripturaire de Jésus en faveur de la résurrection des morts: Marc 12:26–27." *Revue Biblique* 66 (1959): 213–224.

Droge, Arthur J. "Call Stories." In *The Anchor Yale Bible Dictionary*, vol. 1, edited by David Noel Freedman et al., 821–823. New Haven: Yale University Press, 1992.

Duling, Dennis. "The Therapeutic Son of David: An Element in Matthew's Christological Apologetic." *New Testament Studies* 24 (1978): 392–410.

Dupont, J. *Mariage et divorce dans l'Évangile: Matthew 19,3–12 et parallels*. Bruges: Addaye de Saint-André & Desclée de Brouwer, 1959.

Dwyer, Timothy. *The Motif of Wonder in the Gospel of Mark*. JSNTSup 128. Sheffield: Sheffield Academic Press, 1996.

Eagy, Ryan. "Matthew 9:9–17 and the Divine Bridegroom of Hosea." *Expository Times* 128 (2017): 521–528.

Eco, Umberto. *The Role of the Reader*. Bloomington: University of Indiana, 1979.

Edwards, Richard A. *Matthew's Story of Jesus*. Philadelphia: Fortress, 1985.

———. "Narrative Implications of *Gar* in Matthew." *Catholic Biblical Quarterly* 52 (1990): 636–655.

———. *The Sign of Jonah: In the Theology of the Evangelists and Q*. London: SCM Press, 1971.

Egan, Kieran. "What Is a Plot?" *New Literary History* (1978): 455–473.

Ellis, E. Earle. *The Gospel of Luke*. Grand Rapids: Eerdmans, 1981.

Erasmus, Desiderius. *The Colloquies of Erasmus*. Translated by Craig R. Thompson. Chicago: University of Chicago Press, 1965.

Evans, Craig. *Mark 8:27–16:20*. WBC 34B. Nashville: Thomas Nelson, 2001.

———. *To See and Not Perceive: Isaiah 6:9–10 in Early Jewish and Christian Interpretation*. JSNTSup 64. Sheffield: Sheffield Academic Press, 1989.

Fanning, Buist M. *Verbal Aspect in New Testament Greek*. Oxford: Clarendon Press, 1990.

Farmer, William R. *Jesus and the Gospel: Tradition, Scripture, and Canon*. Philadelphia: Fortress, 1982.

Fenton, John C. *The Gospel of Saint Matthew*. Pelican Gospel Commentaries. Baltimore: Penguin, 1963

Filson, Floyd V. *The Gospel According to Saint Matthew*. BNTC. London: A & C Black, 1977.

Fitzmyer, Joseph A. *Essays on the Semitic Background of the New Testament*. London: Chapman, 1971.

———. *The Gospel According to Luke (I–IX)*. New York: Doubleday, 1981.

———. "Matthean Divorce Texts and Some New Palestinian Evidence." *Theological Studies* 37 (1976): 197–226.

Foster, Paul. *Community, Law and Mission in Matthew's Gospel*. Tübingen: Mohr Siebeck, 2004.

———. "Why Did Matthew Get the *Shema* Wrong?: A Study of Matthew 22:37." *Journal of Biblical Literature* 122 (2003): 309–333.

Fowler, Robert M. "Reader-Response." In *Searching for Meaning: An Introduction to Interpreting the New Testament*, edited by Paula Gooder, 127–134. Louisville: Westminster John Knox Press, 2009.

France, R. T. *The Gospel According to Matthew: An Introduction and Commentary*. TNTC. Downers Grove: InterVarsity Press, 1985.

———. *The Gospel of Matthew*. NICNT. Grand Rapids: Eerdmans, 2007.

———. *Jesus and the Old Testament: His Application of Old Testament Passages to Himself and His Mission*. London: Tyndale Press, 1971.

———. *Matthew: Evangelist and Teacher*. Downers Grove: InterVarsity Press, 1989.

Frankemölle, Hubert. *Jahwebund und Kirche Christi: Studien zur Form- und Traditionsgeschichte des Evangeliums nach Matthaüs*. Münster: Aschendorff, 1974.

Frei, Hans W. *The Eclipse of Biblical Narrative: A Study in Eighteenth and Nineteenth Century Hermeneutics*. New Haven: Yale University Press, 1974.

Fuchs, Ernst. *Studies of the Historical Jesus*. London: SCM Press, 1964.

Fuller, Reginald H. *The Foundation of New Testament Christology*. London: Lutterworth Press, 1965.

Furnish, Victor P. *The Love Command in the New Testament*. London: SCM Press, 1973.

Gaechter, Paul. *Das Matthäus Evangelium*. Innsbruck: Tyrolia, 1963.

Garland, David E. *The Intention of Matthew 23*. NTTS 52. Leiden: Brill, 1979.

———. *Reading Matthew: A Literary and Theological Commentary on the First Gospel*. Reading the New Testament. New York: Crossroads, 1993.

Gathercole, Simon J. *The Preexitent Son: Recovering the Christologies of Matthew, Mark, and Luke*. Grand Rapids: Eerdmans, 2006.

Genette, Gérard. *Narrative Discourse: An Essay in Method*. Ithaca: Cornell University Press, 1980.

Gerhardsson, Birger. "Sacrificial Service and Atonement in the Gospel of Matthew." In *Reconciliation and Hope: New Testament Essays on Atonement and Eschatology Presented to L. L. Morris on His 60th Birthday*, edited by Leon Morris and Robert J. Banks, 25–35. Exeter: Paternoster Press, 1974.

Gibbs, Jeffrey A. "Israel Standing with Israel: The Baptism of Jesus in Matthew's Gospel." *Catholic Biblical Quarterly* 64 (2002): 511–526.

Giblin, Charles H. "The 'Things of God' in the Question Concerning Tribute to Caesar: (Lk 20:25, Mk 12:17, Mt 22:21)." *Catholic Biblical Quarterly* 33 (1971): 510–527.

Gnilka, Joachim. *Das Evangelium nach Markus I*. 2 vols. Zürich: Benziger; Neukirchen-Vluyn: Neukirchener Verlag, 1978–1979.

———. *Das Matthäusevangelium*. 2 vols. Freiberg: Herder, 1986.

Goulder, Michael D. *Midrash and Lection in Matthew*. London: SPCK, 1974.

Grams, Rollin. "Temple Conflict Scene: A Rhetorical Analysis of Matthew 21–23." In *Persuasive Artistry: Studies in New Testament Rhetoric in Honor of George A. Kennedy*, edited by Duane F. Waston, 41–65. Sheffield: Sheffield Academic Press, 1991.

Grässer, Erich. "Jesus in Nazareth (Mark 6:1–6a)." *NTS* 16 (1970): 1–23.

Green, H. Benedict. *The Gospel According to Matthew*. Oxford: Oxford University Press, 1975.

Greeven, Heinrich. "Wer unter euch . . .?" *Wort und Dienst* 3 (1952): 86–101.

Grundmann, Walter. *Das Evangelium nach Matthäus*. ThKNT. 5th edition. Berlin: Evangelische Verlagsanstalt, 1981.

Gundry, Robert H. *Mark: A Commentary on His Apology for the Cross*. Grand Rapids: Eerdmans, 1993.

———. *Matthew: A Commentary on His Literary and Theological Art*. Grand Rapids: Eerdmans, 1982.

———. *The Use of the Old Testament in St. Matthew's Gospel*. Leiden: Brill, 1967.

Guthrie, Donald. *New Testament Theology*. Downers Grove: InterVarsity Press, 1981.

Hagner, Donald. *Matthew*. 2 vols. WBC 33 A–33 B. Dallas, TX: Word Books, 1992.

Hahn, Ferdinand. *The Title of Jesus in Christology: Their History in Early Christianity*. London: Lutterworth Press, 1969.

Hann, R. R. "Judaism and Christianity in Antioch: Charisma and Conflict in the First Century." *Journal of Religious History* 14 (1987): 341–360.

Hare, Douglas R. "How Jewish Is the Gospel of Matthew?" *Catholic Biblical Quarterly* 62 (2000): 264–277.

Harrington, D. J. *The Gospel of Matthew*. Sacra Pagina, vol. 1. Collegeville: Liturgical Press, 1991.

Hasler, Victor. *Amen: Redaktionsgeschichtchtliche Untersuchung zur Einführungsformel der Herrenworte "Wahrlich ich sage euch."* Zürich: Gotthelf, 1969.

Hay, David M. *Glory at the Right Hand: Psalm 110 in Early Christianity*. Nashville: Abingdon, 1973.

Hays, Richard. *Echoes of Scripture in the Letters of Paul*. New Haven: Yale University Press, 1989.

Held, Joachim Heinz. "Matthew as Interpreter of the Miracle Stories." In *Tradition and Interpretation*, edited by Günther Bornkamm, Gerhard Barth, and Heinz Joachim Held, 165–299. London: SCM Press, 1963.

Hengel, Martin. *Studies in Early Christology*. Edinburgh: T & T Clark, 1995.

Heth, W. A., and Gordon Wenham. *Jesus and Divorce*. Nashville: Nelson, 1985.

Hicks, John M. "The Sabbath Controversy in Matthew: An Exegesis of Matthew 12:1–14." *Restoration Quarterly* (1984): 79–91.

Hill, David. *The Gospel of Matthew*. New Century Bible Commentary. London: Marshall, Morgan & Scott, 1972.

———. "On the Use and Meaning of Hosea VI.6 in Matthew's Gospel." *New Testament Studies* 24 (1977): 107–119.

Hirunuma, Toshio. "Matthew 16:2b–3." In *New Testament Textual Criticism: Its Significance for Exegesis*, edited by Eldon J. Epp and Gordon D. Fee, 35–45. Oxford: Oxford University Press, 1981.

Hoehner, H. W. "Herodian Dynasty." In *Dictionary of Jesus and the Gospels*, edited by Joel B. Green and Scot McKnight, 317–325. Downers Grove: InterVarsity Press, 1992.

Horbury, W. *Jews and Christians in Contact and Controversy*. Edinburgh: T & T Clark, 1998.

Howell, David B. *Matthew's Inclusive Story: A Study in the Narrative Rhetoric of the First Gospel*. JSNTSup 42. Sheffield: Sheffield Academic Press. 1990.

Howton, John. "The Sign of Jonah." *Scottish Journal of Theology* 15 (1962): 288–304.

Hughes, John H. "John the Baptist: The Forerunner of God Himself." *Novum Testamentum* 14 (1972): 191–218.

Hultgren, Arland. *Jesus and His Adversaries: The Form and Function of the Conflict Stories in the Synoptic Tradition*. Minneapolis: Augsburg, 1979.

———. *The Parables of Jesus: A Commentary*. Grand Rapids: Eerdmans, 2000.

Hummel, Reinhart. *Die Auseinandersetzung zwischen Kirche und Judentum im Matthäusevangelium*. Beiträge zur evangelischen Theologie 33. München: Kaiser Verlag, 1963.

Hurtado, Larry. *Lord Jesus Christ: Devotion to Jesus in Earliest Christianity*. Grand Rapids: Eerdmans, 2003.

———. *One God, One Lord: Early Christian Devotion and Ancient Jewish Monotheism*. Philadelphia: Fortress, 1988.

Hutchens, Eleanor. "The Identification of Irony." *English Literary History* 27, no. 4 (Dec. 1960): 352–363.

Instone-Brewer, David. *Divorce and Remarriage in the Bible: The Social and Literary Context*. Grand Rapids: Eerdmans, 2002.

———. *Techniques and Assumptions in Jewish Exegesis before 70 CE*. Tübingen: Mohr Siebeck, 1992.

———. *Traditions of the Rabbis from the Era of the New Testament, Vol. 1: Prayer and Agriculture*. Grand Rapids: Eerdmans, 2004.

Iser, Wolfgang. *The Implied Reader: Patterns of Communication in Prose Fiction from Bunyan to Beckett*. Baltimore: Johns Hopkins University Press, 1974.

Janzen, J. Gerald. "Resurrection and Hermeneutics: On Exodus 3:6 in Mark 12:26." *Journal for the Study of the New Testament* 23 (1985): 43–58.

Jeremias, Joachim. "παῖς θεου." In *Theological Dictionary of the New Testament*, vol. 3, edited by Gerhard Kittel and Gerhard Friedrich; translated by Geoffrey W. Bromiley, 406–410. Grand Rapids: Eerdmans, 1964.

———. "Ιωνᾶς." In *Theological Dictionary of the New Testament*, vol. 5, edited by Gerhard Kittel and Gerhard Friedrich; translated by Geoffrey W. Bromiley, 656–716. Grand Rapids: Eerdmans, 1964.

———. *The Parables of Jesus*. Revised edition. London: SCM Press, 1963.

Jones, Ivor Harond. *The Matthean Parables: A Literary and Historical Commentary*. NovTSup 80. Leiden: Brill, 1995.

Juel, Donald. *Messianic Exegesis: Christological Interpretation of the Old Testament in Early Christianity*. Philadelphia: Fortress, 1988.

Keener, Craig S. *A Commentary on the Gospel of Matthew*. Grand Rapids: Eerdmans, 1999.

———. *. . . And Marries Another: Divorce and Remarriage in the Teaching of the New Testament*. Peabody: Hendrickson, 1991.

Kegel, Günter. *Auferstehung Jesu-Auferstehung Der Toten*. Gütersloh: Gütersloher Verlagshaus Gerd Mohn, 1970.

Kelber, Werner H. *The Oral and Written Gospel: The Hermeneutics of Speaking and Writing in the Synoptic Tradition, Mark, Paul and Q*. Bloomington: Indiana University Press, 1983, 1997.

Kilpatrick, George D. *The Origins of the Gospel According to St. Matthew*. Oxford: larendon, 1946.

Kingsbury, Jack Dean. *Matthew as Story*. 2nd edition. Philadelphia: Fortress, 1988.

———. *Matthew: Structure, Christology, Kingdom*. Philadelphia: Fortress, 1975.

———. "Observations on the 'Miracle Chapters' of Matthew 8–9." *Catholic Biblical Quarterly* 40 (1978): 559–573.

———. "On Following Jesus: The 'Eager' Scribe and the 'Reluctant' Disciple (Matthew 8:18–22)." *New Testament Studies* 34 (1988): 45–59.

———. *The Parables of Jesus in Matthew 13: A Study in Redaction-Criticism*. London: SPCK, 1969.

———. "The Title 'Son of David' in Matthew's Gospel." *Journal of Biblical Literature* 95 (1976): 591–602.

———. "The Title 'Son of God' in Matthew's Gospel." *Biblical Theology Bulletin* 5 (1975): 3–31.

———. "The Verb Akolouthein as an Index of Matthew's View of His Community." *Journal of Biblical Literature* 97, no. 1 (1978): 56–73.

Kloppenborg, John S. *The Formation of Q: Trajectories in Ancient Wisdom Collections*. Philadelphia: Fortress, 1987.

Knowles, Michael. *Jeremiah in Matthew's Gospel: The Rejected-Prophet Motif in Matthean Redaction*. JSNTSup 68. Sheffield: Sheffield Academic Press, 1993.

Krieger, Murray. *A Window to Criticism: Shakespeare's Sonnets and Modern Poetics.* Princeton: Princeton University Press, 1964.

Kümmel, Werner G. *Promise and Fulfillment: The Eschatological Message of Jesus.* London: SCM Press, 1984.

Lagrange, M. J. *Evangile selon Saint Matthieu.* 3rd edition. Paris: Gabalda, 1927.

Landes, George M. "Matthew 12:40 as an Interpretation of 'The Sign of Jonah' against Its Biblical Background." In *The Word of the Lord Shall Go Forth: Essays in Honor of David Noel Freedman in Celebrataion of His Sixtieth Birthday*, edited by Carol Meyers, Michael P. O'Connor and David Noel Freedman, 665-684. Winona Park: Eisenbrauns, 1983.

Lanser, Susan S. *The Narrative Act: Point of View in Prose Fiction.* Princeton: Princeton University Press. 1981.

Leitch, J. W. "Lord Also of the Sabbath." *Scottish Journal of Theology* 19 (1966): 426-433.

Levine, Amy-Jill. *The Social and Ethnic Dimensions of Matthean Salvation History: "Go Nowhere Among the Gentiles . . ." (Matt 10:5b).* Lewiston: Edwin Mellen, 1988.

Levine, Etan. "The Sabbath Controversy According to Matthew." *New Testament Studies* 22 (1975/76): 480-483.

Lim, Bo H., and Daniel Castelo. *Hosea.* Two Horizons Old Testament Commentary. Grand Rapids: Eerdmans, 2015.

Linnemann, Eta. *The Parables of Jesus: Introduction and Exposition.* London: SPCK, 1966.

Loader, William R. "Christ at the Right Hand - Ps CX.1 in the New Testament." *New Testament Studies* 24 (1978): 199-217.

———. "Son of David, Blindness, Possession and Duality." *Catholic Biblical Quarterly* 44 (1982): 570-585.

Lohmeyer, Ernst. *Das Evangelium des Matthäus.* 2nd edition. Göttingen: Vandenhoeck & Ruprecht, 1958.

Lohr, Charles H. "Oral Techniques in the Gospel of Matthew." *Catholic Biblical Quarterly* 23 (1961): 403-435.

Lohse, Eduard. "Jesu Wort über den Sabbat." In *Judentum, Urchristentum, Kirche: Festschrift für Joachim Jeremias*, edited by Walther Eltester, 79-89. Berlin: Töpelmann, 1960.

Long, Philip. *Jesus the Bridegroom: The Origin of the Eschatological Feast as a Wedding Banquet in the Synoptic Gospels.* Eugene, OR: Pickwick, 2013.

Lövestam, Evald. "The ἡ γενεὰ αὔτη Eschatology in Mk 13:30 parr." In *L'Apocalypse johannique et l'Apocalyptique dans le Nouveau Testament*, edited by Jan Lambrecht, 403-413. Gembloux, Belgique: J. Duculot, 1980.

Luz, Ulrich. *Matthew: A Commentary.* Hermeneia. 3 vols. Translated by James E. Crouch. Minneapolis: Fortress, 2001-2007.

———. *Studies in Matthew*. Grand Rapids: Eerdmans, 2005.

———. *The Theology of the Gospel of Matthew*. New Testament Theology. Cambridge: Cambridge University Press, 1995.

Lybaek, Lena. "Matthew's Use of Hosea 6:6." In *The Scriptures in the Gospels*, edited by Chris M. Tuckett, 491–499. BETL 131. Leuven: Leuven University Press, 1997.

———. *New and Old in Matthew 11-13: Normativity in the Development of Three Theological Themes*. Gottingen: Vandenhoeck & Ruprecht, 2002.

MacComb, Samuel. "The Irony of Christ." *The Biblical World* 23, no. 2 (1904): 104–109.

Malbon, Elizabeth S. *In the Company of Jesus: Characters in Mark's Gospel*. Louisville: Westminster John Knox, 2000.

———. "Narrative Criticism." In *Searching For Meaning: An Introduction to Interpreting the New Testament*, edited by Paula Gooder, 80–87. Louisville: Westminster John Knox, 2009.

Malina, Bruce. J., and Jerome H. Neyrey. *Calling Jesus Names: The Social Value of Labels in Matthew*. Sonoma: Polebridge, 1988.

Manson, Thomas W. *The Sayings of Jesus: As Recorded in the Gospels According to St. Matthew and St. Luke Arranged with Introduction and Commentary*. London: SCM Press, 1966.

———. *The Teaching of Jesus: Studies of Its Form and Content*. Cambridge: Cambridge University Press, 1963.

McKnight, Edgar V. "Literary Criticism." In *Dictionary of Jesus and the Gospels*, edited by Joel Green, Scot McKnight and I. Howard Marshall, 473–480. Downers Grove: InterVarsity Press, 1992.

McKnight, Scot. "A Loyal Critic: Matthew's Polemic with Judaism in Theological Perspective." In *Anti-Semitism and Early Christianity: Issues of Polemic and Faith*, edited by Craig A. Evans and Donald Hagner, 55–79. Minneapolis: Fortress, 1993.

McNeile, Alan Hugh. *The Gospel According to Matthew: The Greek Text with Introduction, Notes, and Indices*. London: Macmillan, 1952.

———. "Τότε in St. Matthew." *Journal of Theological Studies* 12 (1911): 127–128.

Meier, John P. "Antioch." In *Antioch and Rome*, edited by Raymond E. Brown and John P. Meier, 12–86. London: G. Chapman, 1983.

———. "Historical Jesus and Historical Herodians." *Journal of Biblical Literature* 119 (2000): 740–746.

———. "John the Baptist in Matthew's Gospel." *Journal of Biblical Literature* 99 (1980): 383–405.

———. *Law and History in Matthew's Gospel: A Redactional Study of Mt. 5:17-48*. Rome: Biblical Institute Press, 1976.

———. *Matthew*. Wilmington: Glazier, 1980.

———. *The Vision of Matthew: Christ, Church, and Morality in the First Gospel.* New York: Crossroad, 1979, 1991.
Menninger, Richard E. *Israel and the Church in the Gospel of Matthew.* New York: Peter Lang, 1994.
Merenlahti, Petri. "Characters in Making: Individuality and Ideology." In *Characterization in the Gospels: Reconceiving Narrative Criticism*, edited by David Rhoads and Kari Syreeni, 49–72. Sheffield: Sheffield Academic Press, 1999.
Metzger, Bruce M. *A Textual Commentary on the Greek New Testament.* A Companion Volume to the United Bible Societies Greek New Testament, 3rd edition. New York: United Bible Societies, 1971.
Meyer, Paul. "Gentile Mission in Q." *Journal of Biblical Literature* 89 (1970): 405–417.
Michael, J. Hugh. "The Sign of Jonah." *Journal of Theological Studies* 21 (1920): 146–159.
Moo, Doug. "Jesus and the Authority of the Mosaic Law." *JSNT* 20 (1984): 3–49.
Moore, G. F. *Judaism in the First Centuries of the Christian Era: The Age of the Tannain.* 3 vols. Cambridge: Harvard University Press, 1927–1930.
Moore, Stephen D. *Literary Criticism and the Gospels.* New Haven: Yale University Press, 1989.
Moulton, James H., and N. Turner. *A Grammar of New Testament Greek.* 4 vols. Edinburgh: T & T Clark, 1906–1976.
Muecke, D. C. *The Compass of Irony.* London: Methuen, 1969.
———. *Irony and the Ironic.* The Critical Idiom 13. Second edition of *Irony*. New York: Methuen, 1982.
———. *Irony: The Critical Idiom.* London: Methuen, 1970.
Nestle, Eberhard, Barbara Erwin, and Hurt Aland. *Novum Testmentum Graece*, 27th edition. Stuttgart: Duetsche Bibelgesellschaft, 1898, 1993.
Newport, Kenneth G. *The Sources and Sitz im Leben of Matthew 23.* JSNTSup 117. Sheffield: Sheffield Academic Press, 1995.
Neyrey, Jerome H. "The Thematic Use of Isaiah 42:1–4 in Matthew 12." *Biblica* 63 (1982): 457–473.
Nolan, Brian. *The Royal Son of God: The Christology of Matthew 1–2 in the Setting of the Gospel.* Fribourg: Editions Universitaires Fribourg Suisse, 1979.
Nolland, John. *The Gospel of Matthew: A Commentary on the Greek Text.* NIGTC. Grand Rapids: Eerdmans, 2005.
Novakovic, Lidija. *Messiah, the Healer of the Sick: A Study of Jesus as the Son of David in the Gospel of Matthew.* Tübingen: Mohr Siebeck, 2003.
Ogawa, Akira. *L'histoire de Jésus chez Matthieu: La signification de l'histoire pour la théologie matthéenne.* Pulications Universitaires Européennes 116. Frankfurt am Main: Lang, 1979.

Olmstead, Wesley G. *Matthew's Trilogy of Parables: The Nation, the Nations and the Reader in Matthew 21:28–22:14*. Cambridge: Cambridge University Press, 2003.

Overman, J. Andrew. *Matthew's Gospel and Formative Judaism: The Social World of the Matthean Community*. Minneapolis: Fortress, 1990.

Paget, Valerian. *More's Millenium: Being the Utopia of Sir Thomas More Rendered into Modern English*. New York: John McBride, 1908.

Patte, Daniel. *The Gospel According to Matthew: A Structural Commentary on Matthew's Faith*. Philadelphia: Fortress. 1987.

———. "Speech Act Theory and Biblical Exegesis." *Semiea* 41 (1988): 85–102.

Perry, Menakham. "Literary Dynamics: How the Order of a Text Creates Its Meanings." *Poetics Today* (1979): 35–361.

Peterson, Norman R. *Literary Criticism for New Testament Critics*. Philadelphia: Fortress, 1978.

Ponton, Gary. "Halakhah." In *The Anchor Yale Bible Dictionary*, vol. 3, edited by David Noel Freedman et al., 26–27. New Haven: Yale University Press, 1992.

Porter, Stanley E. *Idioms of the Greek New Testament*. 2nd edition. Sheffield: Sheffield Academic Press, 1994.

Powell, Mark Allan. *The Bible and Modern Literary Criticism: A Critical Assessment and Annotated Bibliography* (with the assistance of Cecil Gray and Melissa Curtis). Westport: Greenwood Press, 1992.

———. "The Plot and Subplots of Matthew's Gospel." *New Testament Studies* 38 (1992): 187–204.

———. "The Religious Leaders in Matthew: A Literary-Critical Approach." PhD diss, Union Theological Seminary in Virginia, 1988.

———. *What Is Narrative Criticism?* Minneapolis: Fortress, 1990.

Pratt, Mary Louise. *Toward a Speech Act Theory of Literary Discourse*. Bloomington: Indiana University Press, 1977.

Quesnell, Q. "Made Themselves Eunuchs of the Kingdom of Heaven (Mt 19:12)." *Catholic Biblical Quarterly* 30 (1968): 335–358.

Repschinski, Boris. *The Controversy Stories in the Gospel of Matthew: Their Redaction, Form and Relevance for the Relationship between the Matthean Community and Formative Judaism*. Gottingen: Vandenhoeck & Ruprecht, 2000.

Resseguie, James L. *Narrative Criticism of the New Testament: An Introduction*. Grand Rapids: Baker Academic, 2005.

———. "Reader-Response Criticism and the Synoptic Gospels." *Journal of the American Academy of Religion* 52 (June 1984): 307–324.

Rhoads, David. "Narrative Criticism and the Gospel of Mark." *Journal of the American Academy of Religion* 50 (1982): 411–434.

Rhoads, David, Joanna Dewey, and Donald Michie. *Mark as Story: An Introduction to the Narrative of a Gospel.* 2nd edition. Minneapolis: Fortress, 1999.

Ricoeur, Paul. "Narrative Time." In *On Narrative*, edited by W. J. T. Mitchell, 165–186. Chicago: University of Chicago Press, 1981.

Robinson, James. "Elijah, John and Jesus: An Essay in Detection." *New Testament Studies* 4 (1958): 263–281.

Rordorf, W. *Sunday: The History of the Day of Rest and Worship in the Earliest Centuries of the Christian Church*, translated by A. A. K. Graham. London: SCM Press, 1968.

Safrai, Zeev. *The Economy of Roman Palestine.* London: Routledge, 1994.

Saldarini, Anthony J. *Matthew's Christian-Jewish Community.* Chicago: University of Chicago Press, 1994.

———. *Pharisees, Scribes and Sadducees in Palestinian Society.* Edinburgh: T & T Clark, 1988.

Sand, Alexander. *Das Evangelium Nach Matthäus. Regensburger Neue Testament.* Regensburg: Verlag Friedrich Pustet, 1986.

———. *Das Gesetz und die Propheten: Untersuchungen zur Theologie des Evangeliums nach Matthaüs.* Biblische Untersuchungen 11. Regensburg: Verlag Friedrich Pustet, 1974.

Sanders, E. P. *Jesus and Judaism.* Philadelphia: Fortress, 1985.

Saucy, Mark. "The Kingdom-of-God Sayings in Matthew." *Bibliotheca Sacra* 151 (1994): 175–197.

Saunders, Stanley. "'No One Dared Ask Him Anything More': Contextual Readings of the Controversy Stories in Matthew." PhD diss., Princeton Theological Seminary, 1990.

Schmid, Josef. *Das Evangelium Nach Matthäus.* 5th edition. *Regensburger Neue Testament.* Regensburge: Pustet, 1965.

Schmit, Karl. L. *Der Rahmen der Deschichte Jesu: Literarkritische Untersuchungen zur ältesten Jesu Überlieferung.* Berlin: Trowitzsch, 1919

Schnackenburg, Rudolf. *God's Rule and Kingdom.* Freiburg: Herder, 1963.

———. *Jesus in the Gospels: A Biblical Christology.* Louisville: Westminster John Knox, 1995.

Schneiwind, J. *Das Evangelium nach Matthäus.* NTD I/1. 9th edition. Göttingen: Vandenhoeck & Ruprecht, 1960.

Scholes, Robert, and Robert Kellogg. *The Nature of Narrative.* New York: Oxford University Press, 1966.

Schulz, S. *Q, die Spruchquelle der Evangelisen.* Zürich: Theologischer Verlag, 1972.

Schweizer, Eduard. *The Good News According to Matthew.* Translated by David E. Green. Atlanta: John Knox, 1975.

———. *Matthäus und Seine Gemeinde.* Stuttgart: KBW Verlag, 1974.

Scrivener, F. H. A., and Edward Miller. *A Plain Introduction to the Criticism of the New Testament for the Use of Biblical Students.* 2 vols. Eugene: Wipf & Stock, 1997.

Searle, John R. *Expression and Meaning: Studies in the Theory of Speech Acts.* Cambridge: Cambridge University Press, 1979.

Segal, Alan. *Two Powers in Heaven: Early Rabbinic Reports about Christianity and Gnosticism.* Leiden: Brill, 1977.

Segbroeck, Frans van. "Jesus rejeté par sa patrie (Mt 13:5-58)." *Biblica* 49 (1968): 167-198.

Seow, C. L. "Hosea, Book of." In *The Anchor Yale Bible Dictionary*, vol. 3, edited by David Noel Freedman et al., 291-297. New Haven: Yale University Press, 1992.

Shae, Gam Seng. "The Question on the Authority of Jesus." *Novum Testamentum* 16 (1974): 1-29.

Sigal, Phillip. *The Halakhah of Jesus of Nazareth According to the Gospel of Matthew.* Atlanta: SBL, 2007.

Sim, David C. *The Gospel of Matthew and Christian Judaism: The History and Social Setting of the Matthean Community.* Edinburgh: T & T Clark, 1999.

———. "Matthew's Use of Mark: Did Matthew Intend to Supplement or to Replace His Primary Source?" *New Testament Studies* 57 (2011): 176-192.

Simonetti, Manlio, ed. *Matthew: 14-28.* Ancient Christian Commentary Series. New Testament Ib. Downers Grove: InterVarsity Press, 2002.

Smith, Dennis E. "Table Fellowship." In *The Anchor Yale Bible Dictionary*, vol. 6, edited by David Noel Freedman et al., 302-303. New Haven: Yale University Press, 1992.

Snodgrass, Klyne R. *Stories with Intent: A Comprehensive Guide to the Parables of Jesus.* Grand Rapids: Eerdmans, 2008.

Stanton, Graham N. "The Fourfold Gospel." *New Testament Studies* 43 (1997): 317-346.

———. "Matthew's Christology and the Parting of the Ways." In *The Parting of the Ways A.D. 70 to 135. The Second Durham-Tübingen Research Symposium on Earliest Christianity and Judaism (Durham, September 1989)*, edited by James D. G. Dunn, 99-116. WUNT 66. Tübingen: Mohr Siebeck, 1992.

———. "Matthew." In *It Is Written: Scripture Citing Scripture. Essays in Honour of Barnabas Lindars, SSF*, edited by D. A. Carson and H. G. Williamson, 205-219. Cambridge: Cambridge University Press, 1988.

Steinhauser, Michael G. *Doppelbildworte in den synoptischen Evangelien: Eine form- und traditions-kristische Studie.* Würzburg: Echter Verlag, 1981.

Stendahl, Krister. *The School of St. Matthew, and Its Use of the Old Testament.* 2nd edition. Philadelphia: Fortress, 1968.

Strack, Hermann L., and Pual Billerbeck. *Kommentar zum Neuen Testament aus Talmud un Midrasch. Bd. I: Das Evangelium nach Matthäus.* Müchen: Beck, 1956.

Strobel, August. *Untersuchungen zum eschatologischen Verzögerungsproblem auf Grund der spätjüdisch-urchristlichen Geschichte von Habakuk 2,2ff.* NovTSup 2. Leiden: E. J. Brill, 1961.

Stuart, Douglas. *Hosea-Jonah.* WBC 31. Dallas: Word Books, 1987.

Sturch, Richard. "The 'PATRIE' of Jesus." *Journal of Theological Studies* 1 (1977): 94-96.

Tannehill, Robert. "Introduction: The Pronouncement Story and Its Types." *Semeia* 20 (1981): 1-13.

———. *The Sword of His Mouth: Forceful and Imaginative Language in Synoptic Sayings.* Missoula, MT: Scholars Press, 1975.

———. "Tension in Synoptic Sayings and Stories." *Interpretation* 34, no. 2 (1980): 138-151.

———. "Varieties of Synoptic Pronouncement Stories." *Semeia* 20 (1981): 101-119.

Taylor, Vincent. *The Formation of the Gospel Tradition.* 2nd edition. London: Macmillan, 1935.

Thiselton, Anthony C. *New Horizons in Hermeneutics: The Theory and Practice of Transforming Biblical Reading.* Grand Rapids: Zondervan, 1992.

———. "Reader-Response Hermeneutics, Action Models, and the Parables of Jesus." In *The Responsibility of Hermeneutics*, edited by Roger Lundin, Anthony C. Thiselton, and Clarence Walhout, 79-126. Grand Rapids: Eerdmans, 1985.

———. *Thiselton on Hermeneutics: Collected Works with New Essays.* Grand Rapids: Eerdmans, 2006.

Thompson, William G. "Reflections on the Composition of Mt 8:1-9:34." *Catholic Biblical Quarterly* 33 (1971): 365-388.

Tilborg, Sjef van. *The Jewish Leaders in Matthew.* Leiden: Brill, 1972.

Tovey, Derek. *Narrative Art and Act in the Fourth Gospel.* JSNTSup 151. Sheffield: Sheffield Academic Press, 1997.

Trilling, W. "Die Täufertratition Bei Matthäus." *Biblische Zeitschrift* 3 (1959): 271-289.

Tuckett, Chris M. *Q and the History of Early Christianity: Studies on Q.* Peabody: Hendrickson, 1996.

Twelftree, G. H. "Blasphemy." In *Dictionary of Jesus and the Gospels*, edited by Joel B. Green and Scot McKnight, 75-77. Downers Grove: InterVarsity Press, 1992.

Uspensky, Boris. *A Poetics of Composition: The Structure of the Artistic Text and Typology of a Compositional Form.* Translated by V. Zavarin and S. Wittig. Berkeley: University of California Press, 1973.

Vawter, Bruce. "The Divorce Clauses in Mat 5:32 and 19:9." *Catholic Biblical Quarterly* 16 (1954): 155–167.

Venneman, T. "Topics, Sentence Accent, Ellipsis: A Proposal for their Formal Treatment." In *Formal Semantics of Natural Language: Papers from a Colloquium Sponsored by the King's College Research Center, Cambridge*, edited by E. L. Keenan, 313–328. Cambridge: Cambridge University Press, 1975.

Vermès, Géza. *Jesus the Jew: A Historian's Reading of the Gospels*. New York: Macmillan, 1974.

Verseput, Donald J. *The Rejection of the Humble Messianic King: A Study of the Composition of Matthew 11–12*. Bern: Peter Lang, 1986.

———. "The Role and Meaning of the "Son of God" Title in Matthew's Gospel." *New Testament Studies* 33 (1987): 532–556.

Via, Dan O., Jr. "Matthew on the Understandability of the Parables." *JBL* 84 (1965): 430–432.

———. *The Parables: Their Literary and Existential Dimension*. Philadelphia: Fortress, 1967.

Vledder, Evert-Jan. *Conflict in the Miracle Stories: A Socio-Exegetical Study of Matthew 8 and 9*. JSNTSup 152. Sheffield: Sheffield Academic Press, 1997.

Waetjen, Herman C. *The Origin and Destiny of Humanness: An Interpretation of the Gospel According to Matthew*. Corte Madera: Omega, 1976.

Walker, Peter W. L. *Jesus and the Holy City: New Testament Perspectives on Jerusalem*. Grand Rapids: Eerdmans, 1996.

Weiss, Johannes. *Jesus' Proclamation of the Kingdom of God*. Philadelphia: Fortress, 1971.

Wengst, Klaus. *Pax Romana and the Peace of Jesus Christ*. Translated by John Bowden. Philadelphia: Fortress, 1987.

Wenham, Gordon, J. "Matthew and Divorce: An Old Crux Revisited." *Journal for the Study of the New Testament* 22 (1984): 95–107.

Westerholm, Stephen. *Jesus and Scribal Authority*. Lund: CWK Gleerup, 1978.

White, Hugh. C. "Introduction: Speech-Act Theory and Literary Criticism." *Semeia* 41 (1988): 1–24.

Wiebe, P. H. "Jesus Divorce Exception." *Journal of the Evangelical Theological Society* 32 (1989): 327–333.

Williams, D. J. "Bridegroom." In *Dictionary of Jesus and the Gospels*, edited by Joel Green, Scot McKnight and I. Howard Marshall, 86–88. Downers Grove: InterVarsity Press, 1992.

Wink, Walter. *John the Baptist in the Gospel Tradition*. Cambridge: Cambridge University Press, 1968.

Witherington, Ben III. *Matthew*. Smyth & Helwys Bible Commentary. Macon: Smyth & Helwys, 2006.

———. "Matthew 5:32 and 19:9 – Exception or Exceptional Situation?" *New Testament Studies* 31 (1985): 571–576.

Wrede, William. *Vorträge und Studien*. Tübingen: Mohr, 1907.

Wright, N. T. "Jerusalem in the New Testament." In *Jerusalem: Past and Present in the Purposes of God*, edited by Peter W. L. Walker, 53–78. Grand Rapids: Baker Books, 1994.

———. *Jesus and the Victory of God*. Minneapolis: Fortress, 1996.

Yamasaki, Gary. *John the Baptist in Life and Death: Audience-Oriented Criticism of Matthew's Narrative*. Journal for the Study of the New Testament Supplement series 167. Sheffield: Sheffield Academic Press, 1998.

———. *Watching a Biblical Narrative: Point of View in Biblical Exegesis*. Edinburgh: T & T Clark, 2007.

Yang, Yong-Eui. *Jesus and the Sabbath in Matthew's Gospel*. JSNTSup 139. Sheffield: Sheffield Academic Press, 1997.

Zeitlin, Irving M. *Jesus and the Judaism of His Time*. Oxford: Polity Press, 1988.

Zerwick, Maximilian, and Joseph Smith. *Biblical Greek: Illustrated by Examples*. English edition adapted from the 4th Latin edition. Roma: Editrice Pontificio Istituto Biblico, 1963.

www.ingramcontent.com/pod-product-compliance
Lightning Source LLC
Chambersburg PA
CBHW051538230426
43669CB00015B/2648

This study provides valuable insight into the narrative function of the conflict stories in Matthew's gospel, showing their role in the overall design or plot of this gospel. Conflict leads to the passion. The author also rightly highlights the christological function that surfaces in some of these narratives, which reveal Jesus's identity, including its divine aspect.

Craig S. Keener, PhD
F. M. and Ada Thompson Professor of Biblical Studies,
Asbury Theological Seminary, Wilmore, Kentucky, USA

In this fresh and searching exploration of the first gospel, Ye-Atkinson employs literary-critical tools to demonstrate how essential the conflict stories are to Matthew's plot and purpose. Continually, she exposes that, through their querulous questions and strident challenges, Jesus's opponents are struggling, not with legal and theological disputes of their day, much less a later generation's, but with the very identity of Jesus. His opponents eventually learn, just as modern readers of Matthew should, that there is no future in opposition to Jesus, their God and King.

Richard J. Gibson, PhD
Principal, Brisbane School of Theology, Australia

In this insightful and judicious study, Rebecca Ye-Atkinson is putting literary methods to good use by asking the right, theological questions. She aptly guides the reader through Matthew's use of the conflict stories, and she shows how they highlight Jesus's divine authority, the Christ-centered nature of God's people, and the pivot towards the gentile mission. All students of Matthew's gospel will benefit greatly from this book.

Sigurd Grindheim, PhD
Professor, Department of Pedagogy, Religion and Social Studies,
Western Norway University of Applied Sciences, Bergen, Norway

Moving beyond form-critical concerns that center on the *Sitz im Leben* behind the Matthean conflict stories, this study provides a fresh reading of a significant portion of the gospel through a literary-critical lens. Not only does it demonstrate the fruitfulness of a synchronic approach to the ancient text, it also unveils the narrative function of these stories at the intersection of Matthew's ecclesiological and christological concerns. For both its methodological contributions and its exegetical yield, this study deserves to be widely read and studied.

David W. Pao, PhD
Professor of New Testament,
Chair of the New Testament Department,
Trinity Evangelical Divinity School, Deerfield, Illinois, USA

The significance of conflict stories in the narrative of Matthew's gospel has captured scholars' attention since J. D. Kingsbury's ground-breaking study. How these conflict stories function in the narrative remains a field to be ploughed for a richer harvest nonetheless. While scholars take conflict stories for granted, the value of the stories have been reduced to revealing the struggle between the Matthean Christians and their Jewish opponents. Because of this preoccupation, one can speak of the eclipse of the author's concern and the narrative's impact on its readers. Underlying this inadequacy is the failure to read the narrative holistically. Dr Rebecca Ye-Atkinson's effort has filled this void. The selection of seventeen conflict stories provides important data based on which a map of investigation is convincingly drafted. The strategy of narrative and rhetorical reading has provided a nexus in which conflict stories are better understood. Her treatment of the author's interpretation of the Hebrew Scripture has highlighted the theological essence of the stories. More importantly, Dr Ye-Atkinson is found competent in demonstrating how conflict stories in the Matthean narrative impact on the reader. Readers of the Matthean gospel will be benefited by this carefully argued fine piece of work.

Poling Sun, PhD
Professor of New Testament
Taiwan Graduate School of Theology, Taipei, Taiwan

Conflict stories occupy a large portion of the Gospel of Matthew. Dr Ye-Atkinson explains clearly their literary function and cumulative effect, arguing that the conflict stories facilitate Matthew's theological emphasis that Jesus is the Davidic Messiah who possesses the status and authority of God. Relationship to Jesus – not the law – is the foremost criteria for determining one's kingdom inclusion, a turning point marked by the inclusion of the Gentiles. This study helpfully illuminates why Israel and the Jewish leaders ultimately decided to reject Jesus as their expected Messiah and nailed him to the cross.

This study's organized layout and fluent expression will definitely appeal to the readers' appetite and interest in exploring the whole writing. I believe this work will help readers to understand the amazing cumulative effects of these conflict stories. I highly recommend that anyone who has the desire to understand the purpose and message of Matthew's conflict stories should not miss the chance to read this study.

Emily Yeh Wang, PhD
Associate Professor of New Testament,
International Chinese Biblical Seminary in Europe (ICBSIE), Barcelona, Spain